Command	Meaning
move	Moves the contents of data objects
new-line	Creates a new line during list processing
new-page	Starts a new page during list processing
open dataset	Opens a file
parameters	Defines an input parameter on the selection screen
perform	Calls a subroutine
program	Defines a program
raise	Triggers an exception
read dataset	Reads a record from a file
read table	Reads an entry from an internal table
receive	Receives the results of an asynchronous function
refresh	Initializes a control or an internal table
replace	Replaces the first occurrence of a text in a string
report	Defines a report
rollback work	Reverses all database changes made since the last commit
search	Searches a data object for a string
select	Retrieves a set of data from a database table or a view
select-options	Defines a selection criterion on the selection screen
set pf-status	Sets a GUI status
set property	Sets a property of an external object
set screen	Sets the next screen number
shift	Shifts a field
sort	Sorts the entries of an internal table
split	Splits the contents of a string according to a delimiter
start-of-selection	Event before the first Logical Database table access
statics	Defines static variables in a subroutine
submit	Runs a report
tables	Defines a table work area
top-of-page	Event for page header
transfer	Transfers a field to a file
translate	Replaces letters in strings
type-pools	Includes the types and constants of a type group
types	Defines a data type
update	Updates values in a database table
while/endwhile	Conditional loop
window	Displays a dialog box on a list
write	Displays a field on a list

Developing SAP®'s R/3 Applications with ABAP/4®

Rüdiger Kretschmer and Wolfgang Weiss

BPB PUBLICATIONS

B-14, CONNAUGHT PLACE, NEW DELHI-110001

FIRST INDIAN EDITION 1997

REPRINTED 2002

Distributors:

MICRO BOOK CENTRE
2, City Centre, CG Road,
Near Swastic Char Rasta,
AHMEDABAD-380009 Phone: 6421611

COMPUTER BOOK CENTRE
12, Shrungar Shopping Centre, M.G. Road,
BANGALORE-560001 Phone: 5587923, 5584641

MICRO BOOKS
Shanti Niketan Building, 8, Camac Street,
KOLKATTA-700017 Phone: 2826518, 2826519

BUSINESS PROMOTION BUREAU
8/1, Ritchie Street, Mount Road,
CHENNAI-600002 Phone: 8534796, 8550491

DECCAN AGENCIES
4-3-329, Bank Street,
HYDERABAD-400001 Phone: 4756400, 4756967

MICRO MEDIA
Shop No. 5, Mahendra Chambers, 150 D.N. Road,
Next to Capital Cinema V.T. (C.S.T.) Station,
MUMBAI-400001 Ph.: 2078296, 2078297, 2002732

BPB PUBLICATIONS
B-14, Connaught Place, **NEW DELHI-110001**
Phone: 3325760, 3723393, 3737742

INFO TECH
G-2, Sidhartha Building, 96 Nehru Place,
NEW DELHI-110019
Phone: 6438245, 6415092, 6234208

INFO TECH
Shop No. 2, F-38, South Extension Part-1
NEW DELHI-110049
Phone: 4691288, 4641941

INFO TECH
B-11, Vardhman Plaza, Sector-16,
Electronics Nagar, **NOIDA-201301**
Phone: 914-512329, 515917, 515918

BPB BOOK CENTRE
376, Old Lajpat Rai Market,
DELHI-110006 PHONE: 3861747

NOTE: THE CD-ROM INCLUDED WITH THE BOOK HAS NO COMMERCIAL VALUE AND CANNOT BE SOLD SEPARATELY.

This edition is Authorized for sale only in the following countries : INDIA, BANGLADESH, NEPAL, PAKISTAN, SRI LANKA AND MALDIVES.

Printed in India by arrangement with
SYBEX Inc., USA.

Price : Rs. 499/-

ISBN 81-7029-800-8

Published by Manish Jain for BPB Publications, B-14, Connaught Place
New Delhi-110 001 and Printed by him at Pressworks, Delhi.

Warranty

Sybex warrants the enclosed CD-ROM to be free of physical defects for a period of ninety (90) days after purchase. If you discover a defect in the CD during this warranty period, you can obtain a replacement CD at no charge by sending the defective CD, postage prepaid, with proof of purchase to:

BPB PUBLICATIONS
B-14, CONNAUGHT PLACE,
NEW DELHI-110001
FAX: (011) 3266427/3351856

After the 90-day period, you can obtain a replacement CD by sending us the defective CD, proof or purchase, and a check or money order for Rs. 75/-, payable to BPB Publications.

Disclaimer

Sybex and SAP makes no warranty or representation, either express or implied, with respect to this medium or its contents, its quality, performance, merchantability, or fitness for a particular purpose. In no event will SAP or Sybex, its distributors, or dealers be liable for direct, indirect, special, incidental, or consequential damages arising out of the use of or inability to use the software even if advised of the possibility of such damage.

The exclusion of implied warranties is not permitted by some states. Therefore, the above exclusion may not apply to you. This warranty provides you with specific legal rights; there may be other rights that you may have that vary from state to state.

Copy Protection

None of the files on the CD is copy-protected. However, in all cases, reselling or making copies of these files without authorization is expressly forbidden.

Acknowledgments

This book could not have been written without the help, encouragement, and support of many people. First and foremost, we would like to thank Gerhard Rode, head of the ABAP/4 group at SAP AG and inventor of ABAP/4 in the 80s. From our first vague idea of writing a book about ABAP/4 until the final version, he continuously encouraged us in the project and always found the time for stimulating and helpful discussions.

We would like to express our particular gratitude and appreciation to Christina Fales, Dennis Ladd, and Rolf Hammer for their exceptional efforts. Christina Fales steadily improved our writing style, Dennis Ladd helped us to get in contact with Sybex, and Rolf Hammer contributed the sample programs and many helpful ideas for Chapters 19 and 22.

We made an early draft of each chapter available for technical editing to a large group of SAP colleagues: Mary Anthony, Brigitte Becker, Jutta Bindewald, Andreas Blumenthal, Florian Bundschuh, Rainer Ehre, Mathias Hanbuch, Jürgen Heymann, Horst Keller, Walter Kirchgässner, Ulrich Koch, Axel Kurka, Rudolf Niessen, Wolfgang Otter, Brigitte Penther, Helmut Prestel, Brigitte Rousseau, Martin Schneider, Martin Schrepp, Gabriele Schwinn, and Willi Therre. Thanks to you, folks, for reading all the material.

The CD wouldn't exist without the help of Michael Acker and Hans-Jürgen Reiss, who burned it for us on very short notice—thank you. Special thanks also to Peter Reil and Peter Sandmann from the Marketing department for arranging the R/3 demo on the CD.

We would like to thank Celeste Grinage, Linda Good, Kristine Plachy, Melanie Spiller, Amy Romanoff, Stephanie Hollier, and Kimberley Askew-Qasem from Sybex for their hard work and help in setting up the book project. Special thanks to Melanie Spiller, who thoroughly read the early chapters and gave us many useful hints for improving the text.

We gratefully acknowledge the work of our copy editor Michelle Nance, who did a great job in making the manuscript a real book.

CONTENTS AT A GLANCE

TABLE OF CONTENTS

Introduction

SAP's R/3 System is a package of standard international business applications for areas such as Financial Accounting, Controlling, Logistics, and Human Resources. The R/3 System provides an enterprise solution for all these application areas in a distributed client/server environment. Using the R/3 System, a company can manage financial accounting around the world, receive and track orders for goods, and organize and retrieve employee information and records, among many other features. R/3 provides a wide range of user dialogs that apply to everything from an employee's everyday work to decision support for a manager. Many Fortune 500 companies and high-tech companies (including American Airlines, Chevron, IBM, Mercedes, and Microsoft) run their business with the R/3 System.

An integral part of R/3 is ABAP/4, SAP's fourth-generation language. All of R/3's applications and even parts of its basic system are developed in ABAP/4. The simplicity of the language enables you as the developer to quickly create applications for both small- and large-scale businesses. The robustness of the language is evident in the wide range of functionality and high performance that R/3 offers, allowing for applications that can process huge amounts of customer data or print a large number of invoices efficiently.

The R/3 System gives you a great many tools to help you develop applications. With ABAP/4, you can create completely new client/server applications as well as extend existing R/3 modules. The Remote Function Call allows you to develop open applications distributed over several R/3 Systems and even external systems. ABAP/4 applications are portable to a variety of existing database management and operating systems. In particular, ABAP/4 contains a subset of SQL (called Open SQL) that is an integral part of the language. Open SQL and the database interface of the R/3 System form layers between the Database Management System and the application program. This layered architecture enables you to concentrate on conceptual aspects, and you need not worry about technical things like memory management, pointer arithmetic, or network issues.

The R/3 System has many features for teams of developers. The highly integrated tools of the ABAP/4 Development Workbench support team development in a client/server environment. The Development Workbench proves its strength in the development of the R/3 System itself, where more than a thousand developers use the Workbench tools for building an integrated package of business applications. In particular, an integrated Dictionary ensures that data is used consistently throughout the system, thus avoiding redundancy. The ABAP/4 Repository is a source of information for all development and runtime objects. The Repository is made up of the Dictionary, data models, program and screen definitions, and many more elements. The active integrated Dictionary and the Repository Information System are cornerstones of the power and the flexibility of the ABAP/4 Development Workbench.

Is This Book for You?

This book is for everyone who would like to work with ABAP/4 and to develop client/server applications in a distributed environment. As such, the book addresses students, software professionals, and consultants. In addition, R/3 users and planners will benefit from the insights into how R/3 applications are created.

The goal of this book is to give you a basic understanding of how the ABAP/4 language can be used to develop your own applications. You will learn about the syntax of the language and about the tools that support and enhance the language. After you have learned the basics of the language and tools, you'll start building simple programs and applications to try out various features and ideas. As the book progresses, we'll introduce more complex applications, and we'll show you how to integrate these applications with other parts of the system, how to debug and perfect your applications, and how to create a comfortable interface for the programs. By the end of this book, you should be comfortable building your own applications from scratch and implementing them on any kind of R/3 system. This book Complements and enhances the material offered in ABAP/4 training courses.

Throughout the whole text, we will develop a comprehensive application example program, from the first principles up to advanced features, so it will be easy for you to follow all the steps of writing an application with ABAP/4.

The material in this book is based on Release 3.0 of the R/3 System. Since the book contains many conceptual aspects important for application development, it will still be useful to you even if you are working with an older release or don't have an R/3 System at hand.

How This Book Is Organized

Part I briefly sketches the basic principles and the intrinsic advantages of the ABAP/4 language and the ABAP/4 Development Workbench. In Chapter 1, you'll learn to use elementary language constructs, database tables, and internal tables. Multi-language support, re-use of components, and external communication are critical issues for any modern software system, and you'll learn how ABAP/4 supports you with respect to these concepts in this chapter. Chapter 2 is devoted to general questions about the software development process. The ABAP/4 Development Workbench supports the rapid development of completely new applications as well as large-scale business projects. Using the Repository Information System, you can retrieve information about Dictionary definitions, data models, and programs that is always up-to-date. In Chapter 3, you'll work with the Workbench tools, creating a program and working with the ABAP/4 Editor.

In Part II, you learn how to define data objects in ABAP/4. Chapter 4 introduces elementary types and data objects that are local to a program. In particular, the two construction principles (records and internal tables) for building complex data objects are discussed in detail. In Chapter 5, you will work with tables and structures of the ABAP/4 Dictionary. Chapter 6 presents the Data Modeler, a graphical design tool that uses entity-relationship models to visualize the Dictionary tables and their mutual dependencies.

Part III focuses on elementary language constructs, which are common in many programming languages. The event-oriented nature of the language is especially emphasized. In Chapters 7 and 8, the focus is on working with data. Chapter 9 addresses events and the flow of program control. In Chapter 10, subroutines (called forms) and functions are explained: *forms* are modularization units local to a single program, and *functions* are global components that can be called from many different programs.

Part IV introduces database tables, internal tables, and their interplay. Chapter 11 explains the methods used with Open SQL for reading database tables, particularly creating "snapshots" of database tables and holding them temporarily in internal tables. Chapter 12 describes the methods for reading or changing internal tables, which are the most powerful objects in the ABAP/4 language. The last two chapters of this part, Chapters 13 and 14, deal with language commands for changing database tables and with techniques for storing complex data objects to temporary or permanent memory in the database.

In Part V, you will create *reports*—programs that retrieve data from the database, organize it according to different criteria, and present it in the form of a list on the screen or as a printed list. Logical Databases provide re-usable procedures for retrieving complex data from databases. In addition, standard user dialogs for specifying selections are created automatically. The method of writing reports with Logical Databases is explained in this part. Chapter 15 covers the basics of working with Logical Databases.

User dialogs can be further refined as explained in Chapter 16. Designing drill-down features is discussed in Chapter 17, and the last chapter of this part deals with the calling interface for reports.

ABAP/4 provides developers with a wide variety of design tools and language constructs to create dialog programs, and these tools and constructs are the subject of Part VI. The basic building elements are screens covered in Chapter 19, along with menu bars and buttons. Chapter 20 describes ABAP/4's messaging system. To guarantee consistent data even throughout complex application programs with multiple screens, ABAP/4 offers an elaborated transaction concept that is presented in Chapter 21. Chapter 22 discusses advanced GUI features such as table controls. The concepts covered in this section of the book are illustrated by an example application for a travel agency to use in booking airline flights.

Part VII is concerned with dynamic language constructs. In the first chapter of this part, dynamic table operations and dynamic subroutine calls are covered. Chapter 24 introduces the concept of Field Symbols, and Chapter 25 describes how to create and execute a whole program on the fly.

In Part VIII, we discuss various open interfaces to external components like C programs or spreadsheets. Chapter 26 deals with a simple file interface. ABAP/4 supports direct program-to-program communication by an extension of the local function call, the Remote Function Call (RFC), which is the subject of Chapter 27. Finally, in the last chapter, you will see how to directly invoke an application that follows the standard for OLE Automation from within the ABAP/4 language.

The five appendices give you some extra information about important topics. Appendix A describes the architecture of the R/3 System. Appendix B takes a close look at the ABAP/4 Query. In Appendix C, you'll find information on the advanced features of the Development Workbench. Appendix D is about team development work in a distributed environment, and Appendix E wraps up the book with a list of the most important ABAP/4 system fields and their meanings.

Conventions Used in This Book

Throughout this book, we have used some basic conventions to help you understand our instructions. When you see something in **boldface** type, it is generally text that you should key in. Words in *italics* are new terms or concepts you should notice. We have used a special `program` font for all of our code examples to help you distinguish them from the rest of the text.

In addition, there are two elements that point out special kinds of information, as described below.

 A Note contains some additional helpful text about the topic or a reference to another place where you can get more information on the subject.

 A Tip is a useful idea or suggestion for a better way to accomplish a task or to approach a problem.

 A Warning advises you of a common pitfall or problem you should take care to avoid.

About the Companion CD

The free CD inside the back cover of the book contains all of the source code for the examples used in this book. You can use this source code to help you work through the examples. In addition, you can use these pieces of code as templates for your own programs.

The CD also contains detailed documentation about the ABAP/4 commands. Here you'll find all the possible variations of a command and many useful programming examples.

Finally, the CD contains text-based descriptions and demonstrates through PowerPoint presentations, video clips, and white papers the various parts and application areas of the R/3 System. In particular, you'll learn about the benefits of integration in the R/3 System, and you'll see how this integration ensures that all end users work with the most up-to-date operational data, without the need to upload data constantly. The CD also contains various other demonstrations that will help you understand how you can best use R/3 System features to develop relevant, helpful applications for different kinds of businesses.

PART I

Introduction to ABAP/4

- Chapter 1: Key Features of the ABAP/4 Language

- Chapter 2: The ABAP/4 Development Workbench

- Chapter 3: Getting Started

PART 1

CHAPTER

O N E

1

Key Features of the ABAP/4 Language

- **Language structure**

- **Working with types and data objects**

- **Some simple examples**

- **Re-usability in ABAP/4**

ABAP/4 is short for *Advanced Business Application Programming 4GL*. ABAP/4 is SAP's fourth-generation language, and it is the backbone of the R/3 system. All of R/3's applications and even parts of its basis system were developed in ABAP/4. The language's flexibility and ease of use combined with its specially designed commands enable you to quickly design and implement both small- and large-scale business solutions for R/3 systems.

ABAP/4 has many features that make it especially suitable for designing applications for such a large and complex system as R/3. The language is event-driven; that is, user actions and system events control the application's execution. A key feature is the concept of internal tables, which provide a convenient mapping from persistent database tables into runtime objects and vice versa. The ABAP/4 language doesn't stand alone; it is part of a larger development environment called the *Development Workbench*, which offers many tools for planning and implementing applications. You can use ABAP/4 to create completely new client/server applications, as well as to extend existing R/3 modules. Features such as the Remote Function Call (RFC) allow you to develop distributed applications. In addition, ABAP/4 applications are portable to a variety of operating systems and database management systems making it easy to integrate them into a company's existing database framework. The robustness of the ABAP/4 language is evident in the wide range of functionality and high performance that the R/3 system offers.

A Quick Guide to ABAP/4

Through the rest of this chapter, we'll introduce you to the most important features of ABAP/4. We'll point out some of the things that make this language different from others, and we'll let you know how these features benefit you, the developer.

The Structure of the Language

Unlike many other programming languages, an ABAP/4 program can be read like an English text. The underlying design concept is quite simple: a program should not be an assemblage of confusing formulas that only the author and the compiler can understand—the program source should be readable by everyone who is interested in the application. This idea guarantees that ABAP/4 programs have long lives and are easily extended.

In ABAP/4, a program text is built of statements that each end with a period. A statement begins with a reserved keyword followed by additional parameters and data objects. You can combine a sequence of statements that have identical beginnings (the same keyword and sometimes the same parameters and data objects) into a single statement using a colon and commas, with the identical part appearing before the colon. For instance, the following two declarations of integer variables

```
data x type i.
data y type i.
```

can be shortened as follows:

```
data: x type i,
      y type i.
```

Types, Data Objects (Variables), and an Integrated Dictionary

In addition to the straightforward structure of its program text, ABAP/4 features a set of elementary types (including character, integer, and date) and two construction concepts (records and internal tables) to help you build complex types and data objects. In addition, you can create non-elementary types and data structures, store their definitions in the integrated ABAP/4 Dictionary, then use them in all components of the system. In this way, you can save time and effort by avoiding recreating information in your programs.

> **NOTE**   *Non-elementary types* **are also called** *user-defined types*.

Elementary types in ABAP/4 work the same way as they do in any other language. For example, you can define a field `customer_name` of type character and length 25 as shown here:

```
data customer_name(25) type c.
```

You define a non-elementary type in ABAP/4 using the keyword `types`. Using a non-elementary type, you could define the same field as above in this way:

```
types t_name(25) type c.
data customer_name type t_name.
```

In this example, the non-elementary type `t_name` is defined as being type c and length 25. The field `customer_name` is given the type `t_name`. Any number of fields can now use this same `t_name` type.

NOTE For a more complete discussion of types, see Chapter 4.

References tell the program to use the definition of an existing data object for a new data object, so that both objects will have the same information. Any changes to the original data object's definition will be reflected in all the objects that refer to that original. You establish reference to a data object by using the addition like. In the following example, the field vendor_name inherits all information from customer_name:

```
data vendor_name like customer_name.
```

Beyond the simple types and data objects, ABAP/4 supports the construction of complex objects using *records* and *internal tables*. *Records* contain a fixed number of data objects. An *internal table* is a collection of a variable number of records. You can also define nested records and internal tables.

It is fairly easy to define a record. For example, if you wanted to define a record named booking with three fields, you could write the following code:

```
data: begin of booking,
        id(4) type c,
        flight_date type d,
        name like customer_name,
      end of booking.
```

In this example, the record begins with the keywords data begin of. Three fields are defined within the record: id, flight_date, and name. (Note that this last field uses a reference to the customer_name field from the example above). The record ends with the data end of keyword. You can now refer back to this structure throughout your program. When you want to refer back to a field within this record, you write the record name followed by a hyphen and the field name. For example, to refer back to the flight_date field in this example, you would write bookings-flight_date.

7

To define an internal table, you use the addition occurs followed by a number (called the *Occurs Parameter*), which is an estimate of the number of lines in the table. The Occurs Parameter is only a performance parameter, and it does not restrict the maximum size of the internal table. The ABAP/4 runtime system automatically provides extra memory if the number of lines in the table exceeds this estimate.

For example, each entry of the internal table named booking_table defined below has the same structure as the record named booking.

```
data booking_table like booking occurs 100.
```

Many table operations require a record for the information being added to the current line of the table. By using the addition with header line in the defining data statement, a data object with the same structure as a line of the table is created, in addition to the table itself.

NOTE   **We will cover ABAP/4 internal tables in detail in Chapter 12.**

The integrated ABAP/4 Dictionary contains type definitions and data structures that you can use in all components of the system. In particular, since the structure definition of database tables is contained in the Dictionary, you can be sure that these tables will be used consistently in programs and screens. You can refer to a Dictionary table and its fields using the addition like in the same way as we explained above.

NOTE We will cover the ABAP/4 Dictionary in detail in Chapter 5.

A Few Simple Examples

To give you an idea of how a simple ABAP/4 program looks, we'll give you some examples below. ABAP/4 uses many standard commands to perform operations such as moving data and displaying and formatting fields, so most of these examples should be pretty clear.

Commands

You can copy the content of one data object to another using the move command, which takes the form move source to target in ABAP/4. If the type or length of the source and target field are different, ABAP/4 always converts the content of the source field according to the format of the target. Arithmetic expressions behave as usual in other languages, and standard mathematical functions are supported.

Using the write command, you can display the contents of fields in a standard format that depends on the type of the field. For example, the output string 'ABAP/4 is easy.' will be displayed by the following write command:

```
write 'ABAP/4 is easy.'.
```

You can also explicitly set special options to determine a field's format (for example, the color) or position within the list.

TIP

Instead of writing text directly in program code, you can use text symbols. Text symbols are useful if a program will be used in other countries with different languages. Text represented by text symbols is stored in the Repository and is always displayed in the language of the user. The benefit of text symbols is that they can be translated without affecting the source code of a program.

Since ABAP/4 is an event-driven language, a developer can design and implement well-structured dialog programs. At runtime, events are triggered by the user or by the system itself. Whenever an event occurs, all statements between the corresponding event keyword and the next event keyword are processed. For example, if a program provides some drill-down facilities, it must react when a user selects a line. In other words, if the program allows the user to double-click on an object to see more information about it, there must be code in place that causes the screen to change to the right information when the program receives an on-click event. This event's statements are inserted after the `at line selection` command.

```
at line-selection.
  write 'This is displayed after double-clicking a line'.
```

Events thereby determine the external flow of control of the program; that is, events determine how the user is able to interact with the program or how system events influence the program flow. The internal flow of control is given by standard control structures. The `if/else/endif` construct distinguishes between different situations by means of a logical condition, whereas `case/when/endcase` branches according to a fixed set of possible values. An unconditional loop is established by `do/enddo`, and `while/endwhile` is used for a loop with a terminating condition. These constructs work as in other programming languages, and should be familiar to most of you.

Defining Subroutines

ABAP/4 provides two techniques for defining subroutines: forms in ABAP/4 are local subroutines of a single program, and functions are global components that are called by many different programs. Both kinds of subroutines support encapsulation of local data as well as different methods to transfer data via interface parameters (such as call by value or call by reference). Type checks of the interface parameters of forms or functions are executed during the Syntax Check or at runtime.

Functions have a public interface that is created and maintained by an interface description tool. Since functions are usually called by many programs, they are provided with an exception mechanism. An exception can be raised using the raise statement. If this is processed at runtime, execution of the function stops immediately. The caller can either handle the exception explicitly or let the runtime system terminate the current program:

A form is defined by form/endform and called by a perform command. Interface parameters are listed after the additions using or changing, and the parameters are specified by position:

```
perform calc using    a1
               changing a2.
write: a2.
form calc using    f1 like a1
           changing f2 like a2.
   f2 = f1 + ( f2 * 17 ).
endform.
```

A function is defined by function/endfunction and called by call function. In contrast to forms, function parameters are specified by name.

Database Tables and Internal Tables

ABAP/4 contains a subset of SQL (called *Open SQL*) that is an integral part of the language. ABAP/4 programs using Open SQL can access data from all database systems that are supported by the R/3 system. Internal tables and database tables work together. The contents of a database table can be mapped into an internal table at runtime, so that the internal table is a snapshot of a database table. For example, to create a list containing all the entries in a database table, you can read the table contents into an internal table with the same structure and display each line as follows:

```
tables customers.
data all_customers like customers occurs 100
                         with header line.
select * from customers into table all_customers.
loop at all_customers.
  write: / all_customers-name.
endloop.
```

Using a where clause of a select statement, the set of selected records can be restricted according to a logical condition. You can also specify a subset of all table fields and use aggregate functions, such as the number of table entries satisfying a certain condition. Dynamic versions of the select statements are also supported.

ABAP/4 also provides several commands for changing database tables: insert, update, modify, and delete. Using these commands, you can change a single entry as well as a set of entries. The tables of a relational database always have a flat structure (i.e., a structure cannot contain another table). Local objects of a program can be deeply structured, which means that they can contain structures or even internal tables. To store the contents of deeply structured objects in flat tables, you must first break up the objects so that they fit into flat structures. But if you use the export and import commands, you can save and read these complex objects in a single step, without converting them first.

The sort command sorts an internal table according to specified sort fields. You can read a set of lines sequentially using the loop/endloop commands. A loop can be restricted to a specified subset of the table using a where clause. You can access a single line using the statement read table with further parameters specifying the index for the required line or the logical key. If the table is sorted, you can speed up access by specifying the binary search method. Displaying subtotals, headers, and other information about groups of entries in an internal table is possible using blocks of at/endat statements. These blocks are processed whenever the content of some of the relevant key fields changes.

The code below illustrates the use of table operations, using the example of finding out how many seats are available on flights. In this example, the internal table my_flights is filled with information from the database, and the number of occupied seats for each entry is displayed. The output is enhanced by a header and a subtotal of occupied seats for each carrier. (The lines that begin with an asterix are comments.)

```
* Database table with flight data
tables flights.
* Internal table for flights
data my_flights like flights occurs 10 with header line.
* Statistical data
data sum_occupied_seats like my_flights-seatsocc.
* Reading the flights from the database
select * from flights into table my_flights
       order by primary key.
* Displaying the number of occupied seats on each flight
* with headers and subtotals for each carrier
loop at my_flights.
  at new carrid.
    new-page.
    write / my_flights-carrid.
    clear sum_occupied_seats.
  endat.
  add my_flights-seatsocc to sum_occupied_seats.
  write / my_flights-seatsocc.
  at end of carrid.
    write / sum_occupied_seats.
```

```
    endat.
    endloop.
```

This example of everyday life shows the benefit of specially designed language elements for business applications. The like in the definition of the internal table gives it the same structure as the database table—that structure is essentially copied to the internal table. The internal table is filled with data from the database in one single step.

Designing Reports and Dialog Transactions

An ABAP/4 *report* is a program that retrieves data from the database, groups it together according to different criteria, and presents it on the screen or as a printed list. To create a report, you can use the ABAP/4 Query tool, which assists you in designing the list layout and generates the program code automatically (see Figure 1.1). However, if the full flexibility of the programming language is needed, you should create the report either using the basic select commands or using a *Logical Database* that simplifies database access. Logical Databases provide procedures for retrieving complex data from databases, making it easy to develop well-structured reports. If you use the Logical Database to create your report, a selection screen for specifying selection criteria as well as the program code to react on wrong input is created automatically.

NOTE   See Appendix B for a detailed discussion of the Query tool and its uses in ABAP/4. For more information on select commands, see Chapter 11. Logical Databases are covered in Chapter 15.

Logical Databases provide a re-usability that distinguishes ABAP/4 from many other programming languages. The advantages of being

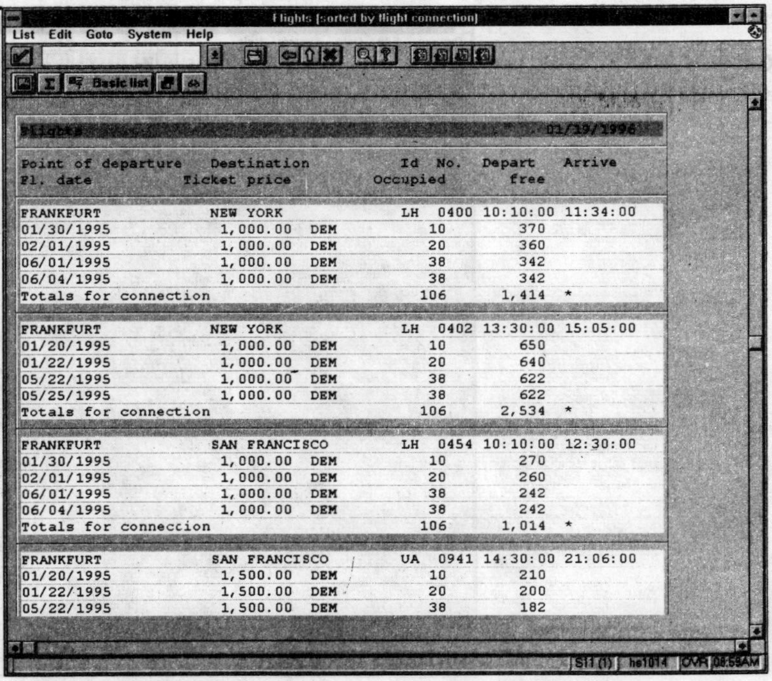

FIGURE 1.1:

The list output from an ABAP/4 query

able to re-use data or methods become obvious if many reports use the same Logical Database. For example, by optimizing the performance of a single Logical Database, you can simultaneously improve the performance of a large number of reports.

Each ABAP/4 report has a standard selection screen for user input. You can create additional input fields in that standard screen by defining Select-Options (see Figure 1.2). For example, the following report has a Select-Option for specifying customer names, and the `select` statement reads the set of data as it were individually specified by each user.

```
tables customers.
data all_customers like customers occurs 100
                    with header line.
select-options sname for customers-name.
select * from customers into table all_customers
       where name in sname.
```

FIGURE 1.2:

Select-Options on a selection
screen

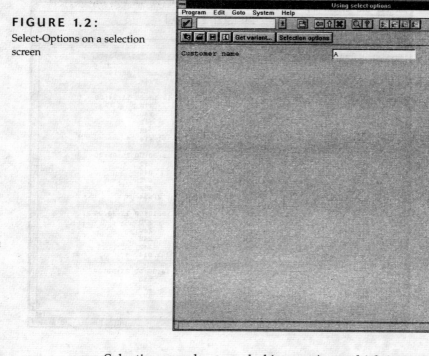

FIGURE 1.2:

Select-Options on a selection
screen

Selections can be recorded in a *variant*, which is a set of values for the selection criteria of a report. If a report is submitted with a variant, the input
fields of the selection screen are automatically filled with the values of
that variant.

ABAP/4 provides many tools and language constructs for designing
applications with dialog boxes and user-input screens with an easy-to-
use Graphical User Interface. Dictionary-based validation rules and
consistency checks provide data integrity even at the user-input level;
that is, the program checks to make sure data is valid at the time the
user inputs it, so that if the data is incorrect, the user has to correct it
right then. Users work with on-screen forms designed to resemble
typical paper forms, and a screen consists of two pieces, the *layout* and
the *flow logic*.

A screen's *layout* is made up of menus, input fields, labels, push buttons, radio buttons, frames, and table controls. You choose these elements from a toolbar or the Dictionary and use drag and drop to place them on the screen.

A screen's *flow logic* is made up of input and output events and events triggered when the user requests help or assistance for possible input. At each event, data is processed as defined by modules of the controlling program. In particular, the sequence of screens is driven by user input and modules of the event `process after input`. If the user provides incorrect input, a messaging system informs the user and provides assistance.

You can see a sample data entry screen showing an inquiry about a flight connection for a flight reservation in Figure 1.3. Figure 1.4 shows a sample screen for booking a flight and entering customer data.

FIGURE 1.3:

An inquiry about a flight connection

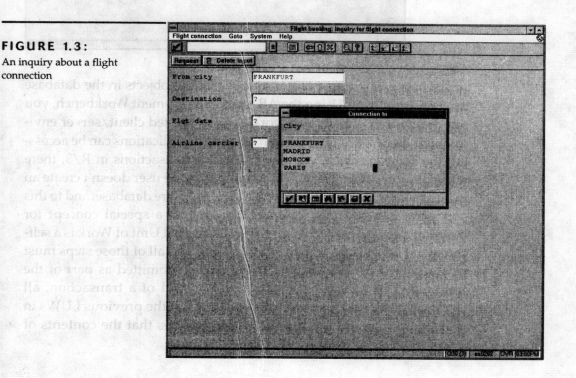

FIGURE 1.4:

A screen for booking a flight
and entering customer data

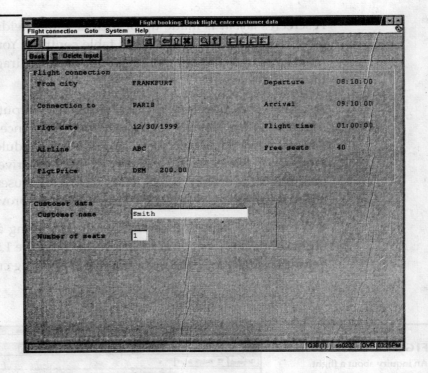

A *transaction* is a dialog program that changes objects in the database
in a consistent way. Using the ABAP/4 Development Workbench, you
can design transactions that work in a distributed client/server environment. Because many different users and applications can be accessing the same database via many different transactions in R/3, there
must be protective measures in place so that one user doesn't create an
incorrect table entry that would damage the entire database, and to this
end there is a separate lock mechanism and a special concept for
defining a *Logical Unit of Work* (LUW). A Logical Unit of Work is a self-
contained set of steps within a transaction, and all of those steps must
be completed correctly before that LUW is submitted as part of the
transaction. If an error occurs before the end of a transaction, all
changes in the current LUW are canceled, but the previous LUWs in
that transaction are not canceled. This ensures that the contents of

database tables are always consistent. A *locking mechanism* ensures that only one user can change a data object at the same time.

Compilation and Runtime Behavior

At runtime, the source code of an ABAP/4 program is compiled to a program code that runs interpretively. This compilation process is also called *generation*. The generated form of a program is stored in the ABAP/4 Repository. Once a program has been generated, it is automatically re-generated if the source code or one of the program's referenced Dictionary objects is changed. The ABAP/4 runtime system generates a program automatically when it is needed, so you don't have to bother with it.

ABAP/4's interpretive nature has some significant advantages for the developer. First, you can rapidly create and test a prototype of an application. Second, changes to Dictionary objects only affect those programs that use the objects and are executed after the change, so the edit-debug cycle is shortened, since changes to an object can be implemented immediately. Last but not least, the generated form of a program can be distributed across a network, such as a distributed R/3 system. Whenever a runtime system is available on a network node, any program that has been put on the network can be executed. In each distributed R/3 system, ABAP/4 programs are executed on the application servers (that is, the nodes of the second level of R/3's three-tier architecture). Therefore, the programs don't have to be run from a single server, but can instead be run on local servers, to optimize the use of local resources.

NOTE   For more information on R/3's three-tier architecture, see Appendix A.

Multi-Language Support

ABAP/4 makes it easy to develop international application programs for worldwide use. You can use language-dependent texts whenever text is displayed on a screen or printed list. These texts can be translated into different languages without requiring you to change or generate a program. At runtime, a language-dependent text always appears in the language the user specified when logging on. ABAP/4 offers language-dependent texts in the following situations:

- Program documentation and program title
- Headers, labels, and help information for Dictionary fields
- Selection texts on selection screens
- Text symbols used in write commands
- Page headers and column headers in report lists
- Menu functions and push buttons
- Interface descriptions of functions
- Text fields on a screen
- Message texts

Re-usability

ABAP/4 supports the system-wide re-use of different kinds of components:

- Structure definitions and types from the Dictionary
- Functions with a flexible interface and exception handling
- Logical Databases for data retrieval in reports

Information about Dictionary table structures and single table fields can be used throughout all of a system's programs and screens. For example, an internal program record structured as a Dictionary table is defined by a `tables` declaration. With the addition `like` in a data declaration, you can refer to complete structures or single fields. In the same way, interface parameters of forms and functions can refer to a Dictionary object. It is also possible to define non-elementary types and constants in type pools of the Dictionary. They can be used in a program through the `type-pools` declaration. If the definition of a Dictionary object is changed and activated, all programs and screens referring to this object are automatically generated the next time they are called.

The ABAP/4 Development Workbench contains a large number of reusable functions. Each function is uniquely determined by its name and belongs to a *function group*—one or more functions that have a similar purpose. For example, there are function groups for printing documents, updating general ledgers, or reading information from complex financial documents. Technically speaking, a function group is a program that lives as long as the caller of a function in the group. If a function in a group is called by the same program that recently called another function in that group, the local data of the group still has the contents of the previous function call.

The interface parameters of a function can be defined as optional, and they can have default values. Therefore, the callers of a function can provide the default values and need not specify all parameters. This flexibility is crucial to re-use and extend function in the life cycle of a system. You can also use functions for displaying dialog boxes or interface screens. The ABAP/4 Development Workbench provides many functions to support standardized dialog boxes, such as functions for confirmation prompt dialogs.

A function can be made public for use by a Remote Function Call (RFC) in a network. The RFC technique is the basis for integrating multiple R/3 systems. This means functions can be made available across the network for re-use in other systems.

Logical Databases provide re-usable methods for data retrieval, as we mentioned above. A change in a Logical Database immediately affects all reports using it. Thus, you can change the runtime behavior of many reports by changing a single Logical Database.

Any re-use concept is only helpful in large-scale software projects if new features can be added with little recompilation and minimum adjustment to existing components, and this is where ABAP/4 offers a high degree of flexibility. First, if a program is executed after Dictionary objects have been changed and activated, the program is only recompiled if it refers to one of the changed objects. This approach avoids the rigidity of using header files. Second, the interface of a function can be extended without affecting existing callers. Finally, a report using a Logical Database can freely choose the tables that are to be read from the database.

Open Interfaces

R/3 system users generally work with many different tools and products in a client/ server environment, so applications written in ABAP/4 should be able to communicate with these components as seamlessly as possible. The ABAP/4 language offers various open interfaces that allow this communication. The simplest one is a file interface, where external data is exchanged through a file. The Remote Function Call (RFC) we mentioned above supports direct program-to-program communication between R/3 systems, between an R/3 system and a mainframe-based SAP R/2 system, or between an R/3 system and external programs such as C/C++ or Visual Basic programs. RFC supports both synchronous and asynchronous communication modes. The RFC relieves you from considerations like communication protocols, network details, or code pages.

Via its Open Object Interface, ABAP/4 supports OLE Automation. This enables you to integrate desktop applications. The ABAP/4's Open Object Interface is not restricted to OLE Automation—it is usable with other object technologies like CORBA, which will be supported in future releases of R/3.

NOTE For more information on using the Open Object Interface with OLE, see Chapter 28.

A Quick Review

Here is a quick review of some of the most important features we have covered in this chapter:

- An ABAP/4 program can be read like a regular text, making it easy for other developers to understand and extend.

- ABAP/4 features a set of elementary types and two construction concepts (records and internal tables) to help you build complex types and data objects.

- The integrated Dictionary contains type definitions and data structures that you can use in all components of the systems.

- Logical Databases provide procedures for retrieving complex data from databases, allowing you to create useful reports.

In this chapter, we have introduced some of the concepts of the ABAP/4 language itself. In the next chapter, we will take a look at the Development Workbench, a set of tools that support and complement the ABAP/4 language.

CHAPTER

T W O

The ABAP/4 Development Workbench

- **Using the Workbench tools**

- **Re-using objects in the Repository**

- **Building graphical representations with the Data Modeler**

- **Managing projects with the Workbench Organizer**

The intrinsic advantages of a programming language are evident not only in the functionality of the language, but also in the development environment that supports that language. The ABAP/4 language is the central tool in the excellent development package called the *ABAP/4 Development Workbench,* and it is the synergy of these two components that guarantees an efficient development process for large-scale enterprise applications across a distributed client/server environment. Using the tools available in the development package, you can concentrate on the conceptual aspects of your new application, without getting mired down in memory management, pointer arithmetic, and network optimization. Although the ABAP/4 language is the real star of the show, you will need to use the entire set of Workbench tools to build and implement applications for R/3. In this chapter, we'll show you how the parts of the Workbench work together to support ABAP/4 and provide you with an effective development environment.

The ABAP/4 Development Workbench proves its strength in the R/3 system itself, where more than a thousand developers used the Workbench tools to build an integrated package of business applications. SAP continues to extend the functionality of the Workbench with new improvements such as integrated desktop applications or business process modeling.

The Development Workbench is made up of the following tools (see Figure 2.1):

- the Object Browser
- the ABAP/4 Language
- the Repository, including the active Dictionary

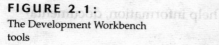

FIGURE 2.1:
The Development Workbench
tools

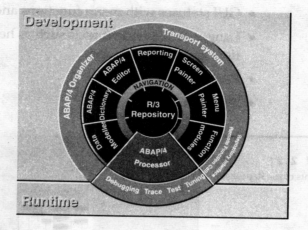

- the Data Modeler
- the Query
- the Workbench Organizer
- various test and analysis tools

We'll begin our exploration of the Workbench with a look at the Repository.

The Repository

The ABAP/4 Repository is made up of the following development and runtime objects (see Figure 2.2):

- Data models
- Dictionary types and table structures
- Programs
- Screens
- System wide re-usable functions

- GUI statuses with menu functions and icons
- Language-dependent texts such as help information, documentation, and error messages
- Report variants
- ABAP/4 queries

FIGURE 2.2:

The elements of the Repository

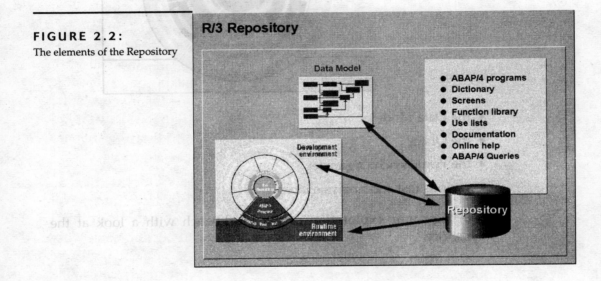

At the center of the ABAP/4 Repository is the Dictionary, which contains descriptive information about things like fields, structures, and database tables. For example, this is where a developer stores the formal description of an entry in a database table (where all the table fields are defined with their types and lengths). You can refer to other fields in the Dictionary. On the programming level, you can also refer to a Dictionary description; for example, by using the addition like in a data declaration or in the interface of a subroutine. The Dictionary ensures that data is used consistently by all development and runtime objects throughout the system, allowing you to avoid repetition.

NOTE   For more information on the Dictionary, see Chapter 5.

The ability to re-use existing objects is only helpful if you can retrieve information from the Repository about those objects and their usage. The Repository Information System allows the developer to search many items, such as programs, tables, and functions, to get information on how to use them. In addition, up-to-date Use Lists, which list all operations that call (or *use*) a specified item, are readily available in the Information System. For example, double-clicking on a subroutine definition in the program code of an application you are developing produces a Use List of all statements that call that subroutine. In a similar way, the Use List of a Dictionary table lists all statements and screens in which that particular table or table field shows up.

The Workbench's Object Browser provides you with identical access to each Repository object by simply drilling down into the object hierarchy. You don't need to use different tools to move around among objects—you can get to all Repository objects by double-clicking. For example, double-clicking on a function call takes you to that function's definition. Similarly, double-clicking on a table name in a program source branches to that table's definition in the Dictionary, as shown in Figure 2.3.

If the Dictionary contains all of the information on how an application's data objects are built, the Data Modeler is the tool that helps you give these objects and their relations a "face."

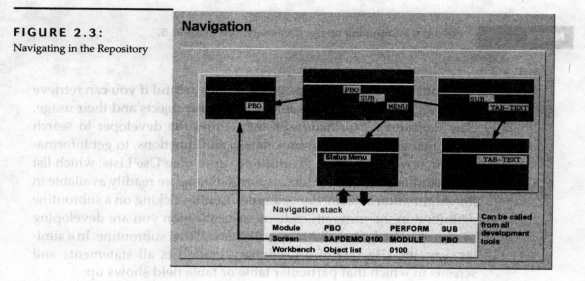

FIGURE 2.3:

Navigating in the Repository

The Data Modeler

The Data Modeler tool supports graphical modeling of software applications, giving complicated "behind-the-scenes" structures and dependencies more user-friendly interfaces. Entity-relationship models (or *ER models*) produce graphical representations of data objects and their dependencies. Technically speaking, the entity type in an entity-relationship corresponds to a table or view in the Dictionary. Because of the tight integration of the Repository's components, the associated Dictionary objects of entity types can be generated automatically. (If there isn't one) In other words, if you create a graphic model for an application, the Dictionary can automatically generate the corresponding table structures. Conversely, changes to a table definition are immediately reflected in the model. You can navigate between the data model and the underlying definitions in the Dictionary by double-clicking on the appropriate object.

Because of its graphical representation, a data model is very useful in documenting large-scale systems. In practice, a model often needs to be adjusted during the life cycle of a system (for example, by adding a new field to a table). There are several reasons for late changes, such as performance considerations or additional requirements from end users. The Data Modeler allows you to re-engineer projects successfully by building a model that graphically displays existing tables and their relationships (see Figure 2.4).

FIGURE 2.4:

A sample data model

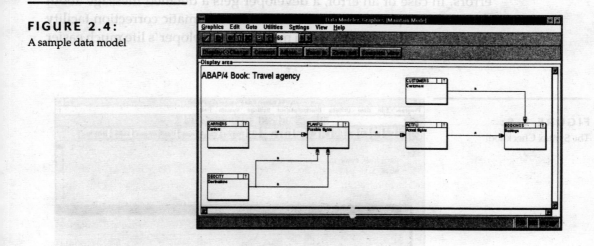

NOTE   For more information on the Data Modeler, see Chapter 6.

Test and Analysis Tools

A set of testing functions and performance measurement tools is integrated into the Workbench. These tools accelerate the development process by allowing you to find errors and trouble spots in your code and applications and correct them early on.

For example, the editor for ABAP/4 programs has a built-in Syntax Check tool, which tests the coding for syntactical correctness and flags errors. In case of an error, a developer gets a detailed message about the error and possible reasons for it. The automatic correction facility suggests a better syntax, which makes the developer's life much easier (see Figure 2.5).

FIGURE 2.5:

The Syntax Check tool

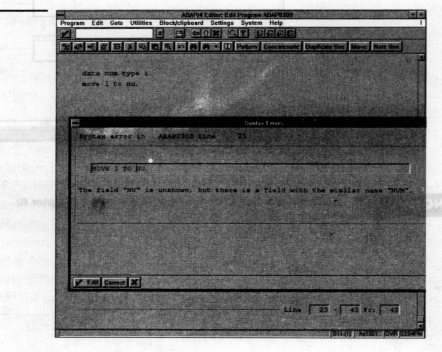

The extended version of the Syntax Check searches out situations that might occasionally result in a runtime error. For example, when the Syntax Check discovers inconsistent interface parameters in a function call, they are flagged so you can correct them.

Analysis tools help you to trace the flow of a program and to find out how much time a particular function or statement consumes. This enables you to tune your application for optimal performance. The Workbench tools also support detailed analysis of all database operations.

NOTE For more information on test and analysis tools, see Appendix C.

The Workbench Organizer

The Development Workbench can be used for both small- and large-scale development projects where many people work together in a distributed system environment. The Workbench Organizer tool maintains multiple development projects and manages their distribution across different systems. The technique of transporting projects between different R/3 systems is independent of platforms in the network. No specific knowledge of the underlying operating system is needed to execute the transports.

Using the Workbench Organizer, you can establish development systems and well-defined transport paths among different systems. This separation guarantees a high degree of security in developing and maintaining a system, since errors in the test phase do not affect the target system.

When many people are working on one development project, they will often need access to the same objects. But at the same time, there must be a way to make sure that no one outside the team can change their objects. The Workbench Organizer supports this kind of team development (see Figure 2.6).

FIGURE 2.6:
Team development and transport management

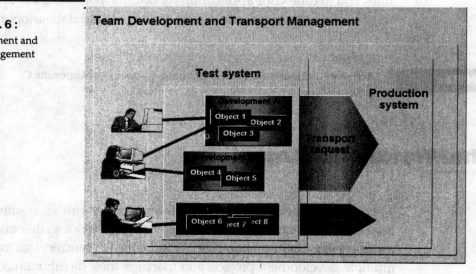

For more information on the Workbench Organizer, see Appendix D.

 NOTE

A Quick Review

Here is a quick review of some of the most important topics we covered in this chapter:

- The ABAP/4 Development Workbench is made up of tools that support the programming language, including the Dictionary, the Data Modeler, and the Workbench Organizer.

- This set of tools supports the team development of small and large business application projects.

- The ABAP/4 language is completely integrated with the Workbench tools, which speeds up the development process enormously.

In the next chapter, we will get down to business: you will learn how to create a simple ABAP/4 application.

A Quick Review

Here is a quick review of some of the most important topics we covered in this chapter.

- The ABAP/4 Development Workbench is made up of tools that support the programming language, including the Dictionary, the Data Modeler, and the Workbench Organizer.

- This set of tools supports the team development of small and large business application projects.

- The ABAP/4 language is completely integrated with the Workbench tools, which speeds up the development process enormously.

In the next chapter, we will get down to business; you will learn how to create a simple ABAP/4 application.

CHAPTER

THREE

Getting Started

- General ABAP/4 syntax rules

- Creating a simple program

- Working in the Editor

- Testing a program

Now that you know the basics about ABAP/4 and the Development Workbench, it's time to get down to business. In this chapter, you will learn how to create a simple ABAP/4 program using the Development Workbench. In the example, we'll explain the syntax rules of the language and demonstrate some elementary statements. You will also learn how to use the basic features of the ABAP/4 Editor, particularly how to make sure that your program is error-free using the Syntax Check.

The Syntax of ABAP/4 Programs

The syntax rules of ABAP/4 are similar to real-life languages. A program text is built of statements (or commands, if you like), and each statement ends with a period. For example, the following sample program is made of two lines of code:

```
report abaptest.
write 'Customer list'.
```

The first statement declares the name of the program as abaptest. Every program must begin with the report declaration. The second command displays the words *Customer list* on the screen. ABAP/4 makes it easy for you to check the syntax of your program: simply click on the Check button in the ABAP/4 Editor. If you've made a mistake, the Syntax Checker describes the error and suggests possible alternatives.

NOTE   For more on the checking the syntax of your program, see the "Syntax Check" section later in this chapter.

Statements and Comments

Here are the basic rules of ABAP/4 syntax:

- A statement is a sequence of words that ends with a period.
- A word in a statement is delimited by blank spaces on both sides.
- A statement always begins with an ABAP/4 keyword such as `write` or `report`.
- A *literal* (a sequence of characters) is enclosed by single quotation marks (').

You may sometimes need to use a single quotation mark within the text of a literal itself. In this case, you must double the single quotation mark to get a single one. So by writing this code:

```
write 'Customer''s Name'.
```

your text will read *Customer's Name*.

Many ABAP/4 commands allow extra parameters that will be referred to as *additions* throughout the book. For example, in the following code, the `write` command has an optional addition named `at` that causes the text to appear at the specified position in the line on the output screen:

```
write 'Customer list'at 10.
```

Although they are not required to make a program run, it is very useful to insert comments in the source code for the sake of better readability and documentation. All text after an asterisk (*) in the first column or after a double quotation mark (") in any column is considered a comment.

There are no serious restrictions on how you format your code. A statement can be extended over several lines, and more than one statement can be in a single line. In practice, of course, you won't spread your code elements around randomly. Instead, you'll order and indent them according to their intrinsic logic, following standard programming conventions and making the programs more readable and maintainable.

Combining Statements

Suppose you have a sequence of statements as follows:

```
write 'Customer list'.
write 'Bookings'.
```

This sequence can also be combined into a single statement using a colon and commas:

```
write: 'Customer list',
       'Bookings'.
```

As a rule, all statements with an identical beginning part can be combined. The part the statements have in common appears before the colon, and the different items in the sequence are separated by commas.

Case Sensitivity

In general, ABAP/4 is not case sensitive. The following three statements produce the same output:

```
write 'X'.
WRITE 'X'.
wRiTe 'X'.
```

The only place where you must distinguish between upper- and lower-case letters is within literals. For example, the statement

```
write 'x'.
```

does not produce the same output as the examples above.

These are all the general syntax rules of the language. Now, for the real mission of this book: creating programs.

Creating a Program

To begin creating your first ABAP/4 program, you must first log on to the R/3 system. This requires you to have a valid user name and password from your system administrator.

Logging on to the R/3 System

When you select an R/3 system by clicking on the R/3 icon on your desktop screen, the Logon screen appears, and you must enter some information to proceed (see Figure 3.1). The first input field on this screen is called Client. Each R/3 system is divided into one or more Clients representing different business units. In most cases, you don't need to worry about entering a Client number, since the default Client is usually already set. Enter your user name and password in the next two fields. You can also specify a language in the Language field (for example, *E* for *English*). If you don't specify a language, your system's default language is chosen. The default language is set by the system administrator or by the user and could be different on different systems.

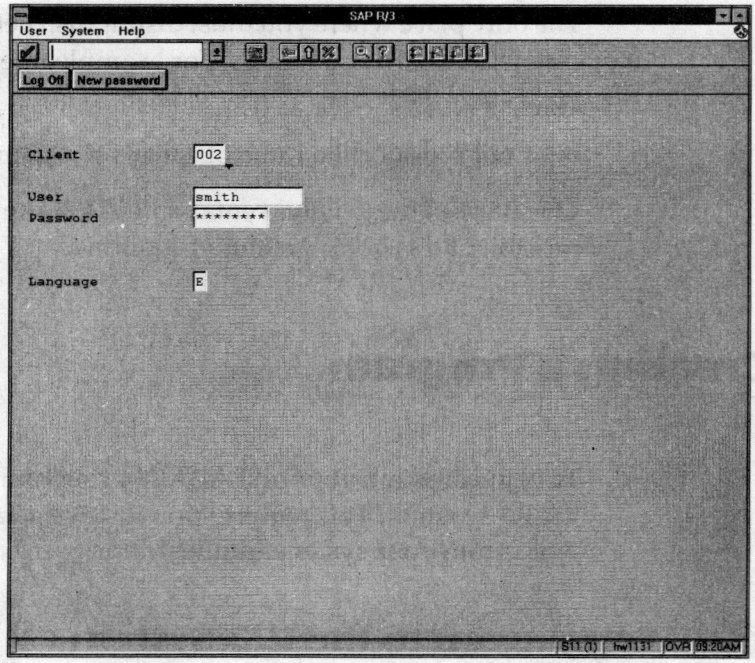

FIGURE 3.1:
The R/3 system's Logon screen

Press ↵, and the system displays a dialog box showing the R/3 system copyrights. Click on Continue to proceed. The next screen is the Start screen, and here the menu bar displays all the major application areas of the R/3 system (such as Logistics, Accounting, and Human Resources), as shown in Figure 3.2. From this menu bar, you can access every application and tool in the system.

FIGURE 3.2:
The R/3 system Start screen

Just below the Start screen's menu bar is one or more toolbars. The upper toolbar is called the *Standard* toolbar, and contains buttons for performing basic operations. The Standard toolbar's buttons are shown in Figure 3.3.

Below the Standard toolbar is a second toolbar, called the *Application* toolbar. It is made up mostly of standard buttons that function the same way throughout the system, with a few application-specific buttons. You can see the Application toolbar's buttons in Figure 3.4.

FIGURE 3.3:
The Standard toolbar's buttons

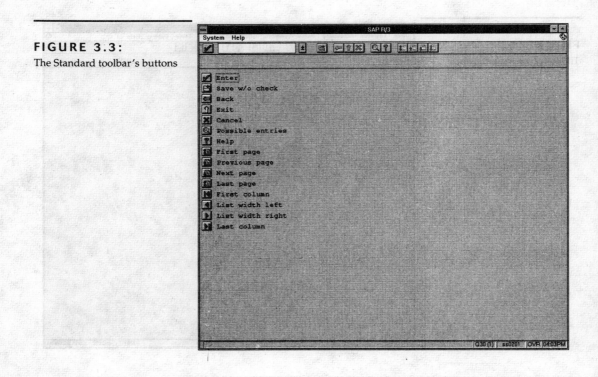

> **TIP**
>
> All functions that are available by clicking on a button can also be accessed via a menu function. However, the opposite is not true—not all menu options have a corresponding button.

Setting the Program Attributes

An ABAP/4 program consists of two basic parts: the *attributes* and the *source code*. The first step in our sample program is to set the attributes:

1. In the Start screen, choose Tools ➤ ABAP/4 Workbench from the menu bar.

FIGURE 3.4:
The Application toolbar's
buttons

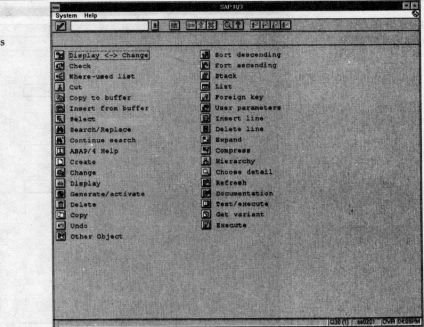

2. The ABAP/4 Development Workbench screen appears. Click on
   the Object Browser button in the Application toolbar.

3. The Object Browser opens, with two groups of radio buttons and
   text boxes. From the Object list group, select the Program radio
   button, enter the name of your program (for our example, **ABAP-
   TEST**) in the corresponding input field, and click on Display (see
   Figure 3.5).

4. A dialog box appears asking whether you want to create a new
   program with that name. Click on the Yes button to move to the
   next screen.

5. A dialog box appears asking you whether you want a TOP Include. Remove the check from the check box, since this is only
   necessary for large programs, and click on the Enter button.

FIGURE 3.5:

Naming the ABAPTEST
program

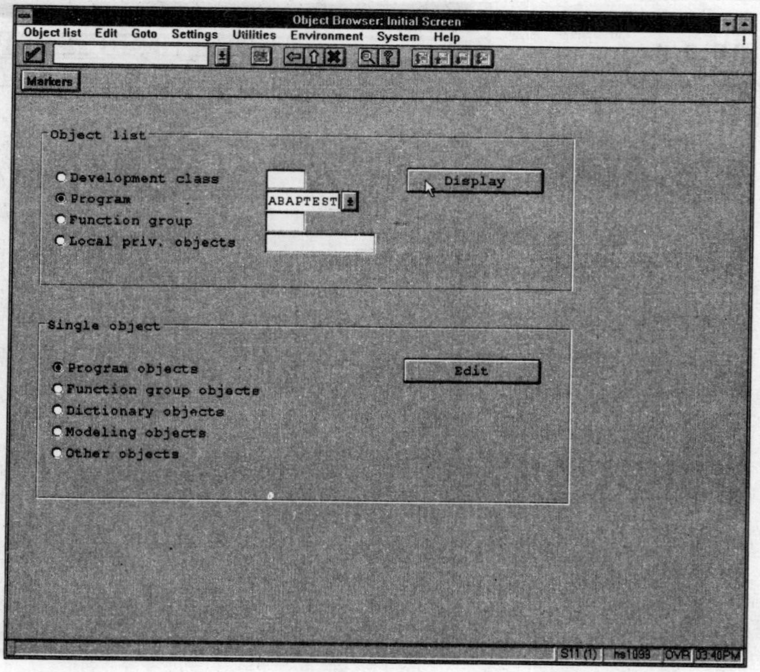

We will explain when to use a TOP Include a little later in this
section.

6. Enter the attribute values on the following screen, as shown
   in Figure 3.6: in the Title box, enter **My first ABAP/4 program**, in the Type box, enter **1** (which represents an executable
   online program), and in the Application box, enter **S** (for *basis*
   or *system* program). Again, we'll explain why you chose these
   options later in the chapter.

7. Save the program attributes by clicking on the Save button in the
   Standard toolbar.

8. The Maintain Object Catalog Entry dialog box appears, where
   you must either choose a development class or specify the program as a local object (more on this below). Click on the Local
   Object button to indicate that the program can only be used in

FIGURE 3.6:

Setting the program attributes for ABAPTEST

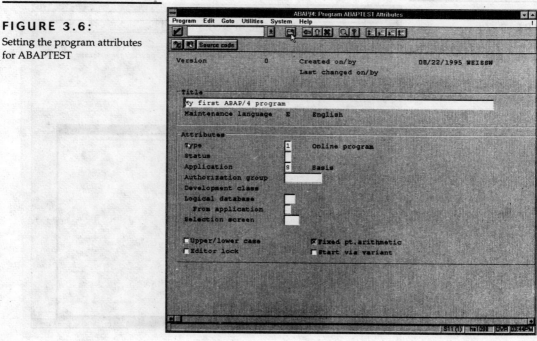

the current system (see Figure 3.7), and you will return to the Attributes screen.

Before you start creating the source code, we should explain some of the choices you made in the steps above.

- Large programs are usually divided into several Include files. An Include is part of a program's source code, but it is stored separately in the Repository like a program. The source code it contains can be inserted into the program using the `include` statement. This allows you to break up the source code of a large program into smaller chunks; for example, an Include might contain the code for all subroutines. A special Include file called TOP Include can be reserved for data declarations, and should be included at the top of the source code, since a variable must be declared before being used. Our first program does not need an Include File since it is

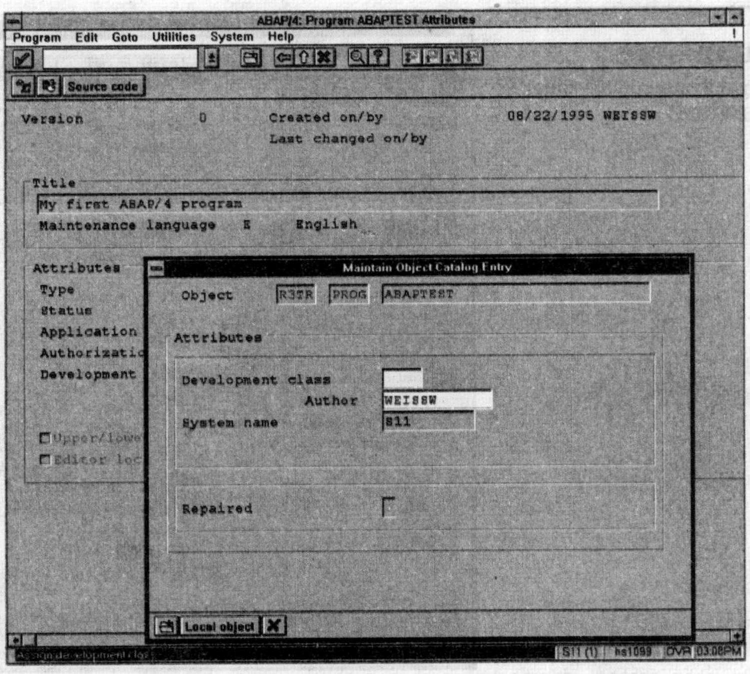

FIGURE 3.7:

Click on Local Object to set the development class

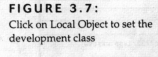

only a small program, and therefore the TOP Include file has been omitted.

- We chose 1 for the program Type. Type 1 is an executable program that can read data and display it on screen (or print it on paper). There are other program types, such as *I*, which is used for Include files, and *M*, which is for dialog programs that change data within the database (this will be covered in Chapter 19).

- Executable program (types 1 or M) are also called *main programs*. In contrast, Include files are not executable.

- We chose *S* (for *basis* or *system programs*) for the Application area. This attribute is used to classify all programs in the R/3 system. You can also choose other values such as F (Financial Accounting), H (Human Resources Planning), or M (Materials Management).

- Since the ABAP/4 Development Workbench supports the development of large applications in teams, you have to decide who will be able to use the program. In the Maintain Object Catalog Entry dialog box, you specify whether the program will be a local object (to be used only in the current system, as we chose) or not. If you intend to transport the program to a production system, you must assign it to a development class. For the examples in this book, you will work only with local objects.

NOTE   The organization of development projects and transports is discussed in Appendix D.

Creating the Program Source

Now that you have set the Attributes for your program, you are ready to get started on the source code.

1. In the Attributes screen, click on the Source Code button on the Application toolbar (refer back to Figure 3.6). The editor screen for the ABAP/4 Editor opens.

2. At the top of the Editor screen, there are seven lines of comments that have been generated automatically by the system. The system also generates the report declaration containing the name you specified for your program. Leave a blank line after the report statement and enter the following code:

   ```
   write 'Customer list'.
   ```

   Your screen should now look like the one shown in Figure 3.8.

3. Save the source code by clicking on Save.

FIGURE 3.8:

Creating the program source

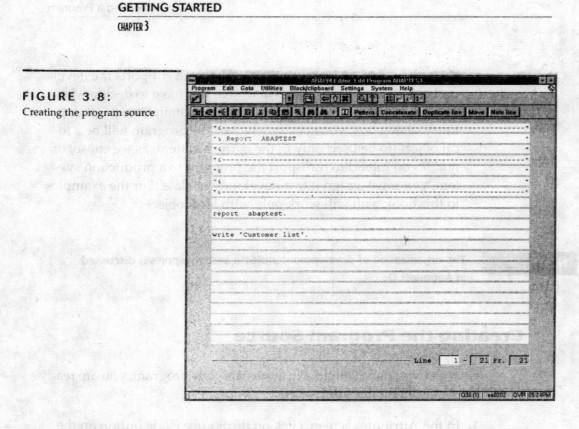

FIGURE 3.8:

Creating the program source

Working in the Editor

You've just had your first opportunity to use the ABAP/4 Editor. The Editor works much like the editors used in many other languages, and you probably won't have any trouble getting used to it. In this section, we'll go over a few of the basic Editor operations. Start by selecting part of the code we just created.

1. In the Editor screen, place your cursor at the beginning of the report statement and click on the Select button.

2. Move the cursor to the end of the write statement (after the period) and click on Select again. The block is now selected, it appears in a different color, and the selected line numbers are displayed at the bottom of the editor screen (see Figure 3.9).

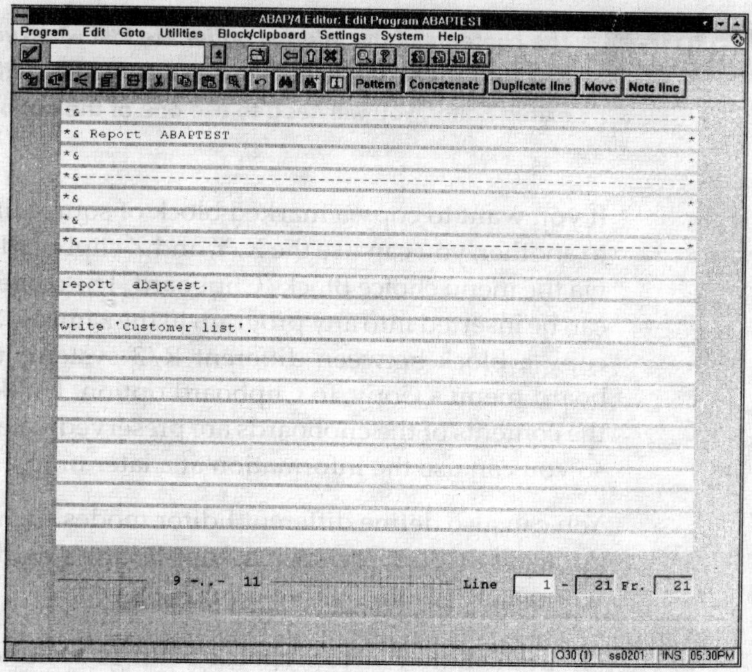

FIGURE 3.9:

The selected block

3. Now cut this block to an internal buffer (a sort of holding zone) by clicking on the Cut button, and then paste it back in by clicking on the Insert From Buffer icon. (The Copy To Buffer button copies the block to the internal buffer so that the block can be inserted elsewhere in the same program.) Your program code should be back in its original position.

If you want to cut or copy a single line, position the cursor on the line and click on Cut or Copy To Buffer. If you want to repeat any line, place the cursor on that line and click on the Duplicate Line button. A copy of the line is inserted below the line you are currently pointing to with the cursor.

WARNING The contents of the internal buffer are lost when you exit the Editor. If you want to use the information in the internal buffer after you've exited Editor, you will need to use one of the options described below.

If you want to copy a marked block of source lines from one program to another, you can use the X, Y, and Z clipboards, which are accessible via the menu choice Block/Clipboard. The contents of these clipboards can be inserted into any program in the same R/3 system. You can even copy a block between different R/3 systems using the Block/Clipboard menu's Copy To Clipboard option. Unlike the internal buffers, the contents of the clipboards are preserved when you leave the Editor, so you can use the information at a later time.

You can also define different Editor modes such as Lower Case or Upper Case display. Try setting your Editor's mode so that your display will match the ones we've used in this book:

1. In the Editor screen, choose Settings ➤ Editor Mode from the menu bar.

2. Select PC Mode Without Line Numbering from the Mode options and Lower Case from the Display options.

Text you key in will now appear in all lowercase letters. Keep in mind that setting Editor modes only affects the program code's on-screen display; it does not affect the results of the program.

Help Information

The Editor provides several features to help you perfect your code. If you don't know the syntax of a keyword like write, you can display help information by placing your cursor on the word and clicking on the ABAP/4 Help button. If you want to figure out the effect of a keyword you have not yet written, click on the ABAP/4 Help button and type in the keyword in the ABAP/4 Key Word text box in dialog box that appears (see Figure 3.10).

FIGURE 3.10:
The ABAP/4 Help dialog box

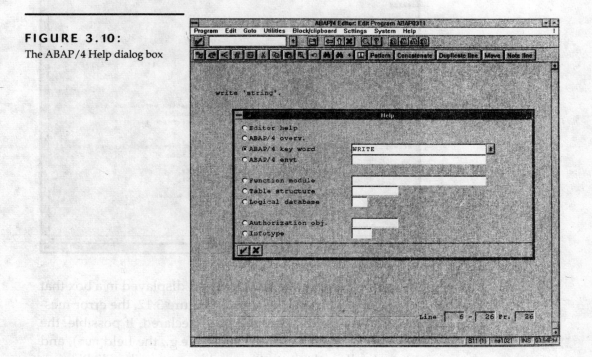

In both cases, you will get a detailed explanation for that command and all its variations, as shown in Figure 3.11. Related keywords can be accessed via hypertext links on the Help page.

Syntax Check

The Syntax Check feature lets the Editor do some of the error-checking work for you. When you click on the Check button in the Editor screen, the system executes a syntax analysis of the current program. If the program is correct, you get a confirmation message. Otherwise, each

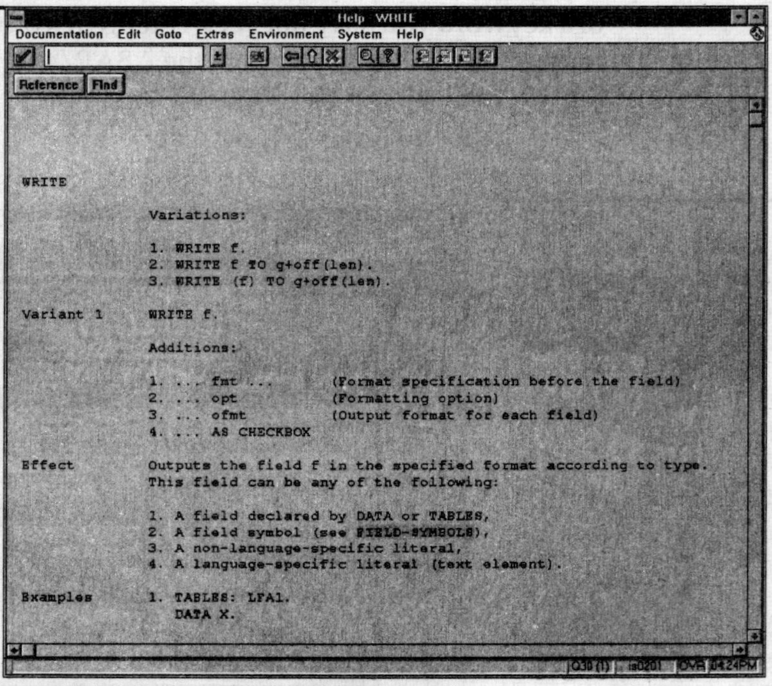

FIGURE 3.11:

Excerpt from the help documentation on write

```
                                      Help  WRITE
Documentation  Edit  Goto  Extras  Environment  System  Help

Reference  Find


    WRITE

                   Variations:

                   1. WRITE f.
                   2. WRITE f TO g+off(len).
                   3. WRITE (f) TO g+off(len).

    Variant 1      WRITE f.

                   Additions:

                   1. ... fmt ...        (Format specification before the field)
                   2. ... opt            (Formatting option)
                   3. ... ofmt           (Output format for each field)
                   4. ... AS CHECKBOX

    Effect         Outputs the field f in the specified format according to type.
                   This field can be any of the following:

                   1. A field declared by DATA or TABLES,
                   2. A field symbol (see FIELD-SYMBOLS),
                   3. A non-language-specific literal,
                   4. A language-specific literal (text element).

    Examples       1. TABLES: LFA1.
                      DATA X.
```

syntax error will be sequentially indicated and displayed in a box that pops up on your screen. In the example in Figure 3.12, the error message indicates that the field nu has not been declared. If possible, the Syntax Check will propose a correct version (e.g., the field num), and you can automatically substitute the correct version by clicking on Correct at the bottom of the screen. You can repeat this process until a confirmation message tells you that there are no more errors.

Testing a Program

Now we can do a little testing on our sample program.

FIGURE 3.12:

A Syntax Check error
explanation

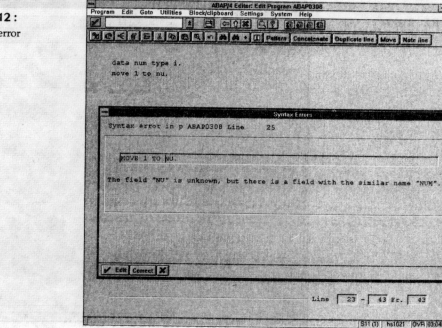

1. First, perform the Syntax Check on your program as described above. You should always run a Syntax Check on a program before you try to execute it. When the program has no errors, a message appears at the bottom of the Editor screen, which says *No syntax errors found.*

2. Execute the program from the Editor screen by selecting Program ➤ Execute from the menu bar.

3. The literal 'Customer list' in the `write` command appears on the screen. The system automatically displays the program title as the list header. The result of your efforts should look like Figure 3.13.

FIGURE 3.13:

The output of our sample
program

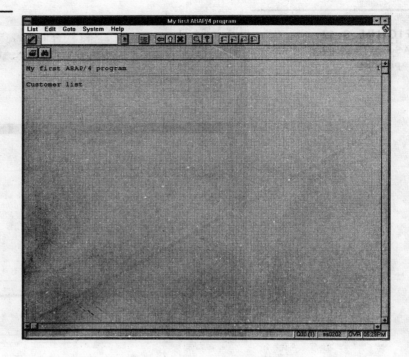

Your code was correct, and you have just successfully run your first
ABAP/4 program.

A Quick Review

Here are some of the more important features we've covered in this
chapter:

- An ABAP/4 program consists of attributes and source code.

- The syntax of the language is very simple. The program source code consists of statements where words are enclosed by blanks and literals by quotes. Statements begin with a keyword, end with a period, and can be combined using colons and commas.

- There is a Syntax Check function to verify the correctness of a program. In case of an error, suggestions for correcting the syntax are given.

- You can execute a program from within the Editor.

In the next chapter, you will be introduced to data structures of the language.

PART II

Data Objects

- Chapter 4: Local Data of a Program

- Chapter 5: Global Tables of the Dictionary

- Chapter 6: Modeling Entities and Relationships

CHAPTER

FOUR

Local Data of a Program

- **Defining ABAP/4 fields**

- **Elementary and non-elementary types in ABAP/4**

- **An overview of records and internal types**

- **Using system fields**

ABAP/4 has a set of elementary types (e.g., character, integer, date) and two construction principles (records and internal tables) for building complex data objects. In addition, the language supports different ways to define types and *variables* (also called *fields*). References to Dictionary fields or structures ensure that data is used consistently throughout all programs of the system.

> **NOTE**   The ABAP/4 Dictionary is covered in detail in Chapter 5.

In this chapter, we will learn how to define types, fields, records, and internal tables. Internal tables are especially useful as temporary copies of database tables or parts of database tables, since you need not know in advance how many entries will be inserted into an internal table at runtime.

> **NOTE**   Working with internal tables is discussed in detail in Chapter 12.

Defining Fields Using Elementary Types or References

A *field* in ABAP/4 is a variable, which cannot be decomposed into smaller parts. A field is defined by a data statement and allocates space in memory depending on its length. Back in Chapter 1, we explained elementary and non-elementary types and additions using an example with a customer name field. Suppose you want to write a program that creates a list of customers and vendors. The customer name field in Chapter 1 was defined as a character field 25 characters long, and the vendor name field in this example has the same definition. In ABAP/4, there are three approaches you can take to write code that will create this list:

- You can use elementary types (such as character, integer, and date).

- You can make a reference to an existing field (in the program or the Dictionary).

- You can make a reference to a non-elementary type (in the program or the Dictionary).

TIP If you need a refresher on this example, refer back to the section "Types, Data Objects (Variables), and an Integrated Dictionary" in Chapter 1.

Using the first approach, elementary types, you might create the code below. In this example, each field is defined separately with the `data` keyword. You must give the field a name and specify the type (c) and the field length (25):

```
data: customer_name(25) type c,
      vendor_name(25)   type c.
```

To accomplish the same thing using the second approach, using the addition `like` for referencing a field, you might create the code shown below. In this example, the field `vendor_name` inherits all types of information (in this case, the elementary type c and the length 25) from the `customer_name` field. In this case, you only have to define the type once, since changes to the definition of the `customer_name` field automatically cause the same changes in the definition of `vendor_name`:

```
data: customer_name(25) type c,
      vendor_name like customer_name.
```

65

Using the third approach, reference to a non-elementary type, you could write the code below. In our example in Chapter 1, we defined the type t_name as a character field 25 characters long, and we'll use that definition here. The definition used for type t_name is applied to both the customer_name and vendor_name fields, and any change to the t_name definition automatically causes the same change in the definitions of both field:

```
types t_name(25) type c.
data: customer_name type t_name,
      vendor_name    type t_name.
```

Which Approach Is Best?

There are some advantages and disadvantages to using each of the approaches above. The first method is less flexible than the latter two, since changes to the definitions of the fields must be made twice—once to each field. This means more work for the developer. The second approach, referencing a field, doesn't require a new type for each field, so you only have to define the type once. The third method, referencing a non-elementary type, is the only one that reflects the fact that both customers and vendors have a name of a certain type and length, which is more general than customer or vendor names. Using non elementary types, you can implement general data structures that can be used in different situations.

The last two approaches are particularly useful if the like or type addition refers to fields or types in the ABAP/4 Dictionary. You can refer to fields and types in the Dictionary that you have defined, or you can refer to those that come with the R/3 system. The Dictionary's active integration guarantees that all changes to the definition of fields and structures are automatically forwarded to all programs utilizing those fields and structures, so your references will always access the most current information. Using the Dictionary is highly recommended whenever you refer to the same fields or structures in more than one application object. The ABAP/4 Dictionary enables you to develop and maintain large program systems where many people work together because it allows everyone to access and use correct, consistent information.

There is no general rule about when to use like, when to define your own types, or when to create Dictionary types. (Keep in mind that all Dictionary types are available in all programs of the system.) Referencing other fields using the addition like is often easier to understand than using non-elementary types, since the non-elementary types introduce a new level of abstraction.

> **NOTE** You can also use dynamic references (called *field-symbols* in ABAP/4) to define fields. This will be discussed in Chapter 23.

In general, changes to your code's fields are easier if you choose one of the more abstract approaches—this is important when many developers work on a highly integrated software project. On the other hand, all programs should be written as clearly as possible, and the more abstract approaches make the code more difficult to understand. In particular, smaller programs or subroutines do not always need long like chains or complicated non-elementary types.

Elementary Types

ABAP/4 has the following elementary types:

Characters	There are two character types: *c* (character) and *n* (numeric text).
Numbers	There are three number types: *i* (integer), *p* (packed number), and *f* (floating point number).
Date	There is one date type: *d* (date).
Time	There is one time type: *t* (time).
Hexadecimal	There is one hexadecimal type: *x* (hexadecimal).

We'll discuss these types in detail a little later in the chapter.

Every field defined by data may refer to these elementary types, as you can see in this example:

```
data: name(25) type c,
      zip_code(5) type n,
      counter type i value 1.
```

The length of a field is determined by the number in parentheses after the field name. In the example above, the name field has the length 25 and the zip code field has the length 5. If the length of a field is not specified within the defining data statement, ABAP/4 assumes a default length.

Length defines how many bytes a field *has*, but the *value* defines what is *in* the bytes. The addition of the word value defines a start value for the variable counter. Every elementary type has its own default value, which is used at runtime if no initial value is defined after data. For instance, the default initial value for type c is space (i.e., the field is filled with blanks), and for type i it is the number 0. You can see the default lengths and values for all elementary types in Table 4.1.

TABLE 4.1: Default lengths and values for elementary types

Elementary type	Length	Initial value
c	1	space
n	1	'0'
i	4	0
p	8	0
f	8	0.0
d	8	'00000000'
t	6	'000000'
x	1	X'00'

You can introduce non-elementary types in the same way as fields. For example, the following declarations define a character type `flag` of length one and a field `address_flag` of this type with the initial value `'X'`. Of course, the type `flag` only defines an abstract type, whereas the field `address_flag` will allocate space in main memory at runtime. In other words, `type` never allocates space and `data` always does.

```
types flag type c.
data address_flag type flag value 'X'.
```

For all types (including non-elementary types, which we will discuss below), you can define constants. Constants are defined like fields using the addition value:

```
constants: company_name(3) type c value 'SAP',
           max_counter type i value 9999.
```

A constant cannot be changed. Any statement trying to change a constant will cause an error message during the syntax check, or it will cause a runtime error if the change can only be detected at runtime (for example, when a constant is used as an actual parameter of a subroutine and this parameter is changed in the subroutine). Note that literals are also treated like constants; that is, a literal cannot be changed with a statement.

You can also use constants to define initial values. Take a look at this code:

```
data counter type i value max_counter.
```

In this example, the value is defined as the constant max_counter, which we defined above as being 9999.

NOTE   Since the syntax of declarations using `types`, `data`, or `constants` is virtually identical, we will only discuss the syntax of one of these things if it differs from the normal syntax shared by all of them.

Now that you understand how types are used, let's take a closer look at the individual types themselves.

Character Types

ABAP/4 has two character types, as we mentioned above. Type c is for characters, or text fields, and type n is for numeric texts.

Character (Text)

Text fields (used for regular text information) are type c (character). This is also the default type when no type is specified. Take a look at this example:

```
data: name(25) type c,
      city(25),
      flag,
      single_character value 'A'.
```

In this example, the `city` and `flag` fields both default to type c, since no type is specified. The `flag` field doesn't specify a length, either, so it contains exactly one character (remember that the default length of character fields is one). For everyday applications, there is no upper limit on the length of character fields. Technical boundary conditions, however, impose a limit, which is 64KB. Above this limit, the syntax check sends an error message. When you run a program, every type c field is filled with blanks if no initial value is explicitly specified in the defining `data` statement. Of course, the contents of a field with initial value may be changed later.

If the field and the literal or constant after `value` have different lengths, the initial value will either be truncated or padded with blanks on the right-hand side:

```
data language(2) value 'ABAP/4'.
```

In this example, the field `language` will have the initial value AB, since the last four bytes of the string ABAP/4 are truncated.

Numeric text

Variables of type n (numeric texts) contain strings of digits (such as *0123456789*). They are appropriate for numbers that are used for identification and as sort criteria for internal tables. For example, type n fields often hold identification numbers such as house numbers, ZIP codes, part numbers, account numbers, and so on.

Where type c fields pad initial values with blanks on the right side, type n fields pad the left side with zeros. Suppose you want to display a list of customer identifiers that have different lengths, so you want them padded with zeros on the left side. You could write the following code:

```
data customer_id(8) type n.
customer_id = '1234'.
write customer_id.
```

The customer identifier will be printed out as 00001234, whereas the same procedure with a character field would display 1234_ _ _ _ (with trailing blanks).

The default length for a field of type n is 1, and the default initial value is a string of zeros of the appropriate length, (e.g., 0000 for a numerical text of length 4).

Numbers

Within the number types, ABAP/4 supports integers, packed numbers, and floating point numbers.

Integers

Fields of type i are mainly used for counting; for example, to determine the number of customers or the number of steps within a loop:

```
data: customer_number type i,
    loop_counter type i.
```

Integers have a fixed length of 4 bytes, and it is therefore impossible to set the length explicitly. The possible values range from -2^{31} to $2^{31} - 1$. At runtime, integers have the initial value 0, but you can also define an initial value, as shown here:

```
data word_length type i value 17.
```

Packed Numbers

Packed numbers (type p) are a way to store numbers internally in a compressed form. Therefore, they cover a wide range of possible values and can be used for all kinds of computations. They are particularly useful in the following situations.

- Very large numbers (up to 31 digits)
- Numbers with decimals
- Rounding according to decimal arithmetic

Suppose you have to determine the population of mosquitoes in an area. You will probably define a variable as follows:

```
data number_of_mosquitoes type p.
```

Not surprisingly, the default initial value is 0. The default length is 8 bytes and within these bytes, up to 15 digits and the sign (+/−) can be stored. In other words, this is the range of possible values for a packed number with the default length (and no decimals):

```
-999,999,999,999,999 to 999,999,999,999,999.
```

If an overflow occurs at runtime, the system will stop immediately and display the current statement and all relevant information (for example, the contents of related fields).

Decimal handling is also supported for packed numbers. Suppose you are employed in an international company that produces airbags, and you want to calculate the price of a new type of airbag. You will probably express your result in US dollars, and you would define a field that looks like this:

```
data airbag_price type p decimals 2.
```

This statement defines a number airbag_price with two decimal places and initial value 0.00.

You can also set the length of a packed number explicitly where the maximum length is 16, which can represent numbers of up to 31 digits plus the sign.

```
data packed_16(16) type p.
```

In this example, the number packed_16 contains 31 digits and the sign. In general, the number of digits in a packed number of length n is given by $(2n − 1)$.

NOTE   The output of numbers will be discussed in Chapter 8.

There is no special benefit to choosing a short length for a packed number. However, it may be helpful for you to choose the maximum length (16) if you think there might be an overflow.

NOTE   Keep in mind that ABAP/4 supports packed numbers on all platforms, even when they are not supported by the hardware. This is particularly important with respect to decimal handling and rounding.

Floating Point Numbers

Floating point numbers (type f) occur in complex arithmetic operations. For example, the number age_of_earth defined below has an initial value 123×10^8 (i.e., with mantissa 123 and exponent 8).

```
data age_of_earth type f value '123E+8'.
```

The values of floating point numbers can be represented in different ways, but they are all equivalent:

```
data: f1 type f,
      f2 type f,
      f3 type f.
f1 = 1.
f2 = '-12.34567'.
f3 = '-765E04'.
```

Floating point numbers have the initial value 0 if the addition value is omitted in the defining data statement. Possible values range from 1E–307 to 1E307. The standard output length of fields of type f is 22.

At runtime, floating point operations on the application server's hardware can often be very fast. However, special care is necessary when using floating point numbers, since rounding errors may occur even in very simple computations. For example, the following simple expression may result in a rounding error.

```
f1 = ( '1.0' / '3.0' ) * '3.0'.
```

Since rounding errors cannot be excluded, you should not use conditions with the operator = or eq when floating point numbers are involved:

```
if f1 = '1'.
```

In this example, the condition f1 = '1' may not be fulfilled. You can replace the condition f1 = '1' by a more complex expression like the following:

```
if '0.9999999999' < f1 and f1 < '1.0000000001.'
```

In the realm of business applications, floating point numbers are mainly used for holding intermediate results of very complex arithmetic operations like graphical representations. They are usually converted to packed numbers later. Note that when using only packed numbers, all intermediate results of a computation will be rounded according to decimal arithmetic. There may be differences in results of calculations including floating point numbers, since binary arithmetic is used in the latter case. Use integers for (small) numbers without decimals. Packed numbers are the best choice if you have large numbers, or if decimals are involved in your calculations.

Date

Date fields are type d with the fixed length 8 and the internal representation YYYYMMDD (year, month, and day). The initial value of a date field is 00000000.

ABAP/4 supports several output formats for date fields that are different from the internal representation. The write command formats dates according to personal settings of the end user.

```
data today type d.
* Get actual date from system field sy-datum and display it
```

```
today = sy-datum.
write today.
```

The first statement in the example code defines the today date field. Then the actual date contained in the system field sy-datum is transferred to the today field, which is displayed on screen by the write command. System fields are discussed below under the heading "Using System Fields". If this small program is run on the last day of the century by an end user in the United States, it will print out the date 12 31 1999 on the screen. However, since Europeans format dates differently, this date would be written as 31 12 1999 in many parts of Europe. If the field today has an output length 10 in the write statement, as shown here:

```
write (10) today.
```

the date will appear as 12/31/1999 in the United States and as 31/12/1999 in Europe.

You can also request special formats by adding an additional parameter to the write command (see Chapter 8) or to the field definition in the ABAP/4 Dictionary (see Chapter 5).

We should mention (even at this early stage) that you can also use date fields to perform computations. A typical example is figuring out the last day of the previous month (often called *ultimo*), which can be calculated as follows:

```
data ultimo type d.
* Set variable to first day of current month.
ultimo = sy-datum.
ultimo+6(2) = '01'.
* Set variable to last day of previous month.
subtract 1 from ultimo.
```

The above-mentioned output formats do not influence the internal representation of date fields. In particular, the day is always contained in the last two bytes internally, regardless of how you have customized your display.

NOTE You will find detailed information about the use of date fields in Chapters 7 and 8.

Time

Time fields are type t with the fixed length 6 and the format HHMMSS (hours, minutes, and seconds). Like date fields, the output is enhanced by the write command or by additional format definitions from the ABAP/4 Dictionary.

Hexadecimal

Hexadecimal (or binary) data is stored in fields of type x. For example, the bit stream 1111000010001001 can be defined as the initial value of a hexadecimal field using the following code:

```
data xstring(2) type x value 'F089'.
```

Note that two hexadecimal digits between 0 and F fit into one byte. In other words, a hexadecimal field of length n contains $2n$ digits and its output length is also equal to $2n$.

Records and Internal Tables

Fields are the basic data objects of ABAP/4. Beyond fields, ABAP/4 supports the construction of complex data objects using records and internal tables. Records contain a fixed number of data objects, and internal tables can collect any number of data objects at runtime. In particular, internal tables are very useful for querying database tables.

Because records (or *structures*) and tables are easy to define and work
with, they are used extensively in almost all ABAP/4 programs.

Using ABAP/4 Records

Records (or *structures*) consist of a fixed number of data objects (also
called *components of the record*) and are defined using the keywords
data begin of and data end of. Suppose you want to store information about a customer in a record. You might define a structure with
fields for the customer identifier, name, and phone number:

```
data: begin of customer,
        id(8) type n,
        name(25),
        telephone(12),
      end of customer.
```

The data begin of keyword marks the beginning of the structure
named customer. This structure contains the three fields for identifier,
name, and phone number (with their respective length specifications),
and it ends with the data end of keyword.

From now on, you can work with the different components as well as
with the structure itself:

```
data vendor like customer.
customer-id = '87654321'.
customer-name = 'Edison'.
customer-telephone = '111-111-1111'.
move customer to vendor.
```

In the code above, the addition like specifies that the vendor structure
will have the same format as the customer structure. Information has
been added for each of the fields. The last command of this example
operates on the whole structure; that is, the contents of all components
of the record customer are copied to the record vendor.

You can also define constant structures, where all fields must be given a fixed value. For example, you might define a record with a path to some directory on your PC as follows:

```
constants: begin of path,
        root(3) value 'a:\',
        home_dir(5) value 'home\',
      end of path.
```

Since the keyword constants together with begin of defines the constant structure path, all components of the structure must have a value. Otherwise, a syntax error message will be sent. As a result, the record path as a whole is equal to the string *a:\home*.

Internal Tables

In contrast to tables in a database, which exist whether or not they are being accessed, internal tables only live during the runtime of the program. They are often used as snapshots of database tables or as containers for volatile data in the program. Internal tables can consist of any number of lines (or entries) of identical type. You need not know in advance how many lines will be inserted into an internal table at runtime. Without having to consider details like memory allocation or garbage collection, you can concentrate on truly important business—developing application programs.

Internal tables are defined using the addition occurs followed by a number (called the Occurs Parameter), which documents the estimated upper limit for the lines of the table. For instance, if you want to collect information about many customers, you can define an internal table, where each line has the same type as the previously defined record customer. Suppose you estimate a maximum number of 100 customers:

```
data all_customers like customer occurs 100.
```

In this line of code, the data statement declares an internal table named all_customers, with each entry having the structure of the record customer. Initially, the ABAP/4 runtime system reserves memory space for the table to contain 100 entries.

> **NOTE** The Occurs Parameter is purely a performance parameter and does not restrict the maximum size of the internal table. The ABAP/4 runtime system automatically provides new memory if more lines are added to the table. In principle, an internal table can contain any number of lines and the developer need not worry about memory allocation.

In the above example, each future line of the internal table has the same type as the record customer. Like records, the line type of an internal table can also be specified using a reference to an elementary or non-elementary type. In the following example, we define a non-elementary type personal_data:

```
types: begin of personal_data,
       name(25),  .
       city(25),
       street(30),
     end of personal_data.
```

Then you can use this type to define an internal table named people where each line refers to this same type, as shown in the next line of code:

```
data people type personal_data occurs 300.
```

Many table operations (such as adding a new line) require an extra record to use to hold the new record's information as you add it. Using the addition with header line in the defining data statement, when the table is created, an additional data object with the same type as an individual line in the table is also created. This record is called a *header line*, and it is used as a default record to hold the record currently being added to the table. If a table does not have a header line, you must provide a separate record to hold the content of the current line.

NOTE   See Chapter 12 for a detailed discussion of internal table operations.

Internal tables are especially useful if you want to work with temporary copies of database tables or parts of them. You can combine the contents of different database tables into one internal table, creating a temporary view. Internal tables are also often used when objects are collected at runtime (for example, for tree structures or linked lists), because they don't have a specific size limitation.

Defining Complex Non-Elementary Types and Data Objects

The syntax description of types and data objects in ABAP/4 is very simple:

1. Fields and types can refer to elementary types (for example, type c) or to Dictionary objects.

2. Records (or structures) are defined using begin of/end of.

3. Internal tables are defined using occurs.

You must always start with elementary types and fields. Afterwards, the above construction principles can be applied in any order. You can also create *nested* structures of records and tables—a structure can contain another structure or an internal table, which in turn can contain an internal table, etc. For instance, a record that contains personal data can contain a record as a component named address that is built of the fields city and street.

```
types: begin of address,
         city(25),
         street(30),
       end of address,
       begin of person,
         name(25),
         address type address,
       end of person.
data receiver type person.
```

In the example above, the person structure is a nested structure. Later you can use the specific components of the structure as follows:

```
receiver-name = 'Smith'.
receiver-address-city = 'Big City'.
receiver-address-street = 'Main Street'.
```

Nested tables are often useful. Suppose you want to build a list of a set of employees, where each person may have multiple phone and fax numbers. You would probably define appropriate types of internal tables and put them together:

```
types: begin of phone_fax_numbers,
         country_code(3) type n,
         area_code(3) type n,
         number(10) type n,
       end of phone_fax_numbers,
       begin of employee,
         name(25),
         phone type phone_fax_numbers occurs 10,
         fax type phone_fax_numbers occurs 5,
       end of employee.
data employees type employee occurs 100.
```

In this code we first defined a record type phone_fax_numbers with three components, each of which is a field. The second record type employee has also three components—the first one is a field and the latter two are internal tables. The data statement then defines a nested internal table named employees with line type employee. Note that each line of the internal table employees contains one field and two internal tables.

The Scope of Data Definitions

You can use data objects everywhere in your program after the defining data statement. Usually the data definitions are placed at the beginning. Larger programs often have a special Include file listing all data definitions.

The data of your program is also available in each subroutine, but you may redefine the data within subroutines (see Chapter 10). Local data objects of a subroutine take precedence over global variables with identical names. For example, if there is a local data object named abc and a global variable named abc, the subroutine will use the local data object instead of the global one.

The variables of one program (that is, all data objects you declared with the data statement in this program) are not available to other programs. If you want to re-use them elsewhere in the system, you can add them to the same Include file that contains the data definitions in different programs. However, the most flexible way to make variables re-usable is to define them as global variables in the Dictionary, which are automatically available in all ABAP/4 programs.

NOTE For more on the Dictionary and defining structures within it, see Chapter 5.

There are three layers of visibility for data objects:

1. Global variables from the Dictionary.

2. Variables of the program, which are local in relation to the system and global in relation to the program itself.

3. Local variables of a subroutine.

Redefining a variable on a lower level always takes precedence over a variable with the same name that has been defined on a higher level.

Using System Fields

The ABAP/4 runtime system offers several system fields that are available in every program. System fields belong to the Dictionary structure sy and contain general information about the current state of the system and the program objects. For instance, the date of the current day is contained in the field sy-datum. Many system fields are set by the runtime system after specific operations (for example, the field sy-tabix is set to the index of the current line of an internal table during a loop. (For more on internal tables, see Chapter 12).

You can get an description of all system fields using the ABAP/4 Help function for the structure sy in the Editor.

NOTE   A list of the most important system fields can be found in Appendix E.

A Quick Review

Here are some of the most important topics we covered in this chapter:

- A data object is defined by the keyword data.
- Non-elementary types can be introduced by the keyword type.
- Constants are declared by the keyword constants.
- Dictionary objects and user-defined objects can be referred to using like or type.

- Records are defined by the keywords data begin of/data end of. They contain a fixed number of objects.

- Internal tables are defined by the addition of occurs followed by a number (called the *Occurs Parameter*). They can contain any number of lines of the same type.

- Complex data objects can be built using records and internal tables.

- There are three possible scopes of variables: Global data in the Dictionary, local data in a program, and local data in a subroutine.

In the next chapter, you will see how to work with global variables from the ABAP/4 Dictionary.

- Records are defined by the keywords data begin-of-data and ... or. They contain a fixed number of objects.

- Internal tables are defined by the addition of occurs followed by a number (called the occurs parameter). They can contain any number of lines of the same type.

- Complex data objects can be built using records and internal tables.

- There are three possible scopes of variables. Global data in the Dictionary, local data in a program, and local data in a subroutine.

In the next chapter, you will see how to work with global variables from the ABAP/4 Dictionary.

CHAPTER

FIVE

Global Tables of the Dictionary

- **The Dictionary's levels**

- **Defining and using tables and structures**

- **Working with data elements and domains**

- **Foreign keys**

Whenever you have a large development project, you probably need a set of data structures that can be re-used in all components of the project. To guarantee a consistent usage of database tables, their structure definition must be available in development and runtime objects. In particular, since internal tables are used as snapshots of database tables, they should refer to the definition of the database table.

The integrated and active ABAP/4 Dictionary takes care of all of these requirements. If a Dictionary object is activated, the new version is automatically available in all objects of the ABAP/4 Repository. For instance, if you change and activate the structure of a database table and start a program using that table, this program is automatically generated with the new version of the table. In other words, changes to a Dictionary object are distributed to all dependent development objects.

A different approach would address the needs mentioned above by using header files, which contain the global definitions and are included in all programs using an element of that header file. However, changing a header file means that all programs referring to it must be recompiled, even if they only use unchanged data definitions. To illustrate this in an example, if you change the way the letter *I* is defined, the word *BLUE* would be affected, even though it doesn't contain an *I*. In contrast, the ABAP/4 Dictionary has the advantage that a program with unchanged source code is only generated if one of its Dictionary objects has been activated since the last generation. This allows you to change and enlarge global definitions without affecting programs that don't use them. Using the Dictionary, if you change the way the letter *I* is defined, the word *BLUE* is unaffected.

Foreign key relations support data integrity in the relational data model. Fields with a foreign key link to primary key fields of another table can assume only those values allowed by the referenced table. In the R/3 system, this check is executed at the time the user enters a value into an input mask.

The Three Levels of the Dictionary

For the sake of better re-usability, the Dictionary's objects reside on three layers:

1. Tables and structures
2. Data elements
3. Domains

Tables and structures are made of one or more fields. *Tables* represent database tables, and *structures* are record declarations that do not correspond to a database table. Structures can be used in all programs and screens, and usually group data from the same application area. For example, instead of defining a record customer in each program, you can define a structure customer only once in the Dictionary and re-use it wherever it is needed.

Each field of a table or structure refers to a data element that describes the meaning of the field. The data element is in turn assigned to a domain, which determines the technical characteristics of the field. Conversely, a domain can be used in various data elements, and a data element can be used for several fields from different tables (see Figure 5.1).

FIGURE 5.1:
Tables, data elements,
domains, and their
relationships

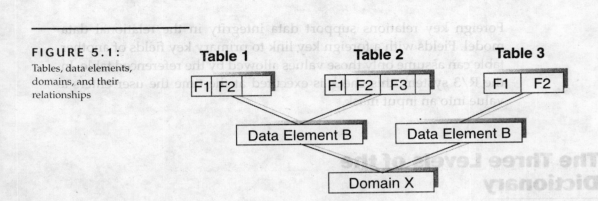

A *domain* describes the technical properties of a table field. It specifies
the set of allowed data values for that field and its output characteristics. In particular, it determines the length and type, a possible foreign key relationship, and the number of decimal places. For example,
the R/3 system has a domain named *Company code* of length four and
type character. A company code is used to define different business
units in an enterprise. The domain Company code is used in data elements that are referred to by fields from several tables (for example, in
the table *Settlement data from payment program*). Changing the domain
would automatically affect the respective field in this table and therefore the table itself.

Data elements represent different roles played by a single domain. They
inherit the properties of the underlying domains. In addition, they provide help information for the fields referring to them. This makes it
possible to provide documentation for each context where a domain is
used. For instance, the R/3 system has two data elements—*Sending
company code* and *Receiving company code*— both of which refer to the
domain *Company code*. The first data element is used in the table *Settlement data from payment program* as explained above, and the second one
in the table *Cost distribution table*. The benefit of this design is that both
kinds of company codes have the same type and length but different
documentation.

Finally, the fields of a table or structure refer to data elements and inherit all of the elements' properties such as documentation, length, and type.

Using this kind of inheritance, you can easily re-use structure information. The concept of re-use is only helpful if you can retrieve information about the usage of an object, and to this end, the Development Workbench provides cross-references for all Dictionary objects. Navigation between related objects (e.g., from a table field to the data element) is always supported.

Tables and Structures

Persistent data is usually stored in transparent database tables. All entries in a table have an identical structure defined in the Dictionary. Each structure contains one or more fields representing the columns of the table.

You can also define a structure without a corresponding database table. This means that you can refer to the structure from within a program, but you cannot store any physical data in the database since there is no underlying table.

Each field refers to a data element and thus also to a domain, assuming their attributes. The attributes of table fields are distributed over three levels (fields, data elements, and domains), since each field refers to a data element which itself refers to a domain. This ensures that fields with equivalent forms and semantics will be consistent. If fields differ from one another in their semantic attributes, a separate data element must be created for each of them. At field level, only information specifically relating to the table is stored. This includes, for example, whether or not the field is a key field. At data element level, semantic attributes (e.g., documentation) are specified, and the domain level contains the technical attributes (such as data type and field length).

Searching table entries can be very time consuming, but you can accelerate the process by using database indexes. These are single fields or groups of fields that identify each entry of the table. In practice, the leftmost fields of a table define the *primary key*; that is, they build a special index to access the rows of the table. The primary key of a table must always be defined and further indexes are optional.

Displaying the Definition

On the Object Browser Initial screen, you can switch to a table definition by clicking to select the Dictionary Objects radio button and then clicking on Edit (see Figure 5.2).

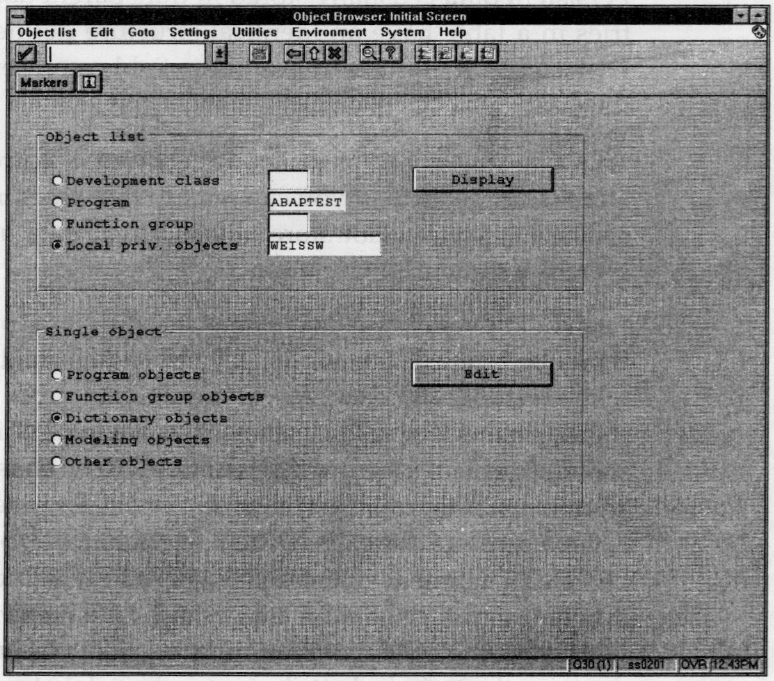

FIGURE 5.2:

The Object Browser Initial screen, where you can switch to a table definition

Enter the name of the table on the next screen and click on the Display button. In the upper part of the next screen, you see the short description of the table and some administrative information, such as the date of the last change (see Figure 5.3).

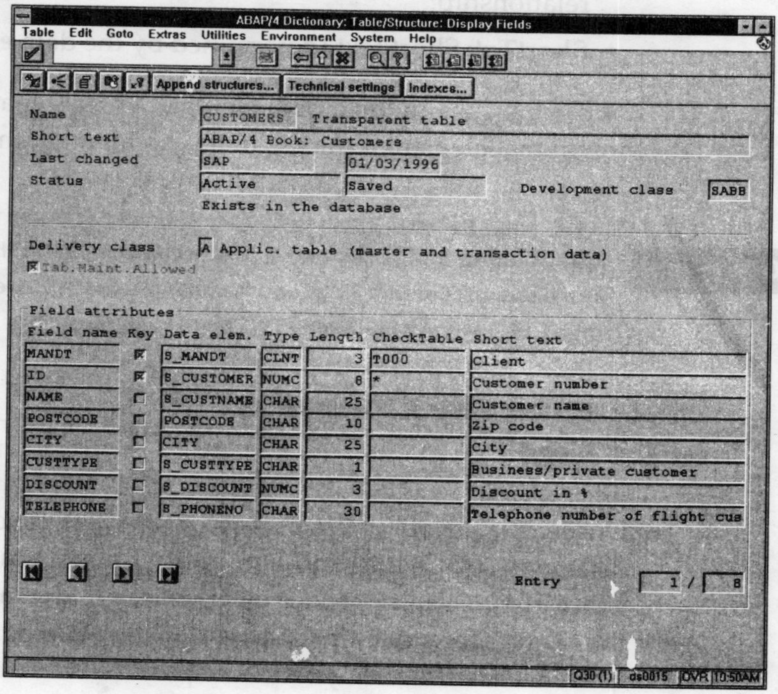

FIGURE 5.3:
A table definition in the Dictionary

The lower part of this screen displays all table fields. The left column contains the name of each field, and the following field attributes are displayed in the other columns along the row:

- **Key**: Box is checked if the field is a primary key field for the database table.

- **Data elem.**: Name of the field's data element.

- **Type**: The field's type (determined by the domain of the data element).
- **Length**: The field's length (determined by the domain of the data element).
- **Chk. table**: Check table—a referenced table of a foreign key relationship.
- **ShortTxt**: Short text (determined by the data element).

By double-clicking on a data element, you can navigate to the definition of that element (which will be explained in the next section).

NOTE   Check tables and foreign keys are discussed later in this chapter under the heading "Foreign Keys and Permissible Entry Values."

Displaying the Contents of a Table

During the development process, you will first consider the structure definition of a table. The Dictionary only contains descriptive data about objects like tables, data elements, and domains. The table entries themselves are stored in database tables. With the Development Workbench's Data Browser, you can display the contents of a database table directly from the table definition screen by choosing Utilities ➤ Table Entries from the menu bar. For example, if you start from the definition of the customers table, a Data Browser selection screen appears, and you can restrict the set of table entries to customer numbers between 0 and 10000000, as shown in Figure 5.4.

Click on the Execute button, and the selected table entries are displayed in the Data Browser (see Figure 5.5).

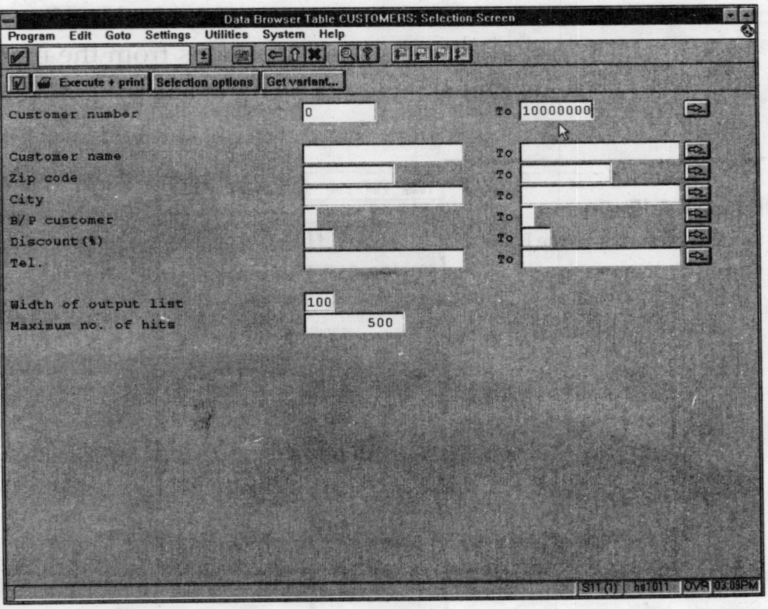

FIGURE 5.4:
Selecting table entries with
the Data Browser

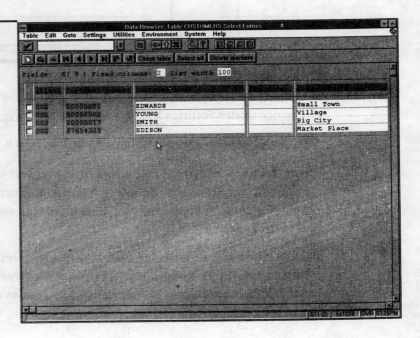

FIGURE 5.5:
The list of table entries from
the Customers table

You can limit the set of displayed table columns by choosing Settings ➤ List Format ➤ Select Columns from the menu bar. The results for the Customers table are shown in Figure 5.6.

FIGURE 5.6:

Selecting columns in the Data Browser

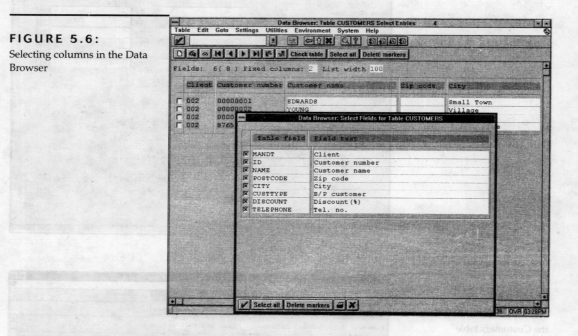

Finally, you can sort the displayed table entries by choosing a sort sequence under Settings ➤ List Format ➤ Sort Sequence (see Figure 5.7).

You can see the results of this sort in Figure 5.8.

From the Data Browser screen, you can insert or change table entries by clicking on the Create Entry or Change Entry buttons. If you click on the Change Entry button, a screen with input fields appears, as shown in Figure 5.9.

Back on the Data Browser screen, you can delete a line of the table by selecting Edit ➤ Delete Entry. The Data Browser supports all elementary table operations and is very helpful as a development tool, providing quick results.

FIGURE 5.7:

Entering sort fields in the Data Browser

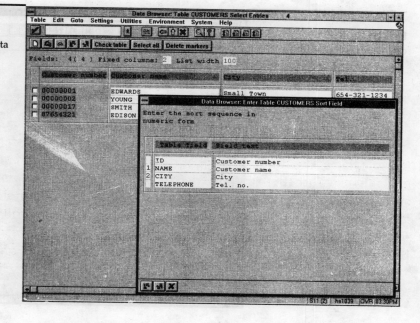

FIGURE 5.8:

The reformatted list of table entries

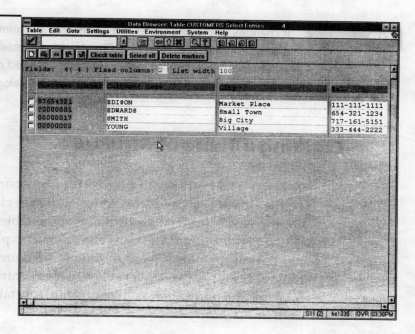

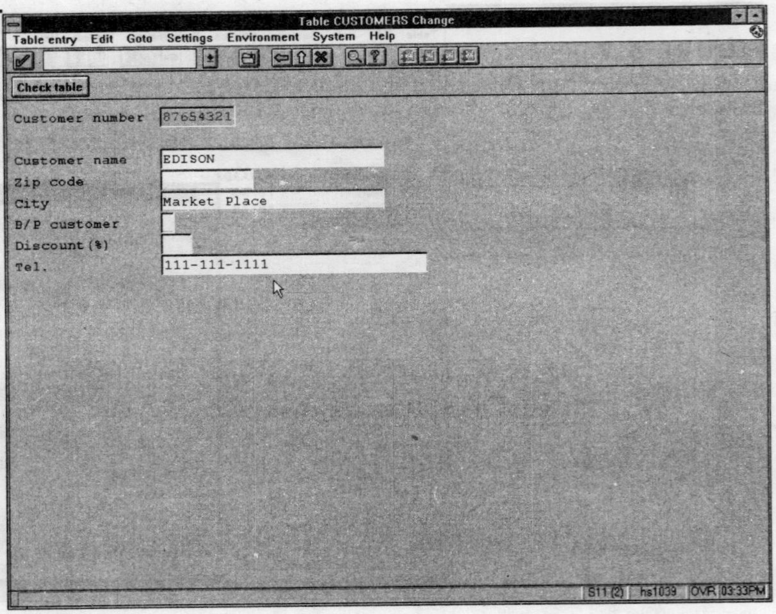

FIGURE 5.9:

Changing a table entry

TIP If changes to existing tables are to become a routine task, design a dialog program as explained in Chapter 19, especially if entries of different but interrelated tables are to be changed or additional features (such consistency checks) of the user dialog are required.

Creating a Table or Structure

To create a table or structure, select the Dictionary Objects radio button on the Object Browser Initial screen and then click on the Edit button. On the next screen, enter the name of the table or structure and click on the Create button. You must enter a short explanatory text in the upper part of the next screen, as shown in Figure 5.10. For a table, you must also specify the delivery class, which controls the degree to which SAP or the customer is responsible for table maintenance and

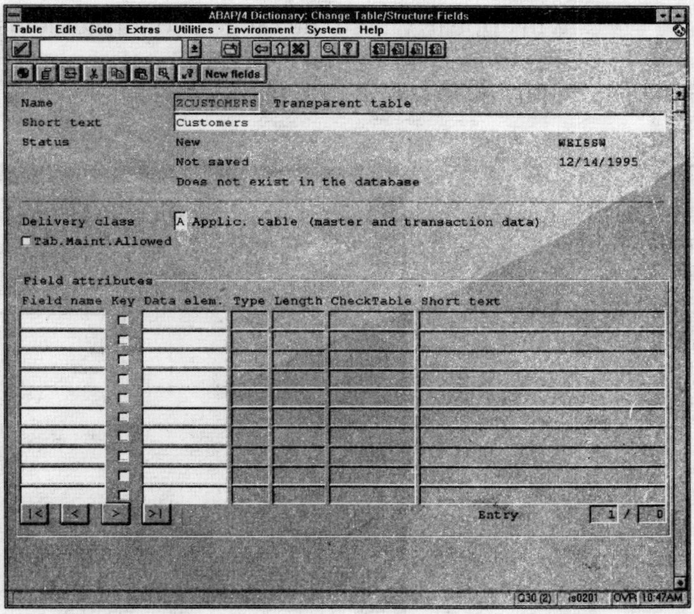

FIGURE 5.10:

Creating a table in the
Dictionary

whether SAP provides the table with or without contents. The delivery class also determines how the table behaves when it is first installed, when there is an upgrade, when it is transported, and when a Client copy is performed. When creating your own table, the delivery classes A (Application table) or C (Customizing table) are good choices.

You can specify fields of the table or structure by entering their names in the left-most column. Click to place a check in the check box in the *Key* column if the field is a primary key field of the database table. The *Data elem.* column must contain the name of the referred data element. The remaining columns are automatically filled with information derived from the chosen data element.

If you already know the name of a suitable data element for your field, enter that element's name in the third column. Otherwise, point to the data element field and click on the arrow that now appears on the right edge of the field to select possible entries from a list. A selection screen will appear, where the range of data elements can be restricted according to several search criteria like the name of the data element or its short description (see Figure 5.11).

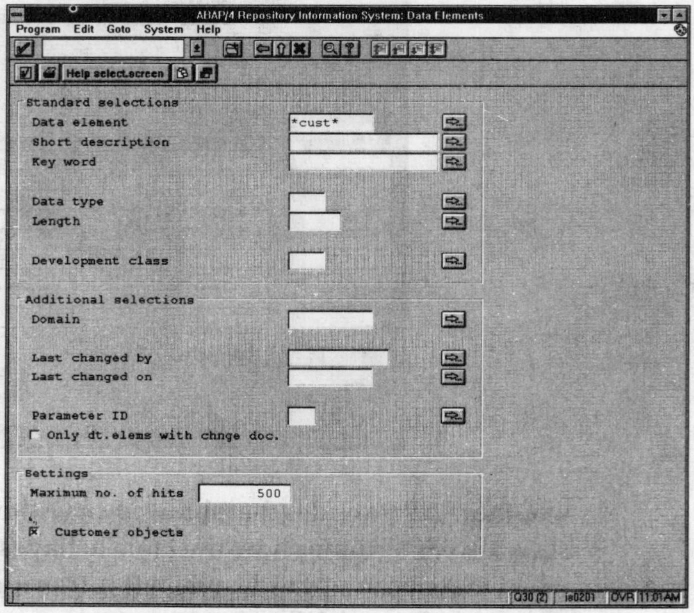

FIGURE 5.11:

Search criteria for data elements

You can then select a data element from the list of matching objects, as shown in Figure 5.12.

If you don't find a data element that can be used for your table field, create a new one by entering its name and double-clicking on this new name. The details about data elements will be discussed in the following section.

When all fields of the table have been entered, you can save this structure by clicking on the Save button. However, the table is not available for other tables or programs until you have activated it by clicking on the Activate button. Afterwards, this table can be used in every program or any other object of the ABAP/4 Repository (for example, in

FIGURE 5.12:

Selecting a data element from the list

other tables of the Dictionary or screens). Note that during activation, the table is also physically created in the database. Therefore, you have to specify the technical settings of the table (see Figure 5.13).

Using Tables and Structures in a Program

Usually, the contents of tables are read or changed by a program. To work on a table from a program, you need first to declare the table via the keyword `tables` followed by the name of the table. ABAP/4 then creates a data object (which is also called the *work area*) for that table. This work area can hold one table record. Because of the reference to the table definition in the Dictionary, all individual table fields are

FIGURE 5.13:

Specifying a table's technical settings

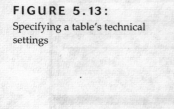

available in the program. For example, you can read and display all entries of the database table customers as seen below:

```
tables customers.
select * from customers.
  write: customers-name.
endselect.
```

This brief program selects all entries in the database table customers (using the select * statement) and displays each name on the screen (using the write: customers-name statement).

 NOTE   The details of the select command will be explained in Chapter 11.

Structures are declared in the same way as tables. A work area is created and all fields of the structure can be used in a program. The only difference is that you cannot use them in `select` statements because a structure doesn't have a database table to which to refer.

In the definition of local data for a program, you can refer to a table, structure, or single fields using `like` (see Chapter 4). For instance, an internal table with the same structure as table `customers` can readily be defined as follows:

```
data all_customers like customers occurs 100.
```

Use Lists of tables are easily accessible from many screens in the ABAP/4 Development Workbench. If you want to know which programs use the table `customers`, click on the Where-Used List button on the table definition screen and select the object type Program from the dialog box that appears. You can then navigate to all occurrences of that table on the resulting Use List (see Figure 5.14).

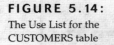

FIGURE 5.14:

The Use List for the CUSTOMERS table

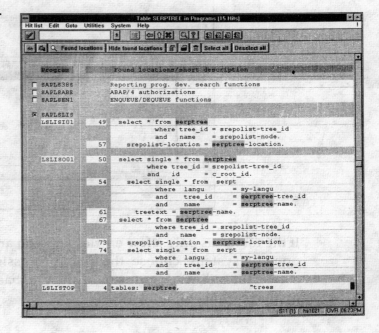

Changing Table Definitions

If you change the structure of a database table and activate the new version, the system automatically performs the necessary actions to adjust the table entries in the database. For instance, adding a new field is executed immediately for all table entries. If you change or delete table columns, a dialog box appears to determine the appropriate way to convert the table entries (see Figure 5.15).

FIGURE 5.15:

The dialog box where you specify how to convert a table

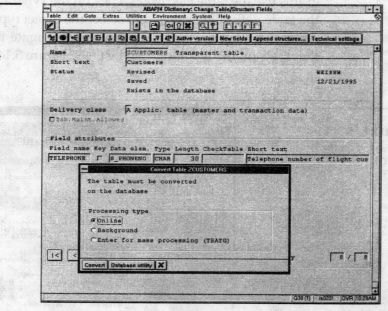

If the table has only a few entries and you are working in a development system, choose the first processing type—Online—to convert it online. A protocol of the database conversion will be displayed immediately.

If you choose the second processing type, Background, a background program for the conversion will be started and you have to set its start time in the dialog box that appears.

In the third alternative, Enter For Mass Processing (TBATG), the table in question is converted by a system program that processes many tables in a special background job.

Changing the structure of a table can be a critical issue, especially if data can be lost or other objects (such as programs or tables) still use a changed or deleted table field. For example, if you delete a key field, the table will be converted to the new structure by a process involving unloading and reloading the data. This process removes any duplicate records that may have been produced, so only records whose key differs from that of records that have already been reloaded will be reloaded into the new table. Data could easily be lost during this operation. The deleted field can still occur in programs that use internal tables of the same structure as snapshots of the database table. These programs will be syntactically incorrect. For these reasons, a table's Use List should be analyzed before a field is changed or deleted.

Including and Appending Structures

Rather than listing all the fields you wish a table or structure to contain, you can choose to include the fields from another structure definition as a *substructure*. If you change and activate a substructure, all tables that include the structure are changed automatically. Individual fields and substructures can be combined as required. Nested substructures are supported; up to nine nesting levels of substructures are allowed.

To include a substructure, switch to the table definition screen, enter the keyword .include (with a leading period) in the left-most column, and type the name of the structure (in our example, SCUSTOM) into the column of data elements, as shown in Figure 5.16. You can also expand all substructures by choosing Extras ➤ Substructures ➤ Expand All Substr.

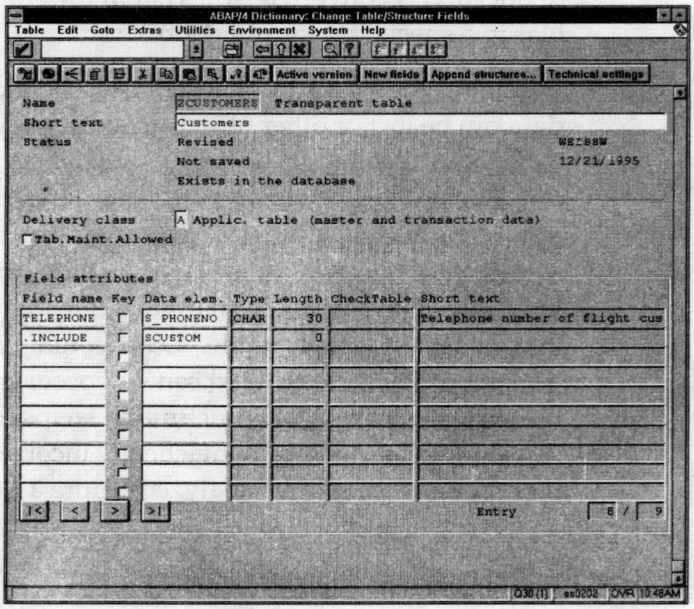

FIGURE 5.16:

Including a substructure

Suppose you want to add new functionality to the standard R/3 system and, among other things, you also need extra fields in the database tables delivered by SAP. You can modify the table's definition by adding fields. After an upgrade from SAP, however, you have to merge your modification with the new version of the table if fields have also been added by SAP. In this case, you must adjust the definition of the table and convert the contents of the database table to the new structure. When new functionality is added in this way, each upgrade creates a certain amount of extra work.

The ABAP/4 Dictionary allows you to avoid these upgrade problems by using *Append Structures*. An *Append Structure* is a structure that is assigned to exactly one table, but each table can have any number of Append Structures.

From the program point of view, Append Structures are always appended at the end of the table structure. However, from the database point of view, the fields of Append Structures remain at their physical position when a new version of the table with additional fields is activated during an upgrade. Thus, adding Append Structures to a table makes it unnecessary to adjust the table definition or to convert the table after an upgrade. When a table is activated, all its Append Structures are found and added to the table.

> **NOTE** Be aware that differences can arise between the sequence of fields in the Dictionary table definition and in the database table.

To create an Append Structure for an existing table, choose Goto ➤ Append Structures from the table definition screen. A dialog box will appear in which you enter a name for the Append Structure. The name must lie within the customer name range—that is, it must begin with Y or Z. This ensures that the structure is protected against being overwritten when the R/3 system is upgraded.

Working with Data Elements

A data element carries field information (valid for every field that refers to this data element) independently of the table in which a given field occurs. The semantic information, as well as its outward representation in the form of on-screen field texts and table captions, is assigned to the data element along with the corresponding online field documentation (that is, the text displayed in the field help for a screen field is taken from the corresponding data element).

A data element describes the role played by a domain in the context of one or more applications. A domain can have various manifestations that possess the same formal attributes (format and value range), but differ in their significance for the applications. This is accomplished by assigning a domain to a number of different data elements. For instance, the data elements *Sender cost center*, *Receiver cost center*, and *Partner cost center* refer to the domain *Cost center*. Therefore, these three data elements all have the same type and length inherited from the domain. They differ in their documentation where the field usage in the respective application is described.

Displaying a Data Element's Definition

On the table definition screen, you can display a data element by double-clicking on it in a table field. You can also select Dictionary objects from the Object Browser and enter the name of a data element. In both cases, you will see the definition of the data element as shown in Figure 5.17.

The upper part of the data element screen contains a short description and some administrative information (the date of the last change and the status). The next lower portion of the screen contains the referred domain with its data type and length, and possibly the attached value table. The lowest portion of the screen (titled *Texts*) contains the field labels (short, medium, and long) and the header. The labels can be used as labels for input fields in screens, and the header for the column heading in a table.

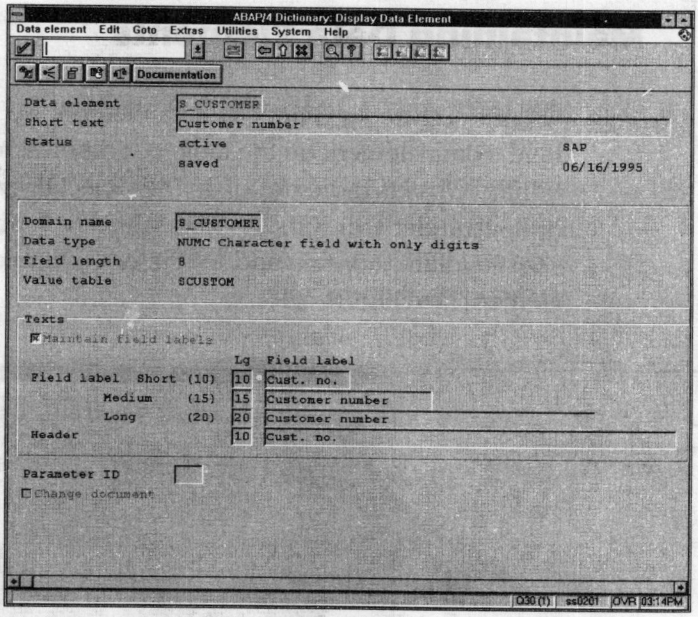

FIGURE 5.17:

Displaying a data element

For more information about using labels from the Dictionary for input fields on a screen see Chapter 19.

The data element's documentation is accessible via the Documentation button. It is displayed as online help for those fields that refer to the data element in question. To call up this information, position the cursor on a field referring to this data element and press F1. The data in the online documentation is always up-to-date, since any changes made to the Dictionary become immediately effective in the help text as well.

Additional attributes, which appear at the bottom of the maintenance screen, are explained in the next section.

Maintaining Data Elements

You can create or change a data element by double-clicking on a table field's data element on the table definition screen or by selecting the Dictionary Objects radio button in the Object Browser and entering the name of a data element. On the data element maintenance screen, enter the short explanatory text and the name of the domain assigned to the data element (see Figure 5.18).

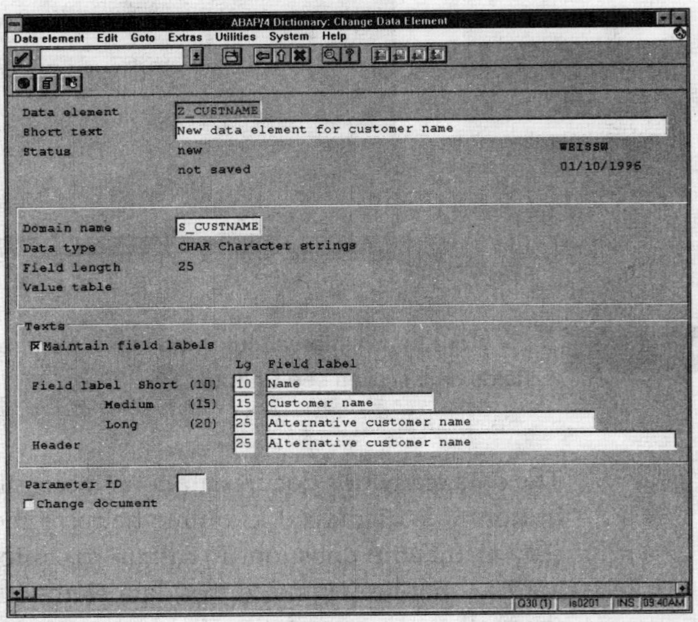

FIGURE 5.18:

Creating a data element

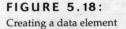

You can enter the name of a new domain or of one that already exists. If the domain is new, a message to that effect is displayed. You can then create the domain by double-clicking on the domain name to branch to the domain maintenance screen (see the section "Creating and Using Domains" below). You can also enter the field labels (short, medium, and long field labels and the header). If you do not wish to maintain the field labels, you can deactivate the Maintain Field Labels check box.

TIP It is not a good idea to deactivate this check box if the labels of data elements appear on screens, because then you need to add labels manually when designing a screen.

You can now save the data element by clicking on the Save button. To activate the data element, click on the Activate button. Afterwards, the data element can be used throughout the system. This also applies for changed data elements—the active version applies for all table fields using the data element.

To create or change the documentation, click on the Documentation button. The documentation you enter here is displayed when the F1 help function is selected.

In the lowest portion of the Data Element Maintenance screen, you can also define a Parameter ID, which can be used to determine the default values for a field. When several screens containing a field designated in this way are displayed in succession, the field is automatically filled with the value entered in the first screen of the series. For example, if you set the customer number on the first screen of an application program, this number is taken by the system as a default for customer number on all subsequent screens. When designing a screen, an appropriate attribute must be assigned to the field.

NOTE For a complete discussion of using the Parameter ID when designing a screen, see Chapter 22.

Creating and Using Domains

A *domain* describes the set of possible values and the output characteristics of a table field. The allowed data values for fields referring to a domain are specified by the value range of the domain. A single domain can be used as the basis for any number of fields that are identically structured. Fields referring to the same domain (via the data elements assigned to them) are changed when a change is made to the domain. This ensures consistency between the fields.

The value range for a domain is defined by specifying a data type and a length on the Domain Maintenance screen. For instance, the domain S_CUSTNAME, which represents the name of a customer, has the data type char (character) and length 25.

Displaying a Domain's Definition

You can display a domain's definition in different ways:

- By double-clicking on a table field to open its data element and then double-clicking on the data element to open the domain.

- By clicking to select the Dictionary Objects radio button in the Object Browser and entering the name of a domain (help for possible entries is available).

In either case, you will see the short text and the attributes of the domain, as shown in Figure 5.19.

The upper part of the domain screen contains a short description and some administrative information (the date of the last change and the status). The following frame contains the data type and the field length.

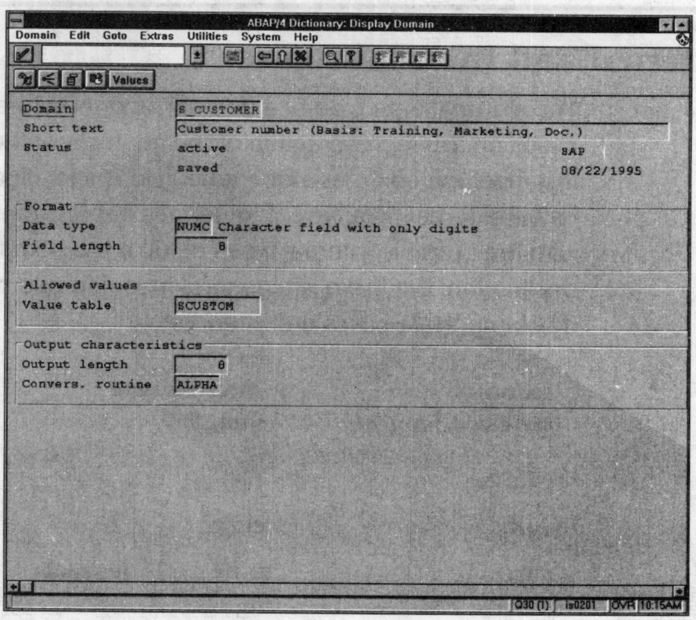

FIGURE 5.19:

Displaying the S_CUSTOMER
domain

The next frame displays information about the allowed values for fields referring to the domain. There are two ways to specify further restrictions of the value range for a domain:

- by using a value table
- by using fixed values

If a value table has been specified, only values contained in the value table can be entered in fields referring to this domain. There is no check on an input mask with a field referring to this domain unless a corresponding foreign key has been defined for this field.

NOTE   We will explain how to define foreign keys in the section "Foreign Keys and Permissible Entry Values" below.

External and Internal types

The external data type of a domain (and therefore of a table field) focuses on the representation of the contents of the field on a screen. For instance, the edit mask for a time field is specified in the representation in the external data type. The set of external types does not coincide with the possible internal types of local program fields defined by a `data` declaration, but there is a general mapping rule between both types. The most important cases are listed below:

External type (x = length)	Internal type (length)	Description
char(x)	c(x)	Character
cuky	c(5)	Currency key
curr	p(n/2 + 1) decimals m	Currency (n digits, m decimals)
dats	d	Date
int4	i	Integer
lang	c(1)	Language
numc(x)	n(x)	Numeric character (only digits)
tims	t	Time

Using fixed values, you can specify the value range for the fields referring to this domain by listing all admissible values. For instance, the fixed values can consist of numbers for months (1, 2, ... 12) or the two values B and P indicating that a person is a business or private customer. You can display the set of fixed values on the domain screen by clicking on the Values button (see Figure 5.20; in the figure, domain S_CUSTTYPE is shown, since domain S_CUSTOMER does not have fixed values).

OF THE DICTIONARY

FIGURE 5.20:

The fixed values of the
S_CUSTTYPE domain

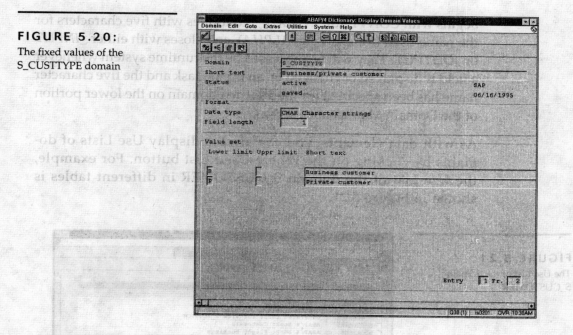

You can also combine both fixed values and a value table. As a result, fields referring to this domain can accept only those values that exist in both the value table and in the fixed values.

The lower frame of the screen in Figure 5.19 contains the output characteristics of a field referring to the domain. For instance, the field Output Length holds the maximum field length including editing characters for input/output. This value is computed automatically, but can be overwritten.

In the ABAP/4 Development Workbench, you can design *conversion functions* to automatically edit field values when they appear on a screen. Conversion functions follow a naming convention: the name begins with *CONVERSION_EXIT_*, continues with five characters for the name itself (for example, *ALPHA*), and closes with either *_INPUT* or *_OUTPUT*. They will be processed by the runtime system whenever a field is displayed or changed on an input mask and the five character name has been specified for the attached domain on the lower portion of the Domain Maintenance screen.

As with data elements, you can always display Use Lists of domains by clicking on the Where-Used List button. For example, the Use List of the domain S_CUSTOMER in different tables is shown in Figure 5.21.

FIGURE 5.21:

The Use List of the domain S_CUSTOMER

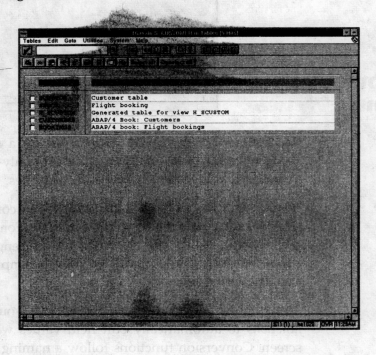

Creating Domains

To create a new domain, you can proceed in the same way as before when you looked at the definition of a domain: double-click on the name of a new domain in a data element or access domain maintenance by selecting the Dictionary Objects radio button in the Object Browser and entering the name of the domain in the next screen. Either way, you must enter explanatory text and select an external data type for the domain. Then select the field length (the valid positions of a field without editing characters such as commas or periods). This defines the type and the length of all table fields referring to this domain. Finally, save and activate the domain.

Foreign Keys and Permissible Entry Values

In a relational data model, tables and relationships between tables are the basic elements of the model. The most important relationship is represented by *foreign keys*, which provide a link between two tables. In its simplest form, this link is established by defining a field in one table whose contents must be contained in a primary key field of the other table. Complex foreign key relations are comprised of groups of fields.

An important function of foreign keys is to support data integrity in the relational data model. Fields with a foreign key link to primary key fields of another table can assume only those values allowed by the referenced table. A field with a foreign key link is called a *foreign key field* and the referenced table is called a *check table* in the ABAP/4 Dictionary. Thus, the primary key of the check table appears as a foreign key in another table.

Using this mechanism, data is handled consistently throughout the system. For instance, if a travel agency's bookings contain information about the customers who have made flight reservations, this information will be stored as identifiers of the customers in a normalized data model. Each identifier, in turn, must occur as a primary key of the table of all customers. In other words, the table bookings has a foreign key field customid, which refers to the check table customers.

In the R/3 system, the foreign key relationships are used to guarantee that only consistent data can be inserted into the system. The system does this by binding check tables to input fields on data entry screens. If the new value does not occur in the check table, the system prompts the user for a new entry with an appropriate error message. Help information on permissible entry values for a field is taken from the Dictionary. If you position the cursor on an entry field and press F4, a pop-up window lists the possible entry values for that field. These values are based on check tables associated with a table field.

NOTE   Using foreign keys to check the user input will be explained in Chapter 19.

The name of the referenced check table is displayed in the column Chk. Table on the table definition screen. To create or change a foreign key relationship, place the cursor on the field in question and click on the Foreign Keys button. On the next screen, enter a short explanatory text and the name of the check table (see Figure 5.22).

The built-in default for a check table is the value table of the underlying domain. For example, in Figure 5.22, the table ACTFLI is the default check table for the domain of the table field ZBOOKINGS-CARRID. You can also enter a different table in the input field after the word Check table. However, the check table itself must be related to the value table of the domain via a single foreign key relationship or a chain of relationships.

FIGURE 5.22:

The check table of a foreign key field

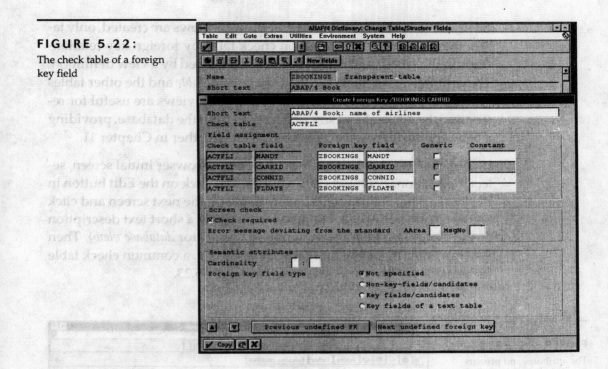

Views

A *view* is a virtual table whose data is taken from one or more tables. This means that the logical definition and the physical storage are different. In a view, only certain data is extracted from the other tables using the following basic rules:

- Projection: Suppressing one or more columns.
- Selection: Transferring only certain rows to the view.
- Join: Combining tables with common columns.

To ensure that only semantically meaningful views are created, only tables that are linked to a common check table by foreign key relationships in the ABAP/4 Dictionary can be connected by a view definition. The common check table is called the *primary table* and the other tables of the join are called *secondary tables*. Database views are useful for restricting the amount and size of data read from the database, providing a better performance. This issue is covered further in Chapter 11.

If you want to create a view, from the Object Browser Initial screen, select the Dictionary Objects radio button and click on the Edit button in the lower part. Then enter the view name on the next screen and click on the Create button. On the next screen, enter a short text description of the view and select the view type *D* (short for *database view*). Then you can enter the name of a primary table (i.e., a common check table for all tables of the view), as shown in Figure 5.23.

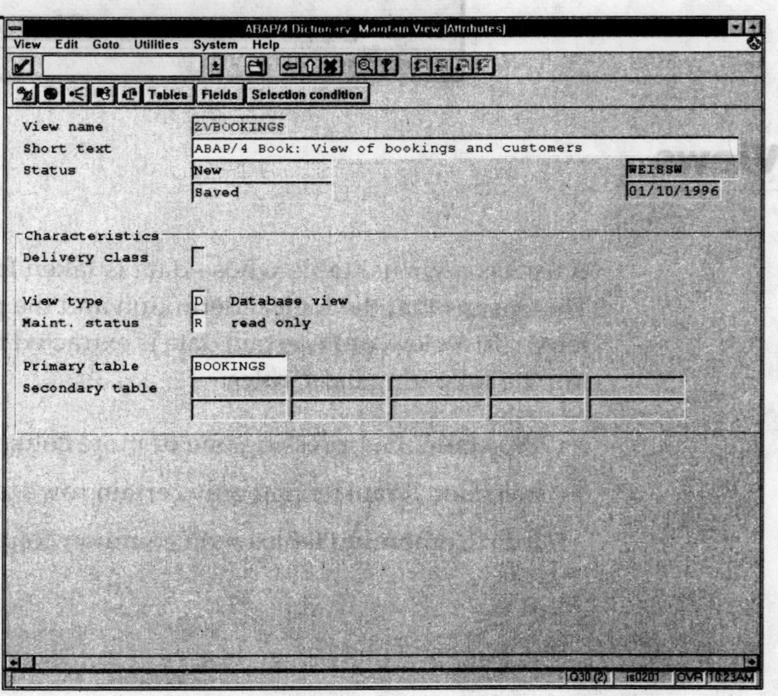

FIGURE 5.23:

The attributes and primary table of a view

You can select further tables for the join operation by clicking on the Tables button (see Figure 5.24).

FIGURE 5.24:
The secondary tables of a view

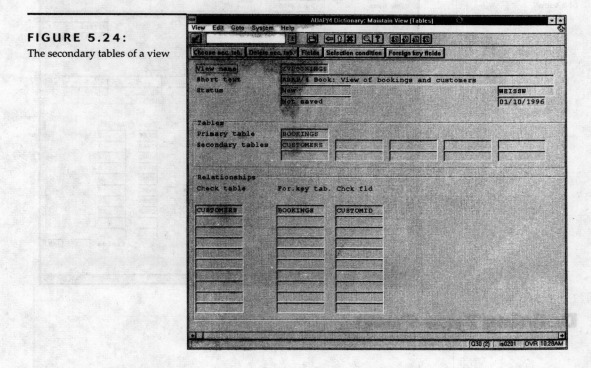

When you click on the Fields button on the Maintain View (Attributes) screen, all key fields of the tables appear. You can delete fields or specify further fields (as shown in Figure 5.25), thus performing the projection operation. Finally, you can select rows by clicking on the Selection Condition button.

Maintaining the fields
of a view

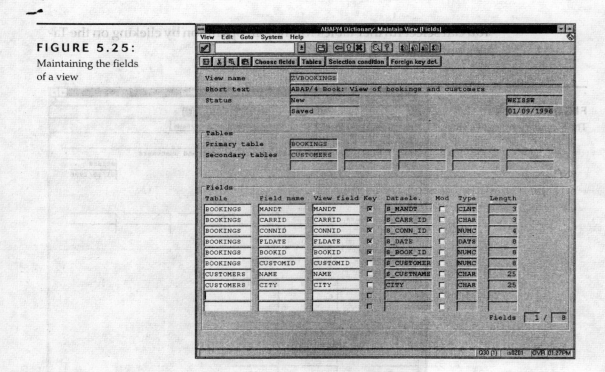

Defining Type-Pools

The above sections describe techniques to define table structures suitable for relational databases. In brief, all tables of the Dictionary have flat rows, containing only fields, and nested tables are not allowed. As you saw in Chapter 4, local data of a program defined by types and data allow not only flat records, but also nested structures and tables. These types can also be re-used in other programs by defining *type pools* in the Dictionary.

To display or create a type pool, from the Object Browser Initial screen, select the Dictionary Objects radio button and click on the Edit button in the lower part of the screen. On the next screen, enter the name of the type pool after Type Group. In much the same way as you make a type definition in a program (see Chapter 4), you can use the same syntax of the types declaration in the Dictionary. For instance, the line type of an internal table containing employee data can be defined in a type pool customer as follows:

```
type-pool customer.
types: begin of phone_fax_numbers,
        country_code(3) type n,
        area_code(3) type n,
        number(10) type n,
      end of phone_fax_numbers,
      begin of employee,
        name(25),
        phone type phone_fax_numbers occurs 10,
        fax type phone_fax_numbers occurs 5,
      end of employee.
```

The types of a type pool can be used in any number of programs using the declaration type-pools:

```
type-pools customer.
data employees type employee occurs 100.
```

Special Table Fields

Many companies have customers in countries all over the world, and each of these countries has a different currency. A customer order document has to be able to handle these currencies. In particular, currency-dependent values must either be converted or the currency must be set separately.

ABAP/4 offers a very flexible method for working with currency. You can define pairs of fields, where one field contains the value and the other the currency. These fields are called *reference fields*. In the definition of a table, the value field has a domain of type curr and the field refers to a table field of type cuky, which contains the currency key (for example, USD for US Dollar). The currency key need not reside in the same table.

In our travel agency example, fields with currency values are not contained in the table customers, but are instead in the table bookings holding all information about flight bookings (see Figure 5.26).

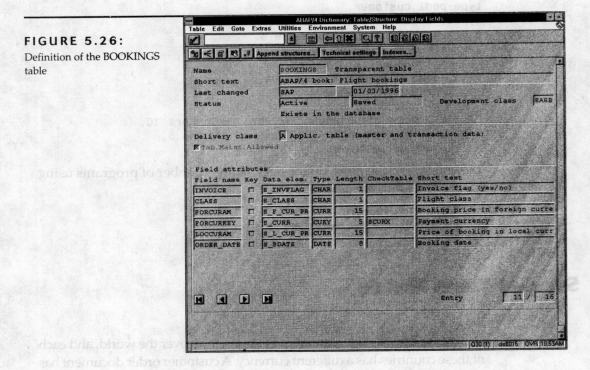

FIGURE 5.26:
Definition of the BOOKINGS table

The field forcuram (the foreign currency amount) has type curr and refers to the field forcurkey (the foreign currency key) of the same table. To see this reference, you can scroll the Table Maintenance screen shown in Figure 5.26 to the right using the scroll buttons in the lower portion of the screen. On the next screen, you see the referenced table and field (see Figure 5.27).

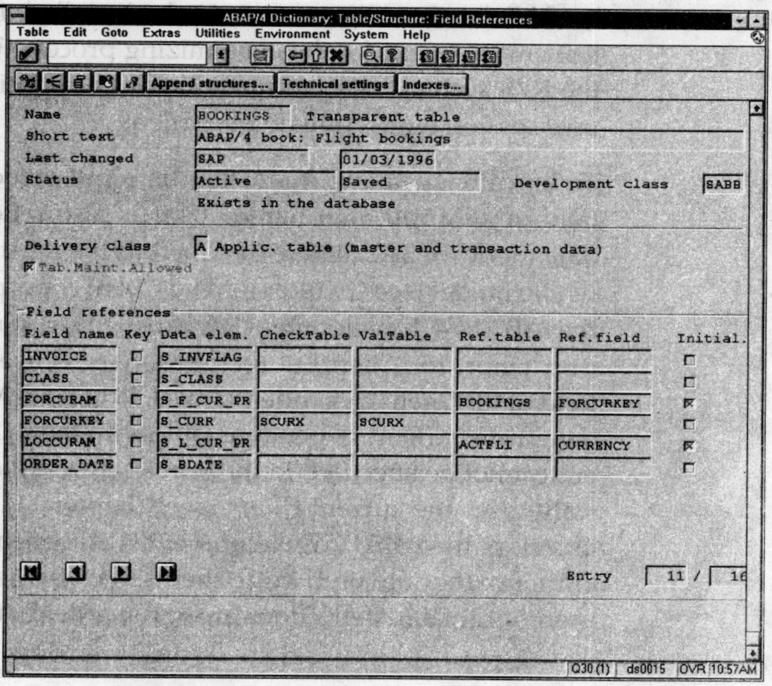

FIGURE 5.27:

Field references of the
BOOKINGS table

```
ABAP/4 Dictionary: Table/Structure: Field References
Table  Edit  Goto  Extras  Utilities  Environment  System  Help

Append structures...   Technical settings   Indexes...

Name              BOOKINGS      Transparent table
Short text        ABAP/4 book: Flight bookings
Last changed      SAP            01/03/1996
Status            Active         Saved            Development class   SABB
                  Exists in the database

Delivery class    A Applic. table (master and transaction data)
X Tab.Maint.Allowed

Field references
Field name Key Data elem. CheckTable ValTable    Ref.table  Ref.field    Initial.
INVOICE     □  S_INVFLAG                                                    □
CLASS       □  S_CLASS                                                      □
FORCURAM    □  S_F_CUR_PR                          BOOKINGS   FORCURKEY     X
FORCURKEY   □  S_CURR     SCURX      SCURX                                  □
LOCCURAM    □  S_L_CUR_PR                          ACTFLI     CURRENCY      X
ORDER_DATE  □  S_BDATE                                                      □

                                                        Entry    11 / 16

                                         Q30 (1)  ds0015  OVR 10:57AM
```

User input into a currency field is automatically supplied with the ap-propriate number of decimal places for that currency (for example, two places for the US dollar: 0.00). Moreover, the reference to the currency key can be used when the field is displayed using the write command (see Chapter 8).

In a similar way, quantities with different units can be handled using the type pair quan and unit. For instance, distances can be measured in miles or kilometers.

The business applications of the R/3 system often use Client-dependent tables. From the application point of view, the whole R/3 system is di-vided into different Clients, where each Client represents the operational data of one business unit. In a typical configuration, one Client is used for the productive data and a second one for a model company delivered by SAP. Further Clients can also be installed; for example, to build a test environment for the customizing process. When a user logs on to the R/3 system, a Client must always be specified. In other words, a user session works only in one Client.

Technically speaking, the Client is represented by the left-most key field of all application tables. This is also reflected in the enterprise data model of SAP, where the Client is the most basic entity type of the whole model (see Chapter 6). The Client concept is fully supported by the ABAP/4 Development Workbench. In particular, the data type `clnt` (short for Client) of the Dictionary is used for the left-most key field of all Client-dependent tables. When an ABAP/4 program reads data from a Client-dependent table with the `select` command, the Client cannot be specified in the `where` clause, since the system automatically uses the current Client (see Chapter 11). System tables and the objects of the ABAP/ Development Workbench are not Client dependent, since they are used in all Clients in the same way. For instance, programs and table definitions are independent of the Client.

A Quick Review

Here are some of the key points you should keep in mind from this chapter:

- The ABAP/4 Dictionary is active and integrated: changes to Dictionary objects are automatically forwarded to all programs referring to them.

- Tables represent database tables and structures are declarations without physical data.

- Each table field refers to a data element, which, in turn, can be used in many fields. Data elements provide help information and labels for the fields referring to them.

- A data element is assigned to a domain, which, in turn, can be used in many data elements. A domain describes the technical properties of a table field. It specifies the set of allowed data values for that field and its output characteristics.

- Table fields with a foreign key link to primary key fields of another table can assume only those values allowed by the referenced table. This check is executed when the user enters a value in an input mask.

- Database views, where data is taken from one or more tables, are helpful to restrict the size of data read from the database.

- Complex types (e.g., nested tables) are defined in type pools. They can be used in different programs by using the command `type-pools`.

- There are special data types for fields with currency values referring to currency keys or quantity fields referring to units.

- Organizing a system with Clients is supported by Client-dependent tables.

In the next chapter, you will see how to graphically design a model of your application data based on the information from the Dictionary.

- A data element is assigned to a domain, which, in turn, can be used in many data elements. A domain describes the technical properties of a table field. It specifies the set of allowed data values for that field and its output characteristics.

- Table fields with a foreign key link to primary key fields of another table can assume only those values allowed by the referenced table. This check is executed when the user enters a value in an input mask.

- Database views, where data is taken from one or more tables, are helpful to restrict the size of data read from the database.

- Complex types (e.g., nested tables) are defined in type pools. They can be used in different programs by using the command type-pools.

- There are special data types for fields with currency values referring to currency keys or quantity fields referring to units.

- Organizing a system with Clients is supported by Client-dependent tables.

In the next chapter, you will see how to graphically design a model of your application data based on the information from the Dictionary.

CHAPTER

SIX

Modeling Entities and Relationships

- **Designing a data model**

- **The entity types of a model**

- **Relationships between entity types**

A Sample Data Model

W hen developing a real-life application program, you will soon find yourself handling many tables and foreign key relationships between these tables. It might be cumbersome to get an overview of all tables and relationships. A graphical representation can help you to visualize the tables and their mutual dependencies. Using the ABAP/4 Development Workbench's Data Modeler, you can display and maintain graphics with entity-relationship models.

A *data model* consists of two key elements: small boxes (called *entity types*) representing the tables and arrows to show the relationships between these tables. Since a data model is based on the Dictionary, changes to a table definition are automatically reflected in the model. For instance, when you add a field to a table, this field will appear in the corresponding entity type. By double-clicking and drilling down, you can also navigate between a data model and the underlying table definitions in the Dictionary.

A Sample Data Model

In this section, we'll show you a data model for a travel agency's bookings. The sample travel agency books flights and maintains a database of customers. We'll use this example to illustrate the key properties of a data model and its connections to the Dictionary.

NOTE We'll also refer to this model in later chapters—for example, when SQL statements or internal tables are discussed—so you should bookmark this chapter.

A table of all of the travel agency's customers will be useful. In addition, the destinations and their geographical position, airlines, connections between different destinations, flights, and bookings are stored in the following tables:

- customers (customers of the travel agency)
- geocity (destinations)
- carriers (airlines)
- planfli (possible flights between destinations)
- actfli (actual flights)
- bookings (bookings of flights by customers)

The left-most column of the table customers contains customer numbers, which serve as unique identifiers for each table entry. In other words, the field id is the primary key of the table customers. This key field will also be used in all tables with a relationship to a customer (such as the bookings table defined below), but the dependent customer data contained in the fields name, city, and telephone is stored in the customers table only, to avoid repetition. You can see the contents of this table in Table 6.1.

TABLE 6.1: The sample contents of the customers table

id	name	city	telephone
00000001	Edwards	Small Town	654-321-1234
00000002	Young	Village	333-444-2222
00000017	Smith	Big City	717-161-5151
87654321	Edison	Market Place	111-111-1111

The city field is the primary key field of the table geocity, and the other fields contain the geographical position of each city. You can see the contents of this table in Table 6.2.

TABLE 6.2: The sample contents of the geocity table

city	longitude	latitude
Frankfurt	10	50
Madrid	1	35
Moscow	30	58
Paris	5	48

The table carriers contains the set of carriers with the identifier of the carrier (field carrid) as its primary key field. The dependent data contains the name of the carrier and its local currency. The contents of this table are shown in Table 6.3.

TABLE 6.3: The sample contents of the carriers table

carrid	carrname	currcode
ABC	ABC Airlines	USD
AL	ALITALIA	ITL
XYZ	XYZ Flights	DEM

The primary key of the planfli table is built of the fields carrid (identifier of the carrier with the check table carriers) and connid (identifier of the connection). The dependent data contains information about the departure and arrival cities (taken from geocity), the total time of the flight, and the time of departure. You can see the contents of this table in Table 6.4.

TABLE 6.4: The sample contents of the `planfli` table

carrid	connid	cityfrom	cityto	fltime	deptime
ABC	1000	Frankfurt	Paris	1	081000
ABC	1234	Paris	Frankfurt	1	175500
xyz	0006	Madrid	Moscow	5	163000
xyz	0007	Frankfurt	Madrid	3	093500

Similarly to the `planfli` table, the primary key of the `actfli` table is built of the fields `carrid`, `connid`, and `fldate` (date of the flight). The `planfli` table is the check table of the fields `carrid` and `connid`. The price of the flight and its currency, and the number of occupied seats are stored in additional fields, as you can see in Table 6.5.

TABLE 6.5: The sample contents of the `actfli` table

carrid	connid	fldate	price	currency	seatsocc
ABC	1000	19991230	200	DEM	110
ABC	1234	19991230	500	DEM	010
ABC	1234	19991231	300	DEM	020
xyz	0006	19990606	100	USD	175
xyz	0007	19990505	110	USD	133

The primary key of the `bookings` table consists of the fields `carrid`, `connid`, `fldate`, and `bookid` (identifier of the booking). The fields `carrid`, `connid`, and `fldate` have a foreign key relation to the `actfli` table. Additional information is given by the customer identifier (with check table `customers`) and the order date, as you can see in Table 6.6.

TABLE 6.6: The sample contents of the `bookings` table

carrid	connid	fldate	bookid	customid	order_date
ABC	1000	19991230	001	00000017	19990101
ABC	1234	19991230	002	00000002	19991229
ABC	1234	19991231	005	00000017	19990101
XYZ	0006	19990606	008	00000001	19990101
XYZ	0007	19990505	007	87654321	19990101

NOTE In reality, the above tables would consist of even more fields, such as a customer type to distinguish between different types of customers (business people or tourists). Since these tables contain application-specific data, they are Client-dependent in a production system—that is, they have a field of type `clnt` as their leftmost key field. We'll assume the existence of additional fields if they are relevant in a later context.

The above tables are connected via foreign key relationships. For example, the `geocity` table is a check table for the fields `cityfrom` and `cityto` of the `planfli` table—that is, the values of these fields are always contained in the key field `geocity-city` of some entry in the `geocity` table. Relationships of this kind are displayed in an entity-relationship model, where the dependencies between tables are shown as connecting arrows. For example, a model for the travel agency is shown in Figure 6.1.

The entity types (nodes) of this model represent the tables. By double-clicking on a node, you can display the definition of the entity type with its documentation. After you double-click on the name of the underlying table, its structure is displayed. As explained in Chapter 5, you can also display the table contents with the Data Browser. An entity type of a data model may also correspond to more than one physical table in the

FIGURE 6.1:

A data model for our sample travel agency

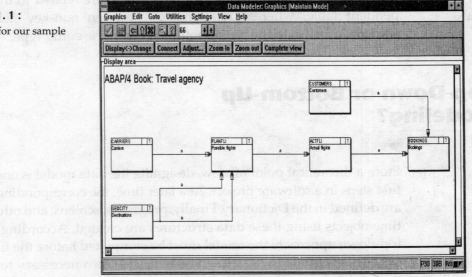

database. In this case, the entity type is related to a view comprising these tables.

The arrows in the data model represent the relationships between the underlying tables of the entity types. For instance, the key field `planfli-carrid` (identifier of the carrier) has the check table `carriers`—that is, `carriers` and `planfli` are connected by a foreign key relationship. This is shown by the arrow starting at `carriers` and pointing to the left edge of `planfli`. The fields `planfli-cityfrom` and `planfli-city to` have the `geocity` table as their check table. This link is represented by two arrows from `geocity` to the lower (or upper) edge of `planfli`, since these fields are non-key fields in `planfli`.

A table pointed to by an arrow is called *dependent*, because its entries depend on the table at the starting point of the arrow. Since arrows always lead from left to right, the dependent objects are located on the right. An arrow pointing to the left edge of an entity type indicates that key fields of the underlying dependent table are related to the independent table, whereas relationships between non-key fields are shown as arrows to the top or bottom edge of the entity type.

Top-Down or Bottom-Up Modeling?

From a theoretical point of view, designing the data model is one of the first steps in a software project. At a later time, the corresponding tables are defined in the Dictionary. Finally, programs, screens, and other runtime objects using these data structures are created. According to this top-down approach, the model must be completed before the first line of code is written. In practice, however, it is often necessary to adjust the model during the life cycle of a system. There are several reasons you might make late changes—the application may not be performing as expected, or users may have additional requirements. Using a bottom-up approach, you can build a model using existing tables and visualize the relationships between them.

The ABAP/4 Development Workbench supports both alternatives: you can either start with the data model and create the runtime objects later (always navigating via double-clicks), or you can build a model to illustrate the behavior of existing table definitions and programs. In addition, a change in the structure of a table automatically appears in the corresponding entity type. In general, a top-down design is preferable for a new project, and the bottom-up method is used for re-engineering projects for large existing systems. You can even choose a mixture of these two design and implementation strategies.

Data Models, Entity Types, Tables, and Views

The nodes of a data model are called *entity types*. They represent either a single database table or a view of one or more tables. On the model layer, the fields of the table or view are called *attributes of the entity type*, the entries in the corresponding table or view are called *entities*.

You can display, create, or maintain a data model from the Object Browser screen by selecting the radio button Modeling Objects and clicking on the Edit button in the lower portion of the screen. On the next screen, enter the name of the data model (a list of possible entries appears if you press F4). If you already know the technical name of the entity type, you can also choose the radio button Entity Type and enter the name. When the data model is chosen, its textual definition is shown on the subsequent screen, as shown in Figure 6.2.

FIGURE 6.2:
The definition of the TRAVEL data model

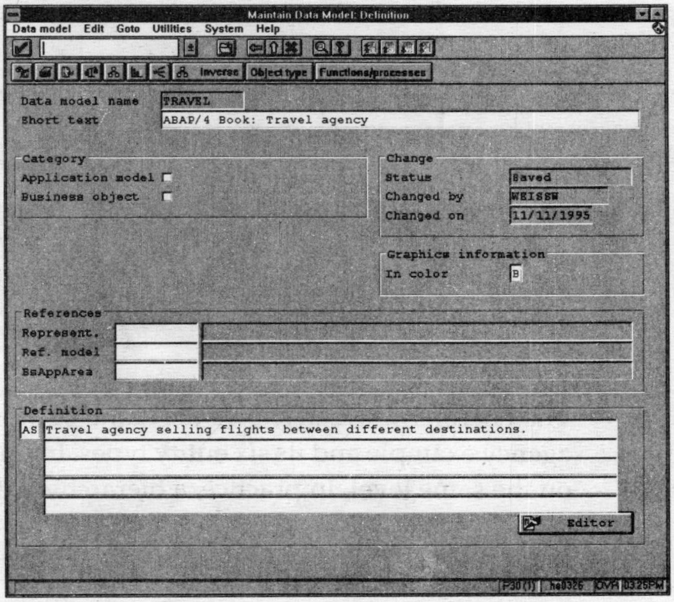

In the upper portion of the data model screen, you see a short explanatory text and some administrative information, such as the date of the last change. The complete documentation of the model is shown in the lowest part of this screen and can be edited by clicking on the Editor button. You can display, create, or change the entity types of the data model by clicking on the Hierarchy button on the Data Model screen. You will then see the Data Model Hierarchy screen as shown in Figure 6.3.

FIGURE 6.3:

The hierarchy of a data model

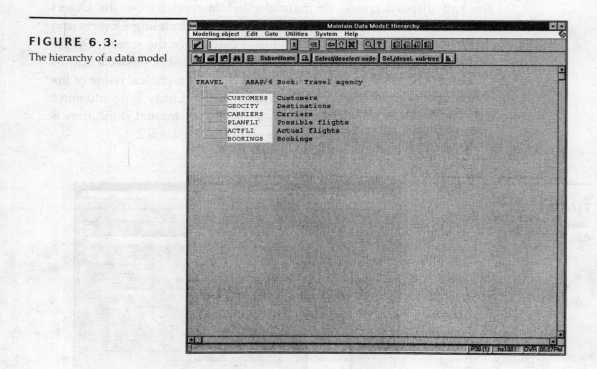

The Hierarchy screen shows the name of the data model for the travel agency example and its six entity types. In this case, all entity types are on the same level. In practice, a hierarchy will consist of many levels.

Creating or Changing a Data Model

To create or change a data model, enter the name of the model on the Object Browser screen, enter the short text of the definition, and edit the model's hierarchy by clicking on the Hierarchy button. Additional entity types can be inserted on the hierarchy screen by clicking on the Subordinate button or by selecting Modeling Object ➤ Insert ➤ On Same Level. Choose Entity Type from the dialog box that appears, and enter the name of the entity type. You can also insert a submodel here. This enables you to group entity types according to their meaning and to build a large model using smaller ones. You can display each model in a different color in the graphical editor, thus structuring the whole picture. The color of a data model is specified in the definition screen (see Figure 6.2, above). In the travel agency example, we have only created the data model, its entity types, and the color of the model; we didn't use submodels.

The hierarchy of a data model is a structured list of all submodels and entity types of the model, but it does not reflect the relationships between the entity types. You can display and change the complete model, including the relationships, in the graphical editor. Before you switch to the graphics screen, select one or more subtrees of your model by clicking on the Sel./Desel. Sub-Tree button. If you wish to omit individual objects in a selected subtree from the graphics, you can deselect these objects by clicking on the Select/Deselect Node button. To open the graphics screen, click on the Graphics button on the hierarchy screen. All selected data models and entity types in the hierarchy list are displayed in the form of a graphic, as shown in Figure 6.4.

In the graphic, you see all entity types and their relationships with the travel agency's data model.

FIGURE 6.4:

The graphic of a data model

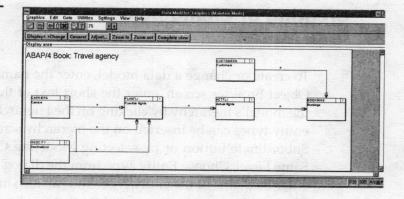

> **NOTE** The arrows in this graphic will be explained in detail in the next section, "Relationships and Foreign Keys".

Displaying or Changing an Entity Type

To display or change an entity type, you can double-click on the name of the entity type in the graphic or in the hierarchy list of the data model. In either case, you will switch to the textual definition of the entity type, as shown in Figure 6.5.

The figure displays the definition of the entity type CUSTOMERS. The short text of this definition also appears in the entity type's box on the graphics screen (see Figure 6.4).

The frame in the center of the entity type screen contains the associated table or view of the Dictionary. This link can be created or changed by clicking on the Dict. button. On the next screen, the name of the associated Dictionary object is displayed (for example the Dictionary table customers). You can see an example in Figure 6.6. You can select the radio button Table or View and enter the name of the corresponding table or view.

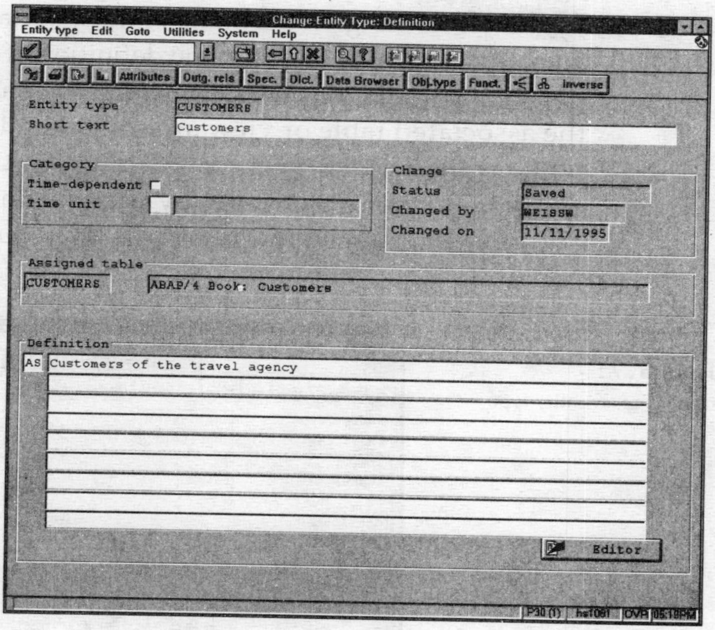

FIGURE 6.5:

The definition of an entity type

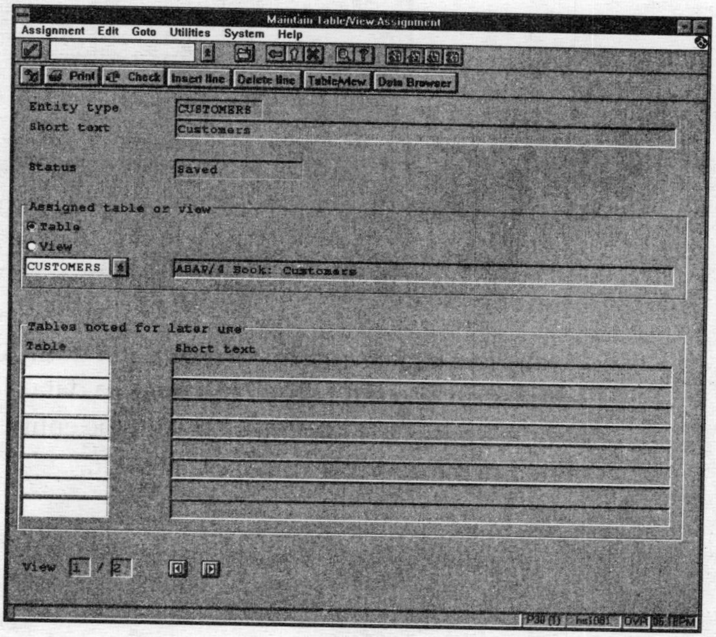

FIGURE 6.6:

The Dictionary assignment of an entity type

By double-clicking on the name of the associated Dictionary object of an entity type, you switch to the definition of this object. You can display fields, underlying data elements, types, and lengths. The fields of the associated table or view are considered attributes of an entity type on the model layer. You can access the attributes from the entity type definition screen by clicking on the Attributes button. The resulting screen for our example is shown in Figure 6.7.

FIGURE 6.7:

The attributes of an entity type

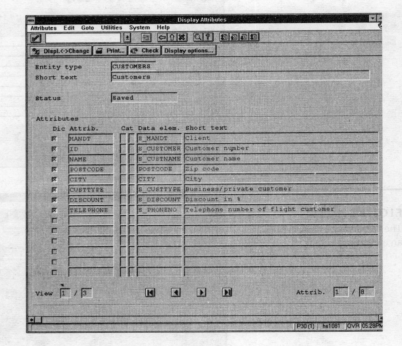

Here you can also define further attributes. As with table fields, each attribute of an entity type can refer to a data element of the Dictionary. For example, the attribute *NAME* of the entity type *CUSTOMERS* is related to the data element *S_CUSTNAME*.

In a top-down design, you first define the attributes of an entity type. Second, you can define the associated table in the Dictionary with fields referring to the same data elements: double-click on the name of the table, create it, and choose Extras ➤ Flds From Ent.Type on the table maintenance screen. All fields from the entity type are copied to the Clipboard and can be inserted as table fields by selecting Edit ➤ Paste.

Relationships and Foreign Keys

Relationships between two entity types are defined by specifying the source entity type (the independent or referenced entity type) and the target entity type (the dependent entity type). Independent entity types are displayed on the left side of the graphic, since arrows representing relationships always lead from left to right.

From a technical point of view, tables can be related via foreign keys in two ways: either key fields or non-key fields of the dependent table refer to the independent table (i.e., the check table). In other words, the target entity type of a foreign key relationship is either existentially dependent on the source entity type or it is not. In the graphic, an arrow pointing to the left edge of an entity type indicates that the key fields of the underlying dependent table are related to the independent table. Relationships to non-key fields are shown as arrows to the top or bottom edge of the entity type.

In the model layer, relationships between non-key fields in the dependent table are called *referential*. For instance, the foreign key relation between `planfli-cityfrom` and `geocity-city` is a referential relation. Foreign key relationships between key fields are further classified as *hierarchical* or *aggregating*. In a hierarchical relation, the existentially dependent entity type is considered a *subobject* or a *refinement of the independent entity*. For example, the relation of `planfli-carrid` (identifier of the carrier) to `carriers-id` is a hierarchical relation. Each entry of the `planfli` table depends on the existence of a referenced entry in the `carriers` table. The target entity type of an aggregating relationship depends on at least two source entity types. The existentially dependent entity type is not a subobject or refinement of the source entity type. The key fields of the aggregated entity type are composed of key fields of the independent entity types. In other words, the key of the dependent table contains the key fields of the check tables. The key can, of course, have additional fields, which do not refer to another table.

Creating Relationships

Relationships between entity types can be created in two ways:

- by drawing arrows in the graphical editor.
- by specifying ingoing or outgoing relationships during entity type maintenance.

To draw a relationship in the graphical editor's maintenance mode, click on the Connect button. The cursor shape changes to a pencil, and you can connect both entity types. For the second alternative, select Goto ➤ Ingoing Relatshps or Goto ➤ Outg. Relatshps, and a list of all relationships is displayed. To create further relationships, click on the Create button and specify the target entity type in the dialog box that appears. In both cases, the relationship must be edited as shown in Figure 6.8.

In this example, both entity types of the relationship appear in the upper portion of the screen. The other portions of the screen are explained in the following text.

You must specify information for the Category and Cardinality input fields on the relationship maintenance screen. In addition to the

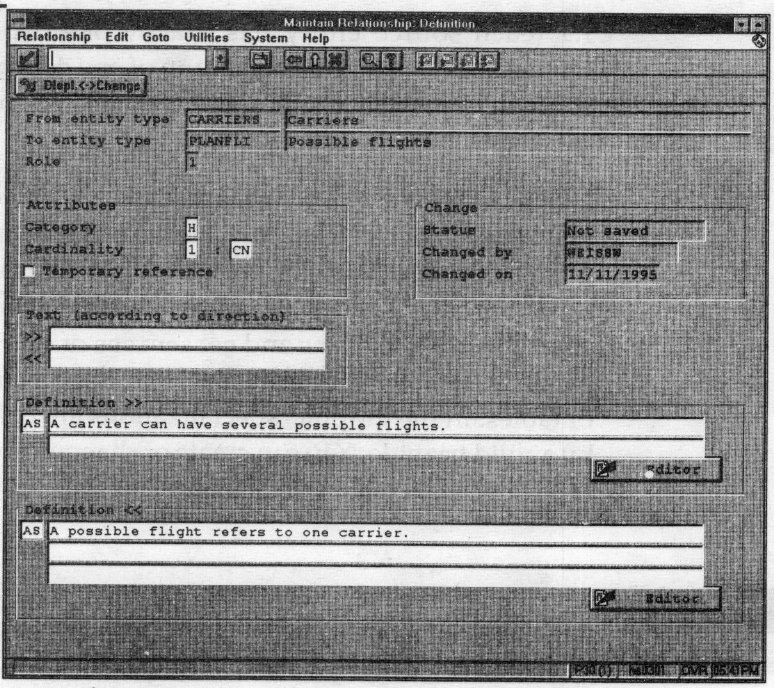

RELATIONSHIPS AND KEY ATTRIBUTES

FIGURE 6.8:

Creating a relationship
between the CARRIERS and
PLANFLI entities

categories mentioned above in the section "Relationships and Foreign Keys" (that is, referential, hierarchical, and aggregating), you can also define a relationship to an object outside the R/3 system, called an *external relationship*, by changing the category to *X*.

The cardinality must be specified for both the source and target entity types of a relationship. In practice, the relationship *1:CN* is often applicable. This cardinality is used if each source entity has an arbitrary number of dependent entities. The number of dependent target objects for the one source object may be zero, one, or any other integer. For instance, in our example each carrier can occur in any number of connections—that is, the relationship between carriers-id and planfli- carrid is of type 1:CN. For this cardinality, it is also possible that a carrier in the carriers table does not occur in any connection with the planfli table. Other useful cardinalities are

1:1 (each source entity has exactly one dependent entity) and *1:C* (each source entity has a maximum of one dependent entity). If the cardinality of the independent entity type is C, each dependent entity has a maximum of one source entity.

Whenever entities are special instances of a general kind of entity, this relation can be modeled as a *specialization*. A specialization is a model of an *is a* relationship. For example, an American carrier *is a* carrier, and a German carrier also *is a* carrier. For this reason, you can define specializations amcarriers and gecarriers of carriers, if necessary. Technically speaking, specializations can be considered as selection views of tables. In the graphic, specializations are drawn as edges pointed at by a solid triangle. You can create or change a specialization on the entity type screen by clicking on the Spec button.

NOTE   In a re-engineering project on an existing system, the relationships between entity types do not always represent foreign key relationships between the underlying Dictionary tables. It is also possible for a relationship between two tables to be established by special programs for database access—for example, by a Logical Database. See Chapter 15 for more information on Logical Databases.

A Quick Review

Here are some of the key points from this chapter that you should keep in mind:

- The data model of an application can be graphically created and maintained using the Data Modeler of the ABAP/4 Development Workbench.

- The Data Modeler can map the models to the ABAP/4 Dictionary.

- Entity types represent either a single database table or a view of several tables.

- The fields of the table or view are called *attributes of the entity type*. The entries of the corresponding table or view are called *entities*.

- Referential relationships in a data model represent foreign key relationships between non-key fields.

- Hierarchical relationships represent foreign key relationships of key fields to a single independent table, whereas aggregating relationships refer to a set of independent tables.

- If entities are special instances of a general kind of entity, this relationship can be modeled as a *specialization* relation.

In the next part, we'll intoduce the elementary constructs of the ABAP/4 language. The first chapter will explain how to work with the different data types.

PART III

Elementary Language Constructs

C H A P T E R

S E V E N

Working with Data

- **Copying fields and complex data objects**

- **Converting fields**

- **Mathematical functions and formulas**

- **String operations**

In the previous chapters, you have seen how to define local data of a program, global data in the Dictionary, and an entity relationship data model of your application. By now you should be starting to understand some of the basics about how applications are implemented in ABAP/4. As you build programs and applications, you will need to manipulate the data they contain by moving it, by calculating arithmetic expressions, or by working with strings (for example, searching for a pattern in a string).

When moving data from one field to another where the fields have different types, ABAP/4 always converts the contents. If the data model for an application is perfectly designed, conversions should not occur. In large software systems, however, conversions from one data type to another are frequently necessary. Using ABAP/4, you need not worry about details of conversion, since the language takes care of this.

If you need to copy records with different structures, ABAP/4 provides a powerful command to automatically copy only those components that have identical names on both sides. On the other hand, if both data objects have the same type, they can be copied in a single step, regardless of how complex their structure is.

Arithmetic expressions behave as usual in most languages, and standard mathematical functions (such as sin, cos) are also supported.

In addition, you can carry out frequently used string operations using special commands, such as those for concatenating and shifting strings, or for searching for patterns.

Copying Fields Using the Move and Compute Commands

The easiest way of working with data in your programs is to move it around using the move command, which is illustrated in the following brief program:

```
data: name(25), counter type i.
move: 'Edison' to name, 17 to counter.
```

After you perform this operation, the field name contains the string *Edison,* and the counter field contains *17.* The move command always copies the contents of the source field into the target:

```
move source to target.
```

If you prefer to write the target on the left side of a statement, you can use the compute command:

```
compute target = source.
```

This statement can be abbreviated by omitting the keyword compute:

```
target = source.
```

The three statements above all accomplish the same thing. It is a matter of your personal taste as to the alternative you prefer for your programming style.

If you want to fill many fields with the same content, you can concatenate compute commands as shown below. For example, if you are preparing an address list and several people on it share the same work telephone number, you might make that telephone number the source field, and then compute each person's work number from that field:

```
phone_4 = phone_3 = phone_2 = phone_1 = source.
```

In this section, you have seen how to copy fields, assuming that they had identical types. In practice, however, source and target fields often have different types, and in the next section you will see how ABAP/4 converts field contents in the copy process.

Converting the Contents of Fields

If the type or length of the source and target field are different, ABAP/4 always converts the contents of the source field according to the format of the target. In practice, this feature is very helpful. For example, suppose you have to compute the sum of two numbers stored in character fields of length four and three. You also want to store the result in an integer field. An ABAP/4 program for this task would look like this:

```
data: number_1(4), number_2(3), result type i.
result = number_1 + number_2.
```

If field number_1 contains the string *1771* and number_2 equals *005*, the field result will contain the number *1776*. You get the same result if number_2 contains _ _5 (two leading blanks), _05 (one leading blank) or 05_ (one trailing blank).

Sometimes, you will work with character fields that have different lengths. For instance, you might have an old database table containing customer names of length 10. You may want to use this old table in a new program where customer names have a length of 25. The solution is simple:

```
data: old_customer_name(10),
      new_customer_name(25).
```

```
move old_customer_name to new_customer_name.
```

After you perform this operation, the field `new_customer_name` contains the content of `old_customer_name`, padded with blanks. If `old_customer_name` equals *Edison*, then `new_customer_name` is equal to *Edison_ _ _ _ _ _ _ _ _ _ _ _ _ _ _ _ _ _ _* (with 19 trailing blanks).

Here is another example. For any given date, you want to determine the date of the same day of the subsequent week:

```
data: any_date type d,
      same_day_of_next_week type d.
same_day_of_next_week = any_date + 7.
```

Starting with *19991231* for your any_date field (December 31, 1999), you will obtain *20000107* for the `same_day_of_next_week` field. If the `any_date` field contains *20000228*, you'll get *20000306* as the date of the same day of the next week.

These examples demonstrate a very important feature of ABAP/4: if the source and target fields in a `move` (or `compute`) statement have a different type or length, ABAP/4 always converts the content of the source field into the format of the target field. A runtime error only occurs in special cases, when a conversion leads to a critical loss of information. For example, when a number field overflows in the computation, the system stops executing and sends an error message about the overflow situation.

Since ABAP/4 supports a variety of types and lengths which can be combined using `move` and `compute`, there are many combinations of conversions: sometimes digits within character fields are viewed as numbers, or the target field is filled with blanks, or the source is truncated, or numbers are converted to dates and vice versa. If you want to read about the details of conversion, read on. Otherwise, you can skip the following sections and continue with "Copying Structured Objects" later in this chapter.

Converting Character Fields

Very often, character fields containing text (for example, names or addresses) do not have the same length in all database tables or files. Suppose you have to store the name *Washington* within two fields of different lengths:

```
data: short_name(8), long_name(16).
move 'Washington' to: short_name, long_name.
```

After these operations, the short_name field will contain the string *Washingt* and the long_name field will contain *Washington_ _ _ _ _ _* (with six trailing blanks). The content of the source is truncated in the first case, and the target field is padded with blanks in the second. Obviously, you lose some information when using short_name, and you will certainly prefer long_name whenever you have enough space in your database table. Sometimes, however, the first eight characters will suffice to identify a person or object (for instance, when your system uses passwords with at most eight significant characters). Another reason for truncating the name field may be that the output list of a report has a very limited line size, and so you print out only the first eight characters.

The following short program produces the same result for short_name but a different one for long_name:

```
long_name = short_name = 'Washington'.
```

In this case, the string *Washington* is first moved into short_name and is truncated. Then the content of short_name (*Washingt*) is moved to long_name, and the rest of the bytes are filled with blanks. As a result, long_name contains *Washingt_ _ _ _ _ _ _ _* (with eight trailing blanks).

Converting Number Fields

Numbers of different types or lengths are also easy to handle. For example, a numeric character field can be used in an arithmetic expression together with integers and packed numbers:

```
data: no_employees(4) type n, no_rooms type p.
data: employees_per_room type p decimals 2.
employees_per_room = no_employees / no_rooms.
```

In this example the numeric character field no_employees is converted into a packed number before the expression is evaluated. The result will be rounded according to the format of the left side of the equal sign—that is, according to the employees_per_room definition in the example.

You should think carefully about how rounding might affect your equations, as the next two examples demonstrate:

```
data: income type i,
      tax type p decimals 2,
      net_income type p decimals 2.
net_income = income * ( 1 - tax ).
```

In this example, if the content of field income is 10,000 and the tax 20% (i.e., 0.20), then the net_income certainly is 8,000.00. In this case, the sub-expression (1 - tax) is evaluated first (giving 0.80, or 80%) and then multiplied by 10,000. The result (8,000) is moved into the field net_income (without conversion, since net_income already has the same type as the right side of the expression).

Numbers sometimes have a different quantity of decimal places. Suppose you have defined the net_income field as an integer field, and you execute the compute statement in a similar way to the code in the previous example:

```
data rounded_net_income type i.
rounded_net_income = income * ( 1 - tax ).
```

In this case, you get the same result for an income of 10,000. Strictly speaking, the result will be 8,000 instead of 8,000.00, but there is no loss of meaningful information. However, there are significant differences if rounding occurs during the calculation: if the income is 10,002, the `net_income` will be 8,001.60, but the `rounded_net_income` will be 8,002.

In general, when the right side of an arithmetic expression is computed by the runtime system, the result is rounded according to the number of decimal places of the result field. Integer fields are treated like packed fields without decimal places. If a floating point number occurs within an expression or a floating-point operation (for example, `cos` or `sqrt`) is applied, all intermediate results are also represented as floating numbers.

Converting Date Fields

Suppose you want to determine the latest possible date that you can send a check to a vendor after receiving a bill. Let's assume this date is 10 days after the reception date. You could use the following code to calculate the date:

```
data: receiving_date type d,
      last_admissible_date type d.
last_admissible_date = receiving_date + 10.
```

This is a short and easily readable program. What happens at runtime? First, the contents of `receiving_date` (let's say *19980223*) are converted internally to a packed number representing the number of days since 01/01/0001. Second, the number 10 is added, and finally the result is converted back into a date field (for our example, *19980305*). Of course, you could have done the necessary computations by yourself, but what happens if the `receiving_date` is *19960223* or *20000223*? The built-in calendar function of ABAP/4 takes care of this, so you don't have to worry about technical difficulties arising from the manipulation of dates.

NOTE   ABAP/4 has the capacity to handle dates above the year 2000. Therefore, a business application written in ABAP/4 will work in the next millennium without any problems, and the transition from 1999 to 2000 shouldn't cause you or your applications any trouble.

We've covered some of the different conversions you will encounter. The most frequently used combinations of different source and target fields are listed in Sidebar 7.1. You will find a complete list of these combinations in the ABAP/4 manual that comes with your software.

Special Conversions

Here are the most frequently used combinations of different types of the source and target fields in a move statement. Consider move commands like the following:

```
move s to t1.
move s to t2.
```

where the source field s and the target fields t1 and t2 have different types and lengths.

Converting type c to type n   Only numeric characters in s are taken into account. They are moved to t, right-justified and padded with zeros on the left (if necessary).

```
data: s(4) value '12x4',
      t1(2) type n,
      t2(6) type n.
```

The result of the move commands would be the following: t1 = '24', t2 = '000124'.

Special Conversions (continued)

Converting type n to type c   The source field s is treated as a character field and the leading zeros remain:

```
data: s(4) type n value '0124',
      t1(2),
      t2(6).
```

The result of this code would be the following: t1 = '01', t2 = '0124__' (two trailing blanks).

Converting type n to type p   The source field s is packed and moved to the target with a plus sign (+). If the target is too short, an overflow error occurs.

```
data: s(6) type n value '012345',
      t1(10) type p,
      t2(2) type p.
```

The result of this code would be the following: t1 = 12345. The second move produces a runtime error.

Converting type p to type n   The source field s is transferred right-justified without a sign and padded with zeros on the left.

```
data: s(4) type p value 124,
t1(2) type n,
t2(6) type n.
```

The result of this code would be the following: t1 = '24', t2 = '000124'.

Copying Structured Objects

To copy structured data objects (records or internal tables), you can certainly copy each component step by step. This requires a lot of editing effort and is susceptible to errors during later modifications. The move-corresponding statement enables you to copy between records those components that have identical names on both sides. So, when you add a new component to the involved structures, the move-corresponding command automatically keeps track of the change without the need to adapt the source code of your program.

If both the source and the target data object in a move statement have the same type (such as an internal table), the content is copied in a single step. In this way, you need not reduce structured data objects to their components to copy them individually, but rather you can transfer the objects all at once.

Suppose two records contain fields with identical names (in our example, id and city). To copy all fields with identical names you can use the move-corresponding command:

```
data: begin of my_customer,
      id(8) type n,
      name(25),
      city(25),
    end of my_customer.
    begin of city_of_customer,
      city like my_customer-city,
      text(30),
      id like my_customer-id,
    end of city_of_customer.
move-corresponding my_customer to city_of_customer.
```

The move-corresponding command copies the contents of the fields id and city in the record my_customer to the corresponding fields of the record city_of_customer. The field city_of_customer-text is not changed, because the source record does not have a field with this name. The preceding example demonstrates that fields with identical names are copied irrespective of their position in both records, since the ABAP/4 compiler only considers the names of the fields. In the example, the field city has position three in my_customer and position one in city_of_customer. If fields with identical names have different types, their contents are converted according to the general conversion rules for fields.

You can also copy structured objects like records or internal tables using the move command. Suppose you have two records with fields of the same type and length:

```
data: current_customer like my_customer,
      begin of previous_customer,
        identifier like my_customer-id,
        name       like my_customer-name,
        city       like my_customer-city,
      end of previous_customer,.
move current_customer to previous_customer.
```

This program copies all fields of the record current_customer to the record previous_customer. In contrast to the move-corresponding command, the field names (e.g., id and identifier) can be different except that they must still have the same elementary type and length.

You can also transfer all lines from one table to another in a single step:

```
types: begin of table_line,
         field_1,
         field_2 type i,
       end of table_line.
data: source_table type table_line occurs 100,
      target_table type table_line occurs 50.
move source_table to target_table.
```

Now you know how to copy fields and complex data objects. The next section covers mathematical computations.

Arithmetic Expressions and Mathematical Functions

Business applications mainly concentrate on accessing database tables and manipulating their contents. Elementary arithmetic operations like multiplication also occur in almost every application program. For particular applications, the language might need to support non-elementary mathematical functions like sin or cos. ABAP/4 provides a set of functions sufficient to cover the needs of most business applications. In the following paragraph, you will learn how you can use them.

You have already encountered arithmetic expressions in some of our earlier examples—for instance, when we calculated a deadline using the simple formula `last_admissible_date = receiving_date + 10`. They are self-explanatory and easy to understand:

```
y = a * x + b.
net_income = income * ( 1 - tax ).
y = x * cos( alpha ).
```

For example, you could use an arithmetic expression to calculate the percentage of black swans within the population of all swans (assuming that there are only black and white swans):

```
data: black_swans type i,
      white_swans type i.
data percentage type p decimals 2.
percentage = black_swans * 100 / ( black_swans + white_swans ).
```

You can build more complex formulas in the usual way arithmetic works, and anyone who is familiar with mathematics will be able to set up these formulas:

```
n5 = ( ( n1 - ( n2 / n3 ) ) * ( n4 + n1 ) / n5 ).
```

In some cases, parentheses can be omitted, if you understand the priority of operations. For example, the statement above yields the same result as the following statement:

```
n5 = ( n1 - n2 / n3 ) * ( n4 + n1 ) / n5.
```

This is because division takes priority over subtraction. The priority of operations is defined as follows:

1. Functions (e.g., cos or sqrt)
2. Exponentiation (**)

3. Multiplication (*), Division (/), Integer Division (div), Remainder (mod)

4. Addition (+) and Subtraction (-)

In addition to these elementary operations, ABAP/4 also supports some other important mathematical functions, which are of first priority according to the previous list:

- Absolute value and sign: abs, sign
- Trigonometric functions: cos, sin, tan, acos, asin, atan, exp, log
- Square root: sqrt
- String length of a character field: strlen

NOTE For a complete list of available mathematical functions, see the ABAP/4 manual under the keyword compute.

Here are some examples of how to set up formulas in ABAP/4 including mathematical functions:

```
y = x * cos( alpha ).
w = exp( b * log( a ) ).
d = n div q.
r = n mod q.
```

Note that parentheses are delimited by at least one blank character when they are used to group sub-expressions. This treatment differs from the way they are used in data statements, where the length is enclosed in parentheses without any surrounding blanks:

```
data name(25).
```

If a non-numeric field occurs in an arithmetic expression, it is internally converted to a number before the expression is evaluated. The conversion is done according to the general conversion rules of the move command.

```
data: n4(4) type n value '12A4',
      n1 type n value '2',
      x type p.
x = n4 * n1.
```

First, the content of n4 is converted to the packed number *124*. Second, the content of n1 is converted to *2*. Multiplication by n1 then yields the result *248* in the field x.

> **TIP**
>
> ABAP/4 supports all kinds of computations that are common for business applications, but the language is not designed for sophisticated technical or scientific calculations. If you need some complex statistical or numerical analysis, you can write a function for the calculation in another programming language such as C and call this function from ABAP/4 via a Remote Function Call. See Chapter 27 for information on Remote Function Calls.

Typical runtime errors in computations are caused by an overflow of a field or division by zero. Some typical runtime errors related to the compute command are briefly discussed in Sidebar 7.2.

String Operations

ABAP/4 has a set of elementary string operations. Using these commands, you can concentrate on manipulating characters and strings, and you need not worry about technical aspects like offsets and lengths.

Typical runtime errors related to the `compute` command

Here are some of the most common errors you might encounter when using the `compute` command.

Overflow   Overflow errors may occur if the content of a number field exceeds the size of that field:

```
data: short_counter(2) type p.
do 1000 times.
  short_counter = short_counter + 1.
enddo.
```

This tiny program leads to a runtime error, since the field `short_counter` admits at most three digits and the sign. Everything would be fine if the counter field had been defined as a packed number of standard length (eight):

```
data: counter type p.
```

In other words, packed numbers with explicit length should be declared only if the content can exceed the size of 15 digits.

Division by zero   Division by zero is a critical issue in business applications, since it is not easy to guarantee that the content of some database field in the system is not equal to zero.

```
data: x type p value 1,
      y type p,
      z type p.
z = x / y.
```

If y is equal to 0 at runtime, the program stops and a runtime error occurs. To avoid this problem, you have to keep track of the divisor:

```
if y = 0.
* divisor zero: do something...
else.
* divisor non-zero: divide
  z = x / y.
endif.
```

Typical runtime errors related to the `compute` command (continued)

However, if both operands are equal to zero, ABAP/4 sets the result to zero. Mathematically, of course, this operation is not defined. For practical purposes, ABAP/4 assumes that the fields arise from database entries with initial contents. In this case, the result should be initial as well.

Concatenating and Splitting Strings

Strings are concatenated using the concatenate command:

```
data: first(25), middle(2), last(25),
      full(54).
first  = 'Con'.
middle = 'ca.'.
last   = 'tenate'.
concatenate first middle last into full.
```

After you perform this operation, the field `full` contains the string concatenate.

If the strings are to be separated by a delimiter (in our example, the strings are the directories and file in a path name), you can specify the delimiter as follows:

```
data: directory_1(2), directory_2(10), file_name(10),
      path(24).
directory_1 = 'a:'.
directory_2 = 'usr'.
file_name = 'programs'.
concatenate directory_1 directory_2 file_name
            into path
            separated by '\'.
```

The contents of the path in this example is `'a:\usr\programs'`. The system return code sy-subrc is set to a non-zero value if the concatenated string is too long for the target field.

The reverse operation is splitting strings at a freely chosen delimiter:

```
data: list(40),
      name_1(25), name_2(25), name_3(25).
list = 'Edison,Smith,Young'.
split list at ',' into name_1 name_2 name_3.
```

You can also split strings at other delimiters (such as blanks, hyphens, or a sequence of characters). If one of the target fields is not large enough, the split component will be truncated and the return code sy-subrc is set to a non-zero value. In addition, if there are more components than target fields, no information is lost, since the last target field contains the remainder of the string. This situation can be avoided using an internal table as the target object, since an internal table can contain any number of lines:

```
data names like name_1 occurs 10.
list ='Edison,Smith,Young,Edwards'.
split list at ',' into table names.
```

The internal table names will contain four lines with the contents *Edison*, *Smith*, *Young*, and *Edwards*, respectively.

Shifting Strings

You can shift strings to the left by one character using the shift command. You can shift strings by multiple characters using the addition by n places. Here is an example:

```
name_1 = 'Edison'.
name_2 = 'Smith'.
name_3 = 'Young'.
shift name_1.
shift name_2 by 3 places.
shift name_3 right.
```

After these operations, the field `name_1` is equal to *dison*, `name_2` to *th*, and `name_3` to *_Young* (with a leading blank). This is sometimes useful when you need to analyze a text and you are sure that you do not need to analyze it from the beginning, but want instead to start it from a certain word.

If you do not want to specify the number of bytes that are to be shifted (maybe you don't yet know this number), you can use several variants of the `shift` command. Suppose you want to search a substring within a string and shift the complete string up to this substring:

```
names = 'Alexander Bill Charles'.
shift names up to 'Bill'.
```

Since a match of the substring *Bill* is found in the field `names`, the contents of `names` will be *Bill Charles* afterwards. If no match is found, the string remains unchanged and the return code `sy-subrc` is set to a non-zero value. Similarly, if the field `names` should be shifted right as long as it ends with a character contained in a predefined set, you may proceed as follows:

```
name = 'Joanne___'.
shift name right deleting trailing space.
```

This `shift` command deletes all blanks after the last non-initial character in the field `name`, returning the result _ _ *Joanne*. Note that `space` is a predefined field consisting of blanks.

Replacing and Translating Characters in Strings

If you need to replace special characters within a string, you can use the `replace` command to replace the first occurrence of a single character (or a substring) within a string:

```
string = 'Variable: &. The variable & is substituted later.'.
replace '&' with 'X' into string.
```

Then `string` will be equal to *Variable: X. The variable & is substituted later.*. If you want to replace all occurrences of *&* with *X*, you can use the `translate` command:

```
translate string using '&X'.
```

Whenever *&* occurs in the field `string`, it will be replaced by *X*; i.e., `string` will be equal to *Variable: X. The variable X is substituted later.*.

The `translate` command allows you to replace more than one character at the same time. The replacement rule is expressed as a sequence of pairs, where the first character is always replaced by the second. For example, you can replace all variables in a mathematical formula:

```
expression = 'a ** 2 + b ** 2 = c ** 2'.
translate expression using 'axbycz'.
```

This will produce the expression $x ** 2 + y ** 2 = z ** 2$.

Searching for Strings in Fields or Internal Tables

Suppose you want to search for the string *California* within a character field:

```
text = 'Texas California New Mexico Louisiana Oregon'.
search text for 'California'.
if sy-subrc ne 0. write 'Not found'. endif.
```

This search will be successful, and the system return code (`sy-subrc`) will be set to zero. Moreover, the system field `sy-fdpos` contains the offset of the matching string (e.g., `sy-fdpos = 6`). The `search` command does not distinguish between lower- and uppercase letters; the following statement would also be successful:

```
search text for 'cAliforniA'.
```

You can also search for substrings that contain blanks:

```
search text for 'New M'.
```

This statement yields the value 0 for the return code sy-subrc and the value 17 for sy-fdpos. If you have to determine whether a substring with trailing blanks occurs in the given string, the substring must be enclosed in periods:

```
data: string(6) value 'ABAP/4'.
search string for './4 .'.
```

The pattern ./4_. does not match, since the field string does not contain a trailing blank, whereas a search for /4_ would be successful.

Searching for strings in internal tables is also supported. Suppose the contents of a letter is contained in the internal table letter defined as follows:

```
types text_line(80).
data letter type text_line occurs 100.
```

If the first line of letter equals *Dear Sir,* and the second *thank you for your letter of 12/31/1999,* then the statement

```
search letter for 'you'.
```

yields the following results: sy-subrc = 0, sy-tabix = 2, sy-fdpos = 6. The system field sy-tabix contains the index of the table line which contains the searched string, and sy-fdpos contains the offset within this line. In addition, you can also restrict the range of lines for the search command:

```
search letter for 'thank' starting at 2 ending at 100.
search letter for 'Sincerely' starting at 3.
```

The first statement restricts the search to all lines between line numbers 2 and 100, and the second to all lines from the third to the last.

Working with Parts of Fields

If the special commands for string operations don't solve your programming problem, you can also work with parts of fields specified by offset and length. Note that the offset of a character in a field is always one character less than the position (for example, the offset of the first character is zero). The following sample program copies three characters starting from the third position of the source field:

```
off1 = 2.
len1 = 3.
off2 = 4.
len2 = 3.
move s+off1(len1) to t+off2(len2).
```

This move statement transfers the characters of the source field between position 3 and 5 to the part between position 5 and 7 of the target field.

A Quick Review

Here are some of the most important topics we've covered in this chapter.

- The following statements are equivalent:
  - `compute target = source.`
  - `target = source.`
  - `move source to target.`
- ABAP/4 always converts the contents of fields whenever the result is meaningful.
- Structured objects can be copied with the move command. In particular, all lines of internal tables are copied.
- Using move-corresponding, all fields with identical names in the source and target record are copied.
- Arithmetic expressions behave as usual in most programming languages, and standard mathematical functions are supported.

- Frequently used string operations can be executed by using special keywords: `concatenate`, `shift`, `replace`, `translate`, `search`.

- Parts of fields can be specified using the notation with offset and length for fields.

In the next chapter, we will see how to show the contents of fields on-screen and get acquainted with different options for presenting fields.

CHAPTER

EIGHT

Writing Data

- **Displaying data on-screen**

- **Enhancing the page layout**

- **Multi-Language Support**

In the last chapter, we discussed moving data around in your programs via the `move` and `move-corresponding` commands. In this chapter, we'll focus on another important operation: writing data to either the screen or the printer using the `write` command. ABAP/4 offers many features for preparing, formatting, and outputting data, one of the most important of which is support for multiple languages—essential in an international system.

Using the `write` command, you can display the contents of fields in a standard format, depending on the type of the field. You can create page headers and footers to help identify pages, but we won't cover these until Chapter 17. You can use symbols, icons, colors, and type-specific output options to enhance the page design. As we mentioned above, multilingual text is supported by text symbols, which appear in the language the user specified when logging on.

NOTE	More advanced topics like drill-down facilities will be discussed in Chapter 17.

Using Basic Layout Formats

`Write` statements print to an *output page* that is sent to the screen or the printer. Output pages created with `write` commands are called *lists* in ABAP/4. In this section you will see how to create a list with basic layout features.

You can create a simple output containing the current date as follows:

```
write: 'This is the current date:', sy-datum.
```

The output will be the string *This is the current date:* followed by the actual date (e.g., 12/31/1999) contained in the system field sy-datum. The two output fields are separated by a blank.

There are special options to determine the format, color, or position of a field, which will be discussed under the heading "Refining the Layout" below. If the format is not set explicitly using one of those options, the contents of a field are displayed according to its type. Character fields are displayed left-justified and numbers right-justified. In addition, decimal points (. or ,) and date formats (e.g., MM/DD/YYYY or DD/MM/YYYY) are represented according to the user's specifications, which can be changed in the Administration menu on the initial screen of the R/3 system.

In this code, the fields have no special formatting:

```
data: string(20),
      int type i,
      packed_number type p decimals 2,
      date like sy-datum.
string = 'Customer list'.
int = 17.
packed_number = 5 / 4.
date = sy-datum + 30.
write: string, int, packed_number, date.
```

The string *Customer list* will be put at the left of the 20-character field string, the number *17* at the right of int (without leading zeros), and packed_number will be written as *1.25*, if the user has chosen the representation . (period) for the decimal point. Finally, the content of the field date appears as *01/30/2000*, if this is the representation chosen by the user (MM/DD/YYYY):

```
Customer list              17         1.25  01/30/2000
```

If the user specifies that the decimal point should be a comma, this same output would look like this:

```
Customer list                    17              1,25  01/30/2000
```

Output fields are separated by single blanks if the position of the field on the line is not specified explicitly. However, if there is not enough space left in the current line, an output field will be put at the beginning of the following line. The line length can be set explicitly using the new-page command with the addition line-size. Otherwise, a default value of 84 characters is used. In general, the new-page statement begins a new page of the list, and it can be used without any addition.

The following short program contains a loop of the form do/enddo, which will be processed 40 times. The loop counter is contained in the system field sy-index, which is moved to the numeric text counter (the details about do/enddo loops are explained in Chapter 9). This program creates a list with 10 lines of size 44. Each line contains four items of length nine and a separating blank between all output fields. The fifth item is not displayed in the first row, since it would not fit into this line.

```
program abaptest no standard page heading.
data counter(9) type n.
new-page line-size 44.
do 40 times.
  counter = sy-index.
  write counter.
enddo.
```

The resulting list is shown in Figure 8.1. Note that the addition no standard page heading in the program declaration drops the standard page title that is provided by the title of the program and is set on the attributes screen.

Output can be put on a new line using the new-line command. The same result can be obtained by using the format option / a write command or

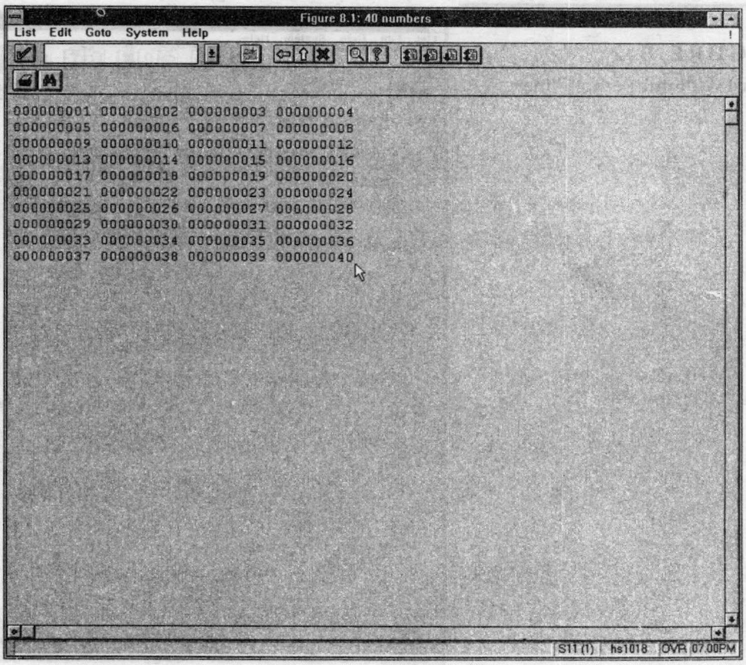

FIGURE 8.1:

The list of 40 numbers with automatic line breaks

```
Figure 8.1: 40 numbers
List  Edit  Goto  System  Help

000000001 000000002 000000003 000000004
000000005 000000006 000000007 000000008
000000009 000000010 000000011 000000012
000000013 000000014 000000015 000000016
000000017 000000018 000000019 000000020
000000021 000000022 000000023 000000024
000000025 000000026 000000027 000000028
000000029 000000030 000000031 000000032
000000033 000000034 000000035 000000036
000000037 000000038 000000039 000000040

                                          S11 (1)  hs1018  OVR 07.00PM
```

by using a skip statement. Both of these approaches are used in the following code, and the result is shown in Figure 8.2:

```
write 'This string will appear on the first line.'.
new-line.
write: 'New line',
     / 'Yet another line'.
skip 3.
write / 'skip 3 produces three empty lines.'.
```

You can set the position of a field in the list by using the addition at in a write statement or by using the command position, which fixes the position for the subsequent output field. You can see both of these options in the code below:

```
write at 5 'position 5'.
pos = 20.
write at pos 'position 20'.
```

FIGURE 8.2:

A list with three empty lines

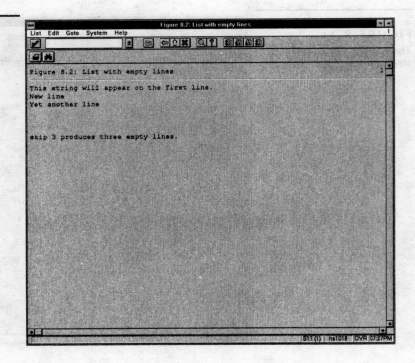

```
position 40.
write 'position 40'.
```

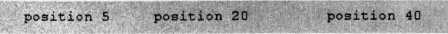

position 5   position 20   position 40

The output length of a field is determined by its type (for example, 2n bytes for packed numbers of length n), but it can also be adjusted dynamically after at:

```
pos = 10. len = 20.
new-line.
write at pos(len) 'position 10, length 20'.
```

Relative positioning is supported by the addition under, which allows you to refer to the position of an already displayed field. In that case, the output field is written in the same column as the referenced field.

Write statements go to an output page that has a logical length. By default, there is only one single output page of infinite length. You can explicitly set a page break using the new-page command. Page headers and footers are written when the events top-of-page and end-of-page happen, as you'll see in Chapter 17.

Refining the Layout

You can make changes to enhance the appearance of your output. Graphical elements such as symbols or icons can be displayed in a list. By including the addition color in the write or format statement, you can set the background color of a field or a part of the list. Finally, you can choose type-specific output options, such as settings for the sign or the number of decimal places in a numeric field.

Symbols and Icons

ABAP/4 has a set of approximately 200 predefined symbols and icons that you can display using the additions as symbol or as icon, respectively:

```
write: / sym_phone      as symbol, 'telephone',
       / sym_fax        as symbol, 'fax machine',
       / sym_left_hand  as symbol, 'hand pointing left',
       / sym_caution    as symbol, 'caution',
       / icon_checked   as icon,   'checked; okay',
       / icon_delete    as icon,   'delete',
       / icon_print     as icon,   'print'.
```

The symbol and icon names are predefined constants that are included with the commands include <symbols> and include <icon>, respectively. The resulting list is shown in Figure 8.3.

FIGURE 8.3:
Several symbols and icons
added to enhance a list

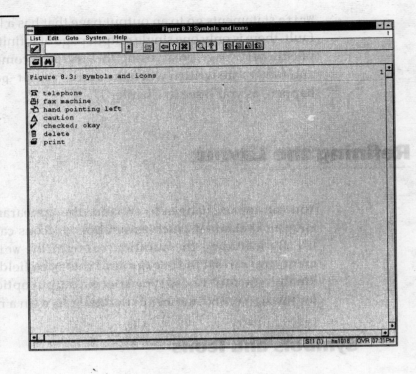

Colors

You can set background colors for each field by including the addition
color in the write statement:

```
write 'Header' color col_heading.
```

The available colors are listed below:

ABAP/4 name of color	Usage	Description of the color
col_heading	headers	grayish blue
col_key	key columns	bluish green
col_normal	list body	bright gray

ABAP/4 name of color	Usage	Description of the color
col_background	background	gray
col_positive	positive threshold value	green
col_negative	negative threshold value	red
col_group	control levels	violet
col_total	totals	yellow

Note that the colors are named according to their usage, but not by their normal color names (like *red*). SAP used this approach because lists in business applications should have a common "look" and "feel"; for example, key columns should always appear in the same color.

The default color for all text is `col_background`. If you set a color using the `write` command, the color is only valid for the current field. Using the `format` command, you can switch the standard color. For example, you can make `col_total` or yellow the standard color for all text:

```
format color col_total.
```

You can reset the current color by using the command `format color off` or by setting another color. You can always override a color by specifying a special color for each field in a `write` statement.

You can also change the color from intensified (the default) to non-intensified, to make the color brighter or darker.

```
write 'total sum' color col_total intensified off.
```

The format from a `format` statement is valid until you set a new format. You can also change the format for a single field in the `write` statement. For example, consider the following program:

```
format color col_heading.
```

```
write 'Header'.
format color off.
skip.
write: / 'Key field' color col_key,
         'Background',
         'Negative' color col_negative,
       / 'Total sum' color col_total intensified off.
```

The output list of this program has a grayish blue header in the first line followed by an empty line. On the next line, fields with background color bluish green, gray, and red are displayed, and a yellow field appears on the last line.

Colors are useful when you want to emphasize pieces of information in a list. To help you figure out the best colors to use when designing your applications, the colors are named according to the results of studies on effective page layout. Of course, you can always choose your own color schemes as well.

Type-Specific Output Options

ABAP/4 offers many special options for displaying fields according to their type. The following examples give you an idea of their effect.

- no-sign: The sign is suppressed.

- currency: Specifies a currency format.

- decimals: The number of decimals that can be set.

- using edit mask: Specifies a format template.

- no-gap: Deletes the gaps between fields in a row.

NOTE You can find a complete list of options and effects in the ABAP/4 Help under the section about the write command.

For example, you can display the time using an edit mask:

```
data time type t value '154633'.
write at (8) time using edit mask '__:__:__'.
```

The output of this code will be displayed as *15:46:33*. When you use the addition `using edit mask`, you must specify the output length explicitly, since the extra symbols require additional space. Otherwise, the output of this code would be *15:46:*, since the implicit output length for type t is six and therefore not big enough for all of the characters.

Multi-Language Support

If your program is going to run in other countries with different languages, the text of the output list must be translated. ABAP/4's text symbols offer a convenient method to display text in the language the user specified when logging on, without the need to change the source code of a program. To cause the text to be displayed in the user's language, simply attach a text symbol to an output literal. You can also use a text symbol without a literal.

```
write: / 'Literal without text symbol',
       / 'Original text of the source code'(001),
       / text-002.
```

By double-clicking on the text symbol in the Editor, you switch to a new screen to create or maintain the text in the current language (see Figure 8.4).

You can see the result of the program above in Figure 8.5.

The use of both text symbols is essentially equivalent. The only difference is that by appending a text symbol to a literal, you can be sure that there is always text on the screen or output page—either the text symbol of the current language or the hard-coded literal, if the text symbol is not maintained. In contrast, when you do not maintain the text using the second alternative, the screen output will be empty.

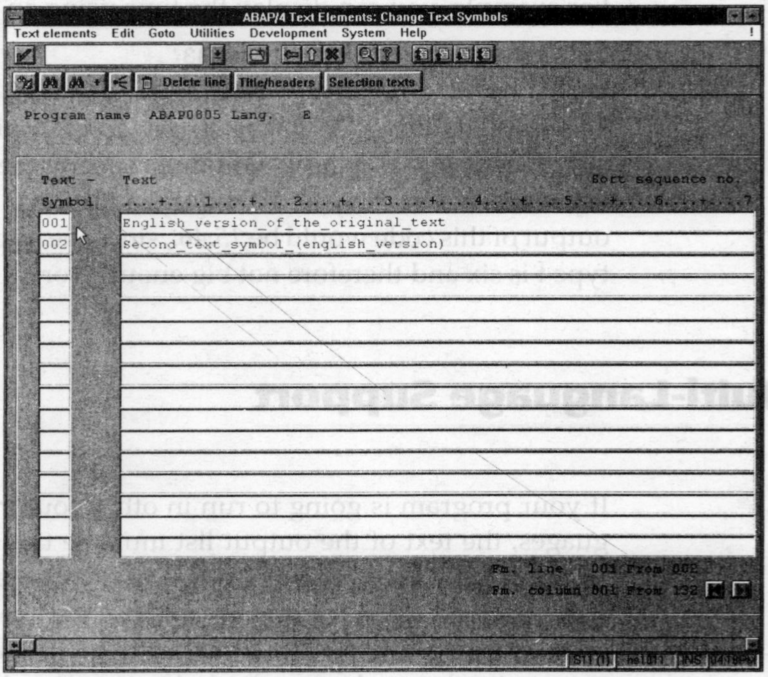

FIGURE 8.4:
Maintaining text symbols

> **NOTE**
> **Multi-language support is explained in detail in Chapter 17 under the heading "Language-Dependent Text Elements."**

A Quick Review

Here are some of the most important topics we covered in this chapter:

- There are standard output behaviors according to the field type: character fields are left-justified, numbers right-justified without leading zeros, and decimal points and dates are displayed according to the user specifications.

FIGURE 8.5:

The output of a program using text symbols

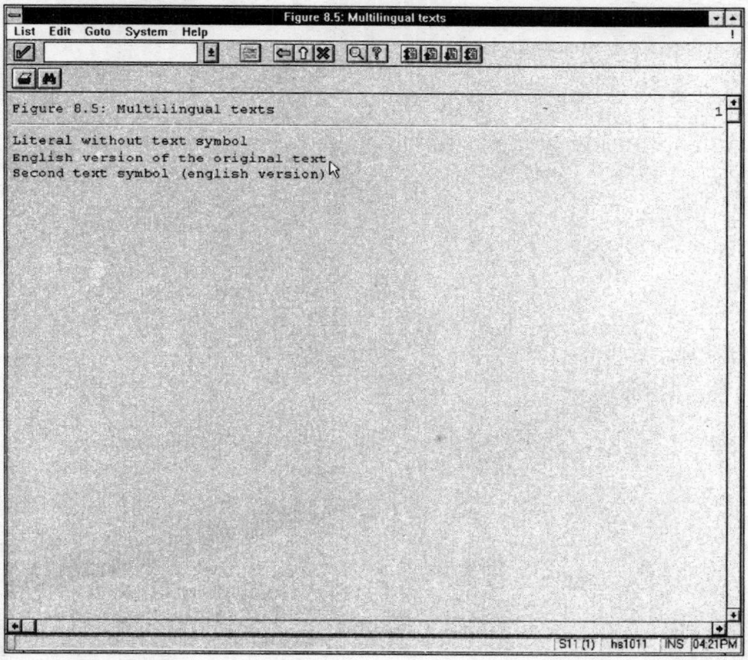

Figure 8.5: Multilingual texts

- Position and output length can be specified by including the addition at in the `write` command.
- You can display predefined symbols and icons by using the additions as `symbol` or as `icon`.
- You can use a set of eight colors. Each color also has a non-intensified version.
- There are several type-specific output options for fields: `no-sign`, `currency`, `decimals`, using `edit mask`, etc.
- By using text symbols, you can cause the output to be translated without changing the source code of a program.

In the next chapter, we will go into more advanced topics of programming larger applications. You will learn how to use events, conditions, and loops.

CHAPTER

NINE

Events and Flow of Control

- **User actions and system events controlling the program flow**

- **Conditions with logical expressions**

- **Loops with terminating conditions**

A BAP/4 is an event-driven language—user actions and system events control the flow of an application. You should be familiar with the concept of an event from your everyday life: suppose you work at the information desk of a company. When the phone rings, you speak with the caller and perhaps initiate some action, such as sending the caller some informational material. Another event occurs when a visitor enters the lobby and asks you where to find the conference room, and you give directions. These events have in common the fact that you cannot foresee when they will occur. At the same time, for each event you know precisely what to do—you have a specific response. In a similar way, a program in an event-driven language can react to various events. For example, a user clicks on a button or double-clicks a line on a list, and the program responds by opening a dialog box or prompting another action.

The event concept of ABAP/4 is a powerful and flexible method for designing dialog programs, because the system automatically handles events. Since events are triggered by the user or the system, they constitute the *external flow of control*. Using control structures like if/else/endif and do/enddo, you can switch to different branches of a program according to conditions that are internal to the program. Therefore, we will also speak of the *internal flow of control*. Dialog programs with many interactive features (such as dialog boxes) usually have many events. On the other hand, a program with complicated algorithms has a lot of internal flow of control. In practice, the external flow of control represented by events documents the main steps at runtime, whereas the internal flow of control is used to structure those parts of the program that are processed sequentially at one event.

In this chapter, we will demonstrate the concept of an event using an example where a user selects a line on a list. More advanced events will be covered in Parts V and VI. We will also describe internal control structures in detail, particularly the if condition. As in every other programming language, loops are very helpful when you need to perform the same operation repeatedly; for example, calculating square numbers from 1 to 100. Unconditional loops can be implemented using do/enddo, and conditional loops using while/endwhile.

External Flow of Control: Events

ABAP/4 has a set of events for user and system actions. Before discussing general properties of events, we will explain the event at line selection, which is triggered by a user double-clicking on a line of an output page.

For example, suppose a program produces a list as follows: all customers of a database table are read using a select loop (see Chapter 11 for an explanation of this database access) and displayed on screen by a write command:

```
select * from customers.
  write / customers-name.
endselect.
```

To provide drill-down facilities, this program must react when a user selects a line. The statements of this event are inserted after the at line selection statement:

```
at line-selection.
  select single * from customers where ...
```

If the user has selected a list item by double-clicking, all commands between at line-selection and the next event statement or the end of the program source are processed.

Now you have seen how to use the event at line selection, but ABAP/4 has many more events. Here are the most frequently used events:

- at line-selection, at user-command: cause a response to user actions (see Chapter 17)

- top-of-page, end-of-page: create and display page headers and footers (see Chapter 17)

- start-of-selection, get, end-of-selection: retrieve data using Logical Databases (see Chapter 15)

- process before output, process after input: occur before and after a screen is displayed by the system (see Chapter 19)

Whenever an event occurs, all statements between the event keyword and the next event keyword are processed by the ABAP/4 runtime system. Each program always contains a default event start-of-selection, which is triggered by the system when the program starts running. You can also insert the event start-of-selection explicitly. The order of the event statements in the source code of a program is completely irrelevant. Their processing order is only determined by the corresponding user or system action.

Internal Flow of Control: Conditions and Loops

ABAP/4 has a small set of language constructs to define the internal flow of control: *logical conditions* and *loops*.

Conditions

Almost every program (written in any programming language) needs to distinguish between different situations by means of a logical condition. For example, when a travel agency books a flight for a customer, the business customer will probably prefer a seat in business class, and the others will probably prefer a less expensive seat in economy class. ABAP/4 provides two basic constructions for determining which situation applies here:

- `if/elseif/else/endif`: branch according to arbitrary conditions
- `case/when/endcase`: branch according to a fixed set of possible values

Here is an example of an `if/elseif/else/endif` condition using the example above: you want to book a business class flight if you have a business customer, and economy otherwise:

```
if customers-custtype = 'B'.
* book business class
...
else.
* book economy class
...
endif.
```

If the content of the field `customers-custtype` equals *B* (for *business*) at runtime, the statements between `if` and `else` are processed. Then the program continues with the statements after `endif`. Similarly, when `customers-custtype` is not equal to *B*, the commands between `else` and `endif` are processed.

`If` statements can also be nested. Suppose you want to increment an integer if it is positive, display *zero* if it is equal to zero, and decrement otherwise:

```
if n > 0.
  n = n + 1.
else.
```

```
if n = 0.
  write 'zero'.
else.
  n = n - 1.
  endif.
endif.
```

Nested if clauses often occur when there are more than two alternatives. So in our example, the alternatives are n > 0, n = 0, and n < 0. In many cases, you can abbreviate the coding using an elseif branch:

```
if n > 0.
  n = n + 1.
elseif n = 0.
  write 'zero'.
else.
  n = n - 1.
endif.
```

In this case, only the statements between if and elseif are processed when n is greater than zero. Otherwise, the condition after elseif is evaluated. If this condition is fulfilled, the part between elseif and else is processed and the program will continue after endif. If the second condition is also not satisfied, the last branch after else is executed. The above short program does exactly the same thing as the preceding one.

In addition to several nested if statements, you can also have several elseif branches. Since deeply nested if clauses are usually hard to understand, using elseif statements is a good idea whenever possible.

Note that in nested if statements, every elseif/else statement goes with the closest if statement. An if statement is not correct until the closing endif occurs. However, the elseif and else branches can be omitted, as you can see in this example:

```
if n = 0.
  write 'zero'.
endif.
```

Whenever you have a set of possible values for a field, you can distinguish between them using case/when/endcase:

```
case color.
   when 'red'.    write 'color is red'.
   when 'green'.  write 'color is green'.
   when 'yellow'. write 'color is yellow'.
   when others.   write 'non-standard color'.
endcase.
```

At runtime, the content of field color is first compared with *red*. If this condition is satisfied, the subsequent statements up to the next when statement are processed. The rest of the case clause is skipped; i.e., the program continues with the statements after endcase. Similarly, if the content of color is not equal to *red*, it will next be compared with *green*. If this condition is satisfied, the corresponding statements after when 'green' are processed. Finally, if all comparisons fail, the branch of when others is processed. This branch can be omitted if you don't want to take into account possibilities other than those explicitly mentioned in the when statements. The sample program above is equivalent to the following one:

```
if color = 'red'.
   write 'color is red'.
elseif color = 'green'.
   write 'color is green'.
elseif color = 'yellow'.
   write 'color is yellow'.
else.
   write 'non-standard color'.
endif.
```

It is primarily a matter of taste as to which alternative you prefer. However, only restricted conditions are supported in a when clause. The field after case is always compared with the values after when with respect to equality. Therefore, it is impossible to express a condition like a > b within a case clause.

Logical Expressions

An if statement consists of two parts: the keyword if itself followed by a logical expression. The above examples already demonstrate two kinds of logical expressions:

- a = b (true, if a equals b)
- a > b (true, if a is greater than b)

ABAP/4 also offers equivalent expressions using characters instead of mathematical symbols:

- a eq b (instead of a = b)
- a gt b (instead of a > b)

Other relations can be expressed in a similar way:

- a ne b (a <> b): a not equal to b
- a lt b (a < b): a less than b
- a ge b (a >= b): a greater than or equal to b
- a le b (a <= b): a less than or equal to b
- a between b and c: (b <= a) and (a <= c)
- a is initial: a has initial value (such as zero for numbers or space for characters)

Conditions can be grouped by parentheses, connected by and or or, and turned into the opposite by not as usual:

```
if ( not ( f1 eq f2 ) ) or ( f3 = f4 and f5 = f6 ).
```

Parentheses can be omitted as long as the usual binding rules are respected. The operator not is stronger than and, which in turn is stronger than or. In other words, the above condition is equivalent to:

```
if not f1 eq f2 or f3 = f4 and f5 = f6.
```

Evaluation of a complex condition is from left to right and stops when the result is already determined by the beginning part of the condition:

```
if f1 = f2 and f3 > f4 and f5 < f6.
```

If f1 is not equal to f2, the condition is false and the runtime system will not evaluate it further.

How to Compare Fields with Different Types

In a logical expression, two fields of different types are often compared. For example, suppose you have to compare numeric texts and packed numbers:

```
data: n(4) type n value '124', p type p.
if n > p.
  write 'n is greater than p'.
endif.
```

You certainly expect that the condition is satisfied for the initial values of n and p (0124 and 0). This is true in ABAP/4, but keep in mind that n and p are of different types. Therefore, one of them must be converted before they can be compared. In this example, the numeric text n is converted to the packed number 124, which can be compared with the content (zero) of p.

In general, if the elements of a relationship (for example, a < b) have a different type or length, the comparison can still be meaningful as long as the following conversion rules are considered. These rules are applied in subsequent order:

1. If both fields are of the same type but have different lengths, the shorter field is padded with zeros or blanks on the left or right side according to the type (see the conversion rules of move as explained in Chapter 8).

2. If one field is of type f, the other will also be converted to type f.

3. If one field is of type p, the other will also be converted to type p.

4. If one field is of type d or t, the other will also be converted to this type. Comparison of date and time fields is not supported and yields a runtime error.

5. If one field is of type n and the other of type c or x, both will be converted to type p.

6. If one field is of type x and the other of type c, the hexadecimal field will be converted to type c.

For example, if both operands have the same type but different lengths, the first rule applies:

```
data: c4(4) value '124', c5(5) value '00124'.
if c4 = c5.
  write 'c4 and c5 are equal'.
endif.
```

Given the initial values *124* and *00124* for c4 and c5, respectively, the condition c4 = c5 is not true: c4 is padded with blanks, not with zeros (i.e., *124_ _* and *00124* are not equal).

How to Compare Character Strings

The preceding examples mainly contain relationships between numbers, such as a > b. Quite often you have to determine whether a character field contains a given character (e.g., *A*) or a string of characters (e.g., *SAP*). ABAP/4 provides the following useful relationships for character fields a and b:

a ca b (*contains any*): a contains at least one character from b

a co b (*contains only*): a contains only characters from b (in any order)

a cs b (*contains string*): a contains the character string b (trailing blanks are ignored; comparison is not case-sensitive)

a cp b (*contains pattern*): a contains the pattern b (* masks any character string, + any single character)

The behavior of these conditions can be seen in the subsequent examples:

```
data: a(6) value 'ABAP/4',
      result(6).
if a ca 'XP'.
   result = a+sy-fdpos(2).
endif.
```

Since the field a contains the character *P*, the condition is true. In addition, the system field `sy-fdpos` (short for *field position*) is set to the offset *P* within field a, which is equal to 3 in this example. Therefore, the field `result` will contain *P/* afterwards. Here is an example of the second string comparison:

```
if a co 'ABP'.
   write 'a only contains A,B, and P'.
endif.
```

Here, the condition of the example is not satisfied, since field a also contains / and 4. Below is an example for the third case:

```
if a cs 'BAP'.
   write 'a contains the string BAP'.
endif.
```

This time, the condition of the example is satisfied, since field a contains the string *BAP*. Finally, here is an example of pattern matching:

```
if a cp '*AP++'.
   write 'a contains AP followed by two more characters'.
endif.
```

The condition is satisfied, since field a contains the string *AP*, which is preceded by an arbitrary string (matching with *) and followed by two characters that are not equal to blank (matching with ++).

Here are some more illustrative examples:

'ABAP/4' co 'AB': false, sy-fdpos = 3 (offset of first character in *ABAP/4* not also in *AB*)

'ABAP/4' cs 'BA': true, sy-fdpos = 1 (offset of start of string *BA* in *ABAP/4*)

'ABAP/4' cs 'AA': false, sy-fdpos = 6 (length of *ABAP/4*)

'ABAP/4' cp '*BA*': true, sy-fdpos = 1 (offset of start of string *BA* in *ABAP/4*)

'ABAP/4' cp '++A+*': true, sy-fdpos = 0 (offset of start of string ++*A*+ in *ABAP/4*)

'ABAP/4' cp '+A*': false, sy-fdpos = 6 (length of *ABAP/4*)

Loops

Now you have seen how to use expressions in conditions to branch to different pieces of code in your program. In this section, you'll learn to work with loops and use conditions to terminate a loop.

You can execute repeated operations using the following elementary loop constructions:

- do/enddo: unconditional loop
- while/endwhile: loop with terminating condition

NOTE   Additional loop constructs are discussed in Part IV, where the use of internal and database tables is explained.

Suppose you want to calculate the first hundred square numbers:

```
do 100 times.
  square_number = sy-index ** 2.
  write square_number.
enddo.
```

When the program starts, the system variable sy-index is equal to one during the first loop. It is incremented automatically at each loop and can therefore be used as a loop counter. The loop is terminated after 100 rounds. Instead of providing a static upper bound, you can also dynamically set this upper bound by using a field, as shown below:

```
data n type i.
n = 200.
do n times.
...
enddo.
```

Quite often, you won't know the number of loop steps in advance. In these cases, you can perform an unconditional loop and terminate it according to some condition:

```
do.
* terminate loop after 5 steps or when the color is red
  if sy-index > 5 or color = 'red'. exit. endif.
* main loop step
  write ...
enddo.
```

The exit command stops the processing of the loop and the program will continue after enddo. The potential risk of this construction is clear: if the terminating condition is not formulated carefully, the loop may never stop. This will cause a runtime error (a *time-out*) in your program.

Using the continue command, you can stop the current step and continue with the next step of the loop:

```
do max times.
  f2 = f1 + f0.
  if f2 < 0. continue. endif.
  f3 = sqrt( f2 ).
enddo.
```

You can also use nested loops using the do/enddo commands. The system field sy-index always contains the correct number of the current step, since it is automatically pushed onto a runtime stack.

Suppose you want to implement a search algorithm for a binary search. Since you do not know in advance how many steps are necessary, you can formulate the terminating condition as follows:

```
min = 0.
max = 1000.
while key <> search_key.
  key = ( min + max ) div 2.
  if key > search_key.
    max = key - 1.
  else.
    min = key + 1.
  endif.
endwhile.
```

As long as the condition after while is fulfilled, the statements between while and endwhile are processed. When the condition becomes false, the program continues after endwhile. You must take care of the condition being satisfied in a reasonable time to avoid a time-out error at runtime. Further terminating conditions can be formulated by means of an exit statement:

```
while a <> b.
..
  if a > b. exit. endif.
endwhile.
```

If the condition a > b is true, processing of the while loop is stopped and the program continues after endwhile. Similar to loops using do/enddo, you can stop the processing of the current step by using continue.

A Quick Review

Here is a review of some of the most important points in this chapter:

- Events: ABAP/4 programs are structured by events that are triggered by the user or the runtime system. All statements between one event and the next belong to the current event.

- `if/elseif/else/endif`: Distinguishes between different situations according to arbitrary logical conditions.

- `case/when/endcase`: Distinguishes between different situations according to a set of possible values.

- Fields of different types or lengths can be compared within logical expressions. Before the comparison is executed, fields are converted according to the general conversion rules of `move`.

- `do/enddo`: Unconditional loop. Can be terminated by an upper bound of loop steps (`do n times`) or by an exit condition in the loop.

- `while/endwhile`: Conditional loop with terminating condition. Can also be terminated by an exit condition in the loop.

The next chapter introduces the use of subroutines and functions. These techniques are necessary to build large, well-designed applications.

CHAPTER

TEN

Subroutines and Functions

- **Local subroutines of a program**

- **Global functions of a system**

- **Interfaces**

- **Exceptions**

ABAP/4 offers a variety of concepts to reduce the complexity of large programs and to re-use software components. This chapter covers the most important modularization techniques:

- Forms (or subroutines): Modularization units local to a single program
- Functions: Global components, which can be called by many different programs

Both techniques support encapsulation of local data as well as different methods to transfer data via interface parameters (for example, *call by value* or *call by reference*). Functions have a public interface maintained by an interface description tool. Because of their character as internally used subroutines, forms can also manipulate global data of the calling program. Since a function can be called by many different programs, the interface rules are more restrictive and allow only the change of the parameters and the local data of a function.

Type checks for the interface parameters of forms or functions are executed during the Syntax Check or at runtime, if the type of the corresponding formal parameter is specified. Otherwise, actual parameters of forms are converted if the formal parameters only have a generic type or even no type at all. Function parameters are identified by their name and form parameters by their position.

Functions provide convenient exception handling. Moreover, if new requirements arise in the life cycle of a function, you can add optional parameters without the need to adjust all calling programs of the function. This property is very helpful in a distributed development environment for large-scale systems.

NOTE   Other modularization concepts (including call of reports and transactions) will be explained in Chapters 18 and 21.

Modularizing Programs Using Forms

A form (or subroutine) is defined by a pair of form/endform statements and is called by a perform statement:

```
data flag value 'G'.
write flag.
perform set_flag.
write flag.
form set_flag.
  flag = 'L'.
  write flag.
endform.
```

When the perform command is executed, all statements between form set_flag and the next endform are processed. Global data defined in the current program (e.g., the field flag) can also be used and changed within a subroutine. In the example above, the output list would be *G L L*.

In ABAP/4, a form does not have a return value. Instead, return information is passed via the parameters of the interface (see below in this chapter under the heading "The Interface of Forms").

The definition of the form is placed at the end of the source in the sample program above. This reflects the general rule that forms are system events. Therefore, any source code after form definitions is only executed at runtime if it belongs to a new form or event (e.g., at line-selection).

Local Data

In the preceding example, the global field `flag` has been changed in the form `set_flag`. If you want to encapsulate data that belongs to the current subroutine only, you can define this local data within the form using the `data` keyword as usual:

```
data flag value 'G'.
write flag.
perform write_flag.
write flag.
form write_flag.
  data l_flag.
  l_flag = 'L'.
  write l_flag.
endform.
```

As a result of this code, the local field `l_flag` is created when the form `write_flag` is called at runtime. The output of this program will be *G L G*.

Note that using a local field named `flag` instead of `l_flag` produces the same result in the example just above. The reason is that the global field `flag` is invisible in the form and changing a local field with an identical name does not affect the global field.

> **TIP**
>
> Using local data increases the readability of the source code. In contrast, manipulating global data in subroutines is error prone, and makes it quite difficult to analyze the source code. Therefore, we strongly recommend that you work with local data as often as possible.

Sometimes you want to retain the contents of a local data object from one invocation of the subroutine to the next, and to do this you should use static variables. For example, you might want to count all calls of a form:

```
perform count.
perform count.
```

```
form count.
  statics calls type i.
  calls = calls + 1.
  write calls.
endform.
```

When the form count is called for the first time, the initial value of the static variable `calls` is incremented by one. In the second call, `calls` is again incremented—the resulting list will display the integers 1 and 2. The syntax of `statics` is parallel to `data`. Static variables can only be defined in forms or functions, and they are particularly useful for local internal tables, because they no longer have to be rebuilt at every call of the subroutine.

WARNING   Static variables are useful, but be careful with them. They make the form dependent on the calling history, and sequence dependencies are the worst problems in debugging.

The Interface of Forms

The forms of the examples above do not have any interface parameters. Parameters are very useful whenever a program is growing. Typically, the algorithm of a subroutine is written in general terms and can be used in different situations. The algorithm needs different actual parameters to produce a correct result for each call. For instance, you can encapsulate calculations of sales tax within a subroutine, and it will be called with many different input values. Some parameters will serve as input and other ones as output parameters. ABAP/4 supports different methods of passing parameters. For the sake of brevity, we'll start with those parameters that can be read and changed in a subroutine and are called by reference. We'll discuss other methods later in the chapter under the heading "Classifying Parameters."

For example, a subroutine is designed to change and display two different name fields:

```
types: t_name(25).
data: name_1 type t_name value 'A',
      name_2 type t_name value 'B'.
perform set_name changing name_1.
perform set_name changing name_2.
form set_name
      changing f_name type t_name.
   write f_name.
   f_name = 'Smith'.
   write f_name.
endform.
```

This program proceeds as follows:

- When the form set_name is called first with the actual parameter name_1, the formal parameter f_name gets the value of the actual parameter name_1.

- In the form, the formal parameter f_name is displayed with its original content *A*, changed to the name *Smith*, and written with its new content.

- At the second call of the form, f_name gets the value of name_2.

- In the form, the formal parameter f_name is displayed with its original content *B*, changed and written with its new content.

In addition, the types of actual and formal parameters are compared and a syntax error occurs if they do not agree.

NOTE   Type checking is explained in detail under the heading "Type Checking" below.

In general, you will have more than one parameter. They can be listed as follows:

```
perform f changing a1
```

```
                        a2
                        a3.
form f changing f1 like a1
                 f2 like a2
                 f3 like a3.
  f3 = f1 + ( f2 * f3 ).
endform.
```

At runtime, formal parameters obtain the values of the corresponding actual parameters:

1. f1 gets the values of a1

2. f2 gets the values of a2

3. f3 gets the values of a3

The number of parameters in the form definition (form) and in the call (perform) must coincide. The Syntax Check of the ABAP/4 Editor checks this before the program runs. The order of the parameters is important: you get a much different result (or a runtime error) if the actual parameters are exchanged. We strongly suggest that you give a formal parameter a name that indicates the role of the corresponding actual parameter. At the same time, the name of a formal parameter should indicate its role as a variable being substituted at runtime. For instance, you can insert a prefix f or f_, but other conventions may also be useful.

Classifying Parameters

Interface parameters belong to one of the following two classes:

- **Read only**: The parameter is read in the subroutine but is not changed.
- **Changing**: The parameter is read and changed by the subroutine.

With respect to memory space and performance, they can also be classified according to the following criteria:

- **Call by value**: At runtime, a copy of the actual parameter is created and the subroutine always works with this copy.

- **Call by reference**: At runtime, only a reference to the actual parameter (i.e., an address) is transferred to the subroutine. Reading and changing operate on the original data.

The list below shows all possible combinations of the above mentioned kinds of parameters, where each cell contains the corresponding ABAP/4 syntax description of a parameter p.

Read/Change	Call by value	Call by reference
Read only	using value(p)	using p
Changing	changing value(p)	changing p

Note that the syntax of the form definition completely determines how a parameter is passed to the subroutine. In particular, the caller need not distinguish between call by value and call by reference. Combinations of different methods are also possible. For instance, a form may have two input parameters f1 and f2, where f1 is called by value and f2 by reference. The output parameter f3 is called by value:

```
perform calc using     a1
                       a2
            changing a3.
write: a3.
form calc using    value(f1) like a1
                       f2   like a2
        changing value(f3) like a3.
  f3 = f1 + ( f2 * f3 ).
endform.
```

When the form calc is called at runtime, temporary local copies of the actual parameters a1 and a3 are created (for example, c1 and c3) and substituted for the corresponding formal parameters f1 and f3. The actual parameter a2 is directly substituted for f2. Afterwards, the body of the form is executed with the values of the actual parameters—in our example, the calculation c3 = c1 + (a2 * c3) is executed with the local copies c1 and c3 and the actual parameter a2. Finally, when the endform statement is reached, the value of the temporary local copy c3 is returned to the actual parameter a3.

In general, the easiest alternative is to change parameters with call by reference. Obviously, you can run into difficulties with call by reference, since damage to or loss of data is not restricted to the subroutine, but will instantly lead to changes to the original data objects. On the other hand, call by value always creates a local copy of the actual parameter, which is inappropriate for huge data objects (for example, internal tables with many lines).

It is important to know that the syntactical difference between using and changing parameters, which are called by reference (that is, the right column of the list above), does not imply that the using parameter cannot be changed in the form. The syntax only documents the role of the parameter, but there is no difference between using and changing at runtime. For the sake of better readability in the source code, we recommend that you also indicate the difference between input (using) and output (changing) parameters in the case of call by reference. Functions in ABAP/4 always guarantee that read-only parameters are never changed (see the "Interface Parameters" section in this chapter).

You can also transfer internal tables with header lines to a subroutine after the addition tables. Table parameters are always passed by reference. This approach dates back to the early days of ABAP/4, when interface parameters did not have a type. For compatibility with older versions, table parameters are still supported. As a substitute for type assignment, you can specify the table structure in the interface. For example, the following form fills an internal table with all customers:

```
data all_customers like customers occurs 50 with header line.
perform read_customers tables all_customers.
...
```

```
form read_customers tables f_customers structure all_customers.
  select * from customers into table f_customers.
endform.
```

Type Checking

In the examples above, formal parameters have references to types or fields through type or like and therefore they also have attached types. If a type has been specified, the technical type of the actual parameter must match the technical type of the corresponding formal parameter. The technical type consists of the elementary ABAP/4 type (c, i, p, n, f, d, t), length, and number of decimal places. If the technical types do not match, the system sends an error message during the Syntax Check or at runtime.

```
data: name_1(25),
      name_3(2).
perform set_name changing name_1.
perform set_name changing name_3.
form set_name changing f_name like name_1.
  f_name = 'Smith'.
endform.
```

The actual parameter name_1 agrees in type and length with f_name, but name_3 does not, since its length is not equal to the length of f_name. Therefore, this program is not correct, and Syntax Check sends an error message.

NOTE   Type checking only refers to the technical type of a field. If two fields have different types but identical technical types, they will pass the type check.

For example, consider the following program:

```
types: t_name_1(25),
       t_name_2(25).
data: name_1 type t_name_1,
      name_2 type t_name_2.
```

```
perform set_name changing name_1.
perform set_name changing name_2.
form set_name changing f_name like name_2.
  f_name = 'Smith'.
endform.
```

This program is correct, since the technical types of the actual parameters and the formal parameter match. The same type check can be achieved using a non-elementary type:

```
form set_name changing f_name type t_name_2.
```

If a parameter is of structured type (a record or internal table), the corresponding components of the actual and formal parameters will be compared down to the elementary type.

Occasionally, type checking parameters might not be useful. For instance, the actual parameters may have different lengths or even different elementary types (e.g., character or numeric text). In these cases, you can omit the type declaration in the interface, and no type check is executed during Syntax Check or runtime:

```
data: string_1(2) value 'AB',
      string_2(8) value '  ABAP/4'.
perform write_first_character changing: string_1,
                                         string_2.
form write_first_character changing f_string.
  shift f_string left deleting leading space.
  write at (1) f_string.
endform.
```

Similarly, you can use generic elementary types in the definition of an interface:

```
form write_first_character changing f_string type c.
```

Here, the type check is reduced to the comparison of the elementary types of the actual and formal parameters, but lengths and decimals are ignored. For example, the first call of the following subroutine is correct, but not the second one, since short_number is not of type c:

```
data short_string(3).
data short_number(3) type n.
```

```
perform write_first_character changing: short_string,
                                         short_number.
```

Generic table types are also supported. You can specify that a parameter must be an internal table without referring to the line type of the table:

```
form sort_and_search_in_table
     changing f_table type table.
  sort f_table.
  search f_table for 'Smith'.
endform.
```

This form can work with arbitrary internal tables. In particular, table-specific operations like sort are possible within the form (see Chapter 12 for operations on internal tables). Without the generic table type, the sort statement would produce a syntax error.

In general, type checking in form interfaces has the following advantages:

- **Security**: Exchange of parameters or false parameters caused by misprints is very unlikely if the type check succeeds.

- **Readability of the source code**: The role of formal parameters is already documented in the interface.

- **Performance**: Many operations are very fast if the technical type is already known during program generation.

Creating Functions to Increase Re-usability

In contrast to forms, functions are usually called by many different programs. For this reason, functions strictly encapsulate data—that is, data of a function can only be changed through the interface. Function arguments are identified by their names (not by their position, as in forms). If new requirements arise during the life cycle of a function, you can add optional parameters without the need to change all calling programs. In addition, functions provide convenient exception handling.

A function is defined by a pair of `function` and `endfunction` statements and is called by a `call function` statement. The name of a function is an uppercase character string.

```
call function 'MY_FIRST_FUNCTION'.
...
function 'MY_FIRST_FUNCTION'.
   write 'My first function!'.
endfunction.
```

When you are using the function interface description tool, you will never edit the `function`/`endfunction` statements or the parameters of the interface in the ABAP/4 Editor, but rather document the function and its parameters (see the section "Interface Parameters" below). To edit a `call function` statement, you can choose Edit ➤ Insert Statement from the ABAP/4 Editor, and the system inserts all parameters and exceptions of the interface.

Function Groups and Functions

To create a function using the ABAP/4 Development Workbench, click to activate the Function Group Objects radio button in the Single Object section on the first screen of the Object Browser (see Figure 10.1).

On the next screen, enter the name of your function in the Function Module text box (we've chosen my_first_function) and click on the Create button, as shown in Figure 10.2.

You are asked to specify the attributes of the function (see Figure 10.3). In our example, we've given the function the description *This is my first function* in the Short Text text box, but we've not yet chosen a function group. Function groups are explained in the next paragraph. We chose Normal for the Process Type.

FIGURE 10.1:

Specifying a function group object

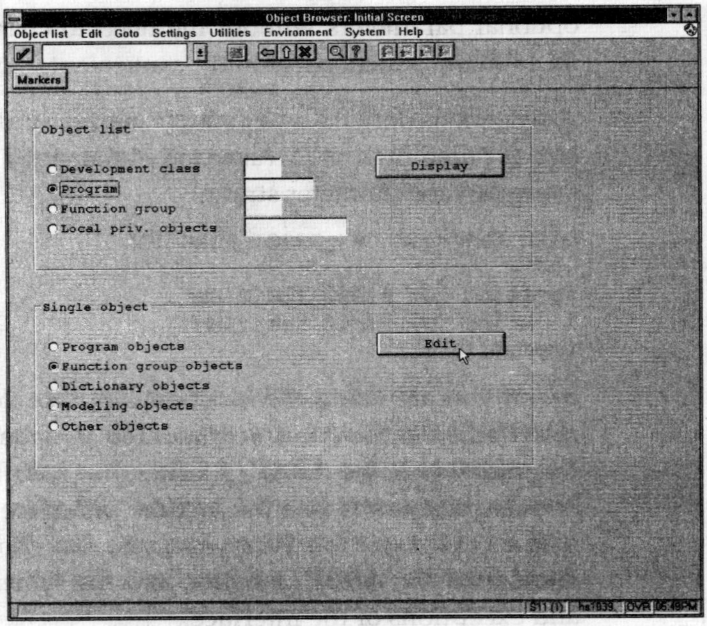

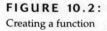

FIGURE 10.2:

Creating a function

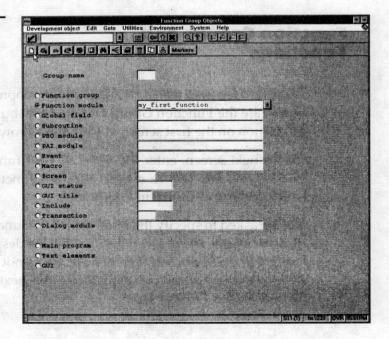

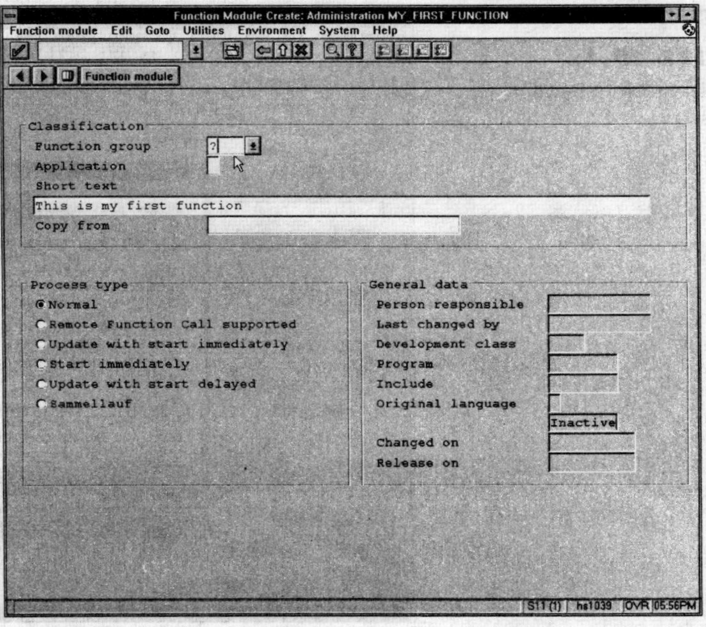

FIGURE 10.3:

Specifying the attributes of a function

A function group is a container for one or more functions that belong together. In particular, all functions in a function group share the same forms that are defined in the function group. Some typical examples of function groups are groups related to printing documents, updating general ledgers, or reading information from complex financial documents.

You can get an overview of all function groups in the Function Module Create screen by placing the cursor in the Function Group input field and clicking on the button Possible Entries right beside the field (or by pressing F4). You'll get a pop-up list like the one shown in Figure 10.4.

In addition to commonly used subroutines, the functions in a function group also share the global data of their group. This property is useful when dialog boxes or full-size screens are displayed by some functions (see Chapters 19 and 22 for details about dialog screens).

FIGURE 10.4:

Possible entries for function groups

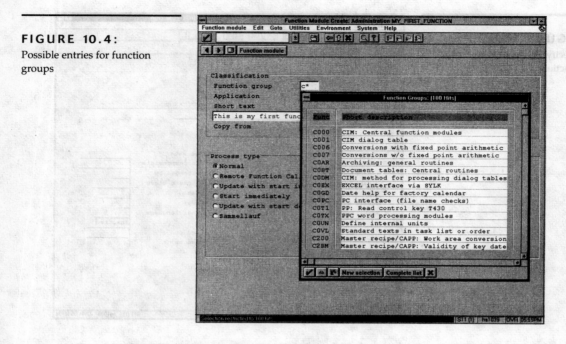

Technically speaking, a function group is a program with one Include File for each function. When a function is called at runtime, the function group is loaded into main memory and the function is executed. Afterwards, the function group remains in memory—that is, it is not loaded twice if the same or any other function of the same group is called again by the main program of the current process.

If you want to associate your function with a new function group, simply enter the new function group name into the Function Group input field in the screen shown in Figure 10.3. The system asks you whether a new group should be created. If you confirm this step, you can enter a short description and the name of the person responsible for this group on the next screen (see Figure 10.5).

FIGURE 10.5:

Specifying a function group

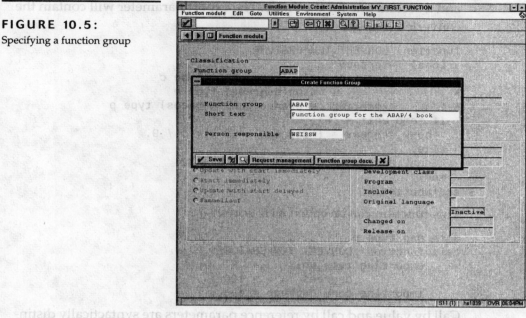

Interface Parameters

The parameters of a function are classified as importing, exporting, or changing parameters. In the call function statement, the formal parameters are listed on the left of an equal sign and the actual parameters on the right. The order of parameters at the calling statement is irrelevant, since the actual parameters are assigned through the formal parameter's name. The additions exporting and importing are always understood from the current point of view—that is, either from the calling program or the called function. Therefore, they exchange their roles between the function definition and the function call. Changing parameters are a combination of importing and exporting parameters.

Suppose you want to write a function to convert temperature degrees between Fahrenheit and Celsius. This kind of function has one import parameter to distinguish whether the input is Fahrenheit or Celsius and a second one for the value. The export parameter will contain the converted degrees.

```
function 'CONVERT_TEMPERATURE'.
* Local interface:
*        importing value(temp_unit) type c
*                  value(degrees) type p
*        exporting reference(conv_degrees) type p
  if temp_unit = 'F'.
    conv_degrees = ( degrees - 32 ) * 5 / 9.
  else.
    conv_degrees = degrees * 9 / 5 + 32.
  endif.
endfunction.
```

This function can be called as follows:

```
data deg type p.
call function 'CONVERT_TEMPERATURE'
     exporting temp_unit    = 'F'
               degrees      = 100
     importing conv_degrees = deg.
```

Call by value and call by reference parameters are syntactically distinguished by the additions value(p) and reference(p). Similar to forms, this distinction is only made at the definition of the function.

Function parameters are always maintained on a special screen of the ABAP/4 Development Workbench. To access this screen, select Goto ➤ Imp./Exp.Interface from any screen where functions are changed or displayed (see Figure 10.6).

For each parameter, you can specify the type either by a reference to a structure or field of the Dictionary or by a reference to a type as shown in Figure 10.7. If you refer to a type, this type must either be an elementary ABAP/4 type (c, n, i, p, d, etc.) or it must be defined in the Dictionary (see Chapter 5).

An importing or changing parameter can have a default value that is used when the calling program does not set this parameter explicitly. You can enter a default value in the Proposal column.

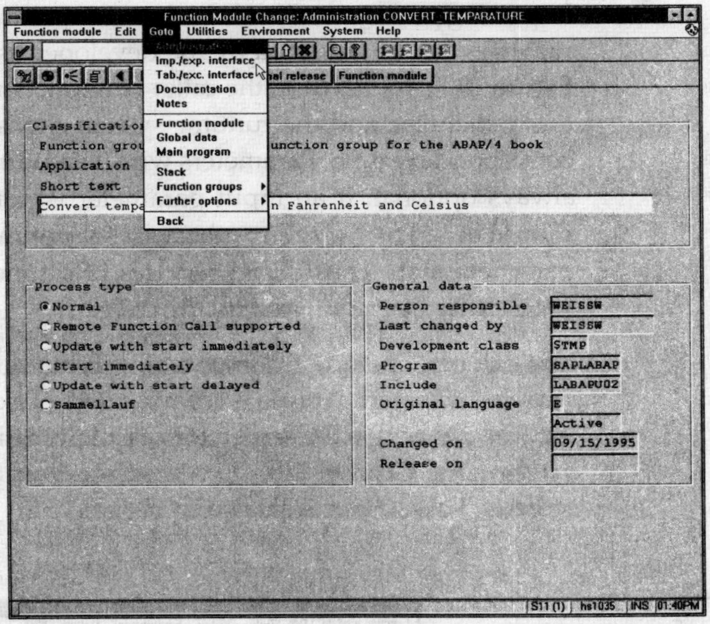

FIGURE 10.6:

Jumping to the interface
parameters from the Attributes
Maintenance screen

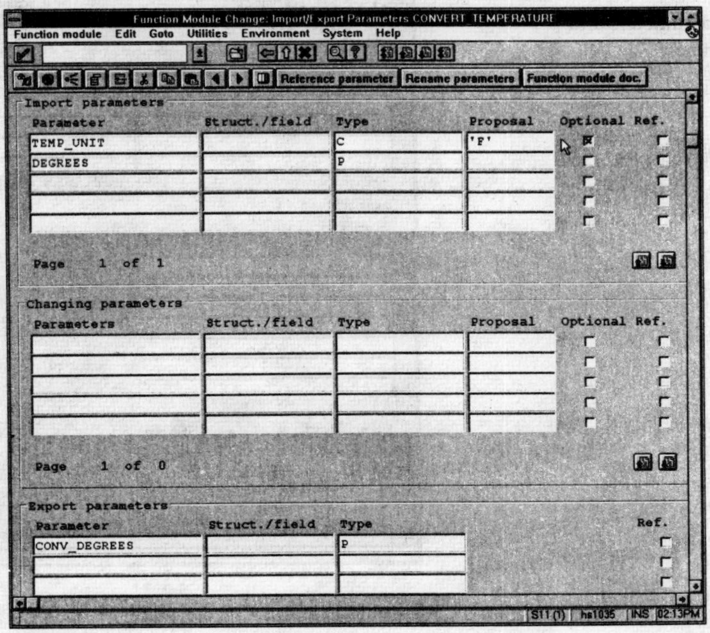

FIGURE 10.7:

Specifying interface parameters

Importing parameters (from the function point of view) and changing parameters can be classified by the developer as optional parameters (see Figure 10.7). In this case, the caller of a function need not pass a value to this parameter, and the runtime system chooses the initial value of the corresponding type. Parameters with a value in the Proposal column are always optional. If an input parameter is not classified as optional, it should be set by the caller; otherwise, a runtime error occurs. Exporting parameters are considered services of a function, and they need not necessarily be mentioned by the caller.

You can also include internal tables in the interface. For performance reasons, an internal table is always used as a call by reference parameter. You can access the screen for maintaining internal table parameters by choosing Goto ➤ Tab./Exc.Interface from all function maintenance screens. This screen is shown in Figure 10.8.

FIGURE 10.8:

Table parameters and exceptions

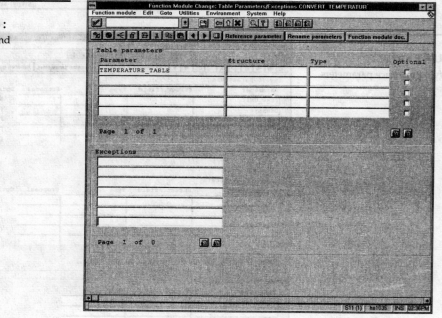

On this screen, you can also enter exceptions, which are explained in the next section.

Exceptions

Since functions are usually called by many programs, they cannot always decide how to react to errors or unpredictable events. Instead, functions should stop their execution and tell the caller what has happened. You can establish this approach using exceptions. You can reach the screen where you define an exception (shown in Figure 10.9) by selecting Goto ➤ Tab./Exc.Interface from any function maintenance screen.

FIGURE 10.9:

The screen where you define exceptions

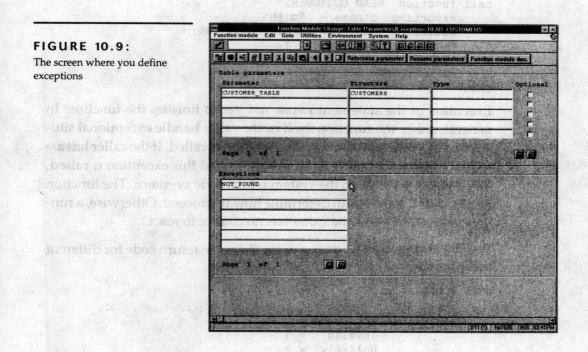

An exception can be raised using a `raise` command. If a `raise` statement is processed at runtime, execution of the function stops immediately, and the caller can identify the exception by its name:

```
function read_customers.
* Local interface:
*        importing  value(i_name) like customers-name
*        tables     customer_table structure customers
*        exceptions not_found
   select * from customers into table customer_table
        where name = i_name.
   if sy-subrc ne 0.
     raise not_found.
   endif.
endfunction.
```

This function can be called as follows:

```
call function 'READ_CUSTOMERS'
     exporting  i_name = 'Smith'
     tables     customer_table = Cust_tab
     exceptions not_found = 1.
if sy-subrc = 1.
  write 'Customer not found'.
endif.
```

Execution of the statement `raise not_found` finishes the function. In general, either the function itself or the caller handle exceptional situations, depending on the way the function is called. If the caller has assigned a specific number to an exception and this exception is raised, this number is stored in the system return code `sy-subrc`. The function returns and the caller can determine how to proceed. Otherwise, a runtime error occurs and the caller has no chance to react.

You can also group exceptions using the same return code for different exceptions:

```
call function ...
     ...
     exceptions not_found = 1
                invalid   = 1
                unlikely  = 2.
if sy-subrc = 1.
```

```
  write 'Error'.
elseif sy-subrc = 2.
  write 'Unlikely case'.
endif.
```

A calling program can react to any exception by means of the standard exception others:

```
call function ...
    ...
    exceptions not_found = 1
               others    = 2.
```

The standard exception others collects all exceptions that are not explicitly listed by the caller. You can also use the addition raising in the message statement. (This technique will be explained in Chapter 20.)

Exceptions can also be raised in subroutines (forms) of functions. In this case, all the forms on the call stack are thrown away and the function stops.

Editing a Function

You can edit the source code of your function by clicking on the Function Module button on the Function Module Create: Administration screen. The function editor screen is shown in Figure 10.10.

To call a function, choose Edit ➤ Insert Statement from the ABAP/4 Editor screen (the ABAP/4 Editor is explained in Chapter 3 under the heading "Basic Editor Operations") and a dialog box will appear as shown in Figure 10.11. Enter the name of your function in the Call Function text box.

When you confirm this step, all parameters and exceptions of the interface and the default values are inserted automatically in the source code part of the Editor screen at the position of the cursor when you started the Insert command (see Figure 10.12).

FIGURE 10.10:

Editing a function in the editor screen

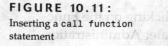

```
Function Module: Edit READ_CUSTOMERS / LARAPU02
Function module  Edit  Goto  Utilities  Block/clipboard  Settings  System  Help

                                                    Pattern  Concatenate  Duplicate line  Move  Note line

function read_customers.
*"----------------------------------------------------------------------
*"*"Local interface:
*"       IMPORTING
*"               VALUE(I_NAME) LIKE   CUSTOMERS-NAME
*"       TABLES
*"                CUSTOMER_TABLE STRUCTURE   CUSTOMERS
*"       EXCEPTIONS
*"                NOT_FOUND
*"----------------------------------------------------------------------


  select * from customers into table customer_table
         where name = i_name.
  if sy-subrc ne 0.
    raise not_found.
  endif.


endfunction.



                                         Line   1  -  19  Fr.  19

                                            S11 (1)  hs1035  INS  03:53PM
```

FIGURE 10.11:

Inserting a call function statement

```
ABAP/4 Editor: Edit Program ABAP1011
Program  Edit  Goto  Utilities  Block/clipboard  Settings  System  Help

                                                    Pattern  Concatenate  Duplicate line  Move  Note line

                        Insert statement

      CALL FUNCTION          read_customers
      MESSAGE           ID     Ty.  E  Number
      SELECT * FROM
      PERFORM
      AUTHORITY-CHECK
      WRITE to struct.
      Internal table
         with LIKE fields fr.
         with INCLUDE STRUCTURE f
      CALL DIALOG

      Other instruct.



                                         Line   5  -  25  Fr.  25

                                            S11 (2)  hs1035  DVR  03:57PM
```

FIGURE 10.12:
A call function statement
inserted by the system

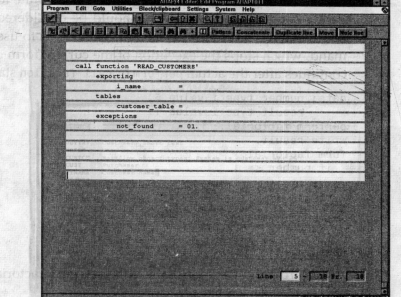

Nested Calls and Exits from Subroutines and Functions

Calls of forms or functions can be easily nested, and you can also use local data in nested calls. However, nested definitions of forms or functions are not possible. The Syntax Check produces an error message if an opening `form` statement occurs before the current definition of a form is completed by an `endform` statement. In other words, forms are global within a program. All functions are defined at the global level of the R/3 system.

Recursive calls are also supported. To avoid infinite loops, the terminating condition of a recursion should be considered carefully. The easiest way to solve this problem in ABAP/4 is to use the exit command, which stops the execution of the current form or function and continues after the actual perform or call function statement:

```
data: number type i value 5,
      result type i value 1.
perform factorial.
write result.
form factorial.
  if number <= 1.
    exit.
  endif.
  result = result * number.
  number = number - 1.
  perform factorial.
endform.
```

Afterwards, the field result will contain the factorial of the given number.

An exit statement is also useful in large forms that are not called recursively. However, you should keep in mind that an exit command always leaves the current unit and the program continues after that unit. The following list shows all pairs of commands where you can use the exit command to leave the current unit (for example, when a loop is left with exit, execution continues after the endloop):

1. Unconditional loop (do/enddo)

2. Conditional loop (while/endwhile)

3. Subroutine (form/endform)

4. Function (function/endfunction)

5. Reading entries of a database table (select/endselect, see Chapter 11)

6. Reading lines of an internal table (loop/endloop, see Chapter 12)

In other words, the `exit` command is context-sensitive and only leaves the inner structure if some of these constructions are nested.

A Quick Review

Here are some of the most important topics we discussed in this chapter:

- Forms and functions support the modularization of programs. Forms are designed for internal use in a single program, and functions are components that are called by many programs.

- Local data are only visible where they are defined.

- Static variables are local data that retain their content over all calls of a subroutine.

- Interface objects of forms and functions can be typed using arbitrary types or data objects. In this case, type checks are made during Syntax Check or runtime.

- Parameters of forms and functions can be classified as read-only or as changing parameters. The method of passing actual parameters to a form is either call by reference or call by value.

- Upon calling, all parameters of a form must be listed in the same order as in the form definition.

- A function has no access to the global data of the calling program, but only to the interface parameters, its own local data, and the global data of its function group.

- Functions support parameters with default values, optional parameters, and exceptions.

- Calls of forms and functions can be nested and even recursive calls are possible.

- An exit command stops the execution of a form or function, and the program continues behind the corresponding calling statement.

In the next part of this book, you will see how to work with database tables and internal tables. The next chapter focuses on reading database tables.

PART IV

Working with Tables

CHAPTER

ELEVEN

Reading Database Tables

- **Selecting data from the database**

- **Dynamic selections**

- **Foreign keys and views**

In this chapter, we'll introduce the use of the `select` statement to read database tables either record by record or as a whole. To select entries that obey certain conditions, you'll use the `where` clause. These conditions do not have to be set statically, but can be formulated dynamically—that is, at runtime—and we'll discuss this in the chapter. You'll learn to perform complex queries involving more than one table, using nested `select` loops or views defined in the ABAP/4 Dictionary. Performance aspects of different strategies for complex queries are discussed at the end of this chapter.

We will frequently use the sample travel agency data model from Chapter 6 to demonstrate the key properties of SQL statements and the use of internal tables, so you might want to review that chapter again.

Creating a Simple Query

You should assume that the `customers` table in the travel agency example contains the information shown in Table 11.1.

TABLE 11.1: Sample contents of the `customers` table

id	name	city	telephone
00000001	Edwards	Small Town	654-321-1234
00000002	Young	Village	333-444-2222
00000017	Smith	Big City	717-161-5151
87654321	Edison	Fort Myers	111-111-1111

Assume that the bookings table contains the information shown in Table 11.2.

TABLE 11.2: Sample contents of the bookings table

carrid	connid	fldate	bookid	customid	order_date
ABC	1000	19991230	001	00000017	19990101
ABC	1234	19991230	002	00000002	19991229
ABC	1234	19991231	005	00000017	19990101
XYZ	0006	19990606	008	00000001	19990101
XYZ	0007	19990505	007	87654321	19990101

Suppose you are a travel agent and all your customer data is stored in a customers table, which you have described in the ABAP/4 Dictionary. The easiest way to create a list of all customers in ABAP/4 would be to write this code:

```
tables customers.
select * from customers.
  write: / customers-name.
endselect.
```

This program selects all entries in the customers database table and displays each customer name on the screen. Using the declaration tables followed by the name of a database table, a data object (called the *work area*) is allocated with the structure of the table as it is defined in the ABAP/4 Dictionary. The select/endselect statements form a loop, where each line of the database table is put into the work area customers. The asterisk at the select statement indicates that all table fields are retrieved.

Instead of using the default work area, you can choose an alternative data object for the current table entry:

```
tables customers.
data my_customer like customers.   "alternative work area
select * from customers into my_customer.
  write: / my_customer-name.
endselect.
```

Note that the first alternative (using the default work area) is suitable for small programs in which the database table in question is only read once. The second approach (using a separate work area with a user-specified name) is appropriate whenever you need different data objects to hold entries of the same table. For example, you might need several different work areas if you wanted to compare values for one of your travel agency tables, such as when you read the last two bookings for a customer. In one work area, you would store the most recent booking, and in the second you would work with the previous one. Usually, all `tables` declarations are placed at the top of the data definitions. The `tables` declarations are also displayed as the Dictionary objects of the program in the Development Workbench's Object Browser.

NOTE For the sake of brevity, we will sometimes omit the `tables` declarations in the following examples.

Elementary Select
Statements for Data Retrieval

Beyond the simple query explained above, ABAP/4 also provides various extensions to the `select` statement, which allow you to specify the amount of data retrieved directly from additions to the statement.

Working with all Table Entries

Still using the travel agency example from above, you can try a different approach to reading database tables. Instead of reading the table entry by entry, you can also read the table contents into an internal table in a single step. Then, you can loop at the internal table and display each line:

```
data all_customers like customers occurs 100
                    with header line.
select * from customers into table all_customers.
loop at all_customers.
  write: / all_customers-name.
endloop.
```

As a result, you obtain a "snapshot" of the database table. To read the individual lines of the internal table, we introduced the loop/endloop construct, which we'll explain in detail in Chapter 12.

At first glance, both sample programs do the same job. They read data from a database table and display each entry. However, there are significant differences between the two approaches:

- The select/endselect loop construct focuses on single entries—that is, only one record is available at each step.

- The command select into table reads a set of entries that is also available afterwards. Working with the lines of the internal table requires an additional loop construct.

The first alternative is preferable if each entry is used only once within the program, whereas the second is very useful whenever the selected set will also be processed later. For instance, after loop/endloop, you might sort the internal table and calculate sums or other statistical figures. Moreover, you can modify or delete entries of the internal table without affecting the consistency of the database.

NOTE   **Operations on internal tables are covered in Chapter 12.**

If the set of selected entries is very large, the second alternative often has better performance than the first, even if you just want to read over the table once. This aspect is discussed under "Foreign Keys and Views" later in the chapter, where we cover nested `select` statements and views.

NOTE   **The `select` statement with the addition `into table` is only correct if the internal table is at least as wide as the database table. In addition to the fields of the database table defined in the Dictionary, the internal table can also have additional columns on the right, which are sometimes useful for flags or other information.**

Using where Clauses

So far, we have always selected *all* database table entries, irrespective of their contents. In practice, you are usually interested in a subset of entries specified by a certain condition—for example, all customer orders placed on 01/01/1999:

```
data customer_orders like bookings occurs 100.
select * from bookings into table customer_orders
        where order_date = '19990101'.
```

Here, the `where` clause restricts the set of selected records to those entries whose order date is 01/01/1999. Note that the name of the table field `order_date` is on the left side of the equal sign, whereas the value of the comparison is on the right. In general, conditions in the `where` clause are composed of a table field, an operator, and a value for the comparison. You can see the possible operators in the list below, which contains alternative mathematical symbols in the second column:

Operator	Symbol	Meaning
eq	=	equal
ne	<>	not equal
lt	<	less than
le	<=	less than or equal
gt	>	greater than
ge	>=	greater than or equal
between a and b	no symbol	interval
like	no symbol	pattern
in (a,b,c)	no symbol	equal a or b or c
in selopt	no symbol	condition is set by user in Select-Option

Several conditions can be combined using the logical operators and and or. For instance, if you want to select all orders after 01/01/1999 from the customer with the customer identifier number 87654321, you would write the following code:

```
select * from bookings into table customer_orders
    where customid   = '87654321'
        and order_date >= '19990101'.
```

Frequently, you'll want to design a query that contains search patterns—for example, all customers whose names begin with an *E*. You can code that request using the like operator:

```
select * from customers into table all_customers
    where name like 'E%'.
```

The percentage character (%) indicates that an arbitrary string can follow the beginning *E*. In other words, *Edwards*, *Edison*, and *E* will meet the condition, but *McElton* will not. To mask single characters, use the underscore character (_). For example, if you wanted to search for a customer whose name was similar to *Bell*, you would use B_ll, which would return *Bell*, *Bill*, and *Ball*.

By using the in operator with Select-Options, you can specify the where clause dynamically. In particular, a report's user can easily determine the required set of data without changing the source code or generating a new report.

> **NOTE**   Using Select-Options is explained in this chapter under the heading "Making Dynamic Selections."

The R/3 system is divided into different *Clients*, where each Client represents the operational data of one business unit. This Client dependency is reflected in application tables, which have a field of type clnt in the left-most position (see Chapter 5). When a program reads data from a Client-dependent table using the select command, the Client cannot be specified in the where clause, since the system automatically uses the current Client.

Reading Single Entries

Whenever you want to read a single entry from a table, you can use the select single command with all primary key fields in the where clause. Then, the system return code sy-subrc indicates whether the database request was successful (value is zero) or not (non-zero value):

```
select single * from customers
       where id = '87654321'.
if sy-subrc = 0.
  write customers-name.
else.
```

```
      write 'Customer not found.'.
endif.
```

Note that a select single statement is only correct if all primary key fields are specified by single values (that is, using the operators = or eq).

Selecting Single Fields

In the above examples, we have always chosen complete table entries with all fields by using the asterisk in the select statement. Sometimes, however, you do not need all fields in an entry, but are only interested in a subset. You can choose specific fields by listing the individual field names (for example, id and name) immediately after the select command. The corresponding fields of the program (for example, cid and cname) are listed after into between parentheses.

```
data: cid   like customers-id,
      cname like customers-name.
select id name into (cid,cname) from customers.
  write: / cid, cname.
endselect.
```

Specifying fields is useful to restrict the size of the data objects in a program. For instance, if you want to read 10,000 entries from a table with 100 fields in each entry, but you are only interested in two or three of the fields, you can significantly reduce the amount of data requested from the database and the amount of time and system resources you need to get it by using the above technique.

Getting Statistical Information

If you only need to know the number of table entries that satisfy a certain condition, you can retrieve this number using the addition count(*) in the select command:

```
data count_bookings type i.
select count(*) from bookings into count_bookings
       where order_date >= '19990101'.
```

After this operation, the field `count_bookings` contains the number of entries that meet the `where` condition. In a similar fashion, you can obtain more statistical values using these additions:

- `max`: maximum value in the specified column

- `min`: minimum value in the specified column

- `avg`: average of the values in the specified column

- `sum`: sum of the values in the specified column

For example, you will get the average number of occupied seats and the maximum number of available seats if you run the following program on our travel agency database:

```
data: average_seats_occupied like actfli-seatsocc,
      max_seats               like actfli-seatmax.
select avg(seatsoccu) max(seatsmax) from actfli
       into (average_seats_occupied,max_seats).
```

Ordering Your Query Results

In general, a `select` statement retrieves a set of data, but the database management system does not necessarily deliver the table entries in a specific order. In ABAP/4, you can sort the results of your query into a certain order by using one of these two alternatives:

- You can insert the addition `order by` into the `select` statement.

- You can sort the internal table containing the result of the query. We'll cover this option in Chapter 12.

Ordering entries via the `select` statement is done using the addition `order by` followed by the names of the sort fields:

```
tables customers.
select * from customers
        order by city name.
```

```
write: / customers-city,
          customers-name.
endselect.
```

If you intend to sort the resulting list according to the key fields of the database table, use the addition order by primary key. In the above example, that would yield a list of customers in the sequence of their identifiers.

Making Dynamic Selections

Up to now, all select statements have been statically defined, in the sense that you foresee the name of the table and the definition of the where clause, but you need not know the content of the compared fields. For some problems, however, you do not know the table name or the precise condition of the where clause when you are writing the program. ABAP/4 offers several alternatives to handle this situation.

Using Select-Options

In the simplest case, you know everything except the logical structure of the where condition—that is, the table name and the fields are known, but the comparison operator is not. A typical example would be that the end user is asked to specify selections before a report starts to read database tables. ABAP/4 reports have a standard user interface (called the *selection screen*) that allows the user to enter arbitrary selection criteria and conditions. At runtime, the user selections are then available in Select-Options, which determine the set of data to be read from the database.

This program offers the end user a screen to enter selection criteria into the Select-Option, and the `select` statement reads the set of data as it was specified by the user:

```
select-options sname for customers-name.
select * from customers into table all_customers
       where name in sname.
```

The order of the user's specifications in a Select-Option does not influence the order of retrieval from the database.

NOTE   The details about how to use Select-Options are explained in Chapter 16.

Dynamic Table Naming

You can also dynamically specify the table name. For example, this allows each user to determine the name of the table from which the data will be read. Within the `select` statement, the table name itself is contained in a field enclosed in parentheses following the `from` parameter:

```
data: tablename(10),
      count_rows type i.
move 'CUSTOMERS' to tablename.
select count( * ) from (tablename) into count_rows.
write: tablename, count_rows.
```

In this example, the table name would be CUSTOMERS.

Using the Dynamic where Clause

Similarly to the process of dynamically specifying the table name, the code of the `where` clause can be taken from an internal table at runtime, and the program will then figure out the where clause based on this information. Suppose you have an internal table conditions_tab that has the contents shown below.

```
name like 'E%'

and city like 'S%'
```

You can use this table in the where clause as follows:

```
select * from customers into table all_customers
       where id between 1 and 999
       and (conditions_tab).
```

This statement reads all customers who have identifiers between *1* and *999* and whose name and town begins with *E* and *S*, respectively.

NOTE Notice that the internal table conditions_tab can only contain literals and constants on the right side of the comparison operator.

Dynamic select statements certainly provide you with flexibility. At the same time, the programs are less readable and less secure, since the syntactical correctness of the dynamic where clause cannot be guaranteed in advance. Therefore, we recommend that you use static SQL statements (including the Select-Options in the where clause) unless the program you are creating needs full flexibility.

Foreign Keys and Views

The data objects of an application are represented as tables in a relational database system, and they are often connected via different relationships. One of the most important ones is the foreign key relationship—an entry in one table is at the same time the primary key of another table. For instance, the contents of the field customid of the bookings table is a key to the table customers. ABAP/4 offers three methods for obtaining all entries from several tables that are related via foreign keys:

- You can read table entries in nested select loops, where the foreign key relationship is reflected in the inner where clause.

- You can read table entries into one internal table from an appropriate view defined in the ABAP/4 Dictionary.

- You can read table entries into many internal tables and use the addition for all entries to establish the foreign key relationship.

To demonstrate these methods, we'll use the customers and bookings tables from our sample travel agency data model. Suppose you want to print a list of all customers who placed an order for a flight on 01/01/1999. Moreover, you may want to display the date of each ordered flight for each passenger. In that case, the resulting list would contain the following data:

Passenger	Flight Date
Edwards	06/06/1999
Smith	12/30/1999
Smith	12/31/1999
Edison	05/05/1999

Obtaining Data with Nested select Loops

We'll first illustrate the method of using nested select loops, where the foreign key relation is reflected in the inner where clause:

```
select * from customers.
  select * from bookings
    where customid  = customers-id
      and order_date = '19990101'.
```

```
      write: / customers-name,
             bookings-fldate.
   endselect.
 endselect.
```

This small program produces the desired list. Note that the inner `select` loop is always determined by the current customer of the outer loop. `Select` loops can also be nested in more than two levels. Both `select` loops can be nested in reverse order. However, if you want to display the names of those customers who have not ordered on 01/01/1999, only the solution in the example above will be useful.

The approach using nested `select` loops is straightforward and easy to implement. Sometimes, however, it isn't the best possible solution as far as performance considerations go, since the flow of control between the ABAP/4 program and the DBMS requires a considerable amount of CPU time at each step in the `select` loop. In particular, if the contents of the database tables will first be moved into internal tables that are to be processed afterwards, then the other two alternatives are preferable.

Using Dictionary Views to Obtain Data

Using previously defined views from the ABAP/4 Dictionary, you can put the result of the query (that is, the output of the `select` statements) into an internal table in a single step. Suppose that a view `vcustbook` of tables `customers` and `bookings` with columns `name`, `fldate`, and `order _date` has been defined in the Dictionary. Its contents might look like Table 11.3.

An internal table can be filled from that view in a single step, and the individual entries are processed at a later time. The resulting list is the same as in the first example using nested `select` loops.

TABLE 11.3: Sample contents of the vcustbook view

name	fldate	order_date
Edwards	19991230	19990101
Smith	19991230	19990101
Smith	19991231	19990101
Young	19991230	19991229
Edison	19990505	19990101

```
data: my_vcustbook like vcustbook occurs 100
                    with header line.
select * from vcustbook into table my_vcustbook
        where order_date = '19990101'.
loop at my_vcustbook.
    write: / my_vcustbook-name.
            my_vcustbook-fldate.
endloop.
```

Using Internal Tables for Selection Criteria

Finally, you can insert the addition for all entries into the select command. Much like nested select loops, the foreign key relationship is reflected in the where clause. However, the different select statements are not nested, but the intermediate results are stored in internal tables. This method is best illustrated by an example:

```
data: all_customers like customers occurs 100
                    with header line,
      all_bookings  like bookings occurs 500
                    with header line.
select * from customers into table all_customers.
select * from bookings  into table all_bookings
        for all entries in all_customers
        where customid   = all_customers-id
          and order_date = '19990101'.
loop at all_customers.
  loop at all_bookings
```

```
          where customid = all_customers-id.
      write: / all_customers-name,
               all_bookings-fldate.
    endloop.
  endloop.
```

In this example, the second `select` statement chooses all entries of the bookings table that satisfy the `where` condition for all customer names of the internal table `all_customers`. The relationship between the two tables is established by the condition `where customid = all_customers` `-id` and the addition `for all entries`. In other words, this `select` statement is equivalent to the following program code:

```
loop at all_customers.
   select * from bookings appending table all_bookings
           where customid   = all_customers-id
             and order_date = '19990101'.
endloop.
```

Note that the addition `appending table` does not overwrite the contents of the internal table, but rather appends the new entries at the bottom of the internal table.

Comparing the Different Techniques

The most important properties of each method can be summarized as follows:

Nested select loops

- Straightforward and easy to implement.
- At each step, all fields of the current table entries are available. Therefore, further fields (e.g., `bookings-connid`) can easily be added.
- No redundancy of data.

- Outer joins can be realized even if the DBMS does not offer this possibility. For instance, you can use the same select loop to display the names of customers who have not ordered on 01/01/1999.

Views defined in the ABAP/4 Dictionary

- For large sets of selected table entries, this approach has a significantly better performance than the nested select statements.

- The internal table can be used afterwards, for example, to sort the entries according to different criteria.

- Some columns of the view might contain redundant data. In the above example, the customer names are redundant in the view vcustbook.

- Outer joins are not supported.

- Addition of further fields requires the change and activation of the view in the Dictionary.

Using internal tables and for all entries

- For large sets of selected table entries, this approach has a significantly better performance than the nested select statements, but it is not as fast as the second alternative.

- Further fields can easily be added.

Keeping these properties in mind, you will probably use nested select loops in the following cases:

- When the amount of data in question is not very large (for example, 50 entries of 200 bytes each).

- When the source code should be written as simply as possible.

- When outer joins are requested; for example, when the result list will also contain the names of customers who have not ordered on 01/01/1999.

- When the internal table corresponding to the view of the second alternative contains too much redundant data.

- When the choice of selected fields will be changed frequently, but views of the Dictionary should not be changed very often.

On the other hand, views of the ABAP/4 Dictionary are very useful if huge sets of table entries are selected without many redundancies, and if the shape of the views remains stable. Finally, the last approach, using the addition for all entries, requires a rather complex source code, but this method is also very flexible.

NOTE Keep in mind that the above list of advantages and disadvantages is not complete. Performance aspects certainly depend on the particular DBMS and on the system architecture (for example, the speed of the network). In general, the performance of SQL statements can be further improved if indices of the DBMS are used.

A Quick Review

Here are some of the more important points we covered in this chapter:

- `select`/`endselect` retrieves the content of a database table entry by entry.

- `select into table` fills an internal table with the selected content in a single step.

- The set of selected entries can be restricted by the `where` clause.

- Uniquely determined entries can be read using the `select single` command. All primary key fields must be specified in the `where` clause by single values (operators = or eq).

- Instead of always using complete entries, you can also select individual fields.

- You can get statistical information in a `select` statement (e.g., maximum, average, or number of specified entries).

- You can sort your query results by using the addition `order by` or by sorting the internal table with the selected entries.

- Dynamic selections are supported by Select-Options, dynamic table names, and dynamic `where` clauses.

- Views of tables that are related via foreign keys can be read using nested `select` loops, using Dictionary defined views, or using the addition `for all entries`.

Now that you have seen how to read data from database tables, the next chapter introduces you into the details of how to work with internal tables.

CHAPTER

T W E L V E

Using Internal Tables

- **Filling an internal table**

- **How to sort the contents of an internal table**

- **Reading single and multiple lines**

- **Changing the content**

- **Working with subtotals**

In Chapter 11, we used internal tables to create "snapshots" of database tables at runtime. When an internal table is filled from a database table, you can easily operate on the data without any additional database access. This property makes internal tables very fast at runtime, in particular in a distributed client/server environment. Internal tables are also useful to you whenever you need to collect data in a container for later processing in the application program.

In this chapter, we will introduce you to the different methods of working with internal tables. We'll discuss the methods for filling an internal table in detail. You'll learn how to sort an internal table according to different criteria (for example, according to different sort fields or in descending order). Different techniques for reading and changing the content of an internal table are presented. In particular, we show how to work with subtotals, and we develop a real-life sample application.

What Is an Internal Table?

An internal table is defined like other data objects using the data declaration. It can be viewed as a snapshot of a database table, and contains some of the rows and columns of that table at runtime. We used internal tables in this context already in the preceding chapter on database select operations. There you saw how to fill an internal table using this code:

```
data all_customers like customers occurs 100.
select * from customers into table all_customers.
```

In many cases, internal tables function as more than simple views of database tables. They may also contain additional columns with temporary information that is only relevant at runtime and therefore not stored in the database table. For example, it is often useful to have a field indicating that the current entry can be deleted, if further checks show that it is not used in other contexts. Sometimes, an internal table may not even be related to any database table at all (for example, if tree structures or general linked lists are built and displayed at runtime).

Using internal tables, you don't have to worry about dynamic storage allocation—the ABAP/4 runtime system does this automatically. In particular, you don't have to know the maximum size of an internal table in advance. The Occurs Parameter (the value after occurs) specifies an estimated maximum and is purely a performance parameter: it does not actually restrict the maximum size of the internal table. In principle, an internal table can hold an unlimited number of lines. The only limitation is set by the virtual memory space of the machine, but these days this is almost never a problem. This flexibility is one of the greatest advantages of internal tables.

Tables and Header Lines

As we mentioned in Chapters 4 and 5, if the defining data statement of an internal table contains the addition with header line, the ABAP/4 system provides you with both the table itself and with an additional data object of the same structure as an individual line, called the *header line*. This object is used as a default record to hold the current line of a table. If a table does not have a header line, you must provide a separate record to hold the content of the current entry for almost all commands dealing with the table.

A *header line* is similar to a *work area* for a database table. A *work area* (or an *alternative work area*) is used as temporary storage for one entry of a database table (see Chapter 11). In a similar way, a header line is used to hold one line of an internal table. If a database table does not have a header line, a separate record to hold the contents of the current entry is also called work area. It is a matter of taste as to which term you prefer to use.

These two approaches (using a header line or providing a separate record) are generally equivalent. Using header lines, you don't need to declare an extra record—ABAP/4 does it for you—and many statements working with internal tables are easier to read. However, embedded internal tables cannot have header lines, since this would lead to ambiguous expressions in some cases. For example, suppose you have defined an internal table as follows:

```
data all_customers like customers occurs 100
               with header line.
```

At runtime, the table would look something like Table 12.1.

TABLE 12.1: The contents of the `all_customers` table

id	name	city	telephone
Header Line			+
00000017	Smith	Big City	717-161-5151
Table Contents			
00000001	Edwards	Small Town	654-321-1234
00000002	Young	Village	333-444-2222
00000017	Smith	Big City	717-161-5151
87654321	Edison	Fort Meyers	111-111-1111

To avoid misunderstandings, we will call the contents of a table (minus the header line) the *body*, to distinguish it from its header line. Many ABAP/4 keywords dealing with internal tables (for example, append or loop) implicitly distinguish between the header line and the body of a table, but some (for example, move) do not. In these cases, you must specify the body explicitly using brackets. Moreover, many statements also have an alternate form for working with a separate record instead of the built-in header line. This version is optional for tables with a header line, but is required otherwise.

Filling an Internal Table

ABAP/4 provides four methods for filling an internal table with data from a database table or from local variables of a program:

- You can read data from database tables via the select command.
- You can append lines using the append command.
- You can insert lines at a specified position using the insert command.
- You can transport complete tables with the move command.

These methods are explained in detail in the subsequent paragraphs.

Reading from Database Tables

We already demonstrated the use of the first method in Chapter 11. Usually, the result of the database query is put into an internal table by inserting the addition into table into the select statement:

```
select * from customers into table all_customers.
```

In this example, the previous content of the internal table is overwritten by the new data. Sometimes, however, you want to keep the old content and add new lines at the end of the table. You do this by using the addition `appending table`:

```
select * from customers appending table all_customers.
```

> **NOTE**
>
> As we've mentioned before, ABAP/4 automatically allocates the correct amount of memory for your table. We'll discuss memory allocation and the Occurs Parameter later in this chapter under "The Size of an Internal Table."

Appending Lines

If you work with `select` loops and internal tables that contain a restricted view of the database table, you can append single lines or blocks of lines. Keeping with our travel agency example, suppose you are interested in creating a table with only the identifier numbers and the city names of your customers (i.e., each line contains two fields of an entry of the database table customers):

```
types: begin of t_customer_city,
          id   like customers-id,
          city like customers-city,
       end of t_customer_city.
data: customer_cities type t_customer_city occurs 100
                      with header line.
select * from customers.
  move-corresponding customers to customer_cities.
  append customer_cities.
endselect.
```

As the name already suggests, the append statement simply adds the content of the header line to the end of the internal table. Here we made use of the fact that this table has been declared with a header line. For instance, if the header line looks like the one shown in Table 12.2, an append command would change the internal table `customer_cities`.

TABLE 12.2: The contents of the `customer_cities` table after the append command

id	name
Header Line	
00000015	Dry Creek
Table Contents	
00000001	Small Town
00000002	Village
00000017	Big City
87654321	Fort Meyers
00000015	Dry Creek

If you hadn't specified a header line in the definition of the table, you would need to explicitly provide a separate record to hold the content of the current line. We'll refer to this record as the *work area*, and it can be used in the append statement as follows:

```
data my_customer like customers.
...
append my_customer to all_customers.
```

The two approaches (header lines and work areas) have different strengths. When you use header lines, you don't have to declare an extra record—ABAP/4 does it for you—and the append statement is easier to read. However, you have to use an extra work area if nested internal tables (tables inside records or other tables) are involved, since they cannot have header lines.

The contents of an internal table can be appended to another table using the addition `lines of`. For example, you can add the internal table `old_customers` to `all_customers` as follows:

```
data old_customers like customers occurs 10.
...
append lines of old_customers to all_customers.
```

Using the addition `from x to y`, you can specify the range of lines in the source table that are to be appended.

> **NOTE** Appending a block of lines using the addition `lines of` is supported starting from R/3 Release 3.0C.

Inserting Lines at a Specified Position

The `append` command fills the table in an order triggered by the flow of the program, but you will often need to insert single lines or a block of lines at a specified position. You can do this using the `insert` statement. The new lines are inserted before a specified line number, and the subsequent entries are scrolled down. Suppose you want to insert a line as the new third row in the table:

```
insert customer_cities index 3.
```

In Table 12.3 below, the Header Line section shows the material that will be added to the internal table, and then the Table Contents section shows the table with that material added to it.

Similarly to `append`, the `insert` statement can be used with an extra work area that is specified after the addition `from`. Moreover, a subset of an internal table can be inserted in a single step using the addition `lines of` and `from x to y`. For example, you can add lines 2 through 5 from `old_cities` into the `customer_cities` table, and they

TABLE 12.3: The customer_cities table

id	name
Header Line	
00000005	Pleasant Site
Table Contents	
00000001	Small Town
00000002	Village
00000005	Pleasant Site
00000017	Big City
87654321	Fort Meyers
00000015	Dry Creek

will be inserted as the new lines 3, 4, 5, 6, and the old line 3 from customer _cities will now be line 7.

```
insert lines of old_cities
      from 2 to 5
      into customer_cities index 3.
```

Whenever a block of lines must be inserted at one position, the version of the insert command we just explained is faster than inserting single lines within a loop.

> **NOTE**   Inserting a block of lines (like appending a block of lines) is supported starting from R/3 Release 3.0C.

Transporting Complete Tables

Finally, you can fill an internal table with the contents of another one in a single step by using the move command. In the following example, the move statement transports the whole internal table all_customers into the table foreign_customers.

```
tables customers.
data: all_customers     like customers occurs 100,
      foreign_customers like all_customers.
select * from customers into table all_customers.
move all_customers to foreign_customers.
```

If an internal table with a header line is involved, this header line (but not the internal table itself) is copied by move. A typical example is shown below, where an entry of a database table is read and copied to the header line of an internal table.

```
tables customers.
data foreign_customers_h like customers occurs 100
                           with header line.
select single * from customers where id = '00000017'.
move customers to foreign_customers_h.
append foreign_customers_h.
```

In this example, the table work area customers is transferred to the header line of foreign_customers_h, and this header line is appended.

The Size of Internal Tables

As mentioned earlier, you don't have to deal with problems like memory allocation—ABAP/4 does it for you. In particular, you don't need to know the maximum size of an internal table in advance. The only size limit is the virtual memory space of the machine—that is, an internal table can essentially hold an unlimited number of lines. However, you can make a program faster if you know the maximum size of an internal table when you are defining it. In ABAP/4, the estimated number of lines of a table is set in the Occurs Parameter, (the value after the addition occurs in the defining data statement of the table). The estimated size of the table in bytes is the main factor influencing the speed of your program. This size is calculated as the product of the width and number of lines in the table:

```
estimated_size = width * number_of_lines.
```

Here, the width is determined as the sum of all lengths of one line, for example, 50 fields of 4 bytes each yield a width of 200 bytes.

When the first table entry is created, the runtime system allocates suitable memory space to hold the whole table or at least a block of approximately 8–16K. So making a good guess at the Occurs Parameter prevents the ABAP/4 runtime system from allocating unnecessary memory space. The number you specify as the Occurs Parameter is particularly important if small tables are contained in one large table with many lines. If the Occurs Parameter is set too large for the tables inside the large table, memory is wasted, since blocks of at least 8K are allocated for each line of the outer table. Whole very large tables cannot be stored in the same region of main memory, and the runtime system swaps some parts of the table. You don't need to worry about the Occurs Parameter for large tables, since the runtime system always determines an optimal size for the swapped parts to find the best combination for using memory space and CPU time.

Since the system allocates memory as necessary, we suggest you use the following guidelines to help you set the Occurs Parameter for your programs:

- Keep in mind that the Occurs Parameter does not affect the actual size of a table; it only affects the performance of table operations.

- If you cannot estimate the size of the table, set the Occurs Parameter to zero and let the system do it for you.

- If the estimated size of the table is below 8K (for example, 500 bytes resulting from 5 lines with a width of 100 bytes each), set the Occurs Parameter equal to the estimated number of lines.

- If the estimated size of the table is larger than 8K, set the Occurs Parameter to zero and let the system do it for you.

For very large internal tables (for example, 10MB), it is sometimes useful to free the memory space that will be needed by the table. You can do this using the `free` statement, which deletes all lines and frees the corresponding memory:

```
free all_customers.
```

You can delete all lines of an internal table by using the `refresh` command, which will be explained below. Local internal tables of a subroutine are freed automatically on return to the caller.

Sorting Internal Table Entries

After filling an internal table using one of the above methods, the entries usually won't appear in any particular order. It is generally more helpful for the user to have the entries ordered according to some sort criteria. You can easily arrange table entries by using the `sort` command. In its shortest form, the `sort` command looks like this:

```
data my_flights like actfli occurs 10.
sort my_flights.
```

The order is implicitly determined by the sequence of fields in the line structure of the table; i.e., the left-most column represents the highest sort criterion.

For example, Table 12.4 shows the contents of the `my_flights` table from our travel agency example before the `sort` command has been applied.

TABLE 12.4: The unsorted contents of the table `my_flights`

carrid	connid	fldate	price	currency	seatsocc
XYZ	0007	19990505	110	USD	133
ABC	1000	19991230	200	DEM	110
ABC	1234	19991231	300	DEM	020
XYZ	0006	19990606	100	USD	175
ABC	1234	19991230	500	DEM	010

Table 12.5 shows what the contents of this same table would look like after they had been sorted using the short form of the sort command, shown in the code above.

TABLE 12.5: The contents of the table `my_flights` after the short form of a `sort` command

carrid	connid	fldate	price	currency	seatsocc
ABC	1000	19991230	200	DEM	110
ABC	1234	19991230	500	DEM	010
ABC	1234	19991231	300	DEM	020
XYZ	0006	19990606	100	USD	175
XYZ	0007	19990505	110	USD	133

Alternatively, you can sort the internal table according to some specified fields.

```
sort my_flights by fldate price.
```

Table 12.6 shows what the same `my_flights` table would look like after being sorted according to this criterion. The first named field, `fldate`, takes precedence, and within that the table is sorted by price.

TABLE 12.6: The contents of the table my_flights after being sorted according to fldate and price

carrid	connid	fldate	price	currency	seatsocc
XYZ	0007	19990505	110	USD	133
XYZ	0006	19990606	100	USD	175
ABC	1000	19991230	200	DEM	110
ABC	1234	19991230	500	DEM	010
ABC	1234	19991231	300	DEM	020

You can also sort in reverse order using the addition descending. The default order is always ascending. For example, in the following code, the table would be sorted first by carrier ID in ascending order and then by flight price in descending order (so the lowest ID would be at the top, and then within that sort, the highest price would come first).

```
sort my_flights by carrid price descending.
```

After this descending sort, the table would appear as shown in Table 12.7.

TABLE 12.7: The contents of the table my_flights after a sort according to carrier ID and descending flight price

carrid	connid	fldate	price	currency	seatsocc
ABC	1234	19991230	500	DEM	010
ABC	1234	19991231	300	DEM	020
ABC	1000	19991230	200	DEM	110
XYZ	0007	19990505	110	USD	133
XYZ	0006	19990606	100	USD	175

> **NOTE**
>
> The shortest form of the `sort` command (without any addition) has a special property: only the non-numeric fields are considered as sort criteria. The reason for this default behavior is that primary key fields are usually character-like fields (types c, d or n). If the sort fields are cited explicitly, this restriction no longer holds, and the table is sorted according to the explicitly cited fields, where the first field you name gets sorted first.

Retrieving Lines from an Internal Table

Once an internal table is filled and its contents are sorted, the next question probably is how to show its contents on the screen. So, we need constructs to retrieve them from the table, either reading each line of the table one by one using a loop or reading individual lines.

Getting All Lines from an Internal Table

The code for a loop reads like this:

```
loop at all_customers.
  write / all_customers-name.
endloop.
```

These statements display the name for all entries of the internal table `all_customers` starting from the first one up to the last one. During the loop, the header line is filled with the current line of the table at each step. In other words, each time the system retrieves a line of the table, it places that line in the header line. The contents of the header line can be changed without affecting the internal table itself.

Similar to `select` loops in database tables, loops in internal tables can easily be nested:

```
loop at all_customers.
  write / all_customers-name.
  loop at new_bookings.
    write / new_bookings-fldate.
  endloop.
endloop.
```

During the loop, the current line number is always available in the system field `sy-tabix`. You can also use this field within nested loops, since it is automatically set by the runtime system according to the currently active loop. Typically, this index is useful if you want to change or delete that line later.

In analogy to the `where` clause of the `select` statement which we discussed in Chapter 11, you can restrict a loop to a subset of entries of the internal table. This is done by adding a `where` clause that specifies the condition:

```
loop at all_customers
    where name = 'Smith'.
  write / all_customers-name.
endloop.
```

The `where` clause can contain all conditional operators that are supported for the `if` statement, as explained in Chapter 9 (for example, eq, =, ne, <>, ge, >=, cp). For instance, if you wanted to display all customers whose names begin with an *E* and who do not live the city Small Town, you could use the operators `cp` (contains pattern) and `ne` (not equal):

```
loop at all_customers
    where name cp 'E*'
    and   city ne 'Small Town'.
  write / all_customers-name.
endloop.
```

In addition, if you already know the range of lines you want to work with, you can specify this interval by explicitly citing the line numbers:

```
loop at all_customers
    from 10 to 15.
```

The lower or upper limit of the selected interval can be omitted. If you omit the lower limit, the loop will run from the first line up to the line you specified. If you omit the upper limit, the loop will run from the line you specified up to the last line in the table.

Looping at internal tables that don't have a header line requires a work area to hold the contents of the current line. This record can be set after inserting the addition into into the loop statement:

```
data my_customer like customers.
loop at all_customers into my_customer.
  write / my_customer-name.
endloop.
```

Reading Single Lines

In general, there are two ways of reading a single line of an internal table: you either specify the line directly by the line number or you specify it by a logical key. Both methods are supported by the read table command. Using the addition index followed by the index of the table entry in question, you can read this line directly:

```
read table all_customers index 3.
if sy-subrc = 0.
  write / all_customers-name.
else.
  write / 'Customer not found'.
endif.
```

The third table entry will be available in the header line if the table actually has at least three entries. Otherwise, the system return code sy-subrc is set to a non-zero value. Much like the loop construction, you can also put the result into another record using the into addition in the read table statement. This separate record is required when the table does not have a header line.

```
data my_customer like customers.
read table all_customers into my_customer index 3.
```

Usually, it is hard to know the number of the table line in advance. Instead, you'll probably have some idea about what the contents of the table entry you want will be. In particular, if you know the primary key fields of the corresponding database table, you can access the associated line of the internal table using the addition with key followed by a specification of the key fields:

```
read table all_customers with key id = '87654321'.
if sy-subrc = 0.
  write / all_customers-name.
else.
  write / 'Customer not found'.
endif.
```

If successful, the read command returns the index of the line in the system field sy-tabix. For example, if line number four of the internal table all_customers contains the ID *87654321*, the system field sy-tabix is set to four and the header line is filled with the corresponding entry. The read table command can also be used with other fields of the table serving as key fields. For instance, if you know the name and the city of a customer, you can read the corresponding table entry using both fields as key fields:

```
read table all_customers
    with key name = 'Smith'
             city = 'Big City'.
if sy-subrc = 0.
  write: / all_customers-id, all_customers-name.
else.
  write / 'Customer not found'.
endif.
```

In this example, the record for the person named Smith who lives in the city Big City would be read from the all_customers table. Note, however, that there may be several customers matching these conditions; perhaps in our example there are both a Robert Smith and a Mary Smith living in Big City. The above version of the read table command loops through the table sequentially and stops when the condition is met. So it will retrieve the first occurrence of an entry satisfying the key condition (for example, it would return Mary Smith's field but not Robert's if the field was sorted according to customer name).

If the internal table is large, a sequential search is slow. You can significantly accelerate the search for an entry in an internal table by specifying the addition binary search in the read table command. In this case, the method of a *binary search* is applied. A binary search algorithm requires that the table entries are sorted according to the specified key fields (we'll explain this further just below). For instance, if you have filled the table all_customers with entries sorted according to the primary key of the database table customers, you can use the binary search method as follows:

```
select * from customers into table all_customers
        order by primary key.
read table all_customers with key id = '87654321' binary
search.
if sy-subrc = 0.
  write / all_customers-name.
else.
  write / 'Customer not found'.
endif.
```

In the binary search method, the system first checks the key condition at the middle entry of the table. If it is fulfilled, all is done and the binary search terminates. Otherwise, it considers the first or the second part of the table, depending on whether the specified key fields are smaller or larger than the middle entry. Then, the middle entry of the chosen half of the table is considered. It is checked against the specified key fields in the same fashion. This procedure is repeated until the search determines whether or not there is a line that meets the conditions. The system return code sy-subrc is set to either zero or not zero.

The binary search method is also applicable when the internal table is sorted according to criteria other than those given by the primary key:

```
sort all_customers by name city telephone.
read table all_customers
     with key name      = 'Smith'
              city      = 'Big City'
              telephone = '717-161-5151'
          binary search.
if sy-subrc = 0.
  write / all_customers-name.
else.
  write / 'Customer not found'.
endif.
```

Changing an Internal Table

We have now covered how to fill an internal table and how to read single or multiple lines from that table. In this section, you will see how to change the table either by modifying existing lines, by adding new ones, or by deleting one or more lines.

Inserting a Set of Lines

Suppose you have searched an entry of a sorted table using the command read table with the additions with key and binary search. If this search was unsuccessful, the system return code sy-subrc is set to a non-zero value. The system field sy-tabix points to the line following the entry that is represented by the key condition, if this entry had been in the table. This behavior enables you to insert the new entry at its appropriate place using the insert command. For instance, suppose that you want to add a new customer to the internal table all_customers, where the table has the content as shown in Table 12.8.

TABLE 12.8: The contents of the all_customers table before inserting the new line

id	name	city	telephone
00000001	Edwards	Small Town	654-321-1234
00000002	Young	Village	333-444-2222
00000017	Smith	Big City	717-161-5151
87654321	Edison	Fort Myers	111-111-1111

```
read table all_customers with key id = '00000005' binary
search.
if sy-subrc ne 0.
  all_customers-id        = '00000005'.
  all_customers-name      = 'Martinez'.
  all_customers-city      = 'Phoenix'.
  all_customers-telephone = '354-321-4567'.
  insert all_customers index sy-tabix.
endif.
```

After the read table statement, the system field sy-tabix equals three, so the new line is inserted before the third line. Now the internal table all_customers looks like Table 12.9.

TABLE 12.9: The contents of the `all_customers` table after inserting the new line

Id	name	city	telephone
00000001	Edwards	Small Town	654-321-1234
00000002	Young	Village	333-444-2222
00000005	Martinez	Phoenix	354-321-4567
00000017	Smith	Big City	717-161-5151
87654321	Edison	Fort Myers	111-111-1111

Using the addition into, you can also insert the contents of a separate work area into the internal table. As explained above, a subset of an internal table can be inserted in a single step using the additions lines of and from x to y.

Modifying a Single Line

In addition to the other things you can do with internal tables (reading lines, inserting lines) you can also change those lines. Typically, you first read the line you want to change, change its content, and then write it back to the internal table. For example, if you wanted to change the line *00000005* in our all_customers table, you can do this with the modify command and this is the code you would write:

```
read table all_customers with key id = '00000005' binary
search.
if sy-subrc = 0.
  all_customers-city = 'Big City'.
  modify all_customers index sy-tabix.
endif.
```

Similarly to append, the modify statement can be used with an extra work area that is specified after the addition from. Changing a single line within a loop/endloop construct does not require you to know the index number of the line, since the current index is used by the system.

Suppose the area code of Big City was changed from 717 to 777 and you need to update your internal table:

```
loop at all_customers where city = 'Big City'.
  all_customers-telephone(3) = '777'.
  modify all_customers.
endloop.
```

With the addition from you can also change a line of the internal table using a separate work area.

Deleting a Set of Lines

In the same fashion, you can delete a single line of an internal table at a specified position:

```
read table all_customers with key id = '00000005' binary
search.
if sy-subrc = 0.
  all_customers-city = 'Big City'.
  delete all_customers index sy-tabix.
endif.
```

Similar to modify, deleting a single line within a loop/endloop construct does not require the index of the line. You can delete a subset of an internal table by specifying a where clause or by specifying a range of lines using the addition from x to y. For example, you might want to delete all customers whose names begin with an E.

```
delete all_customers
       where name cp 'E*'.
```

To delete all lines of a table in a single step, use the refresh statement.

```
refresh all_customers.
```

If the internal table has a header line, it is not changed by the refresh command. The header line can be initialized by clear, if necessary.

Local internal tables defined in a subroutine (form or function) are automatically removed by the system when the subroutine is left. In that case, a refresh statement would be superfluous. However, a static internal table (defined by statics) remains unchanged and can be used at a later call of the subroutine.

Working with Subtotals

Subtotals, headers, or other intermediate results belonging to a block of entries in an internal table can be obtained using blocks of at and endat commands in a loop. The statements between the corresponding at and endat commands are processed in the following situations:

at first/endat: processed at the very beginning of the table.

at new f/endat: processed when the content of the table field f or one of the preceding fields has just changed.

at end of f/endat: processed when the content of the table field f or one of the preceding fields will change at the next entry.

at last/endat: processed at the end of the table.

The program below illustrates the use of the new statements. The internal table my_flights is filled from the database, and for each entry the number of occupied seats is displayed. The output is enhanced by a header and a subtotal of occupied seats for each carrier.

```
tables actfli.
* Internal table for flights
data my_flights like actfli occurs 10
                 with header line.
* Statistical data
data sum_occupied_seats like my_flights-seatsocc.
* Reading the flights from the database
select * from actfli into table my_flights
       order by primary key.
* Displaying the number of occupied seats of each flight
* with headers and subtotals for each carrier
```

```
loop at my_flights.
  at new carrid.
    new-page.
    write / my_flights-carrid.
    clear sum_occupied_seats.
  endat.
  add my_flights-seatsocc to sum_occupied_seats.
  write / my_flights-seatsocc.
  at end of carrid.
    write / sum_occupied_seats.
  endat.
endloop.
```

In order for the at new f/at end of f constructs to work properly, the internal table must be sorted at least by the fields preceding f itself. Otherwise you have to use a local field for the content of the field f of the previous table entry.

Extracting Data

The lines of an internal table always have the same structure. Using the method of extracting field groups, you can also handle groups of data with different structures and get statistical figures from the grouped data.

For instance, suppose you are interested in statistics about connections and flights for each carrier (contained in the tables planfli and actfli). In particular, you want the destination and target of each connection and the number of occupied seats for all flights of a carrier on this connection to be displayed.

One solution would be to define a Dictionary view of the tables planfli and actfli and to define an internal table with the structure of that view. However, using this approach the internal table will contain a lot of redundant information, and this could be a big problem if you have a very large table.

The method of extracting field groups offers an efficient solution for problems of this kind. In principle, this method simulates an outer join of the tables and stores it temporarily in virtual memory using the `extract` command. This set of extracted data can be sorted and the desired statistics can be computed for each group of data.

The following steps are essential for the extract technique: first, the sort criteria for all structures and containers for the contents must be specified using the `field-groups` declaration in combination with a variation of the `insert` command. In a second step, you must store the containers using `extract`. Then, this set of data can be sorted using a `sort` command without any addition. Finally, you can read all entries sequentially using the `loop`/`endloop` construct. Within the loop, statistical figures can easily be calculated in the `at`/`endat` blocks:

```
tables: planfli, actfli.
* Definition of sort criteria and data containers
field-groups: header, connections, flights.
insert: planfli-carrid planfli-connid actfli-fldate into
header,
        planfli-cityfrom planfli-cityto into connections,
        actfli-seatsocc into flights.
* Extracting data
select * from planfli.
  extract connections.
  select * from actfli.
    extract flights.
  endselect.
endselect.
* Sorting the extracted data
sort.
* Reading the extracted data and calculating statistics
loop.
  at new planfli-carrid.
    write: / planfli-cityfrom,
             planfli-cityto,
             sum(actfli-seatsocc).
  endat.
endloop.
```

In the first part of this example, the fields representing the sort criteria are inserted into the field group header. This is a special field group for the sort criteria that must always be present under this name. Moreover, the relevant data structures for the data containers are inserted into the field groups connections and flights. Next, the containers are written to virtual memory by extract commands in nested select loops. The sort criteria of the field group header are automatically filled by each extract statement. Then the extracted data is sorted by a simple sort statement. Finally, all extracted data is read in a loop. The sum of occupied seats is calculated for all flights of each carrier, since it is enclosed by the corresponding at/endat statements.

NOTE

The set of extracted data need not be mentioned by name at the sort command, since a program can only extract one set of containers at runtime. Blocks of at and endat commands can be used in the same way as for internal tables (see the preceding paragraph).

You can also sort the extracted data in a different order:

```
sort by actfli-fldate planfli-carrid planfli-connid.
loop.
  at new actfli-fldate.
    write / sum(actfli-seatsocc)
  endat.
endloop.
```

In contrast to the situation with internal tables, the group logic of the at/endat block follows the order determined by the sort command. This order can be different from the static structure of the field group header, so extracting data provides more flexibility.

Nested Tables

All the statements you can use to manipulate internal tables also apply to nested tables. Remember that tables within a record or a table don't have a header line, so you have to use the versions of table commands without header lines.

For instance, suppose you have data in nested tables about connections and flights as follows:

```
data: begin of flight,
        fldate    like actfli-fldate,
        seatsocc  like actfli-seatsocc,
      end    of flight.
data: begin of conn_fli occurs 10,
        carrid    like planfli-carrid,
        connid    like planfli-connid,
        cityfrom  like planfli-cityfrom,
        cityto    like planfli-cityto,
        flight    like flight occurs 10,
      end of conn_fli.
```

You can read all lines of the outer table `conn_fli` as well as of the inner table `flight` using nested loops:

```
loop at conn_fli.
  write: / conn_fli-carrid,
           conn_fli-connid,
           conn_fli-cityfrom,
           conn_fli-cityto.
  loop at conn_fli-flight into flight.
    write: / flight-fldate,
             flight-seatsocc.
  endloop.
endloop.
```

Note that these nested tables offer an alternative method to the extraction technique for dealing with hierarchical sets of data. In general, internal tables are more flexible.

A Quick Review

Here is a quick review of some of the topics we covered in this chapter:

- Internal tables with an arbitrary number of lines and dynamic storage management are an important feature of ABAP/4.

- If you use a table without a header line, you must provide a separate record to hold the contents of the current entry.

- You can fill a table using the commands select, append, insert, and move.

- The estimated size of a table is documented in the defining data statement by the Occurs Parameter. You don't need to worry about how much memory to allocate.

- The sort command sorts a table according to specified fields.

- By using loop/endloop with a where clause, you can read a set or subset of lines sequentially.

- You can change lines using insert, modify, or delete. The refresh command deletes all lines of the table.

- Group logic is supported by various at/endat blocks in loops.

- Extracting data provides a method for handling groups of assorted data of different structures and for statistical figures related to the grouped data.

- Nested tables can be handled like flat ones, but a separate record must be provided to work with the inner tables.

Now that you have seen how to manipulate the content of internal tables, the upcoming chapter shows you operations for changing database tables, however, it would be tedious to work with nested tables of three or more levels.

CHAPTER

T H I R T E E N

13

Updating Database Tables

- How to insert, change, or delete entries in database tables

- Working with single or multiple entries

- Specifying the table name statically or dynamically

In the preceding chapters, you have seen how to read data from database tables, how to fill internal tables with this data, and how to manipulate the contents of internal tables. These operations are the first steps of a typical application program. In many cases, you will also want to store new or changed data in the database so that this data can be retrieved at a later time. For example, in a dialog program for booking flights, you will first read data about possible flights with free seats. Then the end user will choose a connection and enter the name of the customer and the necessary information (e.g., number of seats). Finally, you will store the booked flight in the database so that the reserved seats cannot be booked by other people.

In this chapter, we'll introduce you to the basic commands for changing database tables: insert, update, modify, and delete. All of these commands are part of the Open SQL subset in ABAP/4. The other important Open SQL command is the select statement, which is used to read entries from database tables as explained in Chapter 11. The four commands allow you to change a single table entry and to change a set of lines contained in an internal table. For example, if a dialog program changes information about a single customer only, you will use the single entry version of the respective Open SQL command. On the other hand, if you have to maintain a lot of customer data at once, you will probably have the data in an internal table in your program. Then you can loop through this internal table and change each corresponding entry of the database table individually. As an alternative, you can use the Open SQL commands, which execute all changes in a single step. At runtime, the second solution (using a mass change) is faster than the first one with the loop. In addition, your program code will probably be easier to read.

For all Open SQL commands changing database tables, the name of the database table can also be set dynamically at runtime. These dynamic versions of the Open SQL commands are especially useful for system programs dealing with any number of database tables.

Inserting New Lines Using the Insert Command

Suppose you want to add new customers to the travel agency database. To do this you would use the insert command as described below. If you add a single customer only, choose the version for single lines. You can establish a mass insert with the version of the insert command that takes the new data from an internal table.

Inserting a Single Line

If you need to insert a single new line into a database table, you use the keyword insert. The simplest way to add a single line is to use the short version of the command, where the new data comes from the default work area defined via the tables keyword:

```
tables customers.
customers-id = '12345678'.
customers-name = 'Brown'.
insert customers.
if sy-subrc <> 0.
  write 'entry already exists'.
endif.
```

Note that the field customers-id has been defined in the Dictionary as primary key. This means that the new entry is inserted only if the table does not already contain an entry with the same value for the key field. Otherwise, the statement is not carried out, and the system return code sy-subrc is set to a non-zero value.

Instead of using the default work area for the new data, you can also enter a new line from an extra record that you specify after the addition values of the insert command. This is helpful when the default work area is already used for a different entry and you don't want to save this entry in a temporary copy. Here is the code you would write to enter a new customer named Green into the customer database using this method:

```
tables customers.
data my_customer like customers.
my_customer-id = '11111111'.
my_customer-name = 'Green'.
insert into customers values my_customer.
```

In this example, customers is the default work area and my_customer is an extra record that is filled with the new data and used as a source for the insert command.

These two methods work just fine for single entries, but there are times when you have a whole group of new lines for a database table. We'll discuss that situation next.

Inserting Multiple Lines

Imagine now that you have to insert a whole bunch of new customers into your customer database table. It would be tedious and time consuming to do this record by record using the methods we described above. By using an internal table that has the same structure as the database table to which you want to add the new entries, you can insert the new set all at once via the addition from table:

```
tables customers.
data all_customers like customers occurs 100
                      with header line.
all_customers-id    = '12345678'.
all_customers-name  = 'Brown'.
append all_customers.
all_customers-id    = '11111111'.
all_customers-name  = 'Green'.
```

```
append all_customers.
all_customers-id    = '12121212'.
all_customers-name  = 'White'.
append all_customers.
insert customers from table all_customers.
```

So what happens in this code? The developer creates an internal table called all_customers, makes it like the customers table, fills the internal table with the new data, and then inserts the contents of that internal table into the database table in a single step. In a real-life application program, the internal table is usually filled by a select command and changed in a loop after the select. Then the contents can be stored in the database table all at once.

This mass insertion only succeeds if all entries from the internal table are inserted. If at least one entry has been rejected by the system because of a duplicate one with the same primary key, then the whole operation is canceled and the program ends with a runtime error.

You can avoid this runtime error by using the addition accepting duplicate keys. When you use this addition, an entry that would duplicate an existing key value is not inserted into the database table, but the remainder of the new entries are inserted without any problem. You can detect this situation because the system return code is set to a non-zero value when at least one line with a duplicate key has been rejected. In practice, you will often check with a select command whether new entries already exist. However, if it is very unlikely that duplicate keys will occur, the mass insert with the addition accepting duplicate key is much faster than a combination of select and insert statements. In contrast, if duplicate keys are likely to occur, you should first find the duplicate keys using select and then insert the unique entries.

You can also add new entries using the `modify` command, which is explained below under the heading "Modifying an Entry with the `modify` Command." This command is useful when you want to add or change an entry whether or not a duplicate key occurs.

In contrast to internal tables, you cannot specify a "line number" or "table index" where you want to insert a new entry in a database table. This is because the question of "where" a line is inserted is left to the database management system of the relational database. From the application's point of view, questions like "Does this entry exist?" or "What is the content of the entry?" are important to answer, but questions like "How is the database table sorted?" or "Where is the physical location of an entry?" are not. This reflects the general philosophy of relational databases that only the content of a table entry is considered, but not its location within a table.

Changing Database Tables with the Update Command

You can change the contents of an entire entry in a database table using the `update` command, in a process much like that for adding a new line. The update command also has versions for changing a single entry and for multiple entries.

Updating a Single Entry

Using our travel agency example, suppose one of your customers moved and you need to change the name of her city. You could write the following code to do this:

```
tables customers.
customers-id = '12345678'.
customers-city = 'Village'.
update customers.
if sy-subrc <> 0.
  write 'entry not existing'.
endif.
```

As in the insert command at the beginning of the chapter, the short version of the update command uses the customers work area defined by the tables declaration to hold the changed information. The entry specified by the key fields is changed only if the table already contains an entry with the same key value. For example, if there is no entry with key 12345678, then the system doesn't add this new information to the table, and the system return code sy-subrc is set to a value other than zero.

Updating Multiple Entries

As with the insert command, you can change a whole group of table entries in a single step using the addition from table. For example, if you have an internal table with changed customer information, you can proceed as follows:

```
tables customers.
data changed_customers like customers occurs 50
                        with header line.
select * from customers into table changed_customers
     where city = space.
loop at changed_customers.
  changed_customers-city = 'City unknown'.
```

```
    modify changed_customers.
endloop.
update customers from table changed_customers.
```

In this example, the internal table `changed_customers` contains all customers whose city has not yet been specified, (e.g., the new customers Brown, Green, and White from the sections above). To make entries with missing cities more visible, the text *City unknown* is inserted for each such customer. This mass update only succeeds if all entries from the internal table already exist in the database table. Otherwise, the system return code `sy-subrc` is set to a non-zero value.

In the previous example, all entries from the database table `customers` with missing city texts are filled in an internal table. Then the city texts are changed in the internal table, and the new entries are stored back in the database. ABAP/4 provides a much more efficient alternative for performing such simple change operations in database tables, as shown in the following example, which performs the same change on the database as the previous example:

```
tables customers.
update customers set   city = 'City unknown'
                 where city = space.
```

In this example, the new value for the `city` field is set to *City unknown* after the addition `set` is inserted into the `update` command. As with the `select` statement, you can specify a `where` clause in the corresponding `update` statement to determine the set of entries that are to be changed.

NOTE If you need a reminder about how the `select` statement and its `where` clause work, turn back to Chapter 11.

Obviously, the program code using `set` and `where` after `update` is easier to read than the previous example with the internal table. In addition, the `update` command with `set` and `where` is faster at runtime than the combination of `select`, `loop`, and `update`. However, you can only perform arithmetic operations after the addition set, but you cannot perform complex operations, call a subroutine, or send a dialog box to get new data. Thus, using an internal table is more powerful and also provides you with a snapshot of the database table.

Here's another example: using our travel agency database, if an airline suddenly canceled a flight and you rebooked your customers on a new flight, you might change all fields containing the old flight date to the new date:

```
tables bookings.
update bookings set    fldate = '19991231'
              where carrid = 'ABC'
              and    connid = '1234'
              and    fldate = '19991230'.
```

Here, all bookings for flight 1234 of carrier ABC are changed from flight date 12/30/1999 to 12/31/1999.

Modifying an Entry with the Modify Command

Often, you don't know in advance whether or not an entry already exists in the database table. You could get this information by using the select command, and then execute the insert or update commands afterwards, depending on the return code. The modify command provides an elegant version to combine the insert and update statements into a single one. Suppose you wanted to change the city name for the record of the customer with the ID number 12345678, but you aren't sure whether there's even a record for that customer yet. You could write the following code to do this:

```
tables customers.
customers-id   = '12345678'.
customers-city = 'Village'.
modify customers.
```

At runtime, the ABAP/4 system checks whether the table entry specified by the key fields (in our example, a customer with the ID 12345678) already exists. Depending on the result, the entry is either inserted or updated. The system return code sy-subrc is not set.

Like the insert and update commands, you can modify a set of table entries in one step using the addition from table:

```
tables customers.
data all_customers like customers occurs 50
                    with header line.
select * from customers into table all_customers
      where city = space.
all_customers-id   = '04295119'.
all_customers-name = 'Gray'.
append all_customers.
loop at all_customers.
  all_customers-city = 'City unknown'.
  modify all_customers.
endloop.
modify customers from table all_customers.
```

In this example, all customers whose city fields are empty are read into internal table all_customers. Then a new customer is added, the contents of the city field is changed to *City unknown*, and the whole internal table is stored in the database.

It is primarily a matter of programming style whether you prefer modify or insert/update. If duplicate keys are unlikely, you will probably use the insert command. In this case, a mass insert is the fastest solution at runtime. Otherwise, using modify simplifies the program source code, since the system makes the decision whether to insert or update for you.

Deleting Database Table Entries Using the Delete Command

You can delete individual or multiple entries from database tables using the `delete` command. In the same way as for `insert`, `update`, and `modify`, you can specify the entries via the default work area, an internal table, or a `where` clause:

```
tables customers.
data all_customers like customers occurs 50
                    with header line.
select * from customers into table all_customers.
customers-id = '12345678'.
delete customers.
delete customers from table all_customers.
delete from customers
      where id like '1%'.
```

Here, the first `delete` statement deletes the customer with ID 12345678, which is contained in the work area `customers`. The second `delete` uses the data from the internal table, and the last one deletes all customers with a leading 1 in their ID.

NOTE   Remember that the percentage sign (%) is used in Open SQL statements to mask any sequence of characters.

The system return code `sy-subrc` is set to a value other than zero if the specified entries don't exist. However, in the mass deletion using an internal table, it is zero only if all lines of the internal table have had corresponding entries in the database before the delete operation.

Dynamic Table Names

All of the commands we've discussed above also have a dynamic version, where the name of the database table is set at runtime. For example, you can just set this code up, and then the end user can type in the name of a table on which to perform the operation. To that end, you can enclose the table name in parentheses:

```
data table_name(30).
table_name = 'CUSTOMERS'.
insert (table_name) from table all_customers.
```

In this nutshell example, the table name is set immediately before the insert. In practice, the table name is often set by another program and transferred through an interface.

A Quick Review

Here is a review of some of the topics we covered in this chapter:

- The basic Open SQL commands are insert, update, modify, and delete.

- All Open SQL statements support changing a single line or a set of lines contained in an internal table.

- You can set the name of the database table dynamically, if it is enclosed within parentheses.

In the next chapter, we'll discuss techniques to export complex data objects (e.g., nested internal tables) to temporary storage or to persistent tables.

CHAPTER

F O U R T E E N

Exporting and Importing Complex Data Objects

- **Working with complex data objects across different programs**

- **Using the ABAP/4 Memory as an interface**

- **Saving complex data objects in the database**

I n ABAP/4, complex data objects can be built using records and internal tables. For example, as we described in Chapter 4, you can use a nested internal table, where each line consists of fields and other internal tables. Until now, we dealt with internal tables only as temporary objects, which only lived as long as the program where they were defined was running.

The operational data of applications in an R/3 system is stored in relational database tables. It can be read or changed using the Open SQL statements we discussed in the previous chapters, such as `select` and `insert`. In contrast to internal tables, these tables always have a flat structure—that is, a table entry consists of fields, but it cannot contain another table. The contents of local program objects like records or internal tables can be stored in tables of a relational database, but first they must be converted to flat structures. Using the `export` and `import` commands, you can also save and read these complex objects in the database in a single step.

Using the `export` and `import` statements, you can combine many complex objects of different types and store and retrieve them as a single object. To avoid unnecessary conversions, you need to be able to import complex objects that have a different number of subobjects, and the `export` and `import` commands allow you to do this.

You can use the `export`/`import` technique to export complex objects to both temporary storage for the current program (the storage is called *ABAP/4 Memory*) and to persistent database tables. Exporting to the ABAP/4 Memory is helpful when you need to transfer many complex objects to called programs, possibly across several calling levels. If you use the second alternative—that is, you create persistent complex objects with the export command—then you don't need to convert deeply structured tables into flat ones.

The export/import technique is especially useful when an application program uses data objects built from more than one table or containing nested internal tables. For example, you might always want to work with internal tables containing customer and booking information at the same time.

Using Temporary Storage

You can export a set of local data objects of your program to temporary storage by using the export statement with the addition to memory and with an identifier after the addition id. Using our travel agency example again, the code below shows how two internal tables named all_customers and all_bookings are exported in a single step as one cluster to a temporary storage area in main memory with the identifier CUSTBOOK (CUSTBOOK is the identifier for the cluster consisting of both internal tables):

```
data: all_customers like customers occurs 100,
      all_bookings  like bookings  occurs 1000.
export all_customers all_bookings
       to memory id 'CUSTBOOK'.
```

The tables of the cluster CUSTBOOK can be retrieved all in one step using the corresponding import statement:

```
data: all_customers like customers occurs 100,
      all_bookings  like bookings  occurs 1000.
import all_customers all_bookings
       from memory id 'CUSTBOOK'.
if sy-subrc ne 0.
  write 'Import failed.'.
endif.
```

In this example, the contents of the internal tables all_customers and all_bookings from the cluster CUSTBOOK are copied to the internal tables of the program with the same name.

NOTE You can also use other names for the data objects to which the tables from the Memory are imported. This is explained in detail below under the heading "Using Local Names for Memory Objects."

The identifier after the addition id can have a maximum of 32 characters. The export command always overwrites the content of the area specified by the identifier in ABAP/4 Memory, so that the actual contents of the cluster in the Memory are the pieces of data you exported with the last export command. The system return code sy-subrc has a non-zero value after the import statement if the ABAP/4 Memory does not contain an object under the specified identifier, and you get a message telling you that there's nothing to import.

TIP You can combine any number of objects in an export or import statement. In particular, you can export or import fields, records, internal tables, and nested internal tables to the same cluster.

Skipping Objects

In an import statement it is not necessary to retrieve the same number of objects as have been exported; that is, you can skip objects of a cluster. For example, using the same cluster as in the example above, you could import only all_bookings, but not the all_customers table:

```
data all_bookings like bookings occurs 1000.
import all_bookings
       from memory id 'CUSTBOOK'.
```

The names of the exported objects (in our example, the contents of CUSTBOOK) and the names in the import statement (in the code above, all_bookings) determine which objects are imported. If an object specified after import has not been exported (is not contained in the Memory object), nothing will be imported for this object. For example, using the cluster CUSTBOOK again, you could use the following program code:

```
data: new_customers like customers occurs 50,
      all_bookings  like bookings  occurs 1000.
import new_customers all_bookings
      from memory id 'CUSTBOOK'.
```

Here, the internal table new_customers remains empty after the import, because we didn't export a table with this name before. You will see in the next section how to use a different name for an object with the same structure.

NOTE When the structures of objects with identical names disagree between export and import, a runtime error occurs.

Using Local Names for Memory Objects

You can also switch the names using the addition to after each object of the import list. For instance, if the internal table to which you want to import the all_bookings table is called new_bookings in the importing program, it can be filled as follows:

```
data new_bookings like bookings occurs 50.
import all_bookings to new_bookings
      from memory id 'CUSTBOOK'.
```

What happens here? A new internal table named new_bookings is declared with the data statement and filled with the all_bookings portion of the CUSTBOOK memory object, without the all_customers portion of that object.

You can switch the names in the export statement using the same technique:

```
data: old_customers like customers occurs 10,
      old_bookings  like bookings  occurs 20.
export all_customers from old_customers
       all_bookings  from old_bookings
       to memory id 'CUSTBOOK'.
```

Here you are exporting the contents of old_customers to a table named all_customers, you are exporting the contents of old_bookings to a table named all_bookings, and you are placing both of the tables into the memory object named CUSTBOOK.

Clearing the Contents of Memory Objects

Using the free memory command, you can free a specified part of the Memory. If you omit the identifier, all parts of the Memory are deleted:

```
free memory id 'CUSTBOOK'.
```

In this example, the contents of the CUSTBOOK cluster are deleted. In addition, the cluster name CUSTBOOK itself is removed by the runtime system.

Working with Memory across Levels

ABAP/4 provides several techniques for calling programs. For example, a dialog program with input screens can be called from another program. The ABAP/4 Memory is retained across several levels of calling programs.

NOTE The details of calling a program are explained in Chapter 18 ("Running a Report") and Chapter 21 ("Transactions").

For instance, if you call a report using the submit command, the caller can export some data objects and the called report can import them. In the same way, data can be transferred to called transactions. The objects in the ABAP/4 Memory live as long as the calling program is active. Other user sessions of the same end user and other end users have their own Memory, and data cannot be transferred among them. So when an end user opens a new session by choosing System ➤ Create Session on any screen of the R/3 system, a new Memory is created by the runtime system.

Using Persistent Tables

In practice, the temporary storage of the ABAP/4 Memory explained above is often used to transfer data objects between programs calling each other. The contents of the ABAP/4 Memory are lost after the program runs. When you want to save these objects for later use in a new program, you export them to permanent storage as explained in this section.

Exporting and Importing to a Database Table

Using a similar syntax to the export and import commands for ABAP/4 Memory, you can store and read complex objects in database tables. For instance, the same internal tables as above are exported to the database table zflight using the following program code. The difference is that here we use a database table to hold the data objects we import and export, where above we used a Memory object to hold the data objects.

```
tables zflight.
data: all_customers like customers occurs 100,
      all_bookings  like bookings  occurs 1000.
export all_customers all_bookings
        to database zflight(zz) id 'CUSTBOOK'.
```

In another program, you can then import the internal tables all_customers and all_bookings as follows:

```
tables zflight.
data: all_customers like customers occurs 100,
      all_bookings  like bookings  occurs 1000.
import all_customers all_bookings
        from database zflight(zz) id 'CUSTBOOK'.
if sy-subrc ne 0.
  write 'Import failed.'.
endif.
```

The two characters zz enclosed in parentheses after the table name are used as an area identifier for a section of that table. This area identifier is obligatory, and the runtime system concatenates it with the identifier after id. The two character ID zz identifies a section of the table zflight to which these internal tables are being exported and from which they will be imported. Since the database table zflight is used as a container for data objects, you as an application developer need not worry about how this container is structured internally—the ABAP/4 runtime system does the administration. This is an advantage of the export/import technique, since otherwise you would have to break up complex data objects into flat lines of database tables. You can choose any two character identifier.

As explained in the next section, you can use different tables for export and import. In practice, different application areas use different tables (e.g., all flight reservation programs use the table zflight). The system return code sy-subrc has a non-zero value after the import statement if there isn't an object in the database table under the specified identifier.

In the same way as for export and import via ABAP/4 Memory, only the names of the objects are important. Thus, you can skip objects during the import step and names can be switched using the addition to (after import) or from (after export).

Skipping an object enables you to add or delete a new data object without affecting existing ones. For example, if you had two internal tables all_customers and all_bookings belonging to an identifier in the first release of your flight reservation program, you could add a new table all_carriers in the next release. In the new release, an import would look like this:

```
data: all_customers like customers occurs 100,
      all_bookings  like bookings occurs 1000,
      all_carriers  like carriers occurs 200.
import all_customers all_bookings all_carriers
       from database zflight(zz) id 'CUSTBOOK'.
```

When a program in the new release imports a cluster CUSTBOOK that has been exported in the old release, the import statement retrieves the contents of all_customers and all_bookings, and the internal table all_carriers remains empty.

Defining a Database Table for Importing and Exporting

You can define your own database table just to use for carrying out export and import statements.

NOTE   When defining a database table for export and import, proceed as explained in Chapter 5 under the heading "Creating a Table or Structure."

The table must have a standardized structure satisfying the following rules:

1. If the table contains Client-specific information, the first field must have the name mandt (Dictionary type clnt).

2. The field relid (Dictionary type char, length 2) contains the area identifier.

3. The two fields mentioned in steps 1 and 2 are followed by table-specific key fields that must all be of type char. They contain the key of the complex objects, which is specified after the addition id in the export/import statements. The developer can freely define this key.

4. The field srtf2 (type int4) is the last field in the key. Its values are assigned automatically through export/import operations.

5. The field in step 4 is followed by any number of fields that are not affected by the export statement. You can assign values to these fields explicitly before an export. These fields are used for administrative data like the date of the export or the name of the user.

6. The data part ends with the fields clustr (type int2) and clustd (type lraw). Both fields are assigned values automatically through export/import operations.

The table's clustd field contains the compressed contents of the complex objects. If they do not fit into one entry, they are automatically distributed over several table entries. The width of the table structure (including all key and data fields) should have a value of approximately 3800 or 7600 bytes. Depending on the database management system, larger table entries may be admissible. An example of an export/import table is shown in Figure 14.1.

Although the identifier after the id addition in the export and import statements appears as a single long character field, you can also specify

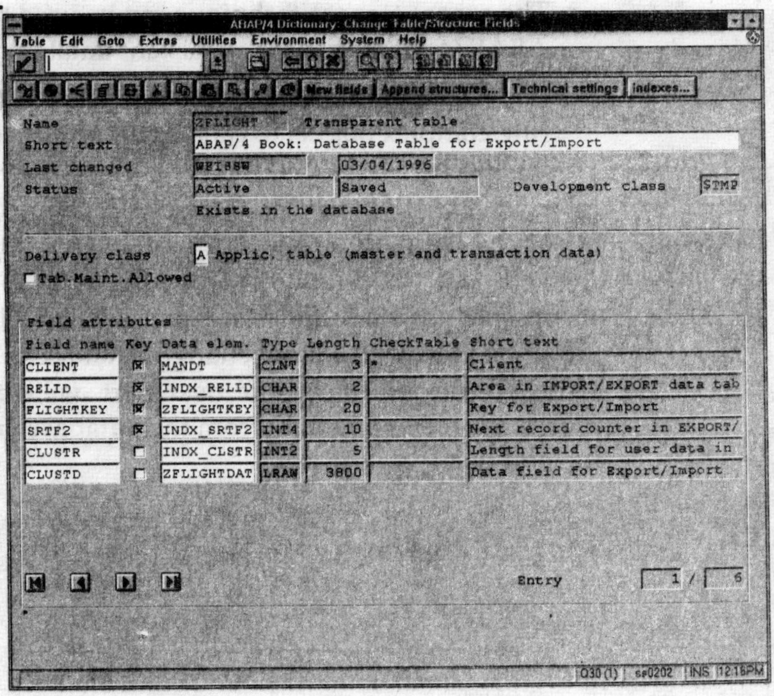

FIGURE 14.1:
The database table ZFLIGHT for export and import

a structure. Define a Dictionary include structure for as many table-specific key fields as you need to use according to the third rule above, and use this structure via a `tables` declaration to overlay the identifier.

A Quick Review

Here is a short review of some of the topics we covered in this chapter:

- The `export` and `import` commands save and read complex objects in a single step. These objects can consist of fields, records, and internal tables of arbitrary structures, so you can avoid having to convert deeply structured objects to and from flat structures.

- The export/import technique can be used to store data in the ABAP/4 Memory or in persistent database tables.

- The ABAP/4 Memory can be used as an interface for transferring complex objects to called programs even across several calling levels.

- Persistent complex objects can be changed without the need to convert already existing ones.

In this part of the book, we discussed the elementary methods of ABAP/4, how to read and change database tables, and how to work with internal tables. In the next part, we'll focus on special techniques for retrieving data from the database and how to present it to the end user.

PART V

Reporting

CHAPTER

F I F T E E N

Retrieving Data Using Logial Databases

- ■ **What is a Logical Database?**

- ■ **Using select commands or Logical Databases**

- ■ **Making complex selections**

- ■ **Working with many tables**

- ■ **Benefits of Logical Databases**

In this chapter, you'll learn what *Logical Databases* are and how they support you in creating a *report* in ABAP/4—i.e., a program that retrieves data from the database, groups it together according to different criteria, and presents it in the form of a list on the screen. First, we'll discuss different methods for accessing data from one or more database tables and for displaying the results.

Creating a Report

You can create a report using any of the following three methods; each one has its special advantages:

- You can define the layout with the *ABAP/4 Query* tool, which generates the program code automatically.

- You can write the program code of the report using a Logical Database, which simplifies database access.

- You can code the report using elementary select commands.

With the *ABAP/4 Query* tool, you design the list layout, and the program code is generated automatically. The ABAP/4 Query is easy to use, and its flexibility enables you to create reports very quickly. You'll probably prefer to use queries whenever standard requests must be fulfilled. However, you should choose one of the other alternatives when you need the full flexibility of the programming language.

NOTE   Working with the ABAP/4 Query is covered in Appendix B.

Logical Databases provide procedures for retrieving complex data from databases. In addition, a Logical Database automatically creates a standard user dialog with a selection screen for specifying selections. The concept of Logical Databases distinguishes ABAP/4 from many other programming languages. Technically speaking, a Logical Database is not a database in the sense of a Database Management System (DBMS), but rather a re-usability concept to simplify and encapsulate the retrieval of data. In particular, the following services are encapsulated by a Logical Database:

- Freely composed views of the data in the database

- A selection screen with a comfortable user dialog for the specification of selection criteria

- The details of the database access (e.g., the particular form of select statements)

Similar to other situations of re-use of data or methods, the advantages of Logical Databases become obvious when a large number of reports are involved: using a Logical Database, you can simultaneously improve the above-mentioned properties of many reports. For instance, making the database access faster in one Logical Database improves the runtime performance of all reports using it.

Finally, if there isn't an appropriate Logical Database for your report, you have to choose the third alternative: using the select commands, as described in Chapter 11.

Comparing Two Sample Reports

The advantages of Logical Databases can best be demonstrated by comparing two reports that produce identical lists but use different methods:

- Using select statements
- Using a Logical Database and get events

For these two examples, Table 15.1 illustrates the contents of the customers table.

TABLE 15.1: The sample contents of the customers table

id	name	city	telephone
00000001	Edwards	Small Town	654-321-1234
00000002	Young	Village	333-444-2222
00000017	Smith	Big City	717-161-5151
87654321	Edison	Fort Myers	111-111-1111

Table 15.2 illustrates the contents of the bookings table.

TABLE 15.2: The sample contents of the bookings table

carrid	connid	fldate	bookid	customid	order_date
ABC	1000	19991230	001	00000017	19990101
ABC	1234	19991230	002	00000002	19991229
ABC	1234	19991231	005	00000017	19990101
AIR	0007	19990430	010	87654321	19990101
AIR	1234	19990901	011	00000002	19990101
xyz	0006	19990606	008	00000001	19990101
xyz	0007	19990505	007	87654321	19990101

Suppose you want to print a list of all customers who will depart after 05/01/1999 and have made flight reservations on 01/01/1999. The list should also contain the flight dates and will look like Figure 15.1.

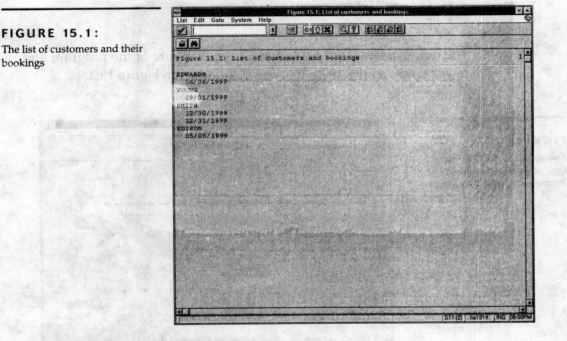

Writing the Program Code

You can create this list with a program using two nested `select` loops:

```
tables: customers, bookings.
select * from customers.
  write / customers-name.
  select * from bookings
        where customid = customers-id
        and   fldate    > '19990501'
        and   order_date = '19990101'.
    write at /3 bookings-fldate.

  endselect.
endselect.
```

The same list will be produced by the following program that uses an appropriate Logical Database and two get events:

```
tables: customers, bookings.
get customers.
   write / customers-name.
get bookings.
   write at /3 booking-fldate.
```

The name of the Logical Database is an attribute of the program and must be set on the attributes screen as shown in Figure 15.2.

FIGURE 15.2:

Filling in the name of the Logical Database in the attributes screen for a report

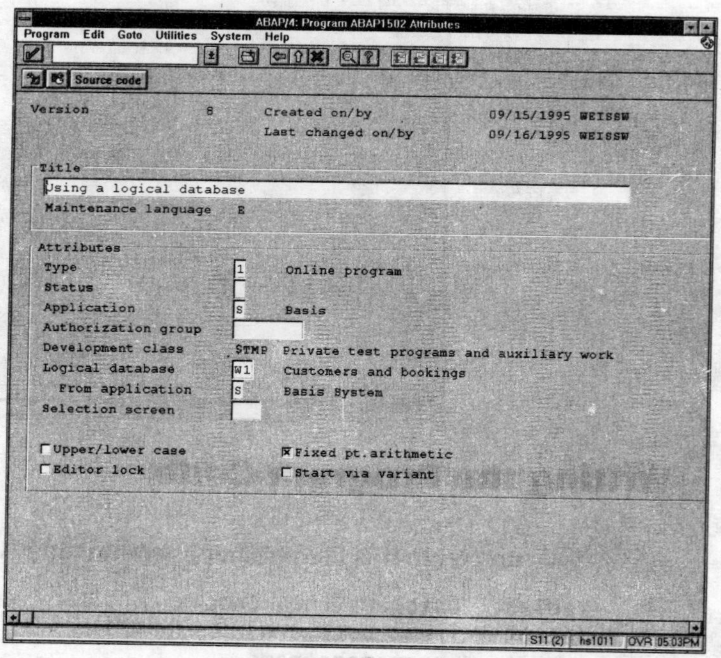

NOTE   If you need a refresher on how to maintain the attributes of a program, look in Chapter 3 under the heading "Setting the Program Attributes."

The R/3 system contains approximately 150 Logical Databases for almost all business applications. For example, Logical Databases are available for the following purposes:

- Financial accounting documents
- Cost centers
- Purchasing documents
- Stock movements
- Orders

Specifying Selection Options

Starting the second of the above sample programs, a selection screen will appear where you can enter the appropriate selections. First, enter the lower bound for the flight date and the order date (see Figure 15.3).

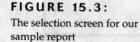

FIGURE 15.3:
The selection screen for our sample report

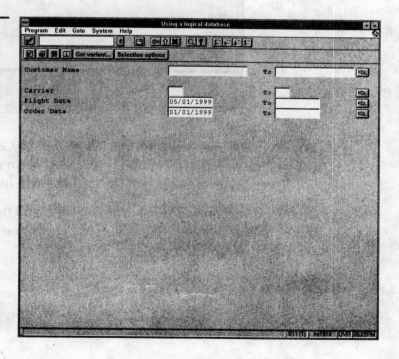

By clicking on the button Selection Options on the selection screen, you can specify the Greater Than operator for the flight date (see Figure 15.4). If you set this option, the search will be for numbers greater than the lower bound.

FIGURE 15.4:

Specifying selection options for the sample report

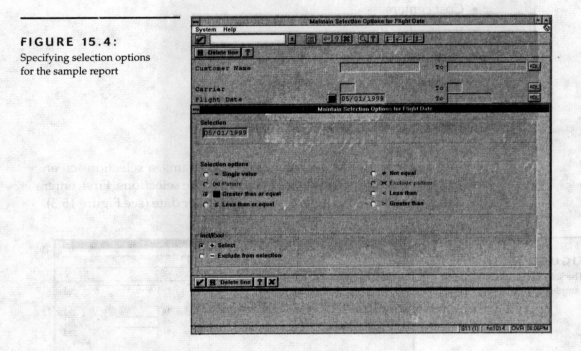

When you confirm this step by clicking on the Copy button, the existence of the selection condition is indicated by an icon beside the value you specified on the selection screen, as shown in Figure 15.5.

When the selection criteria have been filled and the report is executed, the required list of customers and flight dates is presented on the screen (see Figure 15.1).

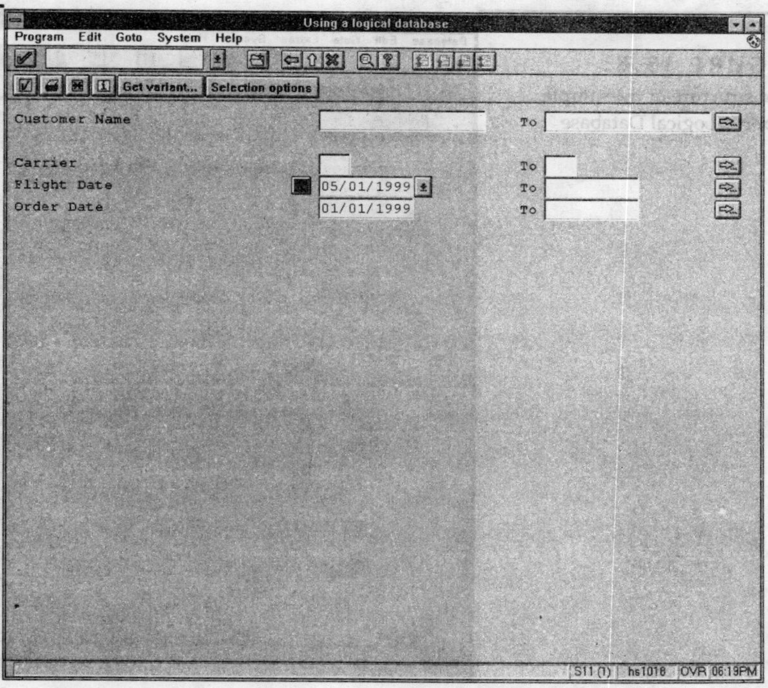

USING LOGICAL DATABASES

FIGURE 15.5:

The completed selection options screen for the sample report

```
┌─────────────────────────────────────────────────────────────────────┐
│                     Using a logical database                    ▼ ▲ │
│ Program  Edit  Goto  System  Help                                 ◈ │
│ ✔            ↑  ⬚ ⇦⇧✕  ⬚?  ⬚⬚⬚                                      │
│ ⬚⬚⬚⬚ Get variant...  Selection options                              │
│                                                                      │
│  Customer Name                [            ]      To [         ] ⬚   │
│                                                                      │
│  Carrier                      [    ]             To [    ]      ⬚   │
│  Flight Date            ▣ [05/01/1999]±          To [         ] ⬚   │
│  Order Date               [01/01/1999]           To [         ] ⬚   │
│                                                                      │
│                                                                      │
│                                                                      │
│                                                                      │
│                                                                      │
│                                                                      │
│                                                                      │
│                                                                      │
│                                                                      │
│                                                   S11 (1) hs1018 OVR 06:19PM │
└─────────────────────────────────────────────────────────────────────┘
```

Processing Data at get Events

The get events of the previous example are processed by the ABAP/4 runtime system in a tree-like order: first, the statements of the event get customers are executed for each customer. Then, the selected bookings are processed one by one—that is, the event get bookings is released for each booking of the current customer. This small example demonstrates that the runtime order of the get events is determined by a tree-like hierarchy of the Logical Database (see Figure 15.6). As you can see in the figure, the customers table belongs to the first level of the structure (and is at the top of the screen), and the bookings table belongs to the second level (as indicated by the line that branches down to it).

FIGURE 15.6:

The structure of the sample report's Logical Database

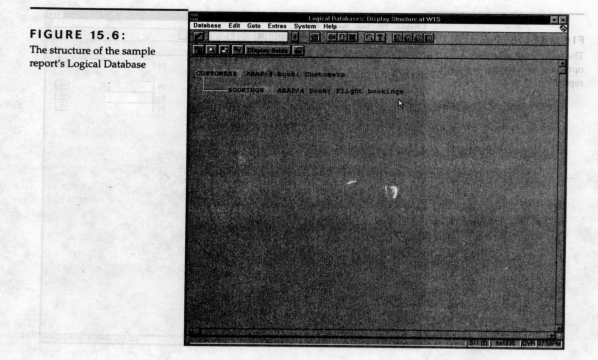

> **NOTE** ⚬ The role of this tree structure will be explained in this chapter under the heading "The Runtime Order of get Events."

Using select **Commands or Logical Databases**

There are some significant differences between the above two sample programs:

- The second report does not have nested select loops, but rather two get events.

- The foreign key relationship between the tables bookings and customers is reflected in the where condition of the first example, but it does not appear in the source code of the second, where it is only modeled in the tree structure of the Logical Database. This structure also determines the order of get events at runtime.

- The selection criteria (flight date and order date) are coded in a where condition of the first example, and they are set dynamically by the end user in the second. So, the selection criteria can be adjusted without changing the source code in this case.

Each report can have only one Logical Database. Conversely, the same Logical Database can be used by many reports, and this is one of the main reasons for using this technique: Logical Databases simplify and encapsulate the data retrieval; you need not specify technical details like where clauses of select commands when you create a report with a Logical Database. Every extension or improvement to a Logical Database immediately applies to all reports using it.

NOTE The advantages of using a Logical Database are discussed below in this chapter under the heading "Benefits of Logical Databases."

Making Complex Selections

The selection criteria of the second example report above show two important cases:

- Single values (e.g., order date = 01/01/1999)
- Lower bounds (e.g., flight date > 05/01/1999)

Moreover, the following selection criteria can also be specified by the end user:

- Intervals (e.g., names between *A* and *M*)
- Generic values (e.g., name with leading *S*)
- Negations of all the above
- Combined selection criteria (e.g., telephone numbers between *111-000-0000* and *666-999-9999* but not equal to *333-444-2222*)

The end user can enter any of these selection criteria. The selected data will be read from the database without changing one line of code.

NOTE   In Chapter 18, we will discuss Variants that enable you to start a report with a set of predefined selection criteria. It is also possible to define report-specific selection criteria that appear on the selection screen below the database specific selections. This technique will be explained in Chapter 16.

The Runtime Order of Get Events

The second example from the previous section demonstrates that the flow of control at the different get events is completely determined by a tree-like hierarchy, which is defined in the Logical Database. In principle, this tree structure reflects the foreign key relationship between the corresponding tables. In the preceding example, the tree structure of the Logical Database contains at least the parent-child relationship between the tables customers and bookings.

It is important to understand that a report based on a Logical Database is not processed sequentially at runtime. Its flow of control is instead determined by the tree structure of the Logical Database. All statements after a get statement and before the next event belong to this get event. They are processed whenever a corresponding table entry has been read by the Logical Database. Thus, the order of the get events in the source code of the report is completely irrelevant. The get events can be thought of as modularization units that are called by the system.

Working with Many Tables

In many cases, a report uses more than two tables. For example, suppose that four tables, ztab1–ztab4, are related as follows:

- ztab1 is a check table of ztab2.
- ztab2 is a check table of ztab3 and ztab4.

Using select statements, these foreign key relationships are reflected in the different nesting levels:

```
select * from ztab1 where ...
  select * from ztab2 where ...
    write 'ztab2'.
    select * from ztab3 where ...
      write 'ztab3'.
    endselect.
    select * ztab4 where ...
      write 'ztab4'.
    endselect.
  write 'end of ztab2'.
  endselect.
endselect.
```

The tree structure of a Logical Database contains a helpful model of the relationships between the tables (see Figure 15.7).

FIGURE 15.7:

The structure of a complex
Logical Database

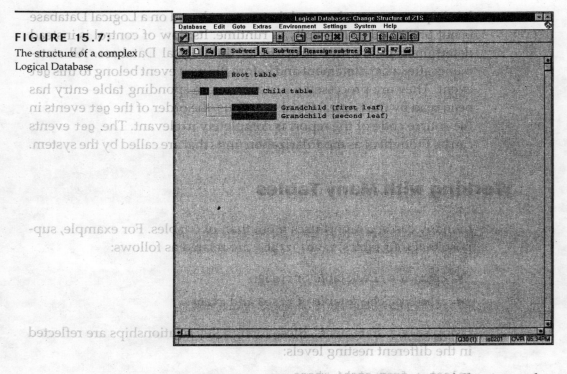

FIGURE 15.7:

The structure of a complex
Logical Database

A report using that Logical Database would have the following code:

```
get ztab2.
  write 'ztab2'.
get ztab3.
  write 'ztab3'.
get ztab4.
  write 'ztab4'.
get ztab2 late.
  write 'end of ztab2'.
```

This report produces the same output list as the preceding one with
nested `select` statements. Note that the event `get late` is processed
when the corresponding entries of all tables hierarchically below `ztab2`

have been processed. At runtime, the entries of table ztab1 are read, even if the corresponding get event does not occur in the report. In general, a table with the structure of the Logical Database will be read at runtime in the following cases:

1. The table corresponds to a get or get late event of the report.

2. The table is an ancestor of some table occurring in 1.

In the previous example, tables ztab2, ztab3, and ztab4 belong to the first case and table ztab1 to the second. According to these rules, a subtree of the structure is not processed (that is, the table entries are not read from the database) if no corresponding get event occurs in the report.

NOTE   The tree structure of a Logical Database is a freely defined logical view of several database tables. In most cases, the parent-child relationship reflects a foreign key relationship, but the tables are sometimes only related via an additional subroutine of the Logical Database, thus establishing the connection at runtime.

Using Outer Joins

Logical Databases also allow you to establish an outer join of different database tables even if that procedure is not supported by the underlying DBMS. Consider again the first example in this chapter, and suppose that you want to display the bookings of customers who are flying after 06/30/1999. Suppose that you also want to start a mailing action for those customers who have not booked for that period, so you are also interested in the names of these customers. If you have a report based on a Logical Database, you need not change the source code of the report, but can instead simply enter the lower bound 06/30/1999 for the flight date on the selection screen and then get the desired list.

Clearly, the same list can be achieved using nested `select` statements, where the changed selection criteria must be adjusted at the appropriate `where` clauses. However, you will only obtain the inner join of the tables `customers` and `bookings` if you use views defined in the Dictionary. For example, you will not get the name of customer Edison, who did not book in that period.

Designing It Yourself

You can also design your own Logical Database using the Object Browser of the ABAP/4 Development Workbench. Basically, you have to define the structure, the relevant selection criteria, and the database access routines. Later, you can use that Logical Database in every report.

> **TIP**
>
> You'll find detailed online information about how to create and maintain Logical Databases in the *ABAP/4 User's Guide*. You can access this guide from the initial screen of the ABAP/4 Development Workbench by selecting Help ➤ Extended Help.

Two Events: start-of-Selection and end-of-Selection

Sometimes, you want to perform some work before the first entry of the database is selected. ABAP/4 offers the event `start-of-selection`, which is processed after the user has specified all selection criteria and before the first `get` event. This event is also assumed as a default for the first event in your report, if you forgot to introduce it.

The event `end-of-selection` is processed after the last `get` event. A typical example of both of these events looks like this:

```
start-of-selection.
  write / 'Start'.
get bookings.
  write: / at 3 booking-fldate.
end-of-selection.
  write / 'Finished'.
get versus select
```

Benefits of Logical Databases

Using `select` statements, you can create a report without referring to a Logical Database in the attributes of the report. However, you get the following advantages by using Logical Databases:

- You need not take care of the key fields and the foreign key relationships between the tables in question.

- A selection screen with appropriate selection criteria is automatically created. You don't have to define this in the report (see also Chapter 16).

- You don't need to program standard authority checks in the report, since they are executed by the Logical Databases (for example, for reading documents or accounts).

- Improvements to the database access methods of a Logical Database immediately improve the performance of all reports using it.

You will certainly design a report with `select` statements, if there isn't a Logical Database with the required tables (which is not very likely, since there are Logical Databases for almost all kinds of business applications). However, if many reports are reading data from the same tables and you cannot find a corresponding Logical Database, you should consider introducing one using the ABAP/4 Development

Workbench. In practice, creating a Logical Database is similar to the design of commonly used function units—that is, Logical Databases can be considered as modularization units for commonly used data retrievals and selection screens.

A Quick Review

Here is a quick review of some of the most important topics we covered in this chapter:

- Logical Databases simplify and encapsulate the database access methods of reports and create a standard user dialog.

- You can easily specify complex selection criteria on the selection screen.

- The relationships between different tables are reflected in the tree structure of Logical Databases.

- A report using a Logical Database is structured according to the get events that are related to tables of the tree structure of the Logical Database. The get events are triggered by the ABAP/4 runtime system.

- A report need not use all get events corresponding to some table of the tree structure. At runtime, only the necessary tables are read by the Logical Database.

- The events start-of-selection and end-of-selection are processed before and after the data has been read during the get events.

In the next chapter, you'll see how to define input fields on the selection screen and handle the user input later; e.g., to check whether the end user has entered valid data.

CHAPTER

SIXTEEN

The User Interface of a Report

- Creating input fields for the selection screen

- Working with Parameters and Select-Options

- How to deal with complex selection criteria

- Using selection screen events

C H A P T E R

S I X T E E N

I f you run a report with a Logical Database, you will first see a selection screen where you can enter the selection criteria. By executing the report using these selections, the Logical Database reads the specified data from the physical database tables and triggers the corresponding get events.

> **TIP** Take a look at Chapter 15 to see how an end user can enter selections for a report with a Logical Database and how the data is read from database tables.

In this chapter, you'll learn to define report-specific input fields on the selection screen, which appear below the predefined selection criteria of the Logical Database. You will also see that the selection criteria from the selection screen help you to write simple and efficient where clauses of select statements. In addition, we'll discuss several events that are useful to set default values of the selection criteria or to check the validity of the user input. The events and language commands of this chapter help you to design a comfortable user interface for reports.

> **NOTE** Designing the user interface of a program that changes data is covered in Chapter 19.

ABAP/4 offers two kinds of input fields on the standard selection screen:

Parameters | Single fields

Select-Options | Internal tables for complex selection criteria (useful for dynamically specified where conditions in select statements)

The definition of Parameters or Select-Options automatically declares the corresponding input fields on the selection screen as well as the data structures of the program for holding the user input.

From a technical point of view, both the selection criteria of the Logical Database and of the report are declared in the same way. The report-specific selection criteria are always displayed below the database-specific selections on the selection screen. The database-specific Parameters and Select-Options can also be used in the report.

Defining Parameters for the Selection Screen

The definition of Parameters is almost identical to the definition of fields by using the data declaration. Using our trusty travel agency example, the code below would define the Parameters for the city, the flight date, and for an additional check box on the selection screen:

```
parameters:
  p_city like customers-city,
  p_fldate like actfli-fldate default '19991231',
  p_flag as checkbox default 'X'.
```

These Parameters will appear on the selection screen as shown in Figure 16.1.

CHAPTER 16

FIGURE 16.1:

A travel agency selection
screen with several Parameters

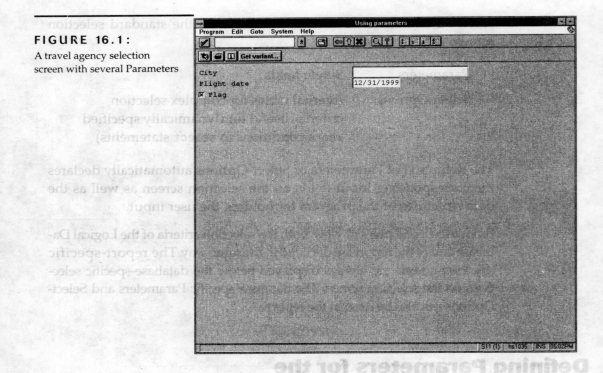

At the same time, every Parameter defines a field that can be used in
the report like a normal field defined by data. When the end user enters data in the input field of a Parameter on the Selection Screen and
runs the report by clicking on the Execute button, the input will be
available in the Parameter field. For example, if an end user types *Big
City* in the input field of Parameter p_city, the following condition will
be true:

```
if p_city = 'Big City'.
* Input value of Parameter p_city is "Big City".
endif.
```

When an end user enters values in a report-specific Parameter or Select-Option, this does not automatically restrict the amount of data retrieved by the Logical Database. If you, the developer, want to access the user input in a `select` statement, place the Parameter in the `where` clause of this `select` statement like an ordinary field.

Because of their role as interface objects on the selection screen, there are some minor differences between the syntax of the `data` and `parameters` declarations:

- Initial values are declared using the addition `default` instead of `value`. They are not mandatory.

- Structured Parameters (similar to records defined by `begin of`/`end of`) are not supported.

- Parameters of type `c` (character) and length one can be displayed as check boxes via the addition `as checkbox` in the `parameters` definition. If you click on the box, the value of the Parameter is equal to X; otherwise it is `space`.

Every Parameter also has an associated language-dependent label that is displayed on the selection screen before the input field (for example, *Flight date* for `p_fldate`). This label can be changed or translated without changing any source code. You can create or change a language-dependent label from the ABAP/4 Editor screen by choosing the menu function Goto ➤ Text Elements. The use of language-dependent texts will also be discussed in Chapter 17.

Working with Select-Options

Select-Options are used for complex selections (for example, a range of values, generic patterns, and even combinations of these). Select-Options appear with two standard input fields on the selection screen where the user can specify standard selections (single values or intervals). Further criteria (for example, multiple selections) can be entered on a separate screen. The ABAP/4 runtime system automatically stores the user input in an internal table of a standardized structure. This internal table can be used for dynamically specified where conditions of select statements.

Using Select-Options in select Statements

Select-Options fit into where clauses of select statements (see Chapter 11). For instance, if the user is interested in a list of all customers with names that begin with letters between *A* and *M*, the program might look like this:

```
tables customers.
select-options s_name for customers-name.
select * from customers
        where name in s_name.
   write / customers-name.
endselect.
```

After starting the report, the user can enter the selection criteria as shown in Figure 16.2.

In this case, the select statement will determine the number of all corresponding customers from the database table customers. In other words, the above report is equivalent to the following one:

```
select * from customers
        where name between 'A' and 'M'.
   write / customers-name.
endselect.
```

The Select-Option enables you to specify additional selection criteria without changing the source code. Suppose you select all customers whose last names begin with *E*, the customer named *Smith*, and all customers with names between *M* and *Shultz*. Then click on the Complex Selections button to the right of the input field for customers. In the

FIGURE 16.2:

Select-Option with an interval

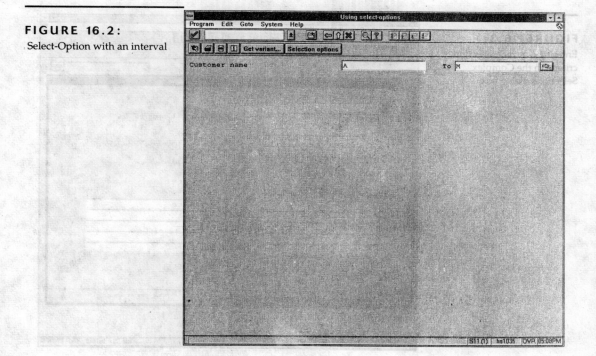

dialog box that follows, type **E*** and **Smith** in the Single Value Selections section, and type **M** and **Shultz** as the range boundaries in the Ranges section, as shown in Figure 16.3. If you click on the Copy button, all selections of this dialog box are copied to the Select-Option and the standard selection screen is sent again, where you can enter more options or run the report. You can also enter different selections by clicking on the Selection options button.

Select-Options are often used by Logical Databases. For instance, the selection criteria of the sample report from Chapter 15 are defined by the associated Logical Database (see Figures 15.3–15.5).

FIGURE 16.3:

Entering complex selection
criteria in the Complex
Selections dialog box

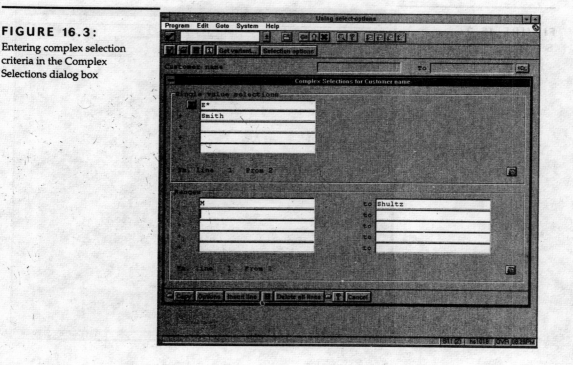

Every Select-Option contains a reference to some field (e.g., `customers-name`) after the addition `for`. Usually, this field is compared with the Select-Option in the `where` clause. The connection between Select-Options and `where` clauses of `select` statements is used by Logical Databases themselves when data is retrieved from physical database tables. Select-Options in `where` clauses are also very useful when you need information from a table not contained in the Logical Database. In particular, you can create a report reading all data without a Logical Database. Select-Options can be used in other SQL statements in the same fashion, and they can also be transferred to a report that is called via the `submit` command (see Chapter 18).

In addition to SQL statements, you can also use Select-Options in the where clause of a loop at an internal table:

```
tables customers.
data all_customers like customers occurs 100
                   with header line.
select-options s_name for customers-name.
select * from customers into table all_customers.
loop at all_customers
      where name in s_name.
  write / all_customers-name.
endloop.
```

In this example program, the internal table `all_customers` is filled with customer data from the database table `customers`. Then, only those lines of the internal table are displayed which are selected by the end user in the Select-Option s_name.

Like Parameters, every Select-Option also has an associated language-dependent label on the selection screen (for example, "Customer name" for the Select-Option s_name). That label is displayed before the input fields of the Select-Option, and the label can be changed and translated without affecting the source code. The labels of Select-Options and Parameters are accessible from the ABAP/4 Editor by choosing Goto ➤ Text Elements.

The Internal Structure of Select-Options

In the above cases, Select-Options function as black boxes in where clauses of `select` statements; that is, you need no special knowledge about the internal structure of a Select-Option to be able to use them. Sometimes, the internal structure of a Select-Option and the contents of the internal table must be treated explicitly. For example, when you want to fill the Select-Option with several default values before the selection screen is sent, you can append one or more lines to the internal table of the Select-Option.

The internal table corresponding to a Select-Option always has four columns: `sign`/`option`/`low`/`high`. For the example shown in Figure 16.3, it contains the entries shown below:

sign	option	low	high
I	CP	E*	
I	EQ	Smith	
I	BT	M	Shultz

Each line of this table corresponds to one selection condition. The first two columns (`sign` and `option`) specify the particular type of condition:

- `sign = I`: "Including" (a positive choice)
- `sign = E`: "Excluding" (a negative choice)
- `option = BT`: "BeTween" (e.g., a name that begins with a letter between *M* and *Shultz*)
- `option = CP`: "Contains Pattern" (e.g., a name that begins with an *E*)
- `option = EQ`: "EQual" (e.g., name = Smith)
- `option = GE`: "Greater than or Equal to" (e.g., id >= 1)

The last two columns (`low` and `high`) contain the values used for the comparison. These columns refer to the corresponding field of the table (for example, `customers-name`); in other words, they have the same type and length. The `high` field is only used for intervals (`option = BT`), and it is left initial otherwise.

At runtime, the internal table associated with a Select-Option is automatically filled with the user input on the selection screen. You can also fill this table with default values before the selection screen is sent. You can work with this table as with any other table (for example, to check the user input for correctness or plausible values). These checks are best executed at one of the events of the selection screen explained in the next section. For instance, you can send an error message to a selection screen if some condition is not satisfied. The selection screen is then displayed again, and the corresponding fields are ready for new input data.

Selection Screen Events

ABAP/4 offers different events to set values on the selection screen and to obtain user input at the selection criteria:

- `initialization`: processed immediately when starting the report and before processing the selection screen
- `at selection-screen output`: processed before the contents of the selection screen are displayed
- `at selection-screen on p/s`: processed after the user has specified the Parameter p or Select-Option s
- `at selection-screen`: processed after the user has specified all selection criteria

The event `initialization` is processed only once, but the event `at selection-screen output` is processed whenever the user presses ↵ while the selection screen is active. After all these events have been processed, ABAP/4 continues with the event `start-of-selection` and then with the top-most `get` event of the tree structure of the Logical Database (see Chapter 15).

Checking User Input

The events at selection-screen and at selection-screen on p/s are particularly useful to check user input for invalid or implausible values. For instance, if a ZIP code is entered that has fewer than five characters, a user of the following report will see a message indicating that the ZIP code is invalid:

```
parameters pcode like customers-postcode.
data parameter_length type i.
at selection-screen on pcode.
  parameter_length = strlen( pcode ).
  if parameter_length < 5.
    message e001 with 'ZIP code invalid'.
  endif.
```

Every error message processed at the event at selection-screen immediately stops the execution of the report and displays the selection screen again. All selection criteria can be changed. If the addition on p/s is also used, only this Parameter or Select-Option will be ready for input. The text of the error message can be created or changed by double-clicking, and it is stored in a language-dependent system table.

NOTE   Message handling will be explained in Chapter 20.

Improving Performance

You can make a report faster if you forbid unrestricted queries on database tables. For large tables, unrestricted queries can take a long time. To avoid this, you can determine the number of lines in a Select-Option that is used in the where clause of a select statement. If the internal table associated with the Select-Option is empty, the user has not specified any selection, and you can send an error message using the following code:

```
select-options s_name for customers-name.
```

```
data number_of_selections type i.
at selection-screen on s_name.
  describe table s_name lines number_of_selections.
  if number_of_selections = 0.
    message e001 with 'Please specify name of customer'.
  endif.
start-of-selection.
  select * from customers
            where name in s_name.
    write / customers-name.
  endselect.
```

The same technique can be applied if a report is based on a Logical Database with database-specific Select-Options or Parameters. The corresponding data objects are also available in the report, and they can be read or changed in the same way as report-specific selection criteria. For example, if a Logical Database has a Select-Option s_id for the field customers-id, the report can check this as follows:

```
at selection-screen on s_id.
  describe table s_id lines number_of_selections.
  if number_of_selections = 0.
    message e001 with 'Please specify ID of customer'.
  endif.
get customers.
  write / customers-name.
```

Note that the Select-Option s_id is available in the report without having been defined explicitly. It is provided automatically when you use the Logical Database. You can display a Logical Database from the Object Browser screen if you choose Single Objects and enter the name of the Logical Database on the screen that follows. First, you see the structure of the Logical Database. Second, you can switch to the selections by selecting Goto ➤ Selections.

The events of the selection screen are useful for designing a user interface. In practice, a comfortable user dialog is very important for the acceptance of a program.

A Quick Review

Here are some of the most important points we covered in this chapter:

- Parameters are single input fields on the selection screen that can be used like ordinary data objects in the report.

- Select-Options support the specification of complex selection criteria. They define internal tables that can be used in the `where` clause of SQL-statements.

- Select-Options can also be treated like normal internal tables with the standard structure `sign/option/low/high`.

- Events of the selection screen (e.g., at `selection-screen`) can be used to check the user input as well as for the definition of default values.

Now you have seen how to design a comfortable user interface of a report. In the next chapter, you'll learn how to create a program with drill-down facilites and advanced list features.

CHAPTER

SEVENTEEN

Drill-Down and Advanced List Features

- **How the program reacts to a double-click**

- **Defining the user interface of a report list**

- **Working with pop-up screens**

- **Foreign language support for reports**

Suppose you want to create a report that provides an overview of all customers of a travel agency. The end user may also be interested in detailed information about individual customers, but the overview should not be crowded with too many details. To this end, you can design an ABAP/4 report with drill-down facilities, so that when the user double-clicks on a customer name in the overview list, the city and the phone number of the selected customer are also displayed.

In general, drill-down facilities are very useful in many situations where a report starts by offering condensed information to the user. In subsequent steps, the user can navigate through the application data and gain more detailed information about selected subjects.

To implement these drill-down facilities, you need to provide the user with things like push buttons and menu functions. In addition, the program must react to the user's actions (for example, pressing a button).

Because ABAP/4 is an event-driven language, it is easy to create programs with a lot of drill-down facilities. A program reacts to a user's double-clicking on a list via the event at line-selection. When the user presses a button or function key, the event at user-command is triggered in the program and that event does different things, depending on what the programmer has specified. For example, you'll learn in this chapter how to display another list (called a *stacked list*) or a pop-up screen by means of a window or call screen command.

The set of menus, menu functions, toolbar buttons, and push buttons that the user interacts with is called a *GUI status*. A GUI status is the key element of the user interface of an ABAP/4 program; the transmission of a user action (clicking a mouse button, pressing a function key, etc.) to a program via one of the functions of the GUI status establishes one direction of that user interface. Conversely, a GUI status can be set by a program dynamically, providing a modification of the available functions on a screen at runtime.

An important consideration for the developer is the ability to make the features and interface of a program useful to people in different countries. The language-dependent text elements of ABAP/4 make it easy to develop applications for international use, since text elements can be translated without changing or generating programs. Language-dependent text elements are used whenever a text is printed or displayed on a screen, and they appear in the language the user specified when logging on. In this chapter, you'll see how to define language-dependent page headers, selection screen text, and text symbols for write statements.

Drill-Down Features

ABAP/4 provides some interactive events on lists such as at line-selection (double-click) or at user-command (pressing a button). You can use these events to move through layers of information about individual items in a list. For example, in an overview of all customers of a travel agency, users may also want more details about individual customers, and drill-down facilities allow them to double-click on a customer's name to display that customer's city and phone number. If users then double-clicked on a field in that record, they would open yet another window.

Double-Clicking: at line-selection

User actions (double-clicking, clicking on buttons) trigger events in the ABAP/4 program. The most important drill-down method is the double-click, which corresponds to the event at line-selection. By default, this event is also triggered by pressing F2. Double-clicking is the way most users will navigate through a program, and it is an essential tool in the user interface. The following small example illustrates the use of the event at line-selection for a response to a double-click:

```
start-of-selection.
  write 'basic list'.
at line-selection.
  write 'New list after double-click'.
```

The new list created by the write commands of the event at line-selection is displayed on a screen that overlays the original list (called the *basic list*), which is produced at the event start-of-selection. The new list is pushed onto a list stack, and so is called a *stacked* list.

> **TIP**
>
> A stacked list is displayed on a full-size screen unless you have specified its coordinates using the window command, which is explained in this chapter under the heading "Pop-Up and General Screens."

The basic list is not deleted when the new list is created, and you can return to it using one of the standard navigation functions: clicking on the Back button (or pressing F3) or on the Cancel button (F12). In either case, the stacked list is *popped*—that is, it is thrown away by the runtime system. Clicking on the standard Exit button (F15) always brings you back to the selection screen of your report, deleting the whole list stack.

> **NOTE**
>
> ABAP/4 supports developers with a built-in set of standard navigation functions on a report list: Back, Cancel, and Exit.

Hotspots are elements you can use to suggest possible actions to users. A hotspot is a list area where the mouse pointer appears as an upright hand symbol. When a user points to that area (and the hand cursor is active), a single-click does the same thing as a double-click. You can create a hotspot in a list by inserting the addition `hotspot on` into a `write` command. For example, in our travel agency list, you might want to create a hotspot at the customer's name, to prompt the user to click on that field:

```
tables customers.
start-of-selection.
  select * from customers.
    write / customers-name hotspot on.
  endselect.
at line-selection.
  write 'New list after single-click on a hotspot area'.
```

In this example, a basic list with all customer names is displayed. When the user points to a customer name, the cursor appears as an up-right hand. Then, a single-click has the same effect as a double-click and produces a stacked list.

NOTE   Hotspots are supported from R/3 Release 3.0C.

General User Action: at user-command

If a user pressed a function key or clicked on a button on the screen, the event `at user-command` occurs in the program. Each menu function, push button, or function key has an associated function code of length four (for example, *FREE*), which is available in the system field `sy-ucomm` after the user action. For example, you can display the number of free seats on a flight in a stacked list. In the code below, we have programmed it so that a function key or an on-screen button equals the "Free" query, and when the user activates that button, the system performs the calculation for free seats:

```
at user-command.
  if sy-ucomm = 'FREE'.
```

```
   free_seats = actfli-seatsmax - actfli-seatsocc.
   write: 'Number of free seats:', free_seats.
endif.
```

You can associate a function code of length four (in our example: *FREE*) with a button or function key on screen in a *GUI status*.

> **NOTE** Creating a GUI status from the Object Browser is explained in this chapter under the heading "Defining a GUI Status."

You can set the GUI status in a program using the `set pf-status` command. Activating a GUI status restricts the menu functions available for user interaction to the set of functions defined for that status, and a GUI status is active until a new status is set.

Defining a GUI Status

To create a GUI status for an application you are designing, click on the Create button in the object list of the report on the Object Browser screen, select GUI Status from the dialog box that appears, and enter a name for the status (e.g., *FLIGHTS*). Then you are asked to enter a short explanatory text and to specify the status type. Since we are defining user actions on a list in our example, we'll choose the status type List as shown in Figure 17.1.

> **NOTE** We'll discuss GUI statuses of other types in Chapters 19 and 22.

After you click on the check mark to confirm your selections, the next screen contains the definitions of menus, menu functions, buttons, and function keys, as you can see in Figure 17.2.

FIGURE 17.1:

Creating a GUI status

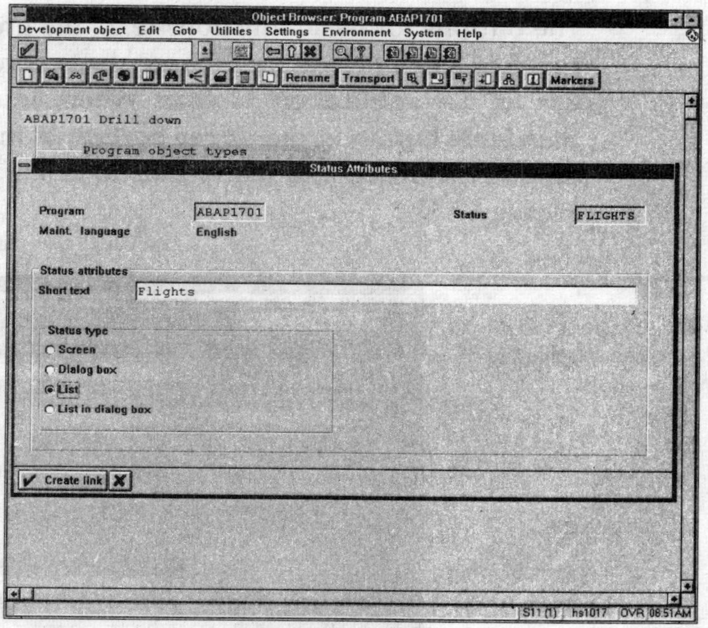

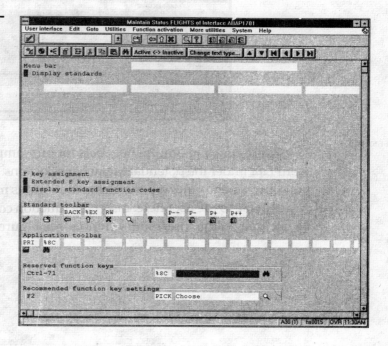

FIGURE 17.2:

Potential components for the GUI status of our sample report list

The buttons for basic functions (e.g., the green arrow for the function *BACK* or a printer for *PRI*) are always present in the system toolbar or the application toolbar. When you click on the Display Standards button in the upper portion of the screen in Figure 17.2, additional menus and menu functions are proposed, as shown in Figure 17.3.

FIGURE 17.3:

Additional standard menus for the sample report list

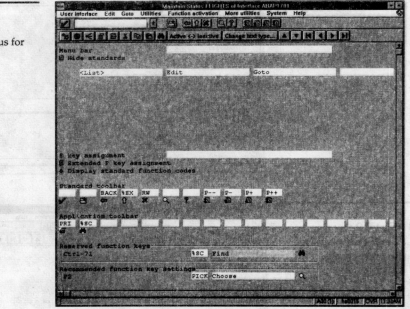

To create a function Edit ➤ Free Seats for our sample report, click on the word *Edit* under the potential Menu bar selections. This displays the Edit pull-down menu, and you can create the various menu options that will be available to the user here: insert the function code and the menu text by clicking on the Insert Entry button (see Figure 17.4).

FIGURE 17.4:
Defining the Edit menu
functions for our report

Insert Entry

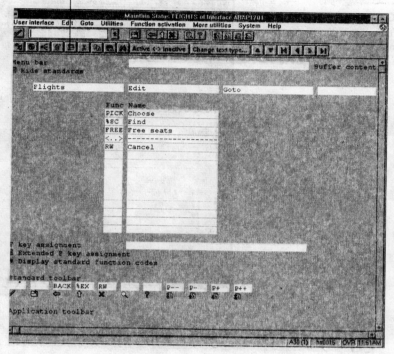

Associating a Function Key to a Menu Function

For quick access to menu functions, you can link function keys and tool-bar buttons or push buttons to menu functions. For example, the function code *FREE* is currently a menu item, but it can also be a function key. To do this, use the right scroll bar in the Maintain Status screen and type **FREE** after F5 in the Freely Assigned Function Keys section to create the function that corresponds to F5 on the keyboard (see Figure 17.5).

When you press ↵, the system automatically inserts the short text *Free Seats*. This text is also displayed when the user presses the right mouse button at runtime.

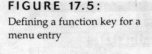

FIGURE 17.5:

Defining a function key for a menu entry

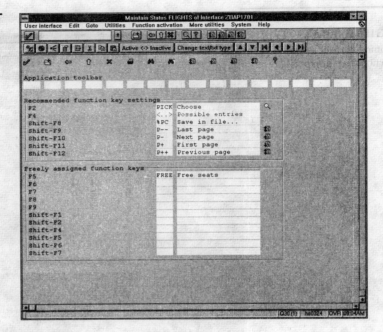

Designing the Application Toolbar

You can also individually design the application toolbar of your report list. Enter the function code *FREE* in one of the empty input fields under the text "Application toolbar" in the lower portion of the screen in Figure 17.6 to associate a push button with a function code. The corresponding short text *Free Seats* will be provided by the system as the name of the push button.

You can also add an icon to a button in the application toolbar. By choosing More Utilities ➤ Propose Icons, you get default suggestions that can be associated to a button. If you think that none of the suggested icons are appropriate, you can choose another icon from the set of predefined ABAP/4 icons. To do this, position the cursor on the function code (e.g., *FREE*) under the Application Toolbar section and

FIGURE 17.6:

Defining a push button

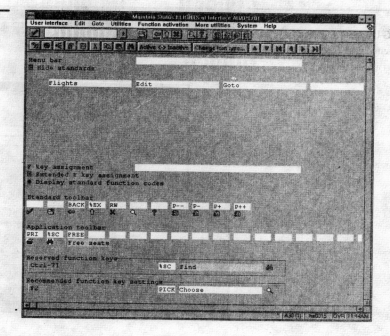

choose Change Text Type. In the dialog box that appears, you are asked to specify the text type. Choose Icon to get a dialog box, where an icon and its text can be specified (see Figure 17.7).

Modifying the Standard Toolbar

So far, we have discussed how to adapt the application toolbar, but we must also consider the standard toolbar. The standard toolbar contains standard icons. Some of these icons already have function codes that are used by the runtime system, such as the function code *BACK* (F3). Other icons are inactive and have no standard function key. You can associate function codes to these icons, as we did for the function code *SAVE* shown in Figure 17.8.

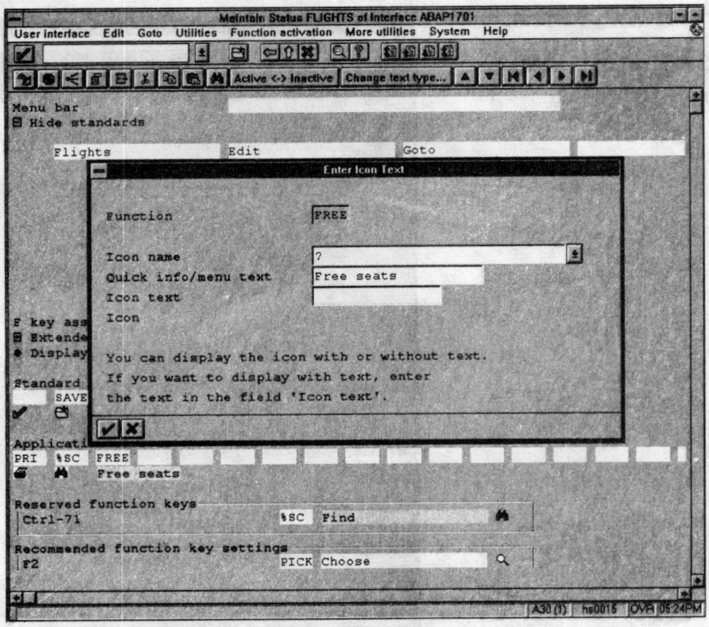

FIGURE 17.7:

Specifying an icon and its text

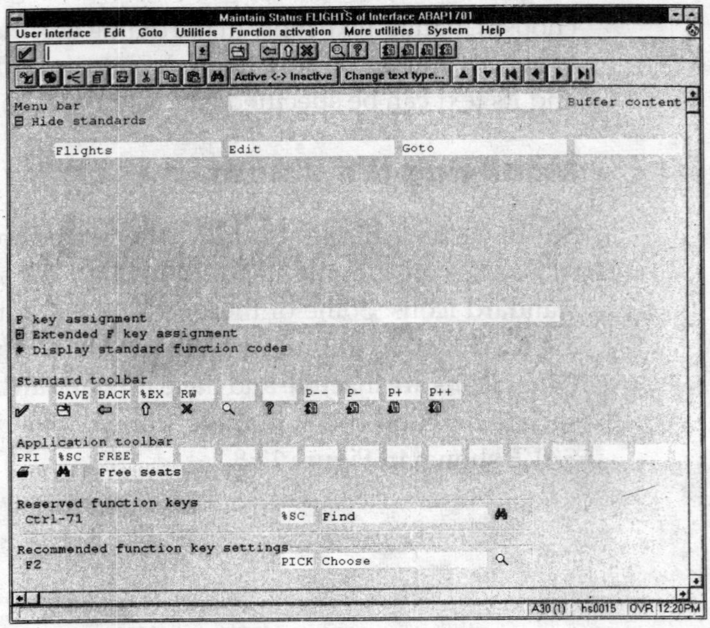

FIGURE 17.8:

Using icons from the standard toolbar

The function codes of standard navigation functions in the standard toolbar can also be redefined. In that case, however, you have to program the navigation explicitly using the techniques of general screens (see Chapter 19).

Working with Multiple GUI Statuses

As a general rule, the end user should always see the same set of menu functions in all screens of an application program. However, some of these menu functions are not applicable on every screen. For example, the *Free seats* function should only be available on the basic list of a report, but not on a stacked list with customer details. In a similar way, a dialog program changing data often has one screen for change operations, and another one for display only, where all change functions are visible but inactive. To achieve this, you need several GUI statuses for one program, where each GUI status represents a set of active menu functions.

You can use the Active <-> Inactive button to deactivate a menu function or push button. An inactive menu function is displayed in a gray color, and an inactive push button disappears. An active button of a GUI status is usable as long as this GUI status is active. Choose Goto ➤ Function List to get an overview of all function codes for the current program.

Once you've made all the selections for a GUI status, you'll need to activate it by clicking on the Generate button. A GUI status is set at runtime with the set pf-status command. The menu functions and buttons of a status remain visible until a new status is set. The name of the current GUI status is available in the system field sy-pfkey. In the following example code, one GUI status, *FLIGHTS*, is set initially for the basic list. A second status, *CHANGE*, is used for change operations, and a third one, *SHOW*, for display only, where all change functions like *SAVE* are visible but inactive.

```
tables actfli.
start-of-selection.
  set pf-status 'FLIGHTS'.
  select * from actfli.
    write: / actfli-carrid,
             actfli-connid,
             actfli-fldate.
  endselect.
at user-command.
  case sy-ucomm.
    when 'SWIT'.
      if sy-pfkey = 'SHOW'.
        set pf-status 'CHANGE'.
      else.
        set pf-status 'SHOW'.
      endif.
    when 'SAVE'.
*     Update customer information
      ...
  endif.
```

When the basic list of the report is displayed, the menus and toolbars of the status *FLIGHTS* appear as shown in Figure 17.9.

Pop-Up and General Screens

The examples above contain full-size stacked lists (that is, the same size as the original screen of the basic list). If you want to display a list in a pop-up screen, use the command window with the additions start-ing at x1 y1 and ending at x2 y2 to set the upper-left and the lower-right corners (see Figure 17.10).

```
at line-selection.
  window starting at 10 10
         ending    at 20 20.
  write 'This is my first window'.
```

The addition ending at of the window command can be omitted. In this case, the lower-right corner of the underlying full screen is used as de-limiter. Similar to stacked lists on full screens, a window automatically has standard navigation functions.

FIGURE 17.9:

A basic list with our sample
GUI status, FLIGHTS

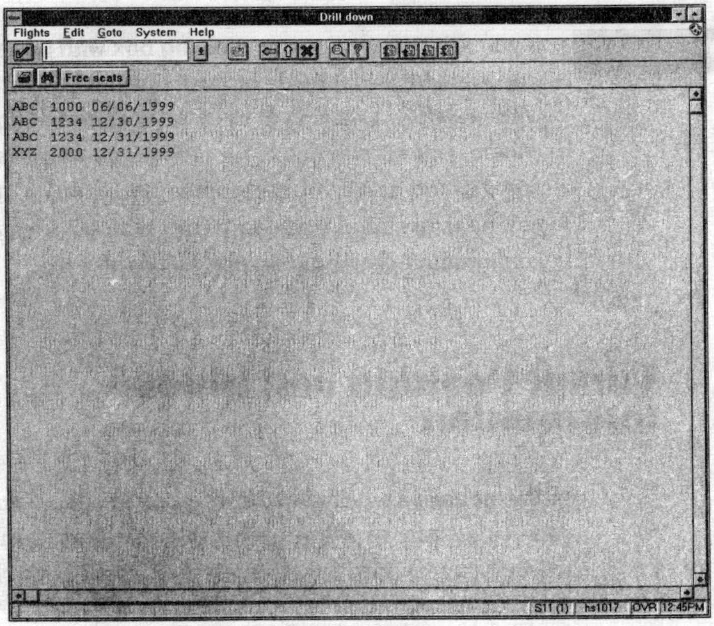

FIGURE 17.10:

A pop-up window on the
sample report list

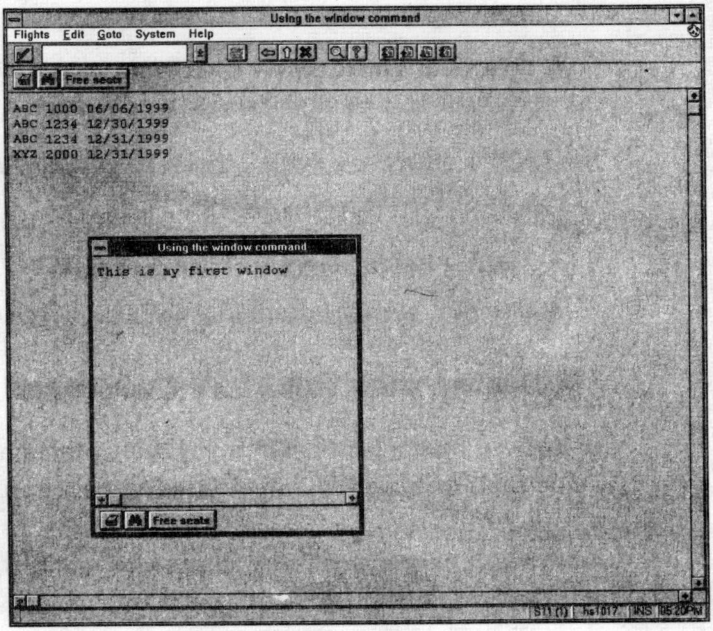

> **TIP**
>
> If you are going to design a dialog box with more general functionality (for example, input fields or push buttons), the statement `call screen` with additions `starting at x1 y1` and `ending at x2 y2` is a good choice. This screen has to be defined as we will explain in Chapters 19 and 22. The ABAP/4 Development Workbench also provides several functions to support standard user dialogs, such as functions for confirmation prompt dialogs (see Chapter 20).

Cursor Position and Hidden Information

At the events at `line-selection` or at `user-command`, the developer will often need information about the selected item on the list to retrieve additional detail data for display in a pop-up screen or stacked list:

1. Fields of the selected line (for example, `customers-id` or `customers-name`)

2. The field name where the cursor was when the user double-clicked and what the content of that field was.

ABAP/4 offers several methods to get this information. We will discuss the following alternatives:

- Hiding fields using the `hide` command.
- The `get cursor` command with the additions `field` and `value`.

Working with the `hide` Command

Suppose that a list of customers is displayed and the identifier of each customer is hidden by the following program:

```
tables customers.
data all_customers like customers occurs 100
     with header line.
```

```
start-of-selection.
  select * from customers into table all_customers.
  loop at all_customers.
    write / all_customers-name.
    hide all_customers-id.
  endloop.
```

The `hide` command temporarily stores the contents of the field `all_customers-id` at the current line in a system-controlled memory (called the *Hide Area*). At an interactive event, the contents of the field `all_customers-id` is restored from the Hide Area. Here's an example to help explain this: if a user selects a line, the field `all_customers-id` will contain the customer's identifier (e.g., *87654321*) and the program can work with this number :

```
at line-selection.

  read table all_customers
            with key id = all_customers-id.
  write / 'Customer detail information:',
         all_customers-name,
         all_customers-city,
         all_customers-telephone.
```

In this example, the Hide Area contains all customer identifiers. When the user double-clicks a line, the event at `line-selection` happens and the field `all_customers-id` contains the number of the selected customer. In the `read table` command, this number is used as a key to retrieve additional information from the internal table `all_customers`. The detail information is then displayed in a stacked list.

Working with the `get cursor` Command

The command `get cursor` is useful if hidden information is not sufficient to uniquely identify the selected line. For instance, this might happen when you create a list with different types of lines. The `get cursor` command returns the name of the field at the cursor position in a field specified after the addition `field`, and the value of the selected field in a field specified after `value`.

```
data: fieldname(30),
      fieldvalue like customers-name.
start-of-selection.
  select * from customers.
    write / customers-name.
  endselect.
at line-selection.
  get cursor field fieldname value fieldvalue.
  if sy-subrc = O and fieldname = 'CUSTOMERS-NAME'.
    write: 'Selected customer:', fieldvalue..
  endif.
```

NOTE   The content of the field `fieldname` is specified in uppercase letters even if you use the lowercase editor mode, since field names are always internally represented by uppercase letters.

Advanced List-Design Features

In this section, you'll learn about several language features that help you to design lists with advanced layout properties. First, you can efficiently create reports for international use with ABAP/4's language-dependent text elements. These text elements can be changed and translated without affecting the source code of programs. At runtime, the language-dependent texts such as page headers and labels on selection screens appear in the language the user specified when logging on. In addition, each text displayed by a `write` command can be related to a language-dependent text symbol.

Second, you can design special page headers or footers using the events `top-of-page` and `end-of-page`. These special events are triggered by the runtime system whenever the first line of a new page is written or the last line of the current page is reached.

Finally, you will learn how to use elementary language constructs for tabular lists. These language commands are demonstrated in a short example.

Language-Dependent Text Elements

Language-dependent text elements are very useful when a text is printed or displayed on the screen, since you can change and translate these text elements without affecting the program source. To create or change text elements, choose Goto ➤ Text Elements on the Editor screen. On the next screen, there are three choices: titles and headers, selection texts, and text symbols (see Figure 17.11).

FIGURE 17.11:
The Text Elements screen

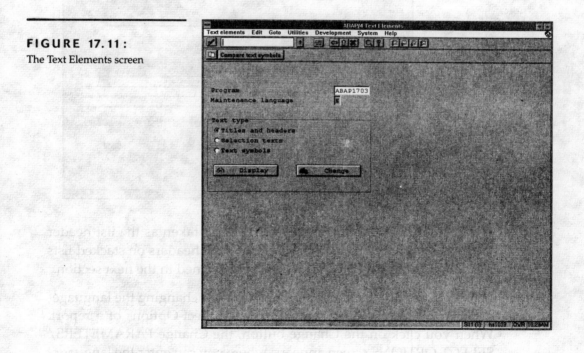

When you want to create or change the report title or the language dependent list headers, select the radio button Titles and headers and
click on the Change button. Every program has a title identical to the
short text that you entered in the program attributes. The list header
and the column headers of a report appear as page headers on the basic
list (see Figure 17.12).

FIGURE 17.12:

Report title, list header, and
column headers

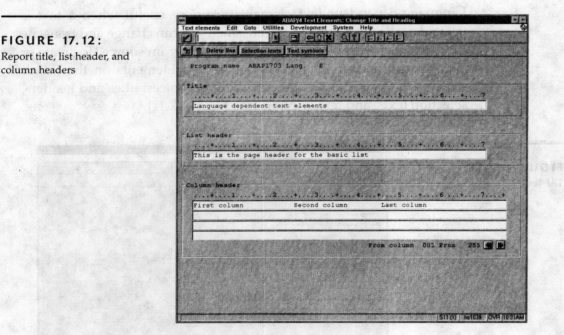

If no list header is defined, the report title is taken as the list header
that appears at the top of each list page. Page headers on stacked lists
are defined at the event top-of-page as explained in the next section.

Back to Figure 17.11, choose Selection texts for changing the language-
dependent labels for the Parameters and Select-Options of a report.
When you click on the Change button, the Change PARAMETERS/
SELECT-OPTIONS screen appears, where you can enter the language-
dependent labels for the selection screen (see Figure 17.13).

FIGURE 17.13:

Changing selection texts

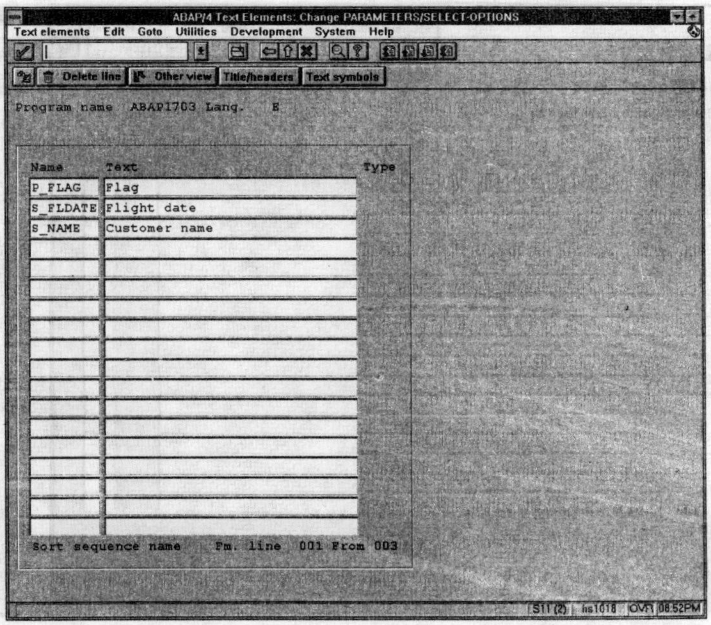

When your report has these selection texts, the selection screen will appear as shown in Figure 17.14. If you didn't specify a label for a Parameter or Select-Option, the technical name (e.g., S_FLDATE) will appear on the selection screen.

In the same way as for titles and headers or selection texts, you can also create or change text symbols. Text symbols can be associated with each literal at a write statement in a program source. For example, if you display a customer's address, you can associate text symbols with the strings *Name* and *City* as follows:

```
write: / 'Name'(nam), customers-name,
       / 'City'(cit), customers-city.
```

In this example, the text symbol nam is attached to the string *Name*, and cit to *City*. After you've written this code, if the user specifies Spanish as his or her language when logging on, the name and city fields would

FIGURE 17.14:

Selection screen with
language-dependent labels

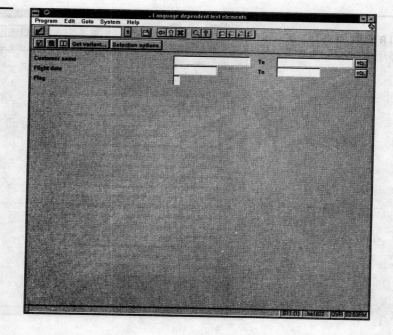

display the symbols for the Spanish equivalents of *Name* and *City*:
Nombre and *Ciudad*.

To create or change the text symbols nam and cit, double-click on the
respective symbol in the program source. The system automatically
takes the text literal in the program as default, which can be modified
later. For example, when you double-click on text symbol cit, a screen appears where you can change *Name* into *Customer name* (see Figure 17.15).

You can translate text elements via the Environment menu on the initial screen of the ABAP/4 Development Workbench. If a text symbol
has not been translated into the Logon Language of a user, the literal
in the write statement is displayed automatically. For example, the
word *Name* from the program's source code would appear instead of
Nombre.

ADVANCED LIST FEATURES

FIGURE 17.15:

Changing text symbols

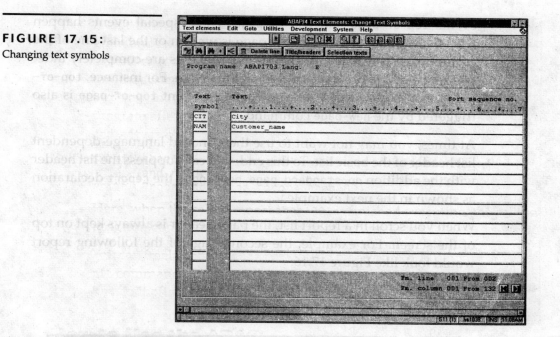

If the same text symbol is used several times in a program, you can use an alternative technique:

```
write: / text-nam, customers-name,
       / text-cit, customers-city.
```

The text symbols `text-nam` and `text-cit` play the same role as above. In this case, no text will be displayed if the text symbol has not been translated into the Logon Language of a user, since the `write` command contains no literal that can be substituted for the text symbol. Thus, this technique is only useful if one text symbol occurs in many places in the program code.

Page Headers and Footers

In addition to the standard language-dependent page headers of a report list, you can also define special page headers and footers at the events `top-of-page` and `end-of-page`. These special events happen whenever the first line of a new page is written or the last line of the current page is reached. Therefore, these events are completely independent of the control structure of the program. For instance, `top-of-page` can occur within a loop. Clearly, the event `top-of-page` is also triggered by the `new-page` command.

At times, you may not want to use the standard language-dependent list header of the basic list. To this end, you can suppress the list header with the addition `no standard page heading` in the `report` declaration as shown in the next example.

When you scroll in a report list, the page header is always kept on top of the screen. For example, the second page of the following report would look like Figure 17.16:

```
report header no standard page heading.
start-of-selection.
```

FIGURE 17.16:

A page header is always kept at the top of the screen, as you can see in this sample list.

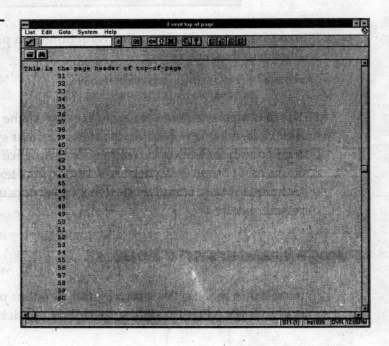

```
     do 100 times.
       write / sy-index.
     enddo.
  top-of-page.
     write 'This is the page header of top-of-page'.
```

By default, report lists that are displayed on the screen have one "logical" page of a virtually unlimited length—the upper bound is 60,000 lines. You can scroll down on a list page via the scroll bar or the standard scroll buttons in the system toolbar. New logical pages are created via the new-page command.

Page headers and the number of lines on a list page become important when you want to print a list. To do this, choose System ➤ List ➤ Print from the menu bar of the report list, and specify the details of the print format on the print screen that appears. The maximum size of a page depends on your printer. You often don't know the print format when the program is created. However, when special forms are printed, the number of lines per page can be set in a report via the addition line-count of the report declaration.

You can design the page footer using the event end-of-page together with a number of lines reserved for the page footer in the addition line-count. For example, the following report reserves three lines for the page footer:

```
report footer no standard page heading
               line-count 44(3).
start-of-selection.
   do 100 times.
     write / sy-index.
   enddo.
end-of-page.
   write 'This is the page footer of end-of-page'.
```

The output of this code is shown in Figure 17.17.

FIGURE 17.17:

A page footer with three lines reserved

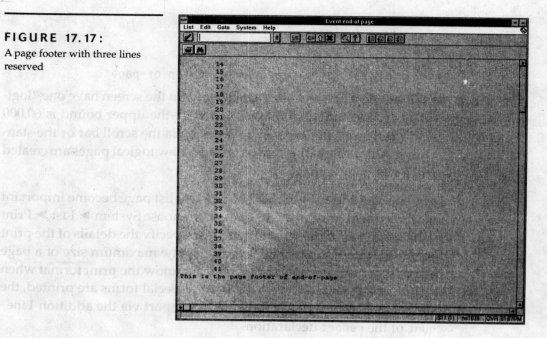

FIGURE 17.17:

A page footer with three lines reserved

In a similar way, you can display page headers on stacked lists by means of the event top-of-page during line-selection. If you want to display different page headers for several stacked lists, define a special GUI status for each stacked list. You can distinguish between the stacked lists by the current GUI status, which is available in the system field sy-pfkey.

Frames

If you want to create a list with enhanced layout features (e.g., table controls), the easiest way is to work with the ABAP/4 Query. But you can also use the various capabilities of the programming language ABAP/4 to design an individual list layout. For example, you can display tabular lists with horizontal and vertical lines (frames) using the uline command and the system field sy-vline (see Figure 17.18).

The list shown in Figure 17.18 was created with the following code:

FIGURE 17.18:

A list layout enhanced with three frames

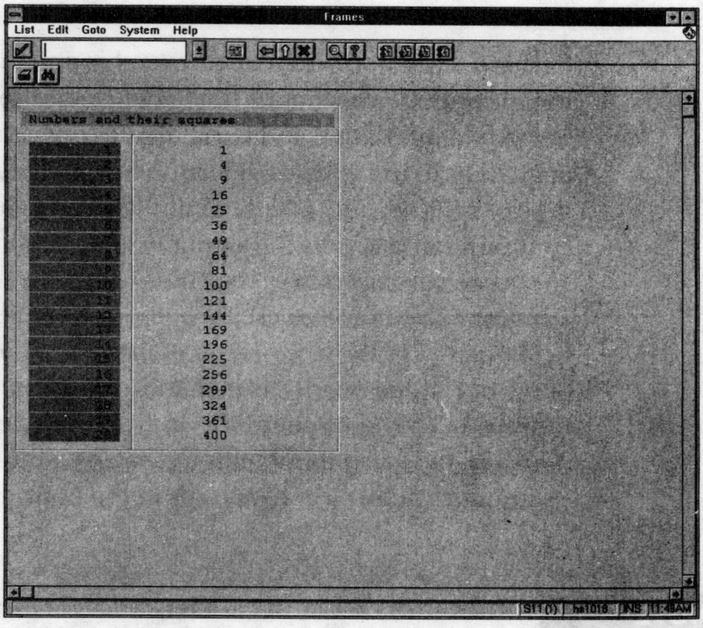

```
constants my_line_size type i value 40.
data square type i.
new-page line-size my_line_size.
uline.
format color col_heading.
write: / sy-vline,
         'Numbers and their squares',
         at my_line_size sy-vline.
format color off.
uline.
do 20 times.
   square = sy-index ** 2.
   write: / sy-vline,
            sy-index color col_key,
            sy-vline,
```

```
        square,
    at my_line_size sy-vline.
enddo.
uline.
```

In this example, the report output is enhanced by three frames around the individual portions of the list using the appropriate commands for horizontal (uline) and vertical lines (sy-vline). At first, the correct size of all lines in the list is determined by the number my_line_size following the addition line-size of the new-page command. Then, the uline command displays the upper horizontal line of the heading frame. The format command sets the color for the heading frame, and the following write command displays the header text enclosed by a pair of vertical lines. The next uline statement is at the same time the lower border of the header frame and the upper boundary for the other two frames. In the do loop, the individual lines with square numbers are displayed, each number being enclosed by vertical lines. The last uline command closes both frames at the bottom.

NOTE   The corners arising at the intersections of horizontal and vertical lines are automatically drawn by the system.

A Quick Review

Here is a quick review of some of the topics we covered in this chapter:

- The events for drilling-down are at line-selection and at user-command.

- Menus, buttons, and function keys make up the GUI status.

- A GUI status can be set using the command set pf-status. The name of the current status is available in the system field sy-pfkey.

- You can display pop-up windows with standard navigation functions by using the `window` command.

- The events `top-of-page` and `end-of-page` are used for page headers and footers.

- You can display tabular lists with elementary language constructs (`uline` and `sy-vline`).

In the next chapter, you will learn how to run a report and supply it with values for the selection criteria.

CHAPTER

EIGHTEEN

Running a Report

- **Executing a report**

- **Using selection criteria as an interface**

- **Working with Variants**

- **Background processing**

An important step in the development process of a program is to test its runtime behavior at an early stage. As the developer, you need to present the user interface to prospective users and improve it according to their suggestions. In addition, ABAP/4's easy-to-use testing facilities help you find out whether your program works as expected. Until now, you have seen how to create a report with a standard selection screen and interactive list features. In this chapter, you will learn how to test a report from the ABAP/4 Development Workbench and how to invoke it from another program. Within a program, a report is executed via the submit command. Each selection criterion of the submitted report can be set by the caller. Instead of specifying each selection criterion separately, you can also specify a Variant—that is, a set of values for the selection criteria of a report. When a report is executed using a Variant, the input fields of the selection screen are automatically filled with the values in the chosen Variant. In this way, the end user need not fill all input fields on the selection screen again and again.

In a production R/3 system, reports are usually executed using Variants. A general directory of all standard reports and Variants (called a *Reporting Tree*) includes more than 1000 standard reports and Variants that come with the R/3 system. The user benefits from using the Reporting Tree in that he or she can easily find reports that deliver information for everyday questions of interest; for example, an inventory list of a department in the company. The Reporting Tree can be refined during the customizing process, and further reports and Variants can be included at a later time. Each application (Logistics, Accounting, Human Resources, etc.) also has special trees that have Variants that are especially suited to that particular application.

If a report reads a lot of data from the database, execution can take a long time, preventing the user from performing other tasks. System resources may also be exhausted, since many users are working at the same time. The usage of system resources can be balanced by setting up jobs running in the background. You will learn in this chapter how to create background jobs and how to schedule them.

Testing Reports from the Workbench

You can execute a report from the Editor screen by choosing Program ➤ Execute. The Editor always uses the current source code, and you don't need to save the code first. When a report is finished executing, pressing the Back function key (F3) brings you back to the Editor.

You can also test a report from the object list of the Object Browser. Click on the report name in the object list, and then click on the Test/Execute button.

NOTE When testing a report, you need not worry about things like compilation or dependencies from other program objects. The ABAP/4 system automatically generates a new runtime version of your program when the source code or a referenced Dictionary object has been changed.

In a large-scale development project, one application area usually needs many reports. In the final version of the application, these reports will be executed via menu functions, buttons, or from the Reporting Tree. However, very often end users need to run reports that are not yet integrated into a user interface. To directly run a report from any screen in the R/3 system, choose System ➤ Services ➤ Reporting, as shown in Figure 18.1.

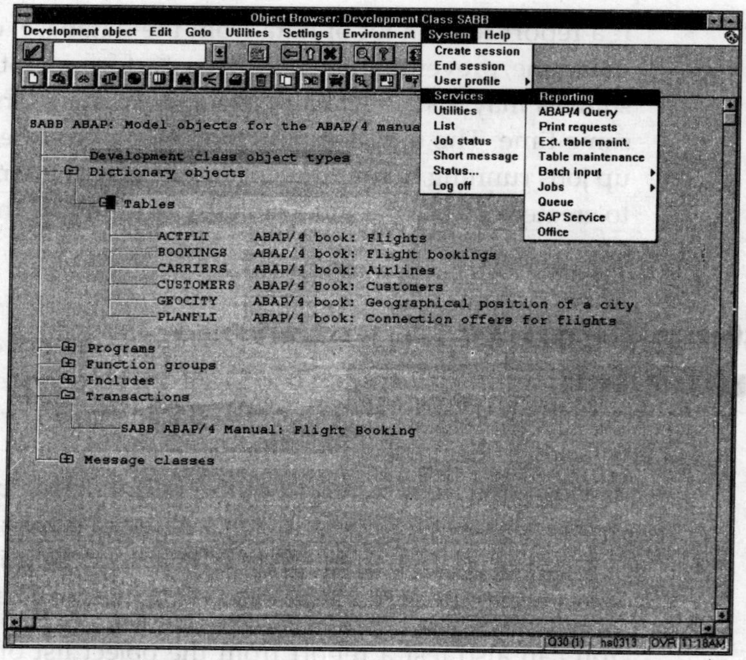

FIGURE 18.1:

Running a report via the menu choice System ➤ Services ➤ Reporting

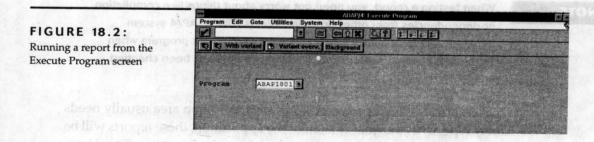

On the next screen, enter the report name (in our example, abap1801) and click on the Execute button (see Figure 18.2).

FIGURE 18.2:

Running a report from the Execute Program screen

When you finish executing the report by clicking on the Back button (F3), you'll return to the screen where you started by choosing the menu function System ➤ Services ➤ Reporting.

Using the Submit Command to Run a Report

To integrate a report into the user interface of an application, ABAP/4 allows you to invoke a report from another program. Similar to calling subroutines or functions, you will probably need to transfer data from the caller to the called report. In this section, we'll discuss two methods to achieve this: first, using the Parameters and Select-Options of the standard selection screen as an interface, and second, using the ABAP/4 Memory.

How to Use Selection Criteria as an Interface

You can start a report from a program using the submit command. Each selection criterion of the submitted report can be set by the caller after the submit command's addition with. For example, the report abap1801 has a Parameter p_date and a Select-Option s_name:

```
report abap1801.
  tables: customers, bookings.
  parameters p_date type d.
  select-options s_name for customers-name.
  select * from customers
        where name in s_name.
    write / customers-name.
    select * from bookings
          where order_date = p_date.
          and   id      = customers-id.
      write: / bookings-carrid,
             bookings-connid,
             bookings-fldate.
    endselect.
  endselect.
```

This sample report reads customer and bookings data from the database and displays it on screen according to the content of the Select-Option s_name. In addition, the Parameter p_date is used to select the order date of the bookings.

If the report abap1801 is not run directly, but is rather started from another program, the selection criteria must be filled by the calling program. For example, the report abap1802 executes abap1801 and fills the selection criteria:

```
report abap1802.
  tables customers.
  select-options s_name for customers-name.
  submit abap1801
         with p_date = sy-datum
         with s_name in s_name.
```

In this example, the selection criteria of the submitted report abap1801 are always on the left side of the relationship after the addition with of the submit command. The parameter p_date is set to the current date (system field sy-datum). The Select-Option s_name of the calling program abap1802 is transferred as a whole to the Select-Option s_name of the submitted report abap1801.

NOTE   Instead of specifying each parameter or Select-Option separately, you can also set all selection criteria at once after the addition using selection-set by using a *Variant*. The concept of Variants is explained in this chapter under the heading "Executing Reports Using Variants."

When a user should have the opportunity to specify the selection criteria of the submitted report, you can display the selection screen using this code:

```
submit abap1801
       via selection-screen.
```

At runtime, the submit command stops the execution of the calling program and executes the submitted report. Therefore, when the list of the submitted report has been displayed and the user clicks on the Back button, the system does not return to the calling program containing the submit command. Sometimes, you want to continue processing the calling program after having invoked a report. For those cases, use the addition and return at the submit statement:

```
submit abap1801
        and return.
write 'Processed after report abap1801'.
```

Here, when the called report abap1801 is finished executing, the calling program continues with the statement behind submit.

You can freely combine the previously mentioned additions of the submit command. For example, you can send the selection screen and return to it after the execution of the report.

How to Use the ABAP/4 Memory as an Interface

If the submitted report needs data different from the Parameters or Select-Options, the caller can export complex data objects to the ABAP/4 Memory using the command export to memory (see Chapter 14). This temporary data can be imported by the submitted report by means of a corresponding import from memory statement. For example, the calling program can export an internal table of customers:

```
report abap1803.
  tables customers.
  data all_customers like customers occurs 100
                  with header line.
  select * from customers into table all_customers.
  export all_customers to memory id 'CUSTOMERS'.
  submit abap1804.
```

Here, all customer data is read from the database and filled into the internal table `all_customers`. Then, this internal table is exported to the ABAP/4 Memory. In a similar way, the submitted report can import this internal table:

```
report abap1804.
  data all_customers like customers occurs 100
                     with header line.
  import all_customers from memory id 'CUSTOMERS'.
  loop at all_customers.
    write / all_customers-name.
  endloop.
```

In this example, the internal table `all_customers` is imported and all table lines are displayed on the screen.

> **TIP** The contents of the ABAP/4 Memory can be used across several calling levels.

Executing Reports Using Variants

A *Variant* is a set of values for all Parameters and Select-Options of a report. When a report is executed using a Variant, the fields of the selection screen are filled with the values of the chosen Variant. For example, you could use a Variant that specifies *19991231* as the value for the Parameter `p_date` of a report, and that uses *A* and *M* as the Select-Option `s_name` of a report. This makes running the report easier, since you don't have to take time out to fill all of these values over and over again. So, Variants support the reuse of selection criteria and they provide maximum security and flexibility.

Creating a Variant

To create a Variant proceed as follows: after you have entered selection criteria on the selection screen of a report, choose Goto ➤ Variants ➤ Save As Variant. On the next screen, enter a name and short explanatory text for the Variant and save it, as shown in Figure 18.3.

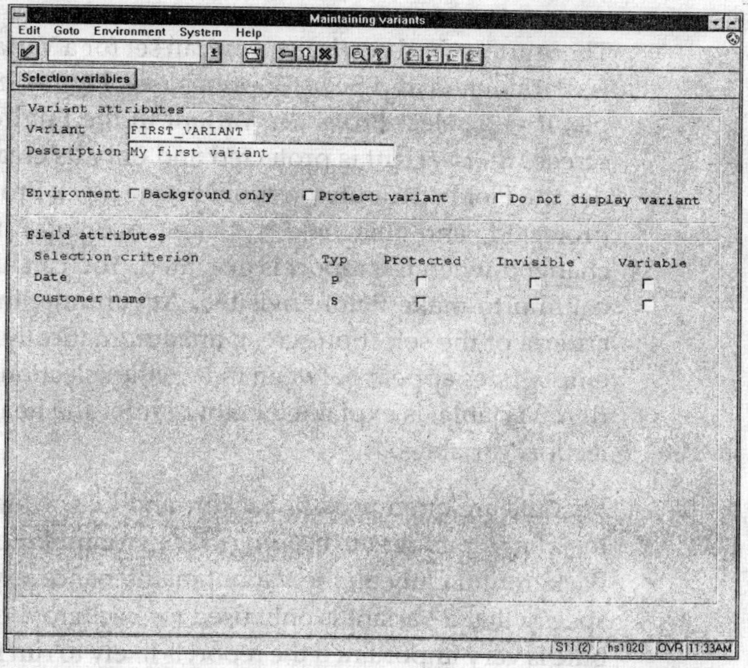

FIGURE 18.3:

Specifying a Variant with Date and Customer name as its selection criteria

On this screen, you can also specify field attributes for the selection criteria on the selection screen. This is covered in this chapter under the heading "Setting Attributes for a Variant."

TIP Complex selections (e.g., all customers between *A* and *M* or with a leading *S*) can also be stored in a Variant, if the user specifies multiple values for Select-Options as explained in Chapter 15.

Setting Attributes for a Variant

There are several attributes you can set for a Variant and its fields—that is, Parameters and Select-Options (see Figure 18.3, above). For example, if you select Protected Variant in the Environment section of the screen, that Variant is protected and only its creator can change it. Under the Field Attributes section, if you check Protected, a single field is protected, and this field appears in display mode and cannot be changed when the report is executed. You can also check the Invisible column to make fields invisible. At runtime, the remaining selection criteria of the selection screen are automatically rearranged so that no empty lines appear between the visible selection criteria. The other option, Variable, is explained below under the heading "How to Use Selection Variables."

Variants are often used in background jobs, which will be explained in this chapter under the heading "Background Processing." Check the box Background Only on the Variant maintenance screen (see Figure 18.3) to specify that a Variant is only used for background processing. This attribute is very important if the report is likely to run for a long time, because the selections of the Variant comprise a large set of data.

How to Use Selection Variables

A flexible way of specifying selection criteria is to use selection variables within Variants. For example, you can create a variable *Z_NAME* for the Select-Option *Customer name*. When the content of *Z_NAME* is *Smith* or *Edison*, the report will run for the customer specified by this value of the selection variable. Every field of a Variant can refer to a selection variable. At runtime, the value of this variable is put into the corresponding field of the selection screen. Many Variants of different reports can refer to the same variable. To create a reference to a variable from the Variant maintenance screen, select the check box Variable for a field of a Variant and click on the Selection Variables button. On the next screen, enter the name of a variable (e.g., *Z_NAME*), which is used to fill the field (e.g., *Customer name*) on the selection screen (see Figure 18.4).

FIGURE 18.4:

Setting a selection variable (Z_NAME) for a Variant

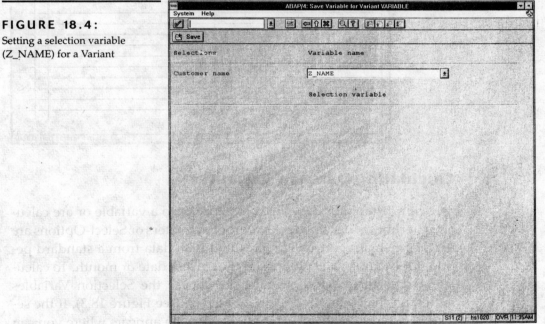

If this variable does not yet exist, you can create it by double-clicking on the variable's name and specifying its values, as shown in Figure 18.5.

In this example, the selection variable *Z_NAME* specifies all customer names between *A* and *M* or with a leading *S*.

Calculating Dates in Variants

Selection criteria for date fields either refer to a variable or are calculated at runtime. Calculated dates for Parameters or Select-Options are useful when a report will be executed with data from a standard period; for example, all bookings of the current date or month. To calculate a date for a selection criterion, choose the Selection Variables button on the Maintaining Variants screen (see Figure 18.3). If the selection criterion refers to a date field, a screen appears where you can determine how the date is calculated (see Figure 18.6).

Setting the current date for a
calculated date

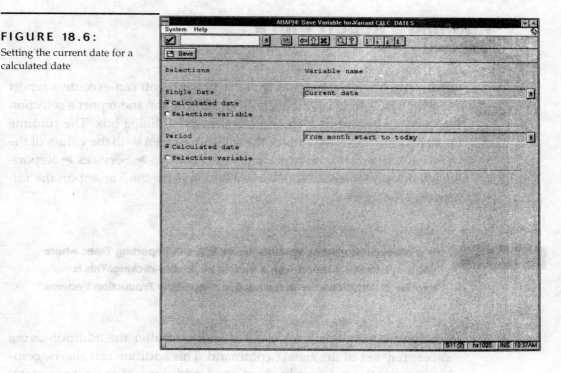

On this screen, you can choose from various alternatives for calculating a date. In our example, we use the current date. You can also calculate a date before or after the current date (e.g., current date + 10). Select-Options for date fields also allow complex calculations. For example, you can choose the following periods by clicking on the down arrow at the right edge of the Period section and choosing from a dropdown list box:

- From month start to today
- First quarter of a year
- Preceding month

Running a Report with a Variant

Once you have created and saved a Variant, you can execute a report with it by clicking on the Get Variant button on the report's selection screen and choosing a Variant from the next dialog box. The runtime system fills the input fields of the selection screen with the values of the chosen Variant. If you start a report via System ➤ Services ➤ Reporting, click on Execute With Variant and specify the Variant on the following dialog box.

NOTE   **In a production system, Variants are included in Reporting Trees where you can execute a report with a Variant by double-clicking. This is explained in this chapter in the section "Reports in Production Systems."**

On the program level, a Variant is specified after the addition using selection-set of the submit command. This addition can also be combined with the previously mentioned additions of the submit statement (via selection-screen, and return), as shown here:

```
submit abap1801
       using selection-set 'FIRST_VARIANT'.
```

This program executes the report abap1801 with the Variant *FIRST_VARIANT*.

Reports in Production Systems

Reports can be executed via System ➤ Services ➤ Reporting as shown in Figure 18.1 (earlier). A user must enter the technical name of thereport in this case. In contrast, you need not know the technical name of the report if you use the directory of all standard reports and Variants, which is accessible through the Information System menu on the initial screen of the R/3 system (see Figure 18.7). This directory is called the *Reporting Tree* and displays each report title. The general Reporting Tree includes more than 1000 standard reports. It is structured according to the different applications in the R/3 system. Each application of the R/3 system (Logistics, Accounting, Human Resources, etc.) also has special Reporting Trees.

FIGURE 18.7:
The general Reporting Tree for all applications

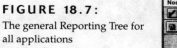

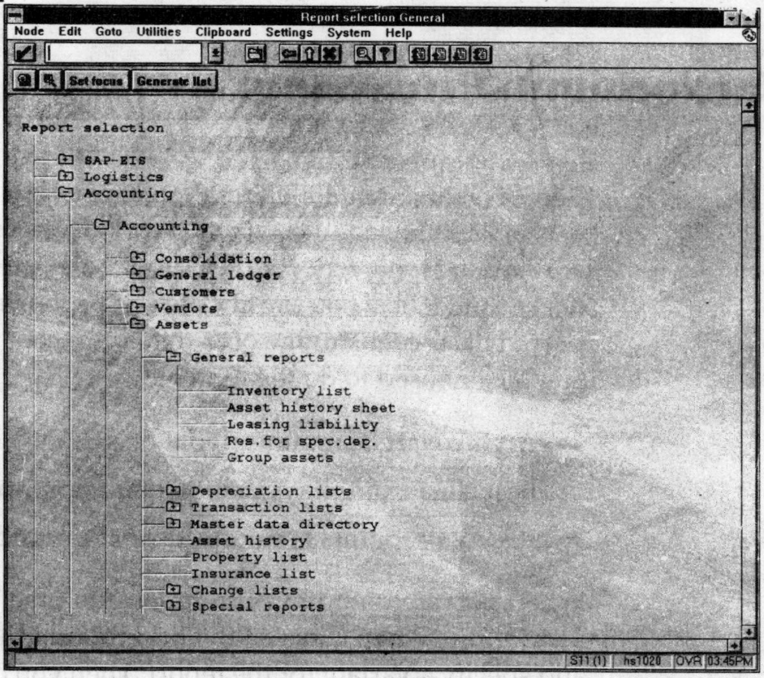

In this example, you see parts of the general Reporting Tree for all R/3 applications. You can easily browse through such a tree and run a report by double-clicking your way.

When customizing your R/3 system, you can change the structure of Reporting Trees (e.g., you can exchange *Logistics* and *Accounting*) and include additional reports and Variants at a later time. For security reasons, you can define authority checks for each subtree of a Reporting Tree. In addition, you can define an individual reporting environment for each position in a company. Each user can choose an entry into the Reporting Tree and select a subtree or suppress reports in every node of the tree. In this way, Reporting Trees are useful, since they allow you to set different users up with different reporting capacities that are most appropriate to their needs.

Background Processing

Reports that read a lot of data can take a long time to execute, but the user will still need to be able to work on other projects. If many users are running large reports, they can exhaust system resources. By using background jobs, you can choose an appropriate start time for each report to balance the usage of system resources. Background processing is typically used to do the following:

- Archive large amounts of data
- Pass data from the system to other applications
- Execute programs periodically or at particular times

When you are going to start a report via the function System ➤ Services ➤ Reporting, choose the Background button on the next screen and specify a Variant for the report. Then you can either execute the report immediately or schedule it for background processing—that is, you instruct the system to process an ABAP/4 program in the background. You can schedule a program as a separate job or add it to an existing job that hasn't yet been processed.

Scheduling a program is just the first part of a two-part process. Before a job can be executed, it must be released. Your job will be released automatically if you are authorized to release jobs and have set a start date or selected the Execute Immediately button. This authorization for releasing background jobs is necessary in large companies. In contrast, if you are working in a small company, your system administrator will probably give everybody this authorization.

Background processing supports many features. For example, if you schedule a job with a start date and time, you can refer to a special calendar of the R/3 system. This allows you to restrict the job start to workdays only and to define exceptions. For example, you will use this feature to start a report every Monday morning at 8:00 that will show how many flights are scheduled that week. Background processing is automatically distributed over any number of servers in your system, thus balancing the workload of the system. You can also specify a single machine for your background job. On all screens, the general functions for background jobs are accessible through System ➤ Services ➤ Jobs ➤ Job Definition and System ➤ Services ➤ Jobs ➤ Job Overview.

The ABAP/4 Development Workbench also includes a set of functions providing the program interface of the background processing system. Using these functions, you can schedule and manage background jobs from your own programs. You can use the programming interface to start both ABAP/4 programs and programs that are external to the system. The programming interface also offers function modules for the following tasks:

- Managing jobs (displaying, copying, and deleting jobs)
- Checking and triggering events, which can be used to start other background jobs
- Displaying the log generated by a background job

A Quick Review

Here is a quick review of some of the topics we've covered in this chapter:

- Using the Execute function on the Editor screen, a report can be started with the current source code, which need not be saved previously.

- A report is started by means of the submit command. With the addition via selection-screen, the selection screen appears; with the addition and return, the calling program continues when the submitted report is finished.

- Variants are made up of a set of selection criteria for a report. They can be used for default values and for hiding input fields on the selection screen.

- Selection criteria can be set after the submit command by specifying a Variant or by transferring values for each Parameter and Select-Option separately.

- At runtime, the values of a Variant can be filled from selection variables that are related to the Parameters or Select-Options in a Variant. Selection criteria for dates can be dynamically calculated.

- In a production system, reports and Variants are started from Reporting Trees. A Reporting Tree is a directory of reports and Variants. Each user can define individual views of Reporting Trees.

- Background jobs can be used to execute certain programs regularly or at particular times.

- With the programming interface of the background processing system, background jobs can be scheduled and managed from every program.

Now you have seen how to work with reports that read data and display on screen. In the next chapter, you'll learn how to design a program with input masks that also changes data in database tables.

PART VI

User Dialogs

CHAPTER

N I N E T E E N

Defining the User Interface

- **Creating a dialog program**

- **Placing elements on a screen**

- **Specifying the Flow Logic**

- **Creating GUI statuses and titles**

The screen, mouse, and keyboard provide the main interface elements for the user to create and change data in the system. In particular, many business operations are based on the manual input of data that must be available at a later time. Therefore, the interface between the user and the system should be as comfortable and friendly as possible. This includes not only the input of data, but also the reaction of the system to wrong or meaningless input. Finally, logical coherence of the data and correct processing should be guaranteed by the system.

For instance, if a group of customers of a travel agency are booking flights, they expect that these transactions will be carried out correctly, so that on the day of departure, they get on the right plane and find their reserved seats. If all seats are already reserved, the customers want to know that when they first try to book the seats at the travel agency.

To fulfill these requirements, a dialog program for the travel agents must provide a convenient Graphical User Interface (GUI) with strong validation rules and consistency checks. In addition, the booking data must be made persistent by storing the data in a database, thus making it available in the future. Finally, it should be easy for agents to correct wrong input data.

ABAP/4 provides developers with a wide variety of design tools and language constructs that enable them to create such applications. A complete ABAP/4 user interface is made up of screens, menu bars, and toolbars. Screens appear within windows and contain graphical elements like radio buttons, check boxes, text fields, and push buttons.

A screen basically consists of two pieces: the *layout* and the *Flow Logic*. Each screen is also attached to a controlling ABAP/4 program. Typically, a dialog application is made up of several screens that are attached to the same program.

The layout of screens is modeled in a WYSIWYG fashion (What You See Is What You Get). *Layout elements* are input fields, labels, push buttons, frames, radio buttons, table controls, etc. They are chosen from the Dictionary or from a toolbar and are placed on the screen via drag and drop.

The *Flow Logic* is structured by events triggered by user actions. At each event, data is processed as defined in modules of the controlling program. The sequence of screens is driven by the user input and modules of the corresponding event. Checks of the manual input data are either done automatically via check tables (for example, valid customer ID) or controlled by the ABAP/4 program itself. In case of erroneous input, a messaging system supports the dialog with the user.

NOTE   Messages are covered in Chapter 20.

A *GUI status* describes the elements that appear in a menu bar and the toolbars. It can be set dynamically in the controlling ABAP/4 program using the command set `pf-status`. In a similar way, a *GUI title* describes the title of a screen and can be set in a program using the command set `titlebar`. The text of GUI statuses and titles is language-dependent and can be translated without changing the program code. If you use the default Workbench suggestions for the GUI status, the user interface of your program will have a standard "look and feel."

NOTE   In this chapter, you'll learn how to create a GUI status for a dialog
program that changes data. GUI statuses for report lists are covered in
Chapter 17.

In this chapter, we will create a user interface for entering flight booking information for our fictional travel agency. In this interface, we'll
show you how to design the layout and set up the Flow Logic. We'll
also build a GUI status for the interface.

An Overview of the Sample Program

Before we get started building the interface, we'll take a minute to
show you what the final product should look like and how it works, so
that you'll know what you are working toward. Then we'll move into
actually creating the screens. The following program is designed to
allow our sample travel agency to make flight bookings. The interface
needs to accommodate two basic steps:

- A request for a flight connection
- A dialog to get the customer's specific data

In the first step, we need information about the city of departure, the
destination, the date, and the airline. Thus the layout of the form for
entering this data should look like the one shown in Figure 19.1.

The screen contains four pairs of labels and input fields. Each field has
a set of properties, such as input fields that require input data (indicated by question marks). When you enter data, the runtime system
checks whether this data is correct (for example, an admissible date).

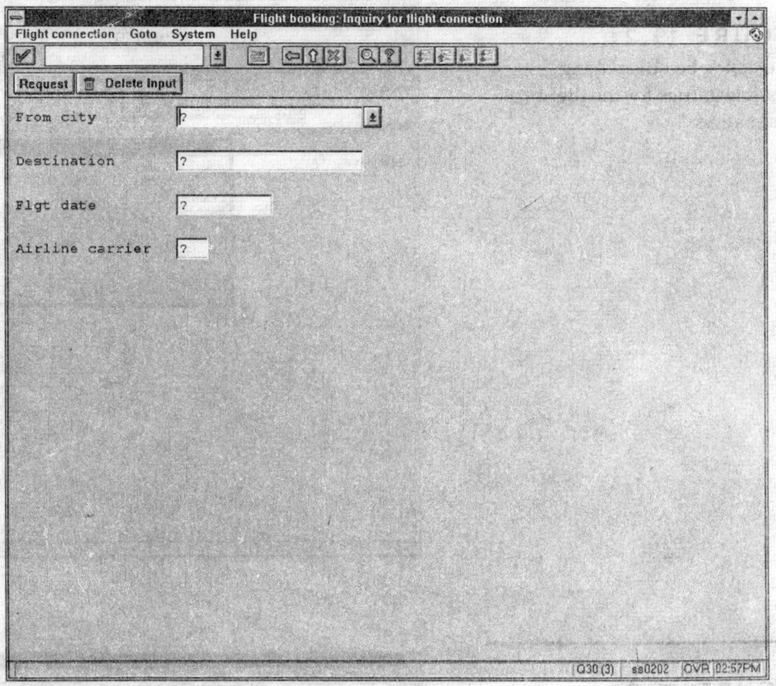

FIGURE 19.1:

Setting up an interface for a
flight request

If you enter an invalid value, the system displays an error message. When you click on the arrow button to the right of each input field, a dialog box with a list of possible entries for the input field is displayed, as shown in Figure 19.2. Any of these entries can be selected by double-clicking, and the dialog box closes automatically.

After you've made all the entries, you can click on the Request button to move to the next screen, where you enter the customer data. This screen is split into two frames. The upper frame displays the data from the previous screen supplemented by further information about the flight connection. None of the fields in the upper portion of the screen is an input field. You can enter the customer name and the number of seats to be booked in the lower frame (see Figure 19.3).

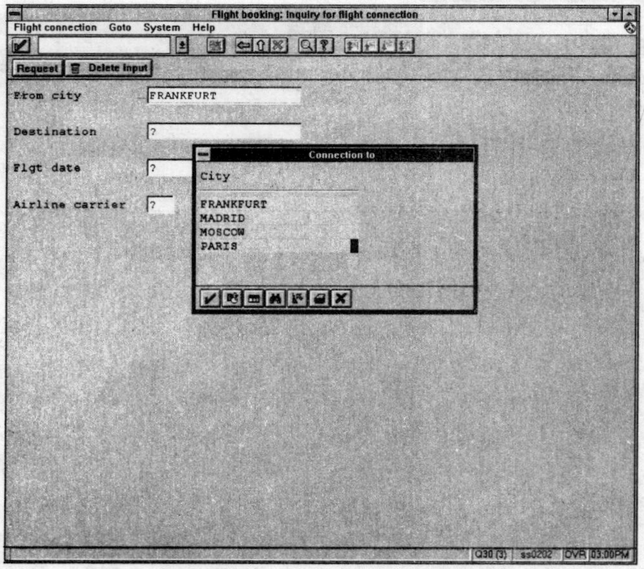

FIGURE 19.2:

The dialog box displaying
possible entries for the flight
destination

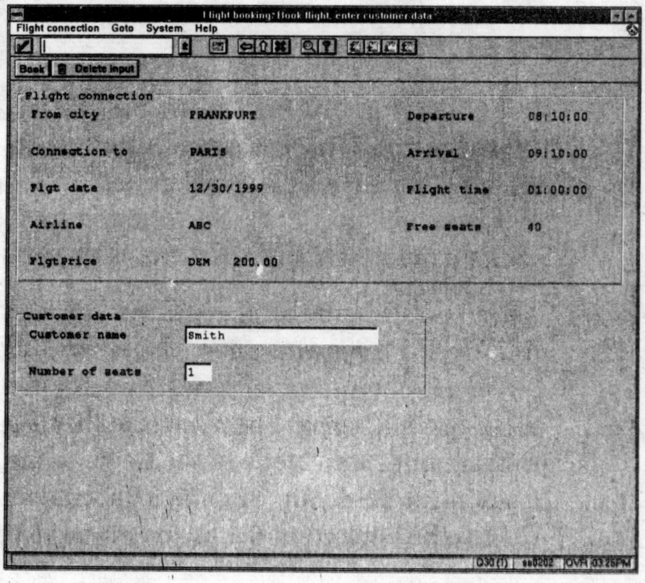

FIGURE 19.3:

The screen where you enter
customer data for booking a
flight

By clicking on the Book button, you can book the flight for the customer. If the operation is completed successfully, you get a message box telling you that a seat is booked. When you quit the message box, the first screen is displayed again so that you can enter data for another flight request.

Creating a Dialog Program

Now that you know what the program will look like when it is finished, we can start building the program. To create a program for this dialog, use the Object Browser as explained in Chapter 3. Give the program a name (we use *SAPMSABB*) and choose the program type *M* to create a Module Pool—that is, a dialog program that changes data in the database. In contrast to a report, you can't start a Module Pool with the submit command or by choosing Test/Execute on the Object Browser screen, since it has no default startup screen. Instead, a Module Pool can be associated with a transaction that is started via a menu function or by a special language construct.

> **NOTE** A *transaction* is a dialog program that changes objects in the database in a consistent way. See Chapter 21 for a detailed discussion of data consistency in transactions.

In our sample program, a transaction is made up of the initial screen shown in Figure 19.1 and the subsequent screens shown in Figures 19.2 and 19.3. You can define a transaction by selecting the Other Objects radio button and clicking on the Edit button in the lower portion of the Object Browser screen. On the next screen, enter the name of the transaction (we used *SABB*), click on the Create button, and select the transaction type Dialog Transaction in the next dialog box. In another dialog box, the system prompts you to specify a short explanatory text, a program, and an initial screen for your dialog transaction (we used program *SAPMSABB* and screen 100).

When a transaction is called, it starts with the initial screen. When a user finishes the transaction, the system returns to the calling program. To test your sample transaction, click on the Test/Execute button on the Object Browser screen.

Creating a Screen

A screen is attached to an ABAP/4 program and can be defined on the Object Browser screen by clicking on the Create button. When a dialog box for different object types appears, select the object type Screen and enter the number of the screen (see Figure 19.4). The screen number consists of at most four digits and is used as an identifier for the screen. In our example, the first screen (see Figure 19.1) has the number 100 and the second 200 (see Figure 19.3).

Then, click on the Create button. On the next screen, enter a short description as shown in Figure 19.5 and save the screen attributes by clicking on the Save button.

You can also specify additional properties of the screen, but for our example the default values are appropriate. You can enter the number of the next screen (for example, 200) in the lower frame. By default, the current screen number is proposed by the system. We'll use the default screen number, since the sequence of screens is set dynamically in the Flow Logic, which we discuss below under the heading "Specifying the Flow Logic."

FIGURE 19.4:

Specifying the number for the first screen of the sample transaction

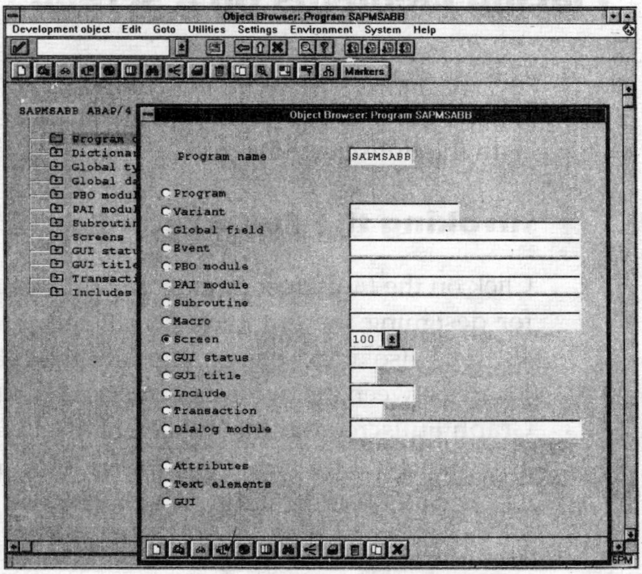

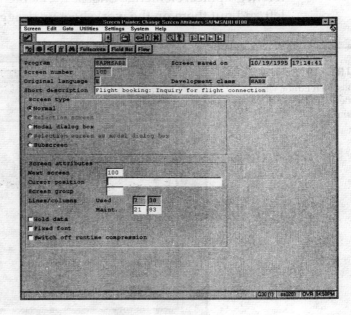

FIGURE 19.5:

Setting the screen attributes for screen 100

Placing Elements on a Screen

Having defined the attributes, you can now go on to define the screen layout. You will see how to define input fields, labels, and titled frames with the Fullscreen Editor.

Invoking the Fullscreen Editor

Click on the Fullscreen button on the attributes screen to open an editor for designing the graphical screen elements, as shown in Figure 19.6. There is also a text-based alternative mode of the editor, and you can toggle between the two editor modes using the menu function Settings ➤ Graph Fullscreen in the Fullscreen Editor screen. It's a matter of taste as to which editor mode you prefer. Throughout this book, we use the graphical Fullscreen Editor.

This editor provides you with a worksheet where you can place the different graphical elements. Choose the elements from the toolbox on the left and put them on the worksheet by dragging and dropping them.

FIGURE 19.6:

The Fullscreen Editor, where you'll define the screen layout for your program

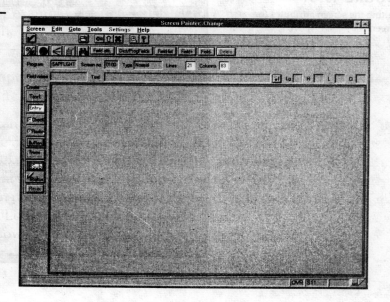

Defining Labels and Input Fields

To define a label for some field on your screen, you can select the Text button. A label text box appears and you then drag it to where you want to place it. When you have placed the label by clicking the left mouse button, you are asked to enter a name for the label and the text in the highlighted input fields at the top of the screen, Field Name and Text (see Figure 19.7).

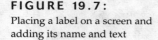

FIGURE 19.7:
Placing a label on a screen and adding its name and text

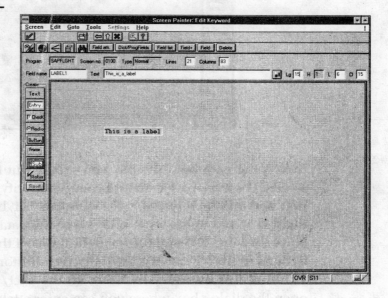

In a similar way, you can use the Entry button to place an input field on the worksheet, as shown in Figure 19.8. You can make any field longer by dragging its right or left edge. You can also change the position of any graphical element on the screen using drag and drop. You can key in a name for the field after Field name at the top. The Text field only displays the length of the field.

FIGURE 19.8:

Placing an input field on the
screen

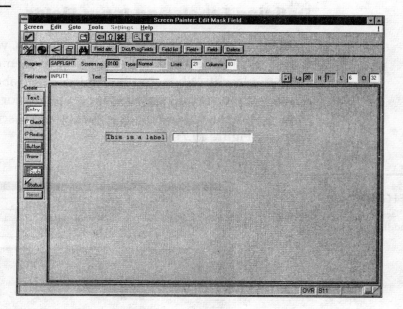

In keeping with our example, you should put flight data on the first
screen. The information about a connection (city of departure, destination, and airline) is stored in the table planfli, but the actual date of a
flight is stored in the table actfli (see the data model in Chapter 6).
Since the label text and format definitions of these fields are already
defined in the Dictionary, the Fullscreen Editor offers the possibility
to re-use this information. Click on the Dict/ProgFields button to
open the dialog box where you can enter a table name (e.g., *PLAN-
FLI*) in the upper input line (see Figure 19.9). Press ↵, and all fields
of the table appear in the lower part of the dialog box. Click on the
Yes radio button under Template and on the Average button under
Key Word, and the length and label text are displayed for each of the
screen fields, too.

When you select a Dictionary field by double-clicking on it, you are
asked to place it on the worksheet. Note that both the label with the

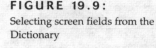

FIGURE 19.9:

Selecting screen fields from the Dictionary

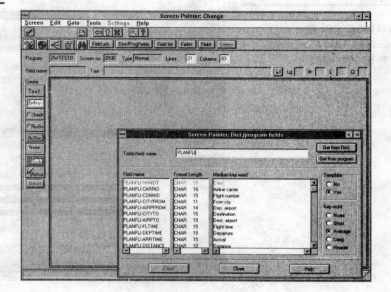

selected keyword and the template are put on the screen. If you don't need keywords, simply choose the None radio button under Key Word.

For our example, we need the fields cityfrom, cityto, and carrid from the planfli table. You can pick them from the Dictionary step-by-step as described above. You can also put them on the worksheet in a single step by holding down Ctrl while clicking on the fields from the list in the dialog box with the mouse (see Figure 19.10).

Having selected fields and templates from the Dictionary, you can rearrange them using drag and drop. To group several fields, draw a box around them with the mouse. Place the mouse pointer inside that box if you want to drag and drop the whole group.

Whenever you place Dictionary fields on the screen, the corresponding tables declaration must be included in the program of the screen. On the other hand, if you want to use fields not contained in the Dictionary, you can select fields that are already defined or will be defined in the associated program.

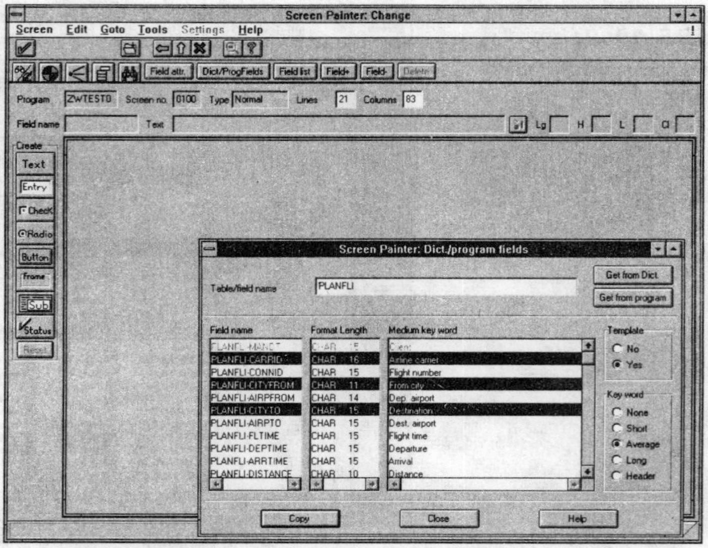

FIGURE 19.10:

Selecting several screen fields
from the Dictionary

Defining a Titled Frame

Another graphical element, the titled frame, can be used to group fields visible on the worksheet as shown previously in Figure 19.3. Click on the Frame button and place the mouse pointer where you want the upper-left corner of the frame to be. Hold down the left mouse button and drag the pointer to the right and down, then release it when the dotted outline of the frame is the size you want. Then enter the text of the title of the frame as shown in Figure 19.11.

You can drag and drop a frame and all the fields inside the frame by clicking and dragging on the square handle on the frame's upper border. The size of a frame can be changed by dragging the diamond handles on its border.

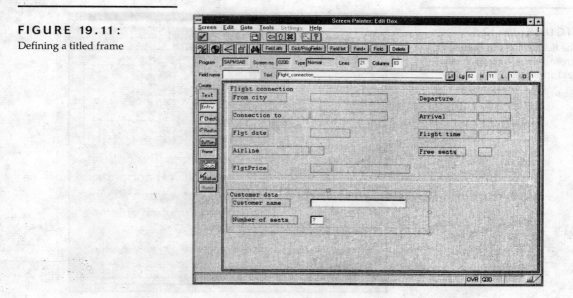

FIGURE 19.11:
Defining a titled frame

Attributes of Screen Elements

Each object on the screen has some special properties, such as to be an obligatory input field or to allow case-sensitive input and so on. Click on the Field List button in the Fullscreen Editor to open a dialog box where you can change the field attributes. ABAP/4 offers a lot of attributes that can be associated with a field on the screen (see Figure 19.12).

Let's take a look at the attributes of the field planfli-cityfrom. Note that there are two entries with the name planfli-cityfrom, but they have different field types (attribute Ftype). Entries of type Text represent labels, and entries of type I/O represent the actual input/output fields. Place the cursor in the second entry (I/O) and click on the Attribs. For 1 Field button. Figure 19.13 shows the dialog box that appears with the actual settings for the attributes of the field planfli-cityfrom. Alternatively, you can open this dialog box by double-clicking on the field in the Fullscreen Editor.

FIGURE 19.12:

The field list for our sample screen, where you can change field attributes

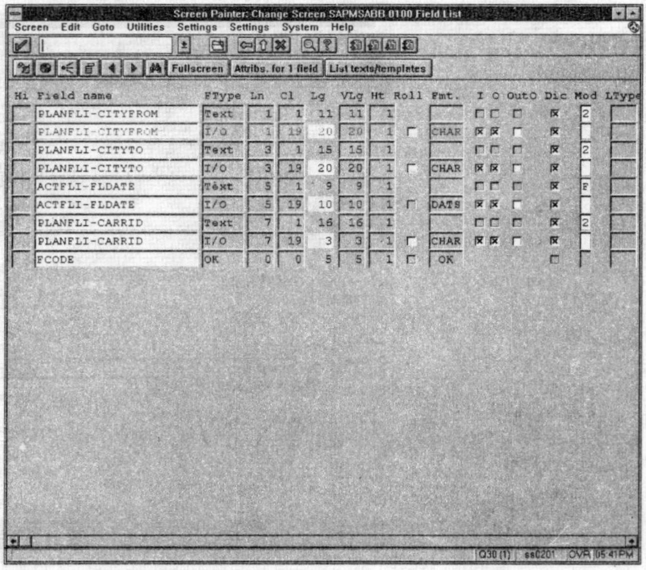

FIGURE 19.13:

Setting the attributes for a single field (PLANFLI-CITYFROM)

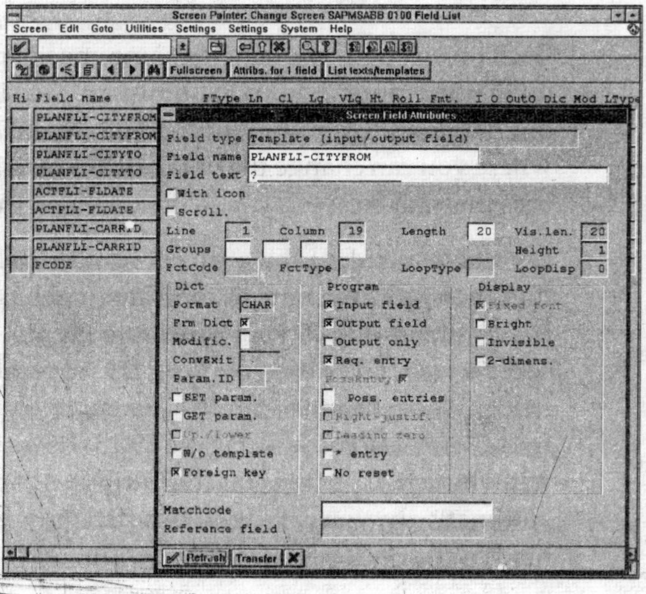

As you can see, the field is taken from the Dictionary and is used for input and output. In our example, we need the field attribute Obligatory Input—that is, at runtime, the system will prompt the user for input and the user won't be able to do anything else unless she or he enters something there. To set this property, activate the check box Req. Entry. A question mark appears in the input field, signaling that input is requested. If you want to see a list of admissible entries for the field, click to activate the check box Foreign Key. At runtime, a down arrow button will appear on the right edge of the input field if you place the cursor on it. Clicking on the button brings up a dialog box with a list of city names, and the system sends an error message if you try to enter a value that isn't on the list.

NOTE   The check box Foreign Key can only be set if a check table or a set of fixed values is associated with the corresponding table field in the Dictionary (see Chapter 5).

Finally, set display options by activating the check boxes in the right-most frame. For instance, a text field is displayed with intensified colors if the Bright check box is set.

TIP   We just described how to change the attributes of a single field. You can also modify the attributes of all fields at once in the field list itself by clicking on check boxes or entering values in input fields. Always use the right-most button in the application toolbar (e.g., the List Texts/Templates button in Figure 19.12) to get additional attributes that don't appear in the field list.

The last field of the field list plays a special role: it has the field type *OK* and is called the *OK Code Field*. This field is used to accept the user actions and send them to the application program. Enter any name you want for this field (e.g., fcode for function code) and also define a field with an identical name in the program. The program field must be a character field of length four:

```
data: fcode(4) type c.
```

At runtime, when the user selects a menu function, a push button, or a toolbar button, the associated function code is put into the OK Code Field.

NOTE   For more on the definition and maintenance of function codes, see the section "Creating GUI Statuses and Titles" later in this chapter.

We'll discuss how the program reacts to the function code in the next section on the Flow Logic of the screen.

Specifying the Flow Logic

The Flow Logic of a screen drives the processing sequence for that screen. In particular, the Flow Logic describes how to determine default values for screen fields and how the program reacts to user actions. For these purposes, you can use several events:

- process before output(PBO): Processed before a screen appears; generally used to initialize screen fields.

- process after input (PAI): Processed when a user selects a menu function, a push button, or a function key.

- process on value request (POV): Processed when the set of possible entries is requested (key F4).

- process on help request (POH): Processed when help information is requested (key F1).

The program code of each event determines how the contents of screen fields are set or read by the application program. For each field, a special subroutine can be called. The value of a field is set in a subroutine of the event process before output. Field values can be read in subroutines of the other events (PAI, POV, POH). The special subroutines of the Flow Logic are called *modules*. See Figure 19.14 for a schematic description of the flow of control for the sample program; the possible user actions are shown on the edges.

The editor for defining the Flow Logic is called by choosing Goto ➤ Flow Logic on the Field List screen. By choosing a screen from the object list of a program, you will directly enter the editor of the Flow Logic.

FIGURE 19.14:

Flow of control for the sample program

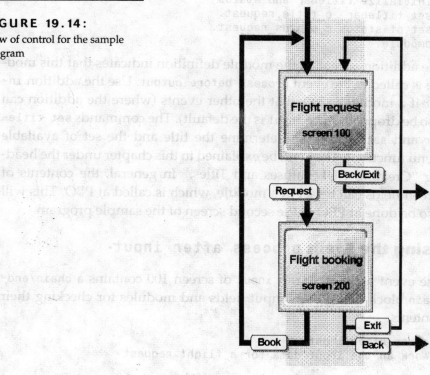

Using the Event `process before output`

First, we'll describe how to program the event `process before output` for screen 100 of our sample program:

```
process before output.
* Set title and status
  module init_request.
```

Here the module `init_request` is called without any reference to a field. Therefore, it is related to all fields of the screen. The module itself can be defined as follows: double-click on the name of the module, choose an include from the next dialog box, and insert the code between `module` and `endmodule` as shown:

```
module init_request output.
* Initialize titlebar and status
  set titlebar  c_title_request.
  set pf-status c_status_request.
endmodule.
```

The addition `output` in the module definition indicates that this module is called at the event `process before output`. Use the addition `input` if a module is called at the other events (where the addition can also be dropped, since `input` is the default). The commands `set titlebar` and `set pf-status` determine the title and the set of available menu functions. They will be explained in this chapter under the heading "Creating GUI Statuses and Titles." In general, the contents of screen fields can be set in a module, which is called at PBO. This will also be done at PBO of the second screen of the sample program.

Using the Event `process after input`

The event `process after input` of screen 100 contains a `chain/end-chain` block that groups input fields and modules for checking their contents:

```
process after input.
* Work an the input data for a flight request
```

```
chain.
   field: planfli-cityfrom,
          planfli-cityto,
          actfli-fldate,
          planfli-carrid.
   module action_request.
endchain.
```

The module `action_request` is associated with the screen fields specified after the `field` statement. If an error occurs while the module `action_request` is executed, the flow of control returns to the screen and the fields within the chain are ready for input again, so the developer can correct them all at once.

The above chain includes a single module. You are free to join several modules to the fields of a chain, too. They are executed in the order of their appearance in the chain. The source code of the module `action_request` looks like this:

```
module action_request input.
   case fcode.
     when c_fcode_request.
*      Check for a valid connection
       perform flight_request changing flag_found.
       if flag_found = false.
          message e001.        " Flight connection not available
       else.
          set screen 200.      " Next screen
          leave screen.
       endif.
     endcase.
endmodule.
```

In this example, the field `fcode` is the OK Code Field of screen 100 and therefore contains the user command. In general, different user commands are checked in a `case`/`endcase` block of a PAI module. We followed this scheme even in this small example of the module `action_request` for only one user command. When the function code is equal to c_fcode_request, the subroutine flight_request is called. This form checks whether the input values represent a valid flight connection. If the check gives a negative result (i.e., the actual parameter flag_found has the value false), an error message is sent using a message statement. Then, all fields of the chain are ready for input. You can define the message text by double-clicking on the message number. The text is language dependent and can be translated without changing the source code. The prefix e, (which here stands for *error*), characterizes the message type. Other types (information or warnings) will be explained in Chapter 20.

If the check of the flight_request subroutine is successful (i.e., the actual parameter flag_found has the value true), the next screen is set with the command set screen 200 and the current screen is left by leave screen. When you leave a screen, the event process before output of the following screen will be processed. The subsequent screen is statically defined in the screen attributes and it can be dynamically redefined using the set screen statement. In our example, we used the default setting for the static successor—that is, the same screen. Thus, the screen is sent again if the next screen is not redefined dynamically. In particular, when you press ↵, the event process before output of the actual screen is processed, and the actual screen is sent again.

You can also send another screen using the command call screen followed by the number of the screen. The called screen is displayed above the current screen—that is, as a dialog box (also called a *pop-up screen*). When you leave the called screen, the runtime system processes the next statement after the call screen statement in the Flow Logic of the calling screen. This technique will be described in detail in Chapter 22.

Completing the Application Example

Let's now look at the Flow Logic of the second screen:

```
process before output.
* Set title and status, initialize screen fields
  module init_booking.

process after input.
* Work an the input data for a customer's flight booking
  chain.
    field: customers-name,
           seats_required.
    module action_booking.
  endchain.
```

The module `init_booking` sets the title and status of the screen and initializes the screen fields `seats_free`, `seats_required`, and `customers-name`. The latter field is cleared together with all fields of the work area of the customers table by the statement `clear customers`.

```
module init_booking output.
* Initialize titlebar and status
  set titlebar  c_title_booking.
  set pf-status c_status_booking.
* Get number of seats free
  seats_free = actfli-seatsmax - actfli-seatsocc.
* While processing the booking screen, the contents of the
* input fields are kept (e.g., if ENTER is pressed).
  if flag_keep_input = false.
    clear customers.
    seats_required = 1.
    flag_keep_input = true.
  endif.
endmodule.
```

In our example, all PBO modules are also processed after you press ↵, so input data in the fields `seats_required` and `customers-name` doesn't need to be changed if the actual screen is sent again. We've used the global flag `flag_keep_input` to indicate that the input must be kept.

The PAI module `action_booking` performs the booking of the flight and returns to the first screen:

```
module action_booking input.
  case fcode.
    when c_fcode_booking.
*     Make the booking
      perform flight_booking.
*     Return to previous screen for another request.
      flag_keep_input = false.
      set screen c_screen_request.
      leave screen.
  endcase.
endmodule.
```

The subroutine `flight_booking` performs the core business of the booking procedure. The main steps of this form are listed below:

1. Check if seats are available

2. Check for a valid customer

3. Update the bookings table

4. Update the number of occupied seats in the `actfli` table

5. Display an information message

The source code of the form `flight_booking` looks like this:

```
form flight_booking.

  data: l_customers  like customers occurs 10
                     with header line,
        l_line_count type i,
        l_index      like sy-tabix.

* 1. Check if seats are available
  if seats_required > seats_free.
    message e003 with seats_free.     "Not enough seats
  endif.
```

```
* 2. Booking is only allowed for registered customers. Thus,
*    check if a customer ID is available in table CUSTOMERS.
  select * from  customers into table l_customers
          where name = customers-name.

* Check number of matching entries
  describe table l_customers lines l_line_count.
  if l_line_count = 0.
    message e004 with customers-name. "No Customer ID
  elseif l_line_count > 1.
*   Process dialog to select the appropriate customer
    ...     " To be implemented: set L_INDEX
  endif.

  l_index = 1.      " Must be deleted if L_INDEX is set above
  read table l_customers index l_index.
  if sy-subrc <> 0.
    message a006.     "Internal booking error: missing entry
  endif.

* 3. Update bookings information in table BOOKINGS
  move-corresponding actfli to bookings.
  perform set_bookid changing bookings-bookid.
  bookings-customid   = l_customers-id.
  bookings-order_date = sy-datum.

  insert bookings.
  if sy-subrc <> 0.
    message a005.     "Internal booking error: duplicate entries
  endif.

* 4. Update number of occupied seats in table ACTFLI
  add seats_required to actfli-seatsocc.
  update actfli.
  if sy-subrc <> 0.
    message a006.     "Internal booking error: missing entry
  endif.

* 5. Message: booking successful for customer ...
  message i002 with actfli-connid customers-name.

endform.
```

The identifier for a booking is calculated in the separate subroutine set_bookid:

```
form set_bookid changing f_bookid like bookings-bookid.
* Get maximum bookid and increment it by 1
  select max( bookid ) into (f_bookid) from bookings.
  add 1 to f_bookid.
endform.
```

If a customer name does not uniquely identify a customer, you should provide another dialog box to determine the customer. The second part of form flight_booking is already prepared for this refinement. Techniques for adding another dialog are described in Chapter 22.

> **NOTE**
>
> The modules of the Flow Logic are similar to subroutines defined by form/endform. They can be called from different screens, which is very useful when some check of the user input is to be done on different screens. Data exchange between screen and modules in the associated ABAP/4 program is done via shared data areas—that is, global variables (defined by data) and table work areas (defined by tables).

So far, the sample program fulfills most of the requirements. However, we have not yet described how to define the menu functions and buttons. This is covered in the next sections. We will also describe how to interrupt the sequence of screens. For instance, when you wish to leave the booking screen without making an actual booking, the first screen will be displayed. Also, we'll discuss different methods for sending pop-up windows.

Creating GUI Statuses and Titles

A GUI status describes the elements of the menu bar and the buttons of the toolbars below the menu bar. A GUI title determines the title of a screen. The texts for GUI statuses and titles are language-dependent: they appear in the language the user specified when logging on. GUI statuses and titles can be translated without affecting the source code of the program.

You can define a GUI status on the Object Browser screen using the Create button. Select the object type GUI Status from the dialog box that appears after clicking on the Create button, enter a name for the status, and specify the attributes as shown in Figure 19.15. In our example, we chose the type Screen for the status REQUEST of the first screen, since it is used as a full screen.

NOTE The status type List is used for lists of reports (see Chapter 17), and the other status types will be described in Chapter 22.

Defining Menus

When you've specified the status attributes, you can define the menu functions and buttons on the next screen (see Figure 19.16). Enter a short explanatory text for the menu bar in the top line. Standard menus are proposed by the system when you double-click on the symbol to the left of Display Standards, as shown in Figure 19.17. To add or remove items you can pull down or collapse a menu by double-click.

FIGURE 19.15:

Creating a GUI status for our sample program's first screen

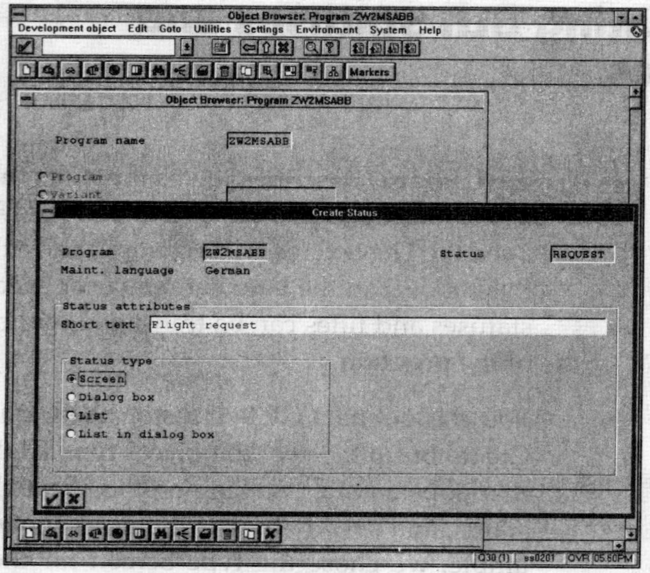

FIGURE 19.16:

Specifying attributes for the GUI status for our sample screen

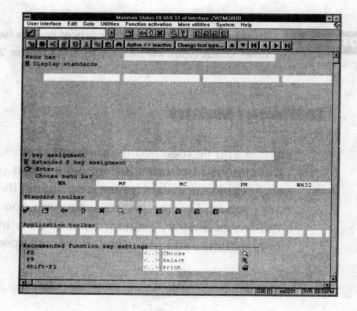

FIGURE 19.17:

The standard menu entries proposed by the system for our GUI status

```
Maintain Status REQUEST of Interface ZW2MSABB
User interface  Edit  Goto  Utilities  Function activation  More utilities  System  Help

Active <-> Inactive   Change text type...

Menu bar
⊟ Hide standards

  <Object>              Edit              Goto              Details

Func Name
<..> Other <object>
<..> Create
<..> Change
<..> Display
<..> Copy from
<..> -----------
<..> Save
<..> -----------
<..> Print
<..> -----------
<..> Delete
<..> Exit



F key assignment
⊟ Extended F key assignment
↵ Enter..
  Choose menu bar
    WN            MF            MC            PM            WN32

Standard toolbar

✓   🗁  ⇦  ⇧  ✖  🔍  ?  ⧉  ⧉  ⧉  ⧉

                                              Q30 (1) ss0201 OVR 05:57PM
```

In general, the first menu is used for operations of the current object such as Create, Change, Save, or Delete. In our example, the first menu is named Flight Connection. Other menus (Edit, Goto, Details, and Environment) are also provided. In the example in this chapter, we only need the Goto menu in addition to the Flight Connection menu. To delete a menu, place the mouse pointer on it and click on the Cut button. You can delete menu functions in the same way.

The program for flight bookings provides the following functions:

Function code	Purpose
REQU	Request for a flight connection
BOOK	Booking a flight
CLEA	Delete current input

Function code	Purpose
BACK	Back to previous screen
EXIT	Exit from the program

To define a menu function on the GUI status maintenance screen, insert the function code in the left column and type a short text into the right column for the pull-down menu (see Figure 19.18).

Since the booking operation is related to the second screen, it must be inactive on the first screen. You can deactivate a menu function in a status by clicking on the button Active <-> Inactive on the GUI status maintenance screen. Inactive functions are displayed in a different color than the active functions. Menus with many functions can be structured by inserting lines via Edit ➤ Insert ➤ Separator Line.

FIGURE 19.18:

Defining menu functions for the Flight Connection menu

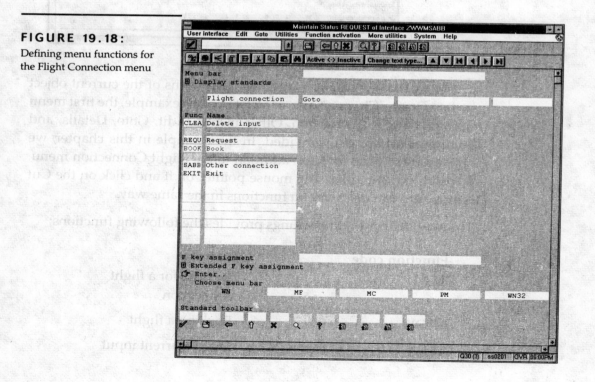

As explained above in section "Attributes of Screen Elements," function codes are used to propagate user actions to the application program. When, at runtime, a user selects a menu function, the associated function code is put into the OK Code Field (for example, fcode). Its contents are used by the PAI modules to react to the user action. In practice, function codes are defined as constants in the program.

```
types
  function_code(4) type c.
constants:
  c_fcode_request  type function_code value 'REQU',
  c_fcode_booking  type function_code value 'BOOK',
  c_fcode_clear    type function_code value 'CLEA',
  c_fcode_back     type function_code value 'BACK',
  c_fcode_exit     type function_code value 'EXIT'.
```

Before a GUI status becomes active at runtime, you have to generate it separately by clicking on the Generate button on the GUI status maintenance screen or on the Object Browser screen. This means that you can edit a status without affecting the running program. The status of a screen is usually set in a PBO module using the command set pf-status followed by the name of the status. The runtime system always uses the same status that has been set previously. So, if you do not set a status at the event PBO of the second screen, the status of the first screen will be used again.

Function Keys and Buttons

For quick access to menu functions, you can attach function keys, push buttons, and toolbar buttons to menu functions. For those users who prefer to use function keys instead of mouse clicks, each push button should refer to a function key.

For example, in the status REQUEST, we use the buttons Request and Delete Input. The latter is combined with a toolbar button. To relate the function code REQU to the function key F5, type **REQU** in the framed area Freely Assigned Function Keys in the appropriate line, and press ↵. The short text *Request* will be inserted automatically, since it has already been defined in the Flight connection menu. This text is also displayed when the user clicks the right mouse button at runtime anywhere on the screen.

You can enter the function codes REQU and CLEA in the application toolbar to associate push buttons with the function codes. The corresponding short texts *Request* and *Delete Input* will be provided by the system, as shown in Figure 19.19.

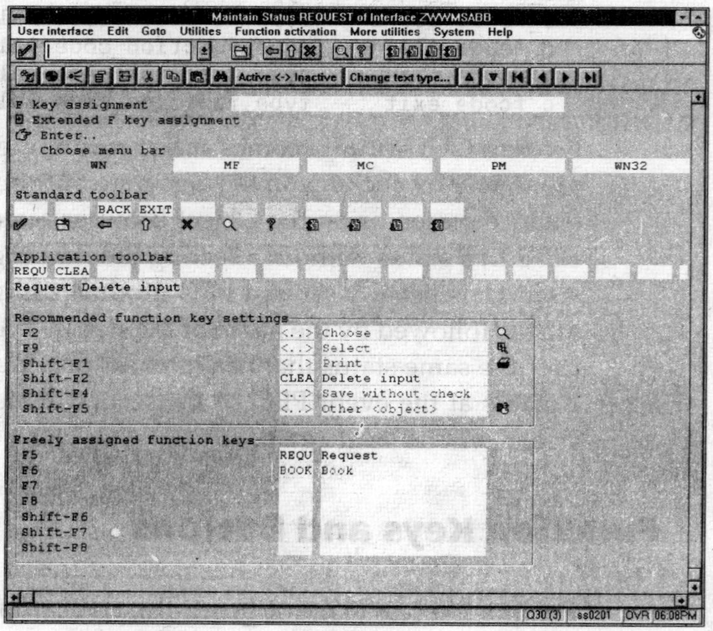

FIGURE 19.19:

Defining function keys and push buttons for the REQU and CLEA function codes

You can also attach a toolbar button to the function code. By choosing More Utilities ➤ Propose Icons, you get a proposal of standard buttons, which can be associated with the push buttons. To add text to the button, activate the Text check box. If the proposal is not appropriate for a push button, you can also attach an arbitrary toolbar button. Select the push button in the application toolbar and choose Change

Text Type. On the next dialog box, you are asked to specify the text type. Choose Icon to get a dialog box, where the toolbar button and its text can be specified (see Figure 19.20).

FIGURE 19.20:

Specifying a toolbar button for the CLEA function

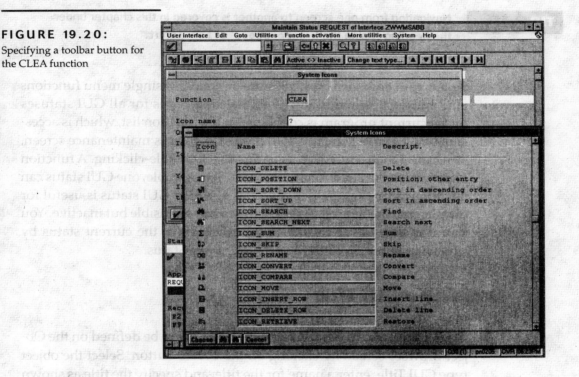

The standard toolbar contains standard buttons. For example, when you design a GUI status for a report list, some of the toolbar buttons already have function codes that are used by the runtime system for navigation and scrolling (see Chapter 17). For different status types, function codes are not associated automatically. If you want to activate a standard toolbar button, enter a function code of your choice and implement the corresponding functionality in a PAI module. For example, backward navigation to a previous screen must be programmed using the commands set screen and leave screen if the GUI status is not of type List.

Navigating from one screen to another is covered in this chapter under the heading "Using the Event process after input."

So far, you have seen how to create or maintain single menu functions and buttons. An overview of all function codes for all GUI statuses of the current program is contained in the function list, which is accessible via Goto ➤ Function List on the GUI status maintenance screen. You can change any function on this list by double-clicking. A function code can be used in different statuses. For example, one GUI status can be defined for changing operations. A second GUI status is useful for display only, where all changing functions are visible but inactive. You can also activate or deactivate all functions of the current status by choosing Function Activation ➤ In Current Status.

Defining a GUI Title

A GUI title determines the title of a screen. It can be defined on the Object Browser screen by clicking on the Create button. Select the object type GUI Title, enter a name for the title, and specify the title as shown in Figure 19.21. In our example, we entered the title *Flight booking: Inquiry for flight connection.*

The title of a screen is usually set in a PBO module using the command set titlebar followed by the name of the title. As with GUI statuses, the runtime system always uses the title, which has been set previously. For instance, the PBO module init_request of the first

FIGURE 19.21:

Creating a GUI title for the first screen of the sample program

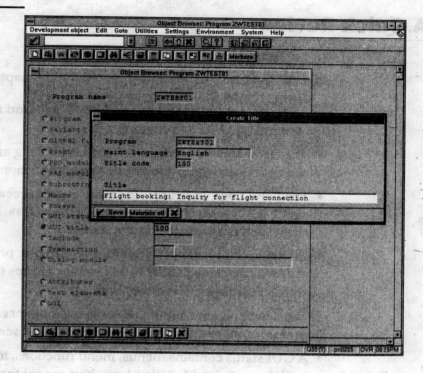

screen of our sample program looks like this:

```
module init_request output.
* Initialize titlebar and status
   set titlebar  c_title_request.
   set pf-status c_status_request.
endmodule.
```

Here we followed the convention of declaring constants in the program for GUI titles and statuses, since they are often used in different places. However, you can also use literals:

```
module init_request output.
* Initialize titlebar and status
   set titlebar  '100'.
   set pf-status 'REQUEST'.
endmodule.
```

A Quick Review

Here are some of the topics we covered in this chapter:

- A screen consists of layout and Flow Logic, and it is attached to a controlling ABAP/4 program.

- The elements of the layout are placed via drag and drop. They can be chosen from a toolbar or from the Dictionary.

- The Flow Logic is structured by the events process before output (PBO), process after input (PAI), process on help request, and process on value request.

- Within each event, modules of the controlling program can be called. They can be attached to fields or groups of fields (keywords fields or chain/endchain).

- You can navigate among screens using set screen or call screen. You exit the current screen via leave screen.

- A GUI status contains menus, menu functions, toolbar buttons, push buttons, and function keys. You can set the status in a program using the command set pf-status.

- At runtime, a user action is automatically translated into a function code of the GUI status and put into the OK Code Field of the current screen. The controlling program can react to this function code at the event process after input (PAI).

- A GUI title is the title of a screen, and you can set the title in a program using the command set titlebar.

- The texts for screens, GUI statuses, and titles are language-dependent, and they can be translated without affecting the program source.

In the next chapter, you'll see how to display dialog boxes after invalid user input.

CHAPTER

TWENTY

Messages, Standardized Dialog Boxes, and Exceptions

- **Using different types of error messages**

- **Sending standard dialog boxes**

- **Working with exceptions of a function module**

A dialog program often asks the user to enter new data when input data was invalid. A success message is sent when data has been changed in the database. These elementary user dialogs are easily implemented using the message command combined with different message types and a language-dependent text. If the dialog requires alternative user actions (such as selecting Yes, No, or Cancel), the ABAP/4 Development Workbench provides some standard functions for these purposes, and we'll discuss them in this chapter.

Whenever many programs are involved in real applications, the following situation arises: a function called by many programs detects an error, but each caller of the function wants to continue in a different way after the error. For example, one caller enables the user to enter new data and another caller terminates the program, since the error cannot be corrected by a user action. Under these circumstances, the called function must provide detailed information about the error type without terminating the calling program. The exceptions of ABAP/4 functions fulfill these requirements. Several techniques are provided to handle exceptional situations that the calling program does not intend to handle explicitly, and we'll discuss this in this chapter. This flexibility of the interface of ABAP/4 functions is very useful when new exceptions are introduced during the life cycle of a function.

Working with Messages

In this section, you will learn how you can use error messages in your programs and how to edit message texts. Messages have different types, and you will learn how these types affect the runtime behavior of a program after a message has been sent to the end user.

Sending a Message from a Program

If a user enters invalid data into a program, you can arrange for the system to send an error message using the message command, as shown here:

```
message e001.
```

This tiny line of code causes the program to stop and send a message text to the end user. The prefix of the message number specifies the message type; for example *e* is for an error message. You can display or define the message text by double-clicking on the message number in the source code line from the Editor. Then the Display Messages screen appears (see Figure 20.1) and you can edit a message text by double-clicking on the corresponding line. The text is language-dependent and can be translated without changing the source code.

FIGURE 20.1:

The message text display and maintenance screen

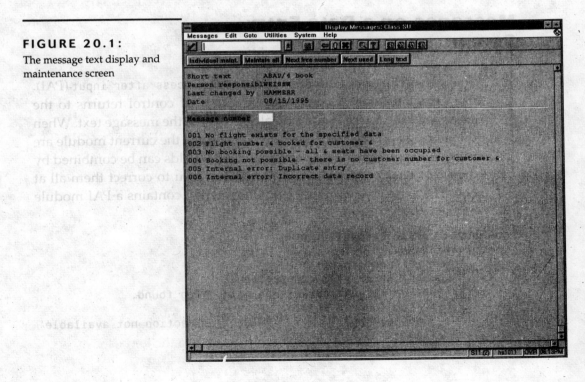

In addition to the message number, the text is determined by a two-character message identifier. The message identifier is usually specified after the addition `message-id` of the `program` declaration:

```
program sapmsabb message-id su.
```

You can also set the message identifier and type dynamically at the message command:

```
data: msgid like sy-msgid value 'SU',
      msgty like sy-msgty value 'E',
      msgno like sy-msgno value '001'.
message id msgid type msgty number msgno.
```

Using the & character, you can include a maximum of four variables in the message text. You set the values for the text variables after the addition `with` in the message statement:

```
message i002 with actfli-connid customers-name.
```

Messages on a Data Entry Screen

You can send an error message at the event `process after input` (PAI). If an error message is processed, the flow of control returns to the screen and the system sends a dialog box with the message text. When the message is confirmed, the fields related to the current module are ready for input again. For example, several fields can be combined by means of `chain` and `endchain`. This allows you to correct them all at once. The example program from Chapter 19 contains a PAI module with an error message:

```
module action_request input.
  case fcode.
    when c_fcode_request.
*     Check for a valid connection
      perform flight_request changing flag_found.
      if flag_found = false.
        message e001.        " Flight connection not available
      else.
```

```
        set screen 200.      " Next screen
          leave screen.
        endif.
      endcase.
    endmodule.
```

When this error occurs, the message text is displayed in a small dialog box, as shown in Figure 20.2. In our example, this could happen when no flight exists for the chosen destinations, date, and carrier.

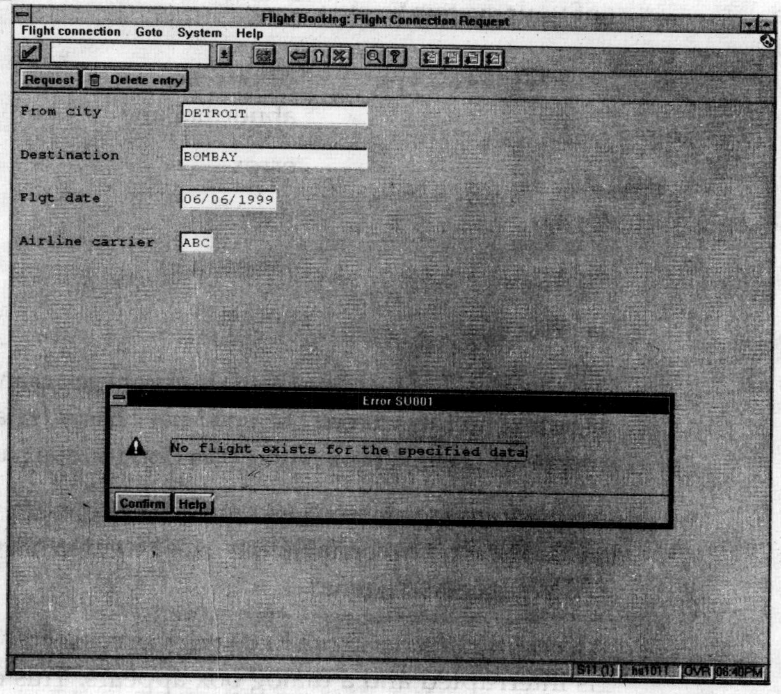

FIGURE 20.2:

A dialog box displaying an error message following an end user's data input error

When clicking on the Confirm button on the dialog box, the end user is returned to the same screen with all fields on the screen ready for input again. Detailed information about the error situation can be displayed through the Help button on the dialog box of the error message.

The developer can create this help information by clicking on the Long text button on the Message Display screen.

Different Message Types and Their Effect on a Program

ABAP/4 supports the following message types, which are listed ordered by their severity (i.e., how seriously they interrupt the operation of your system):

Message Type	Meaning
a	abnormal end
e	error
w	warning
i	information
s	success

An *abnormal end* terminates the current program and displays the message text on the screen. The end user has no chance to correct the data, and must select a new menu function to start another dialog.

An *error message* interrupts the flow of control in a PAI module, sends a dialog box, and enables the user to enter new data. Then the event PAI is processed again.

A *warning* behaves much like an error message: the current PAI module is interrupted and a dialog box appears. This dialog box contains the message text and two alternatives for the subsequent user action as shown in Figure 20.3. The user can either choose New Entry on the dialog box to change the input data or can click on the Continue button to proceed with the interrupted PAI module immediately after the `message` statement.

FIGURE 20.3:

An example of a warning
dialog box, with two choices
for the user

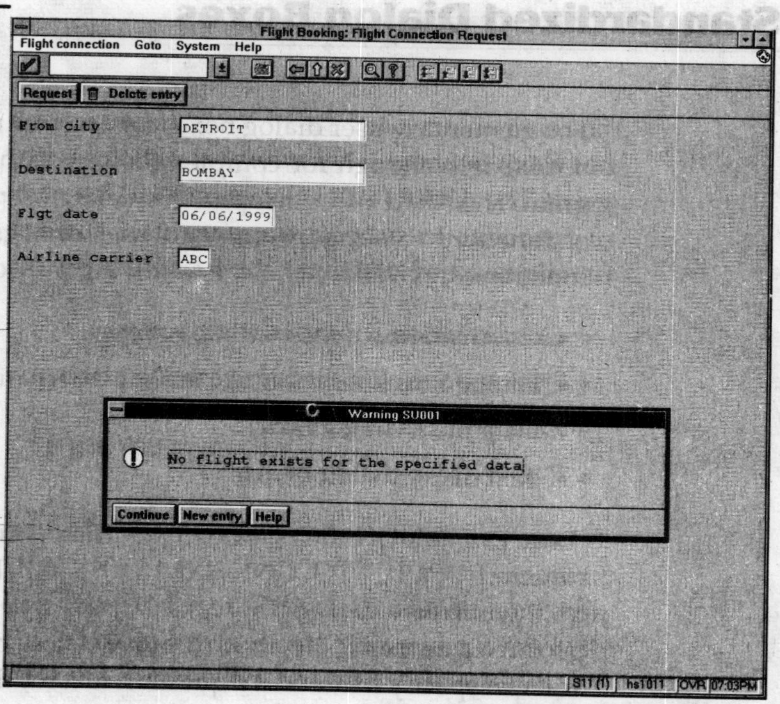

An *information message* also displays the message text in a dialog box. However, there is no way to interrupt the program. The flow of control of the program always continues immediately after the message statement.

Finally, a *success message* works like an information message. The only difference is that the message text is displayed on the next screen.

The above message types are primarily designed for dialog programs that have screens for the user input. They are also helpful to check user input on the selection screen of a report—that is, at the event at selection-screen (see Chapter 16). If you try to send an error message at a later report event like start of selection, get table, or end of selection, the runtime system always terminates the report with the message type *e* converted to type *a*, since there is no screen available to correct the input data.

Standardized Dialog Boxes

The elementary user dialog boxes for an error message or warning are not flexible enough for complex dialogs with the end user of a program. The ABAP/4 Development Workbench provides a large number of functions to support standard user dialogs. For example, several functions are available for the following purposes:

- Confirmation prompt dialog boxes
- Dialog boxes for choosing among alternatives
- Data print dialog boxes
- Text display dialog boxes

As an example of the first category of dialog functions, you can use the function POPUP_TO_CONFIRM_LOSS_OF_DATA. With this function, you create a dialog box to ask users whether or not they wish to perform a processing step with possible loss of data (see Figure 20.4). You can specify a title and a question text for the dialog box. The function provides warning text that says data will be lost and suggests possible responses. The user must answer Yes, No, or Cancel. In the interface, the response No is pre-selected as the default, and you cannot set a different one. The user response (Yes, No, or Cancel) is returned in the parameter answer. For example, the function call can look like this:

```
call function 'POPUP_TO_CONFIRM_LOSS_OF_DATA'
    exporting
        title     = 'Leave customer list'
        textline1 = 'Really quit?'
    importing
        answer    = user_answer.
```

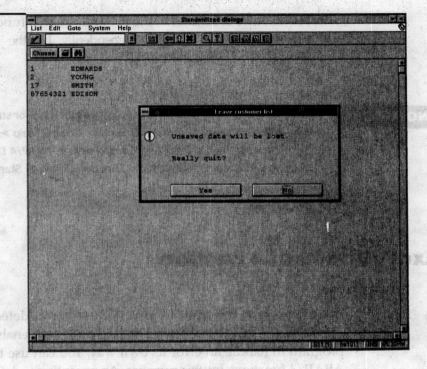

FIGURE 20.4:

An example of a warning dialog box, with two choices for the user

As an example for a function of the second category, the function POPUP_TO_DECIDE creates a dialog box in which the user is asked to choose between two processing alternatives, or to cancel the action. Action, question, and alternative actions are passed as parameters. The user action (Alternative 1, Alternative 2, or Cancel) is returned in a parameter.

Using the functions TABLE_PRINT_STRUCTURE_KNOWN and TABLE_PRINT_STRUCTURE_UNKNOWN from the third category, you can print database tables. With a parameter, you can control whether the table records are output with a standard list format or whether the user can specify the print format in a dialog box. The user can choose fields, specify a sort sequence, and specify the column sequence and titles in these dialog boxes. Using the function TABLE_PRINT_STRUCTURE_KNOWN, you pass data from tables whose structure is known in the program to this function. Otherwise, this structure data is fetched independently by the function TABLE_PRINT_STRUCTURE_UNKNOWN.

NOTE You can find complete documentation of the functions for standardized dialogs in the Online Help of the R/3 System. Choose Help ➤ R/3 Library from any screen. Then select Basis Components ➤ ABAP/4 Development Workbench ➤ Extended Applications Function Library ➤ Standardized Dialogs.

Exceptions of a Function

If a function is called from many programs, errors detected by the function should be given back to the calling programs, enabling each calling program to handle an error its own way. You can use the exceptions of ABAP/4 functions for this purpose. An exception is defined in the interface of a function (see Chapter 10). To trigger an exception, you can either use the `raise` statement or the addition `raising` of the `message` statement. For example, the exception `not_found` can be raised in a function as follows:

1. `raise not_found.`

2. `message e001 raising not_found.`

In both cases, if the `raise` or `message` statement is processed at runtime, the function is terminated immediately. If the program calling the function handles the exception, control returns immediately to that program and the export parameters of the function are not given back. The above-mentioned alternatives differ when the caller does not handle the exception: if the `raise` statement is processed in the function, a general system runtime error occurs and the calling program is also terminated. On the other hand, the specified message in the `message` command is sent if the caller does not handle the exception specified after the addition `raising`.

In practice, new exceptions will be introduced during the life cycle of a function, but it would be tedious to adapt all calling programs. Using the standard exception `others`, the callers of a function can define how they want to handle unforeseen exceptions. If a function always raises exceptions with the `message` command followed by the addition `raising`, the calling programs need not work with the exception `others`.

Exceptions can also be triggered by subroutines (forms) of functions. In this case, all the forms on the stack are popped, the function is terminated, and the calling program can handle the exception.

A Quick Review

Here is a quick review of some of the topics we covered in this chapter:

- Messages are sent using the `message` command followed by a message identifier, a type, and a number. The message identifier can also be specified in the `program` or `report` declaration.

- There are different message types for abnormal end, error, warning, information, and success messages.

- The message number refers to a language-dependent text, which can be translated without affecting the source code of the program.

- Standardized user dialogs are supported by several functions. For example, confirmation prompt dialog boxes or dialog boxes for choosing among alternatives are available.

- Exceptions of functions can be triggered by the raise statement or by the addition raising of the message statement. These alternatives are treated separately by the system when the calling program does not handle the exception.

In the next chapter, we'll introduce the R/3 transaction concept and cover how to change data consistently in the database.

CHAPTER

TWENTY-ONE

Changing Database Objects Using Transactions

- **The concept of a transaction**

- **Locking objects for a transaction**

- **Working with an Update Task**

To guarantee consistent data even throughout complex application programs, ABAP/4 offers an elaborated transaction concept that is independent of the underlying database management system. For example, if you book a flight through a travel agency, it should be guaranteed that you really will get a boarding pass card on the day of departure. On the other hand, if the flight is already fully booked, you expect the people at the travel agency to let you know while you are making the reservation. It is also important that other travel agencies reserving seats for the same flight have accurate information about the number of seats available at the moment of reservation so that the flight doesn't get overbooked.

A *transaction* is a dialog program with one or more screens that changes objects in the database in a consistent way. The program logic of a transaction is divided into one or more Logical Units of Work (LUW). If an error occurs, all changes in the current LUW are taken back, so that the contents of database tables are always consistent. A locking mechanism for transactions ensures that only one user can change a data object at the same time. Locks are set and released by standardized functions that are automatically created by the ABAP/4 Development Workbench. The lifetime of locks also defines the Logical Units of Work.

With the ABAP/4 Development Workbench, you can design transactions that work in a distributed client/server environment. The database server is often the bottleneck of the whole system. Using the concept of an Update Task, you can both minimize the response times for all dialog users and guarantee data consistency. The concept of a transaction and of a Logical Unit of Work is well-known among database developers and users. However, since the R/3 system supports different database management systems, and because of the three-tier architecture of the R/3 system, a separate lock mechanism and a special concept for Logical Units of Works are necessary.

Logical Units of Work

In the flight reservation program from Chapter 19, several measures already guarantee the data integrity to a certain extent. For example, check tables prevent the user from booking nonexisting flights. In addition, a special subroutine checks whether enough free seats are available. If two or more travel agencies use this flight reservation program at the same time, it is possible that too many seats will be booked. To avoid this inconsistency, you can use the lock mechanism of the ABAP/4 Development Workbench.

The R/3 Locking Mechanism

To lock an object, you can call a standardized function that creates a corresponding entry in a global system table. You can release a lock with a standardized function call or let the system make the release at the transaction's end. If another user tries to lock the same object while the lock entry still exists, the locking function returns an exception. The locking mechanism defines Logical Units of Work. The LUW starts when a lock entry in the system table is created, and it ends when the lock is released.

The R/3 locking mechanism is portable to all database management systems. A developer can freely define lock objects without worrying about the organization of data in database tables. In contrast, many database management systems lock a set of table entries even if only a single record lock is sufficient. As a consequence, situations are likely to happen where end users can't access a database object because they must wait for the lock to finish, and deadlocks can even occur. These problems are avoided when locks of a small granularity are created with the R/3 lock mechanism.

Since the R/3 system is designed for multi-user applications that can have up to several thousand users, it is necessary to share common resources among them. One such resource obviously is the database. Therefore, many users of the R/3 system are mapped onto a single database user, and a native database commit is processed whenever a screen is sent for one R/3 user. In other words, an LUW of the R/3 system is made up of one or more database LUWs. To guarantee the overall data consistency of an application, all database changes must be processed within one database LUW. To achieve this, choose one of the following alternatives:

1. Collect all data of the transaction in internal tables and perform the database changes at the event PAI on the transaction's last screen.

2. Use a system service functionality called an *Update Task* that collects the data and changes the database (see below).

NOTE The flexible way of defining lock objects in the R/3 lock mechanism requires that all programs changing the same object should also use the same lock object.

Creating a Lock Object in the Dictionary

To create a lock object, choose Dictionary Objects on the Object Browser screen and enter the name of the new object after Lock Objects on the next screen. Specify a short explanatory text and the name of the database table as shown in Figure 21.1.

FIGURE 21.1:

Creating a lock object

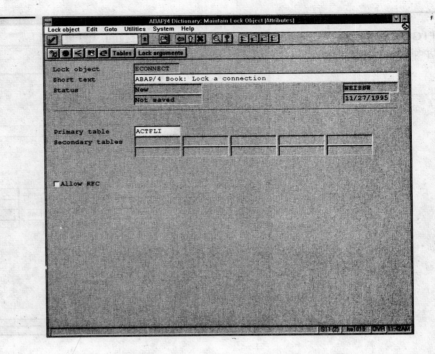

In general, a lock object can refer to several database tables. For each table of the lock object, you can specify fields as lock arguments (see Figure 21.2).

Click on the Generate button to activate the lock object. The system then generates functions to set and release a lock at runtime.

Setting a Lock Entry

The functions that are generated by the R/3 system when you activated a lock object are called *Enqueue* and *Dequeue* functions. The function names are normalized to ENQUEUE_ and DEQUEUE_ followed by the name of the lock object. To set a lock entry for an object you would write the following piece of code:

```
call function 'ENQUEUE_ECONNECT'
```

FIGURE 21.2:

Specifying lock arguments

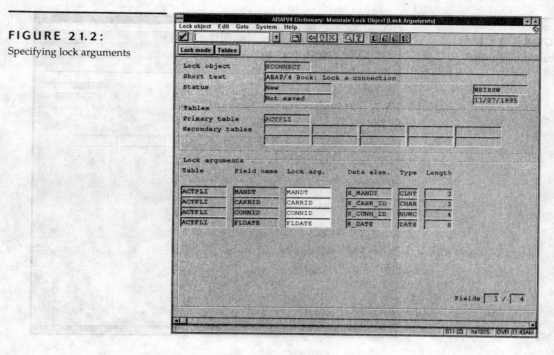

```
exporting  carrid    = actfli-carrid
           connid    = actfli-connid
           fldate    = actfli-fldate
exceptions foreign_lock = 1
           others    = 2.
case sy-subrc.
    when 1.
    message e010 with actfli-carrid actfli-connid
    actfli-fldate.
  when 2.
    message a011.
endcase.
```

The exception foreign_lock is raised by the Enqueue function when a lock entry already exists. Other exceptions can occur after a system failure. In both cases, the program should send the user a message and terminate.

The R/3 locking mechanism covers different levels of granularity. If all key fields of a table are specified in the interface of the Enqueue function, a single record is locked. On the other hand, when no field is set by the Enqueue function, the whole table is locked. Intermediate locking levels are possible by specifying a proper subset of the table fields. Complex objects of the application program can be locked in a single step if the lock object is made of more than one database table.

Once you have established locks on all database objects you intend to change, you can make the database changes, for example, by inserting a new record in a table. The commit work command makes persistent all database changes initiated in the current LUW. If an error occurs, you can use the rollback work command that takes back all database changes of the current LUW.

Deleting a Lock Entry

You can delete a lock entry by calling a standardized Dequeue function. In the example above, the function DEQUEUE_ECONNECT releases the lock that has been created by the function ENQUEUE_ECONNECT. In addition, the end of a transaction terminates a LUW and releases all locks. If you use the service of the Update Task as explained in this chapter under the heading "Using Update Tasks," the commit work command does not execute the database commit immediately, but delegates the commit to an asynchronous process that performs the database changes and releases all locks.

Working with Transactions

As we defined in the introduction to this chapter, a *transaction* is a dialog program with one or more screens that changes objects in the database in a consistent way. In the R/3 system a transaction has a name and needs to be registered in the ABAP/4 Development Workbench.

Creating and Calling a Transaction

To create a transaction, enter the name after the object type Transaction on the Object Browser screen, and select the transaction type Dialog Transaction in the next dialog box as shown in Figure 21.3. In an additional dialog box, the system prompts you to specify a short explanatory text, a program, and an initial screen for your dialog transaction. At runtime, the initial screen is sent when the transaction is called as explained below.

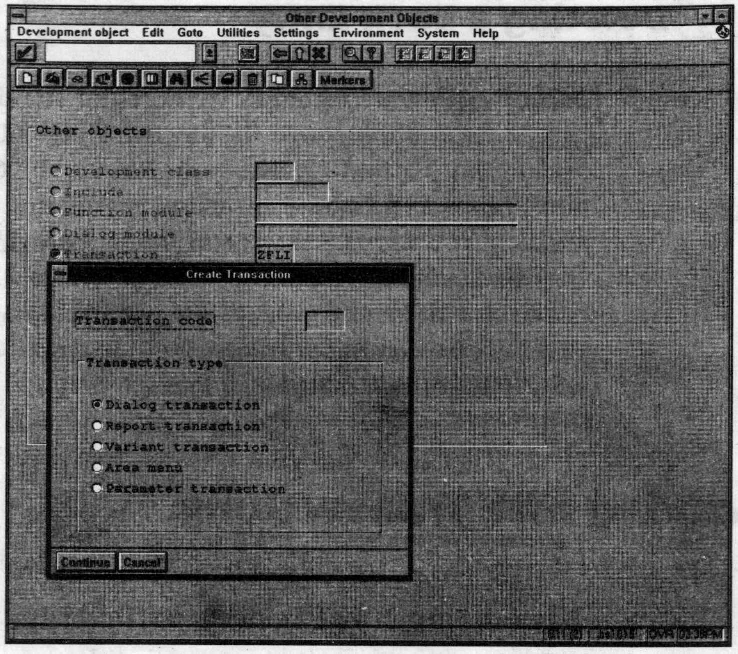

FIGURE 21.3:

Defining a transaction

In addition to dialog transactions, the ABAP/4 Development Workbench supports various transaction types. For example, a Report Transaction executes a report that has a standard selection screen and produces an output list (see Chapters 15–18). A Variant Transaction displays the field values of a transaction variant for one or more screens of the transaction. Like report variants, it is possible to change screen fields to display mode only or even to suppress screen fields. This technique enables you to customize screens without changing the source code.

To call a transaction in a dialog session, create a menu function of type T on the GUI status maintenance screen. For example, the transaction code SABB from Chapter 19 can be added to a menu entry as shown in Figure 21.4.

FIGURE 21.4:

Adding a transaction to a menu

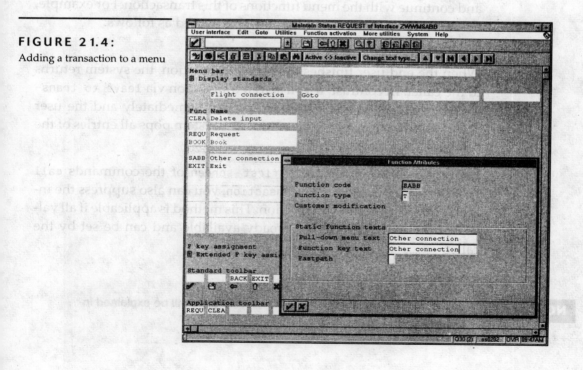

In this example, the transaction SABB appears in the menu Flight connections. At runtime, when the called transaction ends, the system returns to the caller.

On the programming level, you can start a transaction with the following methods:

1. By issuing the command `call transaction`

2. By issuing the command `leave to transaction`

3. By using a standardized function with a variant as parameter

If you start a transaction via `call transaction`, the first screen of the called transaction will appear, and the end user can enter input values and continue with the menu functions of this transaction. For example, the transaction SABB from Chapter 19 is started as follows:

```
call transaction 'SABB'.
```

When the end user finishes the called transaction, the system returns to the caller. In contrast, if you start a transaction via `leave to transaction`, the calling transaction is finished immediately and the user won't come back to that transaction. The system pops all entries of the calling stack for transactions.

Using the addition `and skip first screen` of the commands `call transaction` and `leave to transaction`, you can also suppress the initial screen of the called transaction. This method is applicable if all values of the initial screen are already available and can be set by the caller.

NOTE The method of setting the values of screen fields will be explained in Chapter 22.

Using Transaction Variants

To call a transaction with a variant, you can use the function RS_HDSYS_CALL_TC_VARIANT. Starting from Release 3.0E, variant maintenance is accessible through the System menu that appears on every screen of the R/3 system. First, you specify the transaction and the variant as shown in Figure 21.5.

FIGURE 21.5:

Creating a transaction variant

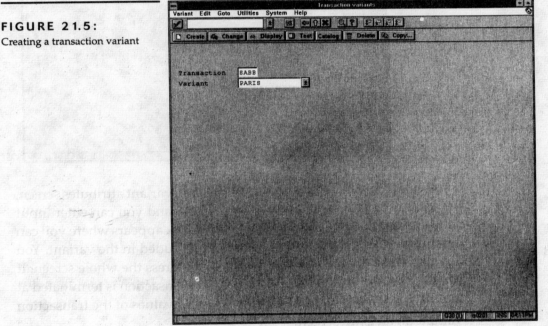

When you click on the Create button, you can enter a short explanatory text for the variant on the next screen (see Figure 21.6) and save the variant by clicking on the Save button.

FIGURE 21.6:

Attributes of a transaction variant

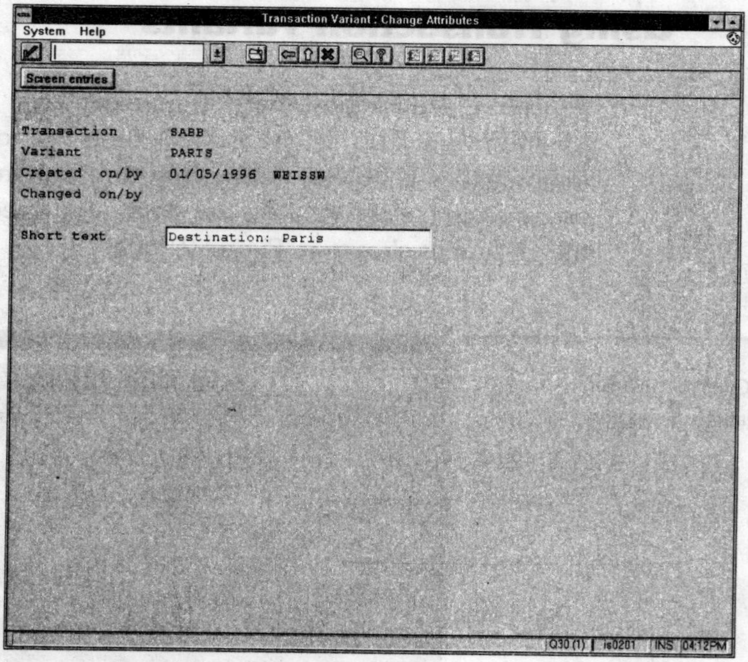

```
Transaction Variant : Change Attributes
System  Help

 Screen entries

Transaction     SABB
Variant         PARIS
Created  on/by  01/05/1996  WEISSW
Changed  on/by

Short text      Destination: Paris

                                                    Q30 (1)  ic0201  INS  04:12PM
```

If you select Screen Entries on the transaction variant attributes screen, the screens of the chosen transaction appear and you can enter input values as usual. After each screen, a dialog box appears where you can determine which input values should be included in the variant. You can also make a screen field invisible or suppress the whole screen. If you click on the button Exit And Save, the transaction is terminated at the current screen and you can save the field values of the transaction variant on an extra screen.

Using Update Tasks

Update Tasks establish a service for asynchronous database changes. Because of the asynchronous nature of Update Tasks, you can minimize the response times for all dialog users and guarantee data consistency at the same time. In general, you expend less programming effort if you use the Update Task technique instead of collecting the transaction data in internal tables and figuring out the proper opportunity for the commit work command. In particular, you need not foresee the program flow if functions are often called from within many different contexts.

Working with Update Functions

When using the Update Task technique, you write a set of functions containing the database change operations for your transaction, such as insert or delete statements. Such an update function needs to be classified in the function administration screen as Update With Start Immediately. In the flight reservation program from Chapter 19, the source code of the update function might look like this:

```
function abap_book_insert_bookings.
   insert bookings from i_bookings.
   update actfli from i_actfli.
endfunction.
```

This update function can be called using the addition in update task:

```
call function 'ABAP_BOOK_INSERT_BOOKINGS'
     in update task
     exporting
        i_bookings = bookings
        i_actfli   = actfli.
* other statements may follow
commit work.
```

Here, the addition in update task in the function call has the effect that the function is not invoked immediately. Instead, the interface data is transferred with the function call to an intermediate system area. When the in update task addition is used, the commit work command does not execute the database commit directly, but delegates the commit to the asynchronous Update Task. The Update Task immediately takes the data from the intermediate system area, executes the update function, and releases all locks of the calling dialog transaction. If a dialog program calls more than one update function, these functions are bundled in an Update Order and all functions of this Update Order are carried out after a commit work statement. The locks are released at the end of the Update Order. In case of a runtime error, the error situation is logged, and a dialog box appears telling the end user that he or she received an express mail in the R/3 mailing system with information about the error. You can query the error status of the Update Order choosing Tools ➤ Administration ➤ Monitoring ➤ Update.

Asynchronous Nature of the Update Task

After the commit work statement, a dialog program does not wait for a response from the Update Task. Thus, an end user can continue working even when the system load is very high. This asynchronous technique minimizes the average response time of the dialog users. In general, the Update Task performs the database changes directly. However, a slight delay might occur when the system is busy. Thus, the LUW of the calling transaction might last longer than the dialog program is active. In any case, data consistency is guaranteed, since lock entries are only released when the Update Order has finished.

To increase the overall performance of the R/3 system, the system administrator can define several Update Tasks. The runtime system dispatches the Update Orders to the Update Tasks, thus balancing the system load.

A Quick Review

Here is a quick review of some of the topics we covered in this chapter:

- The R/3 transaction concept guarantees the consistency of data in a distributed client/server environment independent of database management systems.
- You can create a lock object in the Dictionary.
- An object can be locked by a standardized function that creates an entry in a global system table.
- Logical Units of Work (LUW) are defined by the lifetime of R/3 lock entries.
- A lock entry is deleted by a standardized function or at the end of a transaction.
- Transactions are defined in the Object Browser.
- Transactions are called by menu functions or from programs by the `call transaction` and `leave to transaction` commands.
- Update functions in Update Tasks perform the database changes asynchronously, thus minimizing response times for the users.

In the following chapter you will see how to enhance your dialog programs by using more elaborate GUI features.

A Quick Review

Here is a quick review of some of the topics we covered in this chapter:

- The R/3 transaction concept guarantees the consistency of data in a distributed client/server environment independent of database management systems.

- You can create a lock object in the Dictionary

- An object can be locked by a standardized function that creates an entry in a global system table.

- Logical Units of Work (LUW) are defined by the lifetime of R/3 lock entries.

- A lock entry is deleted by a standardized function or at the end of a transaction.

- Transactions are defined in the Object Browser.

- Transactions are called by menu functions or from programs by the CALL TRANSACTION and LEAVE TO TRANSACTION commands.

- Update functions in Update Tasks perform the database changes asynchronously, thus minimizing response times for the users.

In the following chapter you will see how to enhance your dialog programs by using more elaborate GUI feature.

CHAPTER

TWENTY-TWO

Advanced GUI Features

- **Enhancing the screen layout with check boxes, radio buttons, and table controls**

- **Providing context-sensitive help information**

- **Designing dialog boxes**

This chapter describes supplementary techniques for refining the layout and the functionality of screens by adding check boxes, radio buttons, and push buttons. We'll also discuss adding table controls, which provide full flexibility for interactive table operations.

For complex transactions, you will want to define a menu hierarchy, and we'll cover that in this chapter. Submenus in a hierarchy are defined in the same way as normal menu functions. In a large-scale application, it is helpful to re-use menus, toolbars, and function key settings of a GUI status for several screens. To this end, you can either copy a GUI status or define a reference to a GUI status as a whole or to parts of it.

The standard help information for screen fields—documentation and a set of possible entries—is retrieved from the Dictionary as explained in Chapter 19. In this chapter, you will learn how to implement alternative help functions by defining appropriate events in the flow logic of a screen. Moreover, you can derive a default value for a screen field from the previous user input in a field of the same kind—that is, a transaction can suggest values to support the user at input.

At runtime, the sequence of screens in a transaction is determined by user interaction and by the Flow Logic of each screen. You will see how to implement a sequence of screens either as a queue or as a stack. In addition, when calling a screen as a dialog box, you can specify its size dynamically.

Refining the Layout of a Screen

We described the basic layout elements of a screen in Chapter 19. The layout of a screen is defined using the graphical Fullscreen Editor. In addition to input and output fields, labels, and frames, you can also place check boxes, radio buttons, and push buttons on your screen. Using a table control, the layout of a screen for table display can be changed interactively. For example, a user can resize or change the order of table columns using drag and drop. On the program level, you can also change the layout of a screen at runtime.

Check Boxes, Radio Buttons, and Push Buttons

Check boxes are used for properties with precisely two possible values. In the example program from Chapter 19, a customer can be a frequent flyer or not. To place a check box on a screen, open the sample program from Chapter 19 in the Object Browser, invoke the Fullscreen Editor for screen 200, click on the Check button (see Figure 22.1), and put the mouse pointer where you want the check box to be. You can create a label for the check box as for any other field.

NOTE　If you need a refresher on placing labels on a screen, look back to the section "Placing Elements on a Screen" in Chapter 19.

On the program level, the corresponding program field of a check box is a character field of length one. At runtime, you can determine the state of a check box by comparing the field content with the value space: if the check box is not activated, the field content is space, otherwise it is not equal space.

FIGURE 22.1:
Defining a check box in the
booking screen for our travel
agency

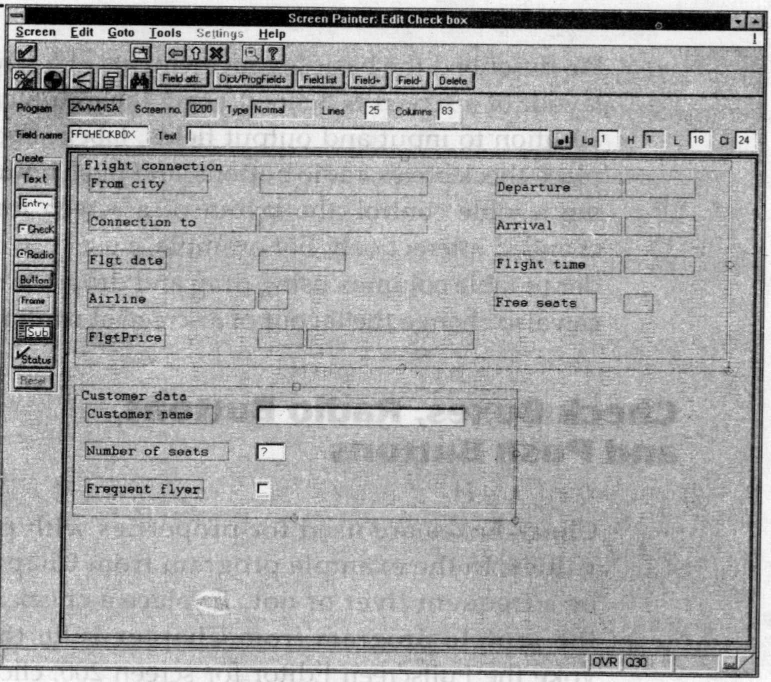

Groups of radio buttons are useful for properties with at least two states, where only one state can be active. In the example of making a flight request, a group of three radio buttons can be used to distinguish between first class, business class, and economy class, as you can see in Figure 22.2. Click on the Radio button in the Create toolbar of the Fullscreen Editor, place the mouse pointer where you want each radio button of the group, and type the text of the radio button (in our example, First, Business, and Economy). When you have created all the radio buttons you want, you have to define the radio button group, which tells the reader how the buttons are related. To do this, place the mouse pointer to the left of the left-most radio button. Hold down the left

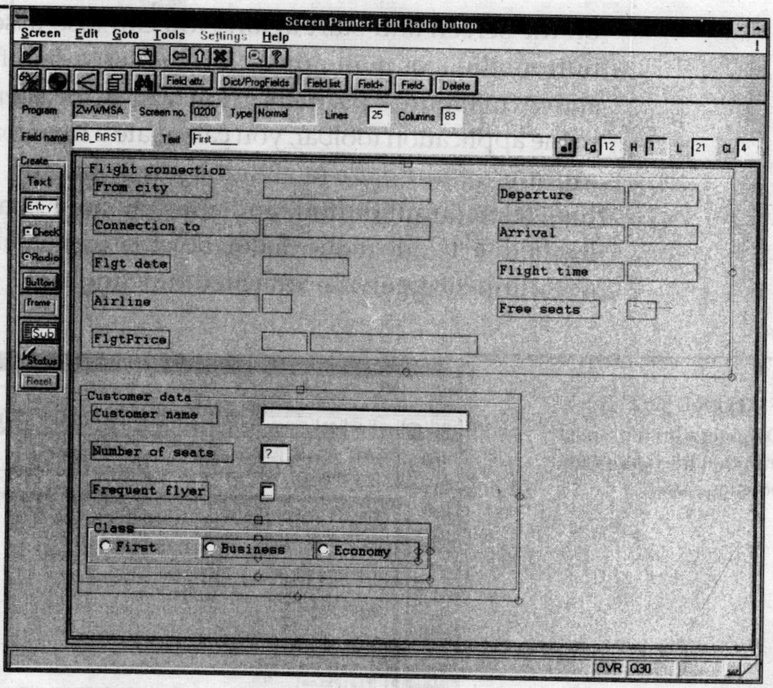

FIGURE 22.2:

Defining a Class radio button
group for the travel agency
booking screen

mouse button, drag the pointer to the right and down, and release it
when the dotted outline of the group includes all radio buttons you
want. Then choose Edit ➤ Radio Button Group ➤ Define and a
group of radio buttons is defined automatically. You will usually define a titled frame for a radio button group. For our example, we used
the title Class. In the same way as for check boxes, the corresponding
program field of a radio button is a character field of length one. At
runtime, the content of a radio button field is either space or not.

In general, push buttons are defined in the GUI status, and they appear
in the application toolbar (see Chapter 19). If you need additional push
buttons in the interior of the screen, click on the Button button on the
left toolbar and place your mouse cursor where you want the new button to be. Then type the text of the button. For our example, we decided
to add a Delete Input button so that the user can clear the information

on the screen and start again. You can also associate an icon with the button; the icon will appear on the left side of the text input field as shown in Figure 22.3. In the same way as for menu functions or buttons in the application toolbar, you can relate a function code to a button in the interior of the screen. Double-click on the button (for example, the Delete Input button) and enter the four character function code in the field FctCode in the dialog box that appears. Clicking on the button at runtime triggers the attached function code.

FIGURE 22.3:

Defining a button (Delete Input) in the interior of the booking screen

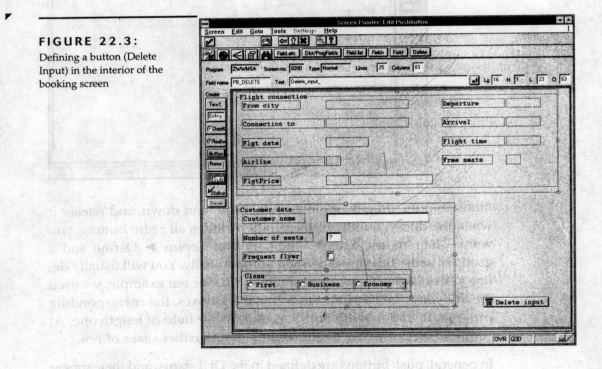

Table Control

A *table control* is used to display the contents of an internal table. End users can change the layout of the table control interactively. For example, they can resize or change the order of columns using drag and drop, as shown in Figures 22.4 and 22.5. In this example, we dragged the last column, City, all the way to the left, making it the first column in Figure 22.5.

FIGURE 22.4:

Displaying a table with a table control

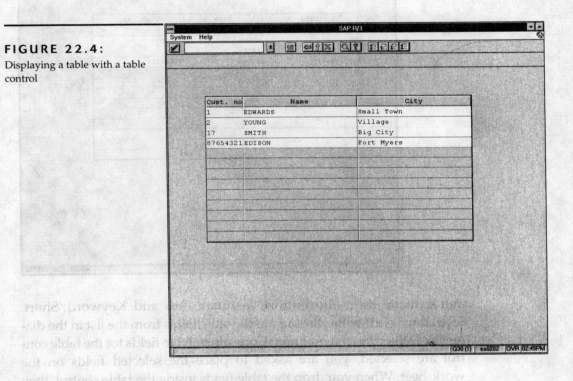

How to Create a Table Control

To create a table control on your screen, select the Table button on the Create toolbar in the Fullscreen Editor. When you have placed the table control where you want it by clicking the left mouse button, you can resize it by dragging the handles at its right or bottom edge. The table control appears as an empty window with scroll bars. Enter the name of the control in the highlighted input field Field Name. To place fields in the table control, you can proceed as usual. For example, if you want to display Dictionary fields, select the Dict/ProgFields button, specify a table name in the upper input line,

FIGURE 22.5:

Changing the layout with a
table control

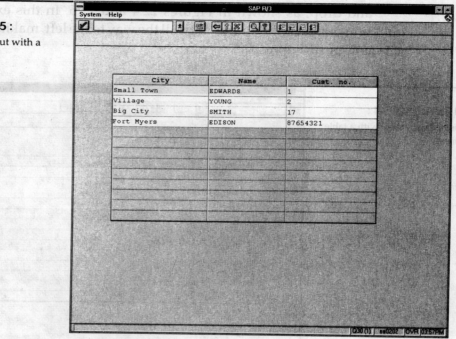

and activate the radio buttons Template/Yes and Keyword/Short.
Hold down Ctrl while clicking on the table fields from the list in the dialog box. When you have chosen Copy after all the fields for the table control are selected, you are asked to place the selected fields on the
worksheet. When you drop the table fields inside the table control, they
are automatically arranged in the order of the Dictionary as columns of
the table (see Figure 22.6). The short texts are used for the column headers.
The width of each column is derived from the length of the template. You
can adjust the frame of the table control by dragging the handle on the
right edge.

In the same way as for other screen elements, you can relate attributes
to a table control. Mark the control by clicking on its frame and select
the Field Attr. button. A dialog box for changing the attributes appears,
as shown in Figure 22.7.

FIGURE 22.6:

Defining a table control for columns Customer No., Name, and City of the database table CUSTOMERS

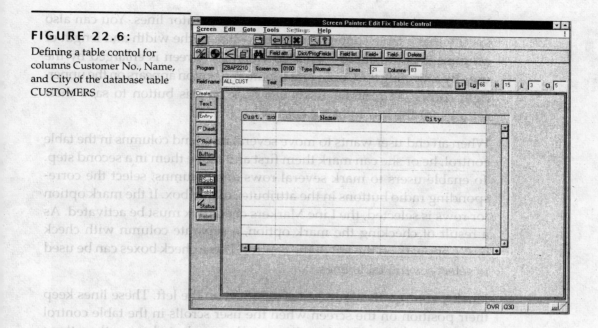

FIGURE 22.7:

Setting the attributes of a table control

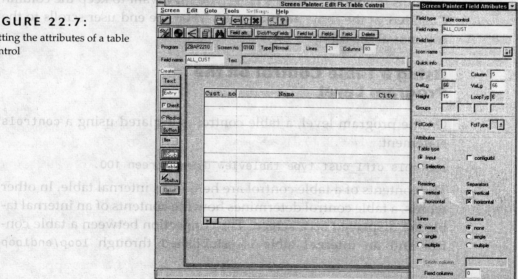

You can activate vertical and horizontal separator lines. You can also specify that a table control is resizable—that is, the width and length of columns is automatically adjusted when the screen is enlarged by the user. By activating the Configurable button, a button appears on the upper-right corner. At runtime, users can click on this button to save their settings for the layout of the control.

When an end user wants to move several rows and columns in the table control, he or she can mark them first and move them in a second step. To enable users to mark several rows and columns, select the corresponding radio buttons in the attributes dialog box. If the mark option for rows is selected, the Line Markers check box must be activated. As a result of checking the mark option, a separate column with check boxes appears on the left of the control. These check boxes can be used to select several table lines.

Finally, you can fix a number of columns on the left. These lines keep their position on the screen when the user scrolls in the table control horizontally. For example, when you have selected more than three columns from the customers table, you may want to keep the column Cust. No. at the same position even when the end user scrolls to the columns at the right.

Using a Table Control on the Program Level

On the program level, a table control is declared using a `controls` statement:

```
controls ctrl_cust type tableview using screen 100.
```

The contents of a table control are held in an internal table. In other words, a table control determines how the contents of an internal table are displayed on a screen. The connection between a table control and an internal table is established through `loop`/`endloop` constructs in the flow logic of a screen. The table control is filled from the internal table at the event `process before output`. Conversely, the contents of the control are transferred to the table at `process after input`. For example, the flow logic of a screen with a table control for a list of customers can be defined as follows:

```
process before output.
  module init_ctrl_cust.
  loop with control ctrl_cust.
    module fill_ctrl_cust.
  endloop.
process after input.
  loop with control ctrl_cust.
    module get_ctrl_cust.
  endloop.
```

The PBO module `init_ctrl_cust` initializes the internal table `all_customers` when the screen is called for the first time:

```
module init_ctrl_cust output.
  if flag_initial = true.
    flag_initial = false.
    select * from customers into table all_customers.
  endif.
endmodule.
```

Within the loop, the PBO module `fill_ctrl_cust` reads a line of the internal table `all_customers`. The index of the table line is determined by the current line of the control. The loop at the table control is finished by the command `exit from step-loop`:

```
module fill_ctrl_cust output.
  read table all_customers index ctrl_cust-current_line.
  if sy-subrc ne 0. exit from step-loop. endif.
endmodule.
```

After an user input, the PAI module `get_ctrl_cust` is used to modify the contents of the internal table line by line:

```
module get_ctrl_cust input.
  modify all_customers index ctrl_cust-current_line.
endmodule.
```

Changing the Layout at Runtime

To change the layout of a screen at runtime, you can modify field attributes within a special loop construct. The layout is changed in a PBO module by means of the command modify screen between loop at screen and endloop. The loop processes every field of the screen. You can modify the following field properties:

- screen-required: Field input mandatory
- screen-input: Field ready to accept input
- screen-invisible: Field not visible
- screen-length: Field length

Use the values 1 and 0 to activate and deactivate a field property, respectively. For example, to make all fields of a screen ready to accept input, the following loop can be used in a PBO module of the screen:

```
loop at screen.
  screen-input = 1.
  modify screen.
endloop.
```

In general, you will only change a subset of all screen fields. The straightforward method to address a screen field is to specify its name in a conditional statement as follows:

```
loop at screen.
  if screen-name = 'CUSTOMERS-NAME'.
    screen required = 1.
    modify screen.
  endif.
endloop.
```

If you want to change properties of several fields at a time, you can combine these fields into a screen group. To associate a field to a screen group, enter the name of the group in the field attributes after Groups. For example, on the second screen of the sample program, you might wish to make the fields for flight time and free seats invisible. Choose a name for the screen group (for example, *INV*), and enter this name after Groups for every member of the group. On the program level, you can detect the group name of a screen field in the field screen-group1 as shown in the following example:

```
module init_booking output.
...
* suppress fields for flight time and free seats
  loop at screen.
    if screen-group1 = 'INV'.
      screen-invisible = 1.
      modify screen.
    endif.
  endloop.
```

In this example, all fields with group name *INV* are made invisible.

It is possible to associate every field to at most four groups. In the Screen Field Attributes dialog box, these groups are entered in the four input fields after Groups. On the program level, you can address the screen groups in the loop using the fields screen-group1 to screen-group4.

Refining a GUI Status

Whenever a dialog program needs many menu functions, submenus are useful to introduce a menu hierarchy. Submenus are defined like top-level menu functions. You can also use fast paths for quick access to any menu function. To create a GUI status for dialog programs with more than one screen, you can use either a copy of an existing GUI status or a reference.

Submenus and Fast Paths

You can also define a hierarchy of pull-down menus. To create a submenu for a menu entry, double-click on the menu entry. An empty submenu is displayed, and you can enter the functions of the submenu as shown in Figure 22.8. In our example, the menu entry *Book* has a submenu with two functions: the menu function *Book* is used for a flight booking as before, and *Book and send* will also send a bill to the customer. The parent menu cannot have a function code, since its only task is to provide a pull-down menu.

FIGURE 22.8:

Defining a submenu

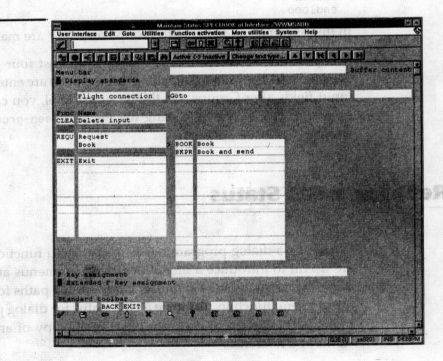

Instead of choosing a menu function by clicking with the mouse, you can also use a *fast path*. A fast path consists of a sequence of characters that are shortcuts to menu functions. You can associate a single character to every function of your GUI status. At runtime, the shortcut character is underlined in the menu entry. You can concatenate a sequence of shortcut characters into a fast path. Enter a period followed by the fast path in the system input field for quick access to the chosen menu function. For example, if *B* is the shortcut of *Book*, and *S* of *Book and send*, the end user can enter *.BS* as a fast path for these menu functions.

To define a fast path for a menu function, double-click on the function in the Maintain Status screen and enter a single character after Fast Path. The chosen shortcut character must be one of the letters of one of the words in the short text of the function; for example, the letter could be *B* and the short text would be *Book a Flight*. Also, the fast path characters of each of the entries of a menu must be unique.

TIP You can get an overview of all shortcut characters in the function list of a GUI status.

Leaving Screens Using Exit Commands

To enable a user to leave a screen without checking the input data further, you can use the *Exit Commands*. Typically, the menu functions Back, Exit, and Cancel are implemented as Exit Commands. You can mark a function code in a GUI status as an Exit Command. Double-click on the function code and enter type E in the Function Type field of the next dialog box.

TIP You can also set the function type of several functions at the same time in the function list of a GUI status.

In the flow logic, modules implementing reactions to Exit Commands are specified by the addition at `exit-command`:

```
process after input.
...
   module exit_screen at exit-command.
...
```

If an Exit Command is executed at runtime, the modules with the addition at `exit-command` are executed first. If such a module performs a leave screen statement, the processing of the current screen is finished.

Using Copies or References

It is common practice that the menu functions of a transaction appear on each screen, even if they are inactive. You can re-use a GUI status or parts of it (pull-down menus, the application toolbar, or function key settings) in two different ways: you can either create a copy, or you can use references. Figure 22.9 shows how to use references for the menus and function keys and a copy of the application toolbar. In the travel agency example, you can re-use the same menus and function keys to achieve a uniform look and feel, but you'll probably use different application toolbars, since different screens will have different buttons.

Changes in the copy of a part of a GUI status obviously do not affect the original one. Since a reference to another GUI status includes menu functions that may be meaningless in a new context, you can deactivate menu functions. At runtime, inactive functions appear in gray.

FIGURE 22.9:
Using references and copies when copying a GUI status

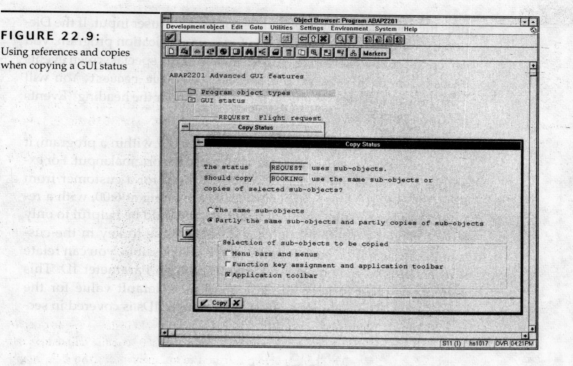

NOTE To see an example of the use of references, look back at the sample program in Chapter 19.

Providing Help Information and Default Values

Help information, check tables, and fixed values for table fields are usually located in the Dictionary. If a Dictionary field appears on a screen, the runtime system provides access to this information and uses the check tables or fixed values to check the user input. If the Dictionary information is not suitable for your application program, you can create context-sensitive help by means of the special screen events `process on help-request` and `process on value-request`. You will learn how to use these events in this section under the heading "Events for Context-Sensitive Help Information."

If users perform the same transaction repeatedly within a program, it would be useful if they could save and re-use the original input. For example, if a travel agent needs to book a flight for a customer from Big City to Fort Meyers for every Friday evening at 6:00, with a return flight every Sunday evening at 6:00, it would be helpful to only have to change the flight dates and not to have to key in the customer's information each time. To make this possible, you can relate screen fields to a memory area identified by a Parameter ID. This memory is used to keep the last input as a default value for the screen field. The technique of using Parameter IDs is covered in section "Default Values of Screen Fields."

Documentation and Check Tables from the Dictionary

Dictionary fields on a screen can provide documentation (function key F1), a list of admissible entries (function key F4), and an automatic check function for the user input (see Chapter 19). If the field attribute Foreign Key is set in the screen definition, and if the Dictionary includes a check table or a set of fixed values (see Chapter 5), the runtime system displays the set of possible entries. The system sends an error message if you try to enter a value that is not in the list of possible entries.

Events for Context-Sensitive Help Information

Use the screen events process on help-request and process on value-request for program-specific help information. For example, if the Dictionary does not contain a check table of customers, you can display a set of possible entries on a separate dialog box. Associate a module to the field in question by using a field statement. At runtime, a down arrow appears on its right edge when the focus is on the field:

```
process on value-request.
  field customers-name
    module values_customers.
```

A template for the module definition is listed below:

```
module values_customers input.
* Display all customers in a dialog box
  call screen 110
        starting at 20 10
        ending   at 50 20.
endmodule.
```

The call screen command with the additions starting at and ending at displays a dialog box with a list of all customers at the specified position. Techniques for pop-up windows and lists in full screens or dialog boxes are explained in the section "Using Full Screens and Dialog Boxes" in this chapter.

Default Values of Screen Fields

To display a default value for an input field, you can use a *Parameter ID*. A Parameter ID can be defined for a Dictionary field or a program field. For example, the Parameter ID CAR for the field planfli-carrid is defined in the Dictionary. To store the user input in memory, activate the check box SET Parameter in the Field Attributes screen. The GET Parameter check box is used for the reverse operation—that is, for reading the previous field content from memory (see Figure 22.10). In our example, the check boxes SET and GET Parameter of input field planfli-carrid after Airline carrier are activated—that is, once the end user has keyed in a carrier (e.g., *ABC*), this carrier is displayed as the default value the next time he or she enters the first screen of the flight booking program.

FIGURE 22.10:
Using SET/GET Parameters for a default value in PLANFLI-CARRID

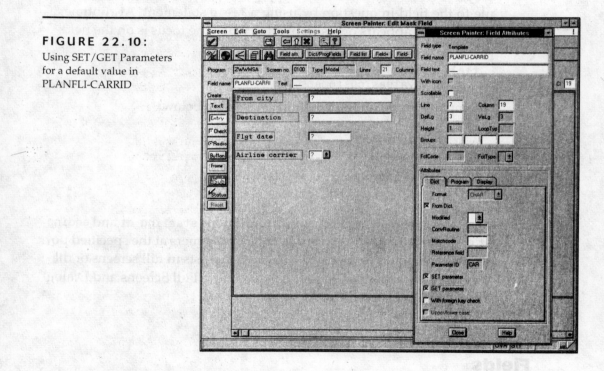

The Parameter ID for program fields can be defined in the field attributes after Parameter ID. On the program level, parameter values can be read and set using the commands get parameter and set parameter as follows:

```
set parameter id 'CAR' field planfli-carrid.
...
```

```
get parameter id 'CAR' field planfli-carrid.
```

The value of the Parameter ID is specified after the addition field.

Using Full Screens and Dialog Boxes

You can establish a sequence of screens either as a queue or as a stack. To implement a queue, you can use the commands set screen and leave screen, whereas the current screen is pushed on a stack by the call screen statement. In addition, the call screen statement is used to call dialog boxes. To display a list in a pop-up window, you can switch to list processing. Then you can use write commands in the same way as in reports.

Switching to the Next Screen

In the example in Chapter 19, we used the commands set screen and leave screen to define a sequence of screens dynamically. If the user leaves a screen via the leave screen command, that screen is thrown away by the runtime system and the new screen appears. In this way, you establish a queue of screens. In contrast, you can define a stack of screens using the call screen command. When you return from a called screen, the flow of control continues after the call screen command. Moreover, the size of the called screen can be specified by the additions starting at and ending at, thus creating a dialog box (or *pop-up window*; see below).

Sending Dialog Boxes with the `call screen` Command

A dialog box is called via the `call screen` command followed by the additions `starting at x1 y1` and `ending at x2 y2`. The numbers x1 and y1 specify the upper-left corner of the pop-up window, and x2 and y2 determine the lower-right corner. For example, the possible entries for customer names in the flight reservation program are displayed in a dialog box that is called via `call screen` as follows:

```
module values_customers input.
* Display all customers in a dialog box
  call screen 110
        starting at 20 10
        ending    at 50 20.
endmodule.
```

When the user selects a customer from the dialog box, the control returns to the calling screen that is still seen in the background (see Figure 22.11).

When a dialog box is active, the contents of the calling screen are also visible, but you cannot perform any action there. The layout and flow logic of a called screen can be designed in the same way as for a full screen. In particular, a general dialog box can contain input fields, radio buttons, frames, and table controls. You will learn in the last section of this chapter ("Lists in General Screens") how to display a list on a dialog box.

NOTE   If you display a report list with `write` statements, you can send a pop-up window like a general dialog box using the `window` command (see Chapter 17). Such a window behaves like a small report list—you can only display fields using `write` commands. The standard push buttons and function keys on lists are automatically available in list windows. For example, the function key F3 leads back to the previous list.

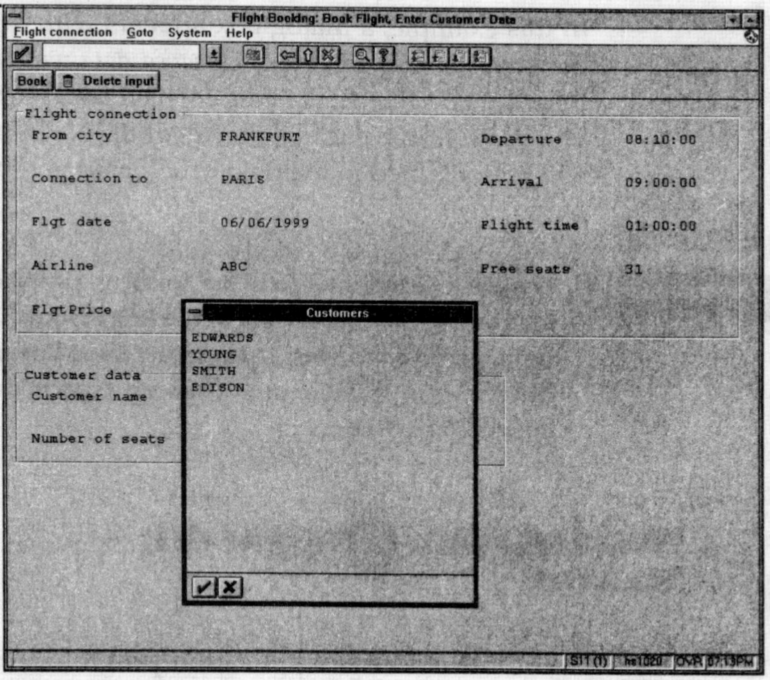

FIGURE 22.11:

Calling the Customers screen with a `call screen` command

Sending Dialog Boxes with Standardized Functions

As explained in Chapter 20, there are several functions to support standardized user dialogs. These functions themselves use the techniques in this chapter, but you don't need to worry about the implementation. For example, you can create a dialog box to ask users whether they wish to perform a processing step that will result in loss of data. The function call could look like this:

```
call function 'POPUP_TO_CONFIRM_LOSS_OF_DATA'
    exporting
        textline1 = 'Really quit?'
        title     = 'Leave customer list'
    importing
        answer    = user_answer.
```

In this example, a dialog box appears with title *Leave customer list*. In the box, the standard text *Unsaved data will be lost* appears first, and then the text line *Really quit?*, which was set by the calling program. The end user can click on the Yes or the No button, and this user action will be contained in the field user_answer of the calling program.

> **NOTE**
>
> Complete documentation of the functions for standardized dialogs can be found in the Online Help of the R/3 System. Choose Help ➤ R/3 Library from any screen. Then select Basis Components ➤ ABAP/4 Development Workbench ➤ Extended Applications Function Library ➤ Standardized Dialogs.

Working with Different GUI Statuses

If you have a large application program with many GUI statuses, you might wish to distinguish between the different statuses. The system field sy-pfkey contains the current GUI status. For example, if you have a subroutine check_data that is called in different situations, you can proceed as follows:

```
case sy-pfkey.
   when 'BOOKING'.
      perform check_data.
*     Perform the booking
   when 'REQUEST'.
      perform check_data.
*     Perform the flight request
endcase.
```

In this example, the form check_data is called both from a screen with the GUI status BOOKING and from a screen with the status REQUEST.

This technique is typically used when the application handles a switch operation between display and change modes. In that case, you work with two different GUI statuses for the same screen, and you distinguish between the GUI statuses in some module or subroutine.

Lists in General Screens

Lists created by write commands usually occur in reports—read-only programs for displaying or printing data (see Part V). Using the command leave to list processing, you can also show a list on a general screen in a dialog program. In this case, it is better for you to suppress the dialog screen itself by means of the command suppress dialog. The list is then displayed instead of the dialog screen.

For example, if you want to display a list of customers in a pop-up window that is called by call screen, you might define the flow logic of the called screen as follows:

```
process before output
   module init_list.
process after input.
   module action_list.
```

The PBO module init_list sets the title and the GUI status, and it prepares the list processing:

```
module init_list output.

* Initialize titlebar and status
   set titlebar  c_title_list_customers.
   set pf-status c_status_list.

* Prepare list
   suppress dialog.
   leave to list-processing and return to screen 0.

endmodule.
```

When defining the GUI status of a list in a dialog box, choose the status type as shown in Figure 22.12. The standard push buttons and function keys for lists on pop-up windows are automatically inserted.

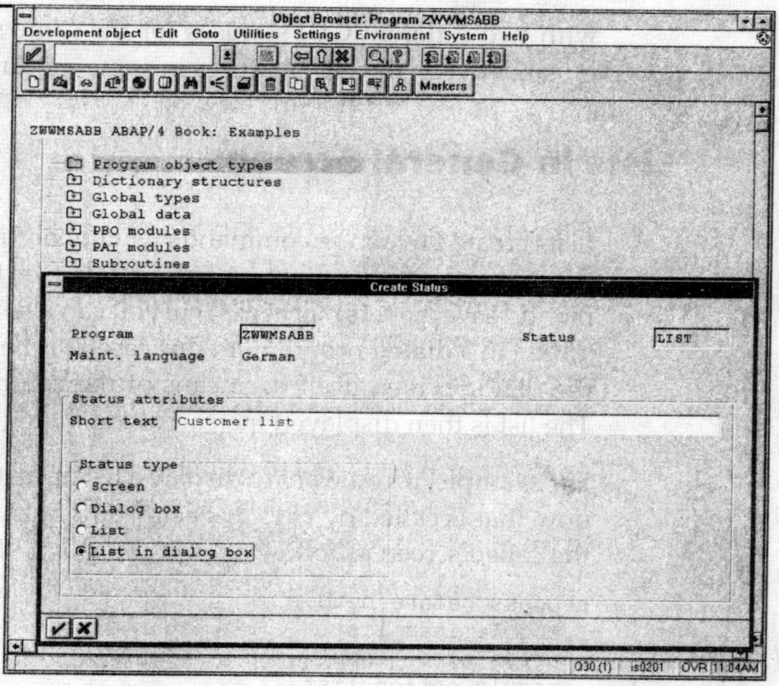

FIGURE 22.12:

A GUI status for a list of
customers in a dialog box

Using the addition `and return to screen 0` of the `leave to list-processing` command, you specify that the flow of control is returned to the caller when the list is finished. The PAI module `action_list` displays the list:

```
module action_list input.

* Read all customers
  select * from customers into table all_customers

* Write all customers
  new-page no-title.
  loop at all_customers.
    write / all_customers-name.
    hide all_customers-id.
  endloop.

endmodule.
```

Here, we have used the `hide` command to store the identifier of each customer in the hide area (see Chapter 17). This information can later be used when the user double-clicks on a customer name:

```
at line-selection.
* Get selected customer and display name
  read table all_customers with key id = all_customers-id.
  if sy-subrc = 0.
    customers-name = all_customers-name.
  endif.
  leave to screen 0.
```

Afterwards, the selected customer name is filled in the corresponding input field of the flight reservation program. Note that we used the shortcut `leave to screen 0` for returning to the caller. This command is equivalent to the following sequence:

```
set screen 0.
leave screen.
```

A Quick Review

Here is a short review of some of the topics we covered in this chapter:

- You can place check boxes, groups of radio buttons, push buttons, and table controls on a screen via drag and drop.

- You can modify the layout of a screen at runtime using the command `modify screen` between `loop at screen` and `endloop`.

- For changing display properties of several fields at a time, these fields can be combined into a screen group.

- Submenus are used to define a hierarchy of pull-down menus.

- You can create shortcuts and fast paths for quick access to menu functions.

- Define Exit Commands to leave a screen without checking the user input.

- You can re-use a GUI status or parts of it either as a copy or by reference.

- Context-sensitive help is implemented by means of the special screen events process on help-request and process on value-request.

- You can set a default value for a screen field using a Parameter ID. On the program level, values of a Parameter ID can be read and set using the commands get parameter and set parameter, respectively.

- You can implement a sequence of screens either as a queue or as a stack. To use a queue, use the commands set screen and leave screen; create a stack by using call screen.

- Specify the size of the called screen by the additions starting at and ending at.

- The system field sy-pfkey contains the current GUI status. You can use it to distinguish between different GUI statuses.

- The system can display a list on a general screen after a leave to list processing statement.

- To display a list on a pop-up window, the command suppress dialog is useful to bypass the dialog screen.

- The GUI status of a list in a dialog box has a special status type. The standard push buttons and function keys for lists on pop-up windows are automatically inserted.

In the next part, you'll learn how to use various dynamic programming features. The next chapter starts with dynamic language constructs (e.g., dynamic operations on internal tables).

PART VII

Dynamic Programming

CHAPTER

TWENTY-THREE

Dynamic Language Constructs

- **Working dynamically with internal tables**

- **Using dynamic database operations**

- **Calling subroutines dynamically**

U p until now, we've discussed *static* commands, in the sense that a reader of the program source code is able to figure out what will happen at runtime. For example, when you are sorting an internal table as explained in Chapter 12, the names of the sort criteria are explicitly mentioned in the program code. Sometimes your programs need to react to requests that can hardly be anticipated in the development phase (for example, an internal table will be sorted according to criteria that are defined by a user's action). So, when users double-click on a column in a list or in a table control, they would expect the table to be sorted according to the values in the chosen column. In general, you can statically implement the same algorithm for all possible variations of sort criteria. This approach might lead to a clumsy source code, and any new variation causes an extra change of the program source. You can avoid these disadvantages using the *dynamic* version of the sort command.

The ABAP/4 language contains several dynamic commands allowing the developer to handle situations where relevant information to carry out a command will be available at runtime only. These dynamic features can increase the flexibility of application programs. In this chapter, you will learn to apply the most important dynamic operations for internal tables, for database tables, and for subroutine calls.

Dynamic language constructs provide a lot of flexibility and allow
elegant solutions to some problems. At the same time, programs with
many dynamic features are less readable and they are less secure,
since error (for example, incorrect field names), cannot be detected by
the Syntax Check, but only by the runtime system.

Table Operations

In ABAP/4, you can operate on both internal and database tables using
dynamic commands. We will first introduce dynamic commands for
internal tables.

If you need a refresher on operations on database tables and on
internal tables, refer back to Chapters 11 through 13.

Dynamic Statements for Internal Tables

There are a variety of dynamic operations you can do with internal
tables. We'll begin with the sort command.

Using the Dynamic sort Command

A typical use of dynamic table operations is explained in the following
example: on a selection screen, a user enters a parameter that controls
the sort criterion of an internal table. Without a dynamic version of the

sort command, such a program needs to anticipate the different input possibilities and would look like the following piece of code:

```
parameters column(10) default 'NAME'.
tables customers.
data all_customers like customers occurs 100
                      with header line.
select * from customers into table all_customers.
case column.
  when 'ID'.
    sort all_customers by id.
  when 'NAME'.
    sort all_customers by name.
  when 'CITY'.
    sort all_customers by city.
  when 'TELEPHONE'.
    sort all_customers by telephone.
endcase.
loop at all_customers.
  write: / all_customers-id,
          all_customers-name,
          all_customers-city,
          all_customers-telephone.
endloop.
```

In the above example code, the default sort field is name and can be changed by the end user on the selection screen before the program runs (see Figure 23.1).

After the database table customers has been read into the internal table all_customers, the lengthy case statement switches between the different sort fields and executes the corresponding sort command, statically written in the code. Finally, the content of the internal table is listed on the screen.

The problem in this example clearly is that all alternatives for sorting the internal table need to be written in the program code. When the internal table or the referenced Dictionary table is changed (for example, a fields name changes), the program code must be adapted.

FIGURE 23.1:

The selection screen for the
sort example

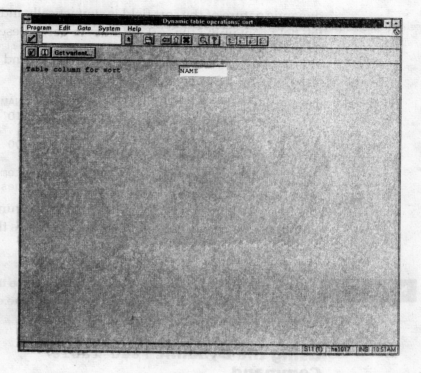

Using the dynamic sort statement, you can considerably reduce the
program code of the above sample program:

```
parameters column(10) default 'NAME'.
tables customers.
data all_customers like customers occurs 100
                  with header line.
select * from customers into table all_customers.
sort all_customers by (column).
loop at all_customers.
  write: / all_customers-id,
           all_customers-name,
           all_customers-city,
           all_customers-telephone.
endloop.
```

If the user enters the name of a table field in the parameter column, the
table is sorted according to the order determined by this column. The

dynamic nature of the sort field is syntactically indicated by enclosing the field containing the sort criterion in parentheses.

You can also add several dynamic sort criteria and use the descending order if you wish:

```
parameters: column1(10)              default 'NAME',
            column2 like column1 default 'ID'.
tables customers.
data all_customers like customers occurs 100
                  with header line.
select * from customers into table all_customers.
sort all_customers by (column1) (column2) descending.
```

It is not necessary to specify all sort criteria at runtime. If the field in parentheses is empty, the sort command ignores this field.

NOTE   **If a field in a dynamic sort statement contains a name that is not part of the table's structure, the system reacts with a runtime error.**

Using the Dynamic read table Command

You are already familiar with reading a single line of an internal table by specifying a key. You can also dynamically set the key fields in a read table command by enclosing them in parentheses:

```
parameters: key1(10)              default 'NAME',
            value1(25),
            key2    like key1 default 'ID',
            value2 like value1.
tables customers.
data all_customers like customers occurs 100
                  with header line.
select * from customers into table all_customers.
read table all_customers
   with key (key1) = value1
            (key2) = value2.
```

```
if sy-subrc eq 0.
  write: / all_customers-id,
           all_customers-name,
           all_customers-city,
           all_customers-telephone.
else.
  write 'entry not found'.
endif.
```

In this example, the default key fields are `name` and `id` and can be set by the user on the selection screen, along with values (see Figure 23.2).

After the database table customers has been read into the internal table `all_customers`, the `read table` command reads the line that has been determined by the end user's input. Here again, an empty key field is ignored.

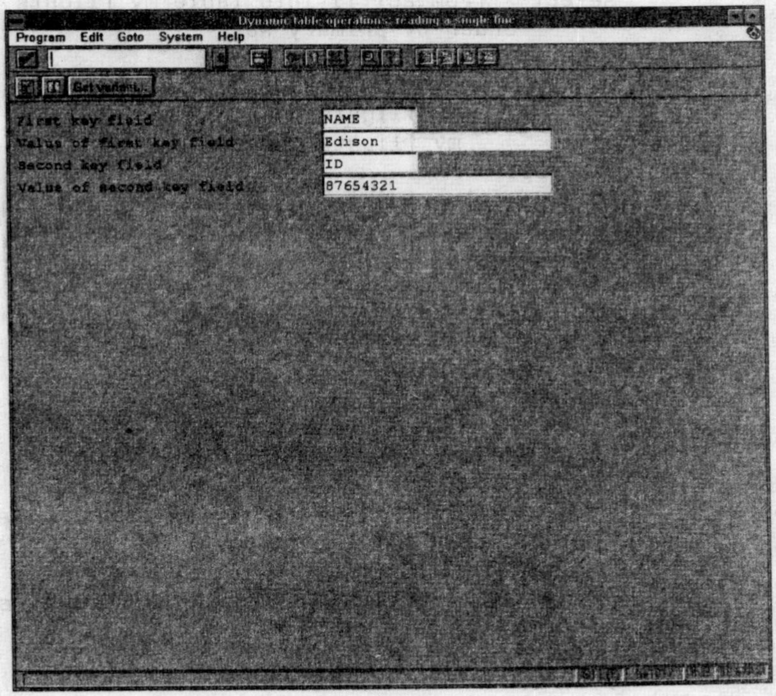

FIGURE 23.2:

The selection screen for the `read table` example

Dynamically Building Subtotals

You can determine subtotals (or other intermediate results belonging to a block of entries in an internal table) using blocks of at and endat commands in a loop. For example, the statements between at new name and endat are processed when the content of the table field all_customers-name or one of the preceding fields has changed. If user input determines which level of subtotals will be evaluated, you can set the name of the table field in the at statement dynamically. We can now modify the example program from Chapter 12 (dealing with subtotals) to react to a user's action as follows:

```
tables actfli.
data my_flights like actfli occurs 10
                with header line.
data sum_occupied_seats like my_flights-seatsocc.
data column(30).
select * from actfli into table my_flights
      order by primary key.
loop at my_flights.
  write: / my_flights-carrid,
           my_flights-connid,
           my_flights-fldate.
endloop.
at line-selection.
* Display subtotals according to end user's selection
get cursor field column.
shift column up to '-'.
shift column.
loop at my_flights.
  at new (column).
    new-page.
    write / my_flights-carrid.
    clear sum_occupied_seats.
  endat.
  add my_flights-seatsocc to sum_occupied_seats.
  write / my_flights-seatsocc.
  at end of (column).
    write: / 'Occupied seats total:', sum_occupied_seats.
  endat.
endloop.
```

In this example the database table `actfli` is read into the internal table `my_flights`, ordered by the primary key fields `carrid`, `connid`, and `fldate`. Then the contents of the internal table are displayed on the screen. When the user double-clicks on a field in the output page, the `at line-selection` event happens, and to get the field name of the clicked column without the table prefix, the `get cursor` and two `shift` commands on the `column` variable are executed. This dynamically specified column name is used in the following `loop`, where subtotals for the occupied seats are computed.

In this section we presented a variety of possibilities you can use to dynamically operate on internal tables. Next, we'll discuss dynamic operations with database tables.

Working with Dynamic Open SQL Commands

As explained in Chapters 11 and 13, the Open SQL commands (`select`, `insert`, `update`, `modify`, `delete`) allow you to set the table name dynamically, so that a dynamic `select` statement looks like this:

```
parameters tablename(10) default 'CUSTOMERS'.
data count_rows type i.
select count( * ) from (tablename) into count_rows.
write: tablename, count_rows.
```

In this small example, the user enters the name of a database table on a selection screen. The dynamic `select` statement with the addition `count( * )` determines the number of entries the database table has. Similar to the examples we had before, the field containing the dynamically set table name is enclosed in parentheses.

In the `select` statement, you can not only set the table name dynamically, but also the `where` clause. To this end, define an internal table and fill it at runtime with the source code of the `where` clause. Suppose you have defined an internal table `where_tab` and filled it as shown in the example code below:

```
data where_tab(80) occurs 10 with header line.
append 'name like ''E%''' to where_tab.
append 'and city like ''S%''' to where_tab.
```

Here, we've filled the internal table with the literals for the `where` condition.

NOTE **Don't forget that single quotes (') in a literal must be doubled (").**

You can use the internal table `where_tab` in the `select` statement that reads the `customers` table as follows:

```
tables customers.
data all_customers like customers occurs 100.
select * from customers into table all_customers
        where id between 1 and 999
        and (where_tab).
```

As a result this program reads all customers who have identifiers between *1* and *999* and whose name and city name begin with the letters *E* and *S*, respectively. Obviously, this example program could have also been written using a `select` command with a static `where` clause:

```
tables customers.
data all_customers like customers occurs 100
select * from customers into table all_customers
        where id    between 1 and 999
        and   name like    'E%'
        and   city like    'S%'.
```

You certainly need a dynamic `where` clause when the table name is unknown, since then you need to determine the fields for the `where` clause at runtime. In addition, when many different user actions are possible, it may be tedious to statically foresee all variations of where conditions in the source code.

One of the most frequent cases for a dynamic specification of the where clause is when a user enters selection criteria for a table field. This kind of dynamic where clause is well-supported by Select-Options, which we covered in detail in Chapter 16.

Calls of Subroutines

When developing programs for a large application, it is sometimes necessary to call a subroutine that belongs to a program other than the current program. It is even possible that the name of the called subroutine or the name of the corresponding program are only known at runtime. Using the following version of the perform command, you can specify the name of an external form. The first program contains the *external* perform command:

```
report chap2307.
write / 'I am program chap2307'.
perform extform in program chap2308.
```

Program chap2308 contains the form definition:

```
report chap2308.
form extform.
  write / 'I am extform in program chap2308'.
endform.
```

At runtime, the program chap2308 is loaded in addition to the current program, and the form extform is executed as usual. You can also use external perform statements within an externally called form—that is, you can build chains of external calls. In addition, you can use interface parameters for externally called subroutines in the same way as for local subroutines.

You can also call an external subroutine dynamically. To this end, include the form name and the name of the other program in parentheses. A frequent application example for this technique is when you work with call back routines—subroutines from the calling program that are called by a subroutine of the called program. The following sample program calls the form extform in program chap2310. The name of the call back routine and of the current program (sy-cprog) are transferred as parameters.

```
report chap2309.
perform extform in program chap2310
        using 'CALL_BACK_FORM'
            sy-cprog.
form call_back_form.
   write / 'I am the call back form in chap2309.'.
endform.
```

Here is the external program with a dynamic perform command for calling the call back form:

```
report chap2310.
form extform
     using f_call_back_form
           f_program.
   perform (f_call_back_form) in program (f_program).
   write / 'I am the form in chap2310.'.
endform.
```

In this example, when chap2309 is executed, it invokes extform in program chap2310, which in turn calls call_back_form in program chap2309. Figure 23.3 illustrates this situation:

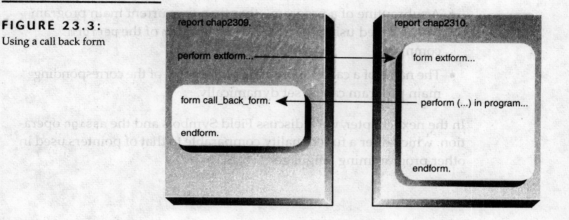

Call back forms are especially useful for frequently called functions that offer a user dialog specific for the caller. For instance, a general function might display hierarchies, and each calling program wants to have its own buttons on the hierarchy list. Then the caller could provide a subroutine display_button installing the button, and the general function contains the dynamic external perform to display_button.

A Quick Review

Here are some of the more important points we covered in this chapter:

- Sort fields can be set dynamically in the sort command.
- Key fields can be set dynamically in the read table command.

- Dynamic at new/endat blocks for subtotals are supported.

- The Open SQL commands (select, insert, update, modify, delete) allow dynamic table names.

- The select command allows a dynamic where clause.

- A subroutine of a program other than the current main program can be called using the addition in program of the perform command.

- The name of a called subroutine or the name of the corresponding main program can be set dynamically.

In the next chapter, we'll discuss Field Symbols and the assign operation, which offer a functionality comparable to that of pointers used in other programming languages.

CHAPTER

TWENTY-FOUR

Field Symbols

- **Defining Field Symbols**

- **Using the `assign` operation**

- **Getting safety and flexibility**

Up to now, all data objects in this book have had a fixed type that could not be changed at runtime. For example, a field has an elementary type and length, or a record has a fixed number of components, where each component also has a fixed type and length. In a similar way, the line structure of an internal table is completely determined by the table definition, and the only change that can be made at runtime is how many lines there are in the table.

Sometimes, however, you might wish to deal with different data objects in a uniform way. A typical application might be that you read external data from a file in a format where the first four bytes represent the length of the immediately following contents. For example, the data might look like this:

`0005Smith0007Edwards0005Young0006Edison`.

When processing this data, you need to have a technique where you can read a portion of data (e.g., five bytes for *Smith*) and then continue reading after it. This can hardly be achieved with data objects of fixed length. In this case, something like a "pointer" would be helpful, which could refer to different positions in a string.

Field Symbols together with the `assign` operation in ABAP/4 offer a functionality comparable to that of pointers used in other languages. Field Symbols are place holders for fields or even arbitrary data objects. A Field Symbol does not occupy memory for a data object, but rather points to the object that has been assigned to the Field Symbol at runtime. After the `assign` operation, you can work with the Field Symbol in the same way as with the object itself. With Field Symbols, you get a high degree of security, since the pitfalls of pointer arithmetic are avoided.

The pointer-like property of Field Symbols makes them powerful, but they need special care: since the references are only established at runtime, the effectiveness of syntax checks is very limited for operations where Field Symbols are involved. This could lead to runtime errors or incorrect data assignments.

Working with Field Symbols

You can define Field Symbols using the `field-symbols` declaration followed by the name of the Field Symbol. The name of a Field Symbol must begin with an opening angle bracket and end with a closing angle bracket, thus distinguishing Field Symbols from ordinary data objects in the source code:

```
field-symbols <fs>.
```

When defining a Field Symbol, you create a place holder for a data object. To work with this Field Symbol, relate it to a data object of your program using the `assign` operation. This is covered in the next section.

Using the `assign` Operation

The `assign` command relates a data object (e.g., a field or a record) to a Field Symbol:

```
field-symbols <fs>.
data field value 'X'.
assign field to <fs>.
```

The Field Symbol `<fs>` inherits all properties from the assigned field, and you can work with the Field Symbol in the same way as with the field itself. For example, you can display a Field Symbol on a list using the `write` statement:

```
write <fs>.
```

A typical use of Field Symbols is shown in the following coding for the example from the introduction of this chapter: suppose you read external data from a file in a format where the first four bytes represent the length of the immediately following contents. If the contents of this data determine the flow of control, you might proceed as follows:

```
data: external_record(4000),
      position type i,
      length type n.
field-symbols <entry>.
read dataset 'external_data' into external_record.
do.
   length = external_record+position(4).
   if length = 0.
      exit.
   endif.
   add 4 to position.
   assign external_record+position(length) to <entry>.
   write <entry>.
   add length to position.
   if position >= 4000.
      exit.
   endif.
enddo.
```

In this sample program, the field `external_record` is supposed to contain the data from the file, e.g., customer names together with length information: *0005Smith0007Edwards0005Young*.

NOTE Reading from a file is covered in Chapter 26.

In the do loop, we first get the length information for the current customer name. If the length is zero, the loop is finished. Otherwise, the position is incremented by four to jump over the length information. Then we can assign the value part in its proper length to the Field Symbol <entry> and display it on screen. The position is incremented by the length, and the loop is finished when the position points after the record.

Variable offset and length specification in an assign statement allow flexible positioning of a Field Symbol. This technique is often applied when working with text strings.

ABAP/4 string operations cover everyday cases of text manipulation. If you need a refresher on string operations, take a look back at Chapter 7.

Besides text manipulation, there are many other occasions to benefit from using Field Symbols, as we'll see in the next section.

Using Field Symbols for Components of a Record

Suppose you want to write an output function for a table with many columns. If you write down all the table components in the source code, you have to adapt the program each time the table structure changes. Using the addition component of structure for the assign command you can write a program that automatically respects the table structure:

```
tables customers.
field-symbols <output>.
select * from customers.
  new-line.
  do.
```

```
assign component sy-index of structure customers to
<output>.
if sy-subrc <> 0.
  exit.
endif.
write <output>.
  enddo.
endselect.
```

As a result, this program reads all table entries from the database table customers. For each entry, the `assign component` command is used in a do loop for assigning one table field after the other to the Field Symbol `<output>`. Here, the system loop counter `sy-index` determines the sequence of assigned table fields. Finally, the contents of field symbol `<output>` pointing to the current table field is displayed on screen.

Safety versus Flexibility

Field Symbols enable you to develop flexible and elegant programs. However, since Field Symbols are anonymous objects, the Syntax Check cannot always detect errors like type conflicts that lead to syntax errors in the static case. For example, the following call of a subroutine will cause a syntax error, since the types of the actual and formal parameters do not match:

```
tables customers.
select * from customers.
  perform display using customers.
endselect.
form display using f1 like bookings.
  write f1-customid.
endform.
```

In this program code, the actual parameter customers does not have type bookings of the formal parameter f1, and therefore, the Syntax Check will send an error message as shown in Figure 24.1.

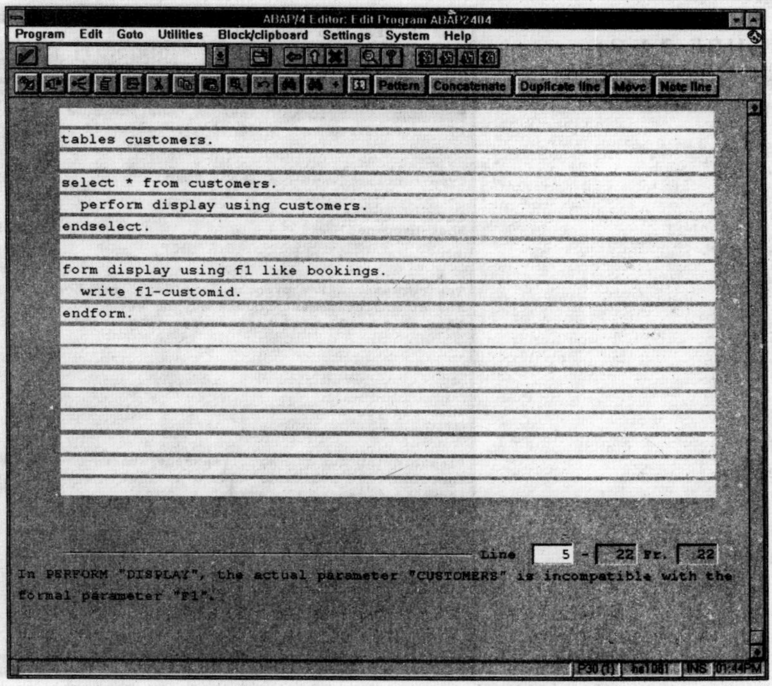

FIGURE 24.1:

A syntax error at a type mismatch

A similar program using Field Symbols looks like this:

```
tables customers.
field-symbols <customers>.
assign customers to <customers>.
select * from customers.
  perform display using <customers>.
endselect.
form display using f1 like bookings.
  write f1-customid.
endform.
```

In this example, the Syntax Check does not send an error message, because the type of the actual parameter cannot be derived from static information in the program code. Instead, a runtime error occurs when you execute the program. The first page of the runtime error display is shown in Figure 24.2, giving general information about the error.

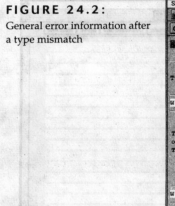

FIGURE 24.2:
General error information after a type mismatch

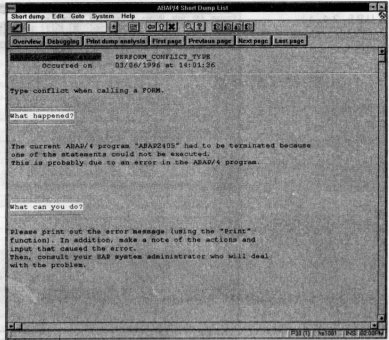

When you scroll down in the error description, you get a lot of detailed information about possible reasons. For instance, you can see the statement in the source code where the runtime error occurred (see Figure 24.3).

To avoid this kind of error, you can declare Field Symbols with a type. The Syntax Check then detects type mismatches for Field Symbols with types. For example, the following program will cause the same syntax error at the perform statement as shown in Figure 24.1, since the actual and formal parameter have different types:

```
tables customers.
field-symbols <customers> like customers.
assign customers to <customers>.
```

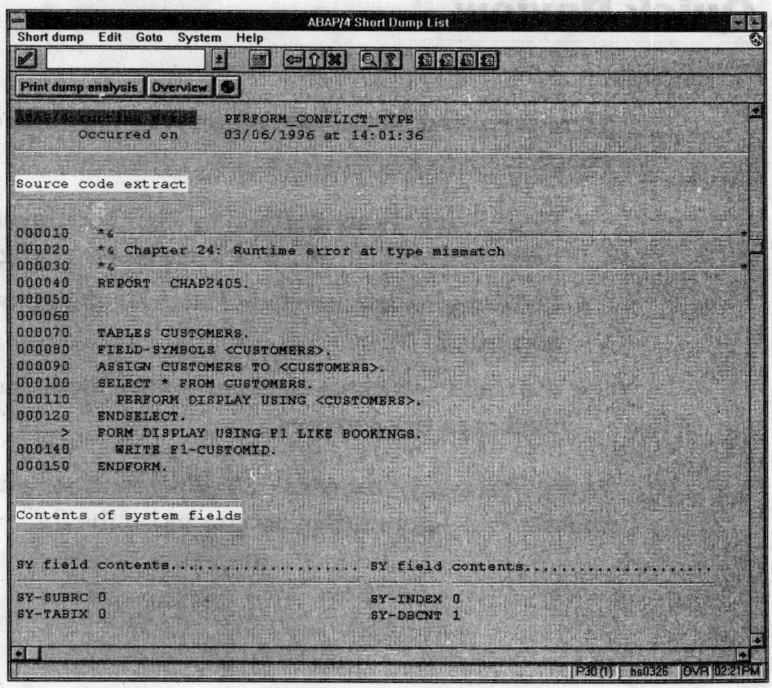

FIGURE 24.3:

The source code showing the statement that caused a runtime error

```
                    ABAP/4 Short Dump List
 Short dump   Edit   Goto   System   Help
 [icons]              [icons]

 Print dump analysis  Overview  [icon]

 ABAP/4 runtime error     PERFORM_CONFLICT_TYPE
              Occurred on      03/06/1996 at 14:01:36


 Source code extract


 000010   *&
 000020   *& Chapter 24: Runtime error at type mismatch
 000030   *&
 000040   REPORT   CHAP2405.
 000050
 000060
 000070   TABLES CUSTOMERS.
 000080   FIELD-SYMBOLS <CUSTOMERS>.
 000090   ASSIGN CUSTOMERS TO <CUSTOMERS>.
 000100   SELECT * FROM CUSTOMERS.
 000110     PERFORM DISPLAY USING <CUSTOMERS>.
 000120   ENDSELECT.
     >   FORM DISPLAY USING F1 LIKE BOOKINGS.
 000140     WRITE F1-CUSTOMID.
 000150   ENDFORM.


 Contents of system fields


 SY field contents...................   SY field contents...................


 SY-SUBRC 0                              SY-INDEX 0
 SY-TABIX 0                              SY-DBCNT 1
```

```
select * from customers.
  perform display using <customers>.
endselect.
form display using f1 like bookings.
  write f1-customid.
endform.
```

From the examples, it is clear that without restricting Field Symbols to a type, you have maximum flexibility for using them in different situations. However, you lose safety in that errors are only detected at runtime. In principle, this conflict between utmost flexibility on the one hand and safety considerations on the other is well known in software development. To achieve the best possible quality in your programs, you can use flexible constructs like Field Symbols and, at the same time, make them as safe as static data objects.

A Quick Review

Here are some of the key points you should keep in mind from this chapter:

- Field Symbols are defined by the field-symbols declaration. The name of the Field Symbol is enclosed in angle brackets.
- Data objects are associated with Field Symbols using the assign command.
- If a Field Symbol is declared with a type, the Syntax Check detects type mismatches.

In the following chapter you will learn about another dynamic feature in ABAP/4—generating programs on the fly.

CHAPTER

TWENTY-FIVE

Automatic Program Generation

- **Creating temporary programs at runtime**

- **Using subroutines in temporary programs**

- **Creating persistent programs on the fly**

AUTOMATIC PROGRAM GENERATION

Using Temporary Programs

The important language constructs of ABAP/4 have dynamic versions: table operations and calls of subroutines can be set at runtime as we saw in Chapter 23, and Field Symbols provide a pointer-like flexibility as explained in Chapter 24. Sometimes, however, you might want to design your programs with even more dynamic features. For example, you can imagine writing a program that displays the contents of a table where the table name is entered by the end user and so is only known at runtime. In ABAP/4, you can accomplish this by creating the whole source of a program at runtime and executing it on the fly, thereby making the program as dynamic as it can be. In other words, you postpone the decision about the final version of the source code of a program to the latest possible moment. This technique can be applied to create normal programs stored in the ABAP/4 Repository as well as temporary programs that vanish after the program's run.

Using Temporary Programs

To create a temporary program during the run of another program, you need first to build up the source code of the temporary program in an internal table. In a second step, you will generate the temporary program using the command generate subroutine pool. Finally, you can execute a form in a temporary program using an external perform command.

NOTE **Generation of a program is explained in Chapter 1 under the heading "Compilation and Runtime Behavior."**

For example, you may want to create a program with a form that executes a single write statement. Then you'll fill an internal table source_table as follows:

```
data: source_table(72) occurs 10 with header line,
      program_name like sy-cprog.
append 'report test.'                           to source_table.
append 'form display.'                          to source_table.
append 'write ''I am a temporary program''.' to source_table.
append 'endform.'                               to source_table.
```

In this example, the internal table source_table contains the report declaration and the definition of form display with a write statement. Then you can generate a temporary program as shown below:

```
generate subroutine pool source_table name program_name.
```

This command generates a program from the internal table source_table and returns its name in the field program_name. This program name is automatically created by the system, and it disappears together with the temporary source code after the program's run. Finally, you can execute a subroutine in this temporary program using an external perform command:

```
perform display in program (program_name).
```

Here, the subroutine display is executed in the program whose name is contained in field program_name.

TIP **Calling a subroutine in another program using the external perform command is explained in Chapter 23.**

As you can see in the example, you'll receive the name of your temporary program from the `generate subroutine pool` command after the addition `name`, and you'll use this name in the external `perform` statement, but you need not know the program name elsewhere.

A temporary program lives as long as the generating program does. Thus, you can call subroutines of a temporary program many times.

Dealing with Syntax Errors

When you create the source code of a temporary program, it is possible that the temporary program has an error in the syntax. However, a temporary program is *not* checked during the syntax check of the generating program, but only at runtime when the `generate subroutine pool` command is executed. If the temporary program cannot be generated because of a syntax error, no program name will be returned in this command and the subsequent external perform will cause a runtime error, since the program name is invalid.

To avoid this kind of runtime error, you can detect syntax errors in a temporary program by querying the system return code `sy-subrc` after the `generate subroutine pool` command. In addition, you can get the error message of the Syntax Check and the erroneous line in the source code. Look at this example code:

```
data: source_table(72) occurs 10 with header line,
      program_name like sy-cprog,
      syntax_check_message(128),
      line_no type i.
append 'report test.'
append 'form display.'                                to source_table.
append 'write ''I am a temporary program''.' to source_table.
append 'endform'                                      to source_table.
generate subroutine pool source_table
                     name    program_name
                     message syntax_check_message
                     line    line_no.
```

```
if sy-subrc ne 0.
  write: / 'Syntax error, message', syntax_check_message,
         / 'in line', line_no.
  exit.
endif.
perform display in program (program_name).
```

As a result, the system return code will have a non-zero value after the `generate subroutine pool` command, since the period after the `end-form` statement is missing in the source code. The text of the error message is contained in field `syntax_check_message` and the line number in `line_no`. In our example, the error text is "The last statement is not complete (period missing)." in line number 4.

A Real-Life Example

In Chapter 24, you saw a program for displaying the contents of one table, namely customers. To create such a display program where the table name is entered by the user and so is only known at runtime, you can generate a temporary program and invoke a form from it. A sample program for this purpose will be explained in this section.

The main steps of the program for general table display look like this:

```
parameters tabname(10) default 'CUSTOMERS'.
data: source_table(72) occurs 100 with header line,
      program_name like sy-cprog,
      syntax_check_message(128),
      line_no type i.
perform build_the_source_code using tabname.
generate subroutine pool source_table
                         name    program_name
                         message syntax_check_message
                         line    line_no.
if sy-subrc ne 0.
  write: / 'Syntax error, message', syntax_check_message,
         / 'in line', line_no.
  exit.
endif.
perform display_table in program (program_name).
```

Here, the end user can enter a table name in the parameter tabname on the standard selection screen. The form build_the_source_code creates the source code of the temporary program including the subroutine display_table. This form is explained in the next paragraph. The generate subroutine pool command and the external perform for subroutine display_table work in the same way as in the previous examples.

Here is the core subroutine of the general table display program:

```
form build_the_source_code using f_name.
append:
'report ztmpprog.                           ' to source_table,
'tables                                     ' to source_table,
         f_name                                to source_table,
'.                                          ' to source_table,
'field-symbols <output>.                    ' to source_table,
'form display_table.                        ' to source_table,
'select * from                              ' to source_table,
               f_name                         to source_table,
'.                                          ' to source_table,
'  new-line.                                ' to source_table,
'  do.                                      ' to source_table,
'     assign component sy-index             ' to source_table,
'              of structure                 ' to source_table,
'              f_name                         to source_table,
'              to <output>.                 ' to source_table,
'     if sy-subrc ne 0. exit. endif.'         to source_table,
'     write <output>.                       ' to source_table,
'  enddo.                                   ' to source_table,
'endselect.                                 ' to source_table,
'endform.                                   ' to source_table.
endform.
```

The formal parameter f_name contains the table name that the user entered at runtime. The content of this formal parameter are appended to the internal table source_table at runtime. Therefore, f_name must not be enclosed in quotation marks in the corresponding append statements.

Generating Persistent Programs

You can also create persistent programs using the `insert report` command, which inserts the source code from an internal table into the database:

```
data: source_table(72) occurs 10 with header line,
      program_name like sy-cprog.
append 'report zgenprog.'                     to source_table.
append 'write ''I am a generated program''.' to source_table.
insert report 'zgenprog' from source_table.
```

In this example, the report zgenprog has only two lines of code: the first statement is the `report` declaration, and the second a `write` command. The `insert report` command takes the source code from the internal table source_table and stores it in the ABAP/4 Repository. Then, you can start the report zgenprog via the submit command. If you want to return to the calling program, use the addition `and return`:

```
submit zgenprog and return.
```

Once the program is in the Repository, you can read it again into an internal table using the `read report` command. For example, if you don't want to create the same program twice, you could proceed as follows:

```
data: source_table(72) occurs 10 with header line.
read report 'zgenprog' into source_table.
if sy-subrc ne 0.
  append 'report zgenprog.'            to source_table.
  append 'write ''Here is zgenprog''.' to source_table.
  insert report 'zgenprog' from source_table.
endif.
submit zgenprog and return.
```

Here, the source code of program zgenprog is retrieved from the Repository and put into the internal table source_table. The system return code has a non-zero value after a `read report` statement, if the program does not exist.

> **WARNING**
> If you generate a completely new program, you should make sure that the program does not yet exist, since the `insert report` command unconditionally overwrites existing programs.

In contrast to temporary programs, where you can only invoke a subroutine using an external `perform` command, you can execute the complete program when it is stored via `insert report`. Certainly, you can use an external `perform` command in this case, too. However, working with a temporary subroutine pool is faster, since saving the source in the Repository produces additional costs.

A Quick Review

In this chapter, we have taken a look at how programs are generated and executed on the fly:

- Temporary programs are generated using the command generate subroutine pool.

- A generated program's code can be made persistent using the `insert report` command.

- The source of a program can be read via `read report`.

In the next part, we'll discuss the interfaces of ABAP/4 to external applications.

PART VIII

Open Interfaces

CHAPTER

TWENTY-SIX

File Transfer

- Opening and closing a file

- Transferring data to a file

- Reading data from a file

So far, all the data we deal with is stored in the database in the form of tables. We haven't yet focused much on how it was entered into the R/3 system. On a more general level, the question is how to communicate with the system. In fact, there are several possibilities to communicate with the system to get data into it and out of it. The most intuitive form is the human-machine communication, where the user enters data manually via the keyboard. Part V explained in detail the various possibilities for manual input via screens of a transaction. This method has the advantage that each value can be checked easily and the user is prompted to interactively correct incorrect values. But the technique is clearly not applicable for mass data input. In addition, human-machine communication is increasingly replaced by machine-machine communication; that is, different computers are connected via a potentially worldwide network. For instance, in many companies, orders are no longer booked manually, but instead come into the system via electronic data interchange mechanisms.

The ABAP/4 language offers various open interfaces to external components. The simplest one is a file interface, where external data is read from a file or internal data is stored to a file in a file system. Other programs can then work with these files. This issue is explained in detail in this chapter.

In the early days of computing, a file interface was the only possibility for exchanging data between different systems. Even today, this technique might be sufficient if the recipient does not need the data immediately—for example, if a floppy disk or CD-ROM is used for data transfer. However, for fast exchange of information, this technique isn't efficient. A better solution is the direct communication between programs, which can even run on different machines in different parts of the world. ABAP/4 supports direct program-to-program communication by an extension of the local function call, the Remote Function Call (RFC). Two R/3 systems can exchange data directly without the deviation to a file. RFC also supports communication with a mainframe-based SAP R/2 system and to external programs. A special use of the RFC is to support the technique of OLE (Object Linking and Embedding) Automation. It is then easy to directly invoke an application that follows the standard for OLE Automation from within the ABAP/4 language. Properties of an external object can be set, methods invoked, and so data can be exchanged between external objects and the R/3 system.

> **NOTE** The Remote Function Call and OLE Automation are covered in Chapters 27 and 28.

Using the File Interface

When you use the file interface, where external data is read from a file or internal data is stored to a file, other programs can work with these files. This technique is sufficient if the recipient does not need the data immediately. Basically, there are three steps when using the file interface:

1. You open a file
2. You write or read the data
3. You close the file

In the travel agency example, suppose you write an ABAP/4 program that extracts customer data from the database table customers into an internal table all_customers, rearranges this table according to the customer's city, and produces a nice list. If you want to export this data for later use in a different application, you can transfer it to a file. The first portion of this program could look like this:

```
tables customers.
data all_customers like customers occurs 100
                   with header line.
select * from customers into table all_customers.
sort all_customers by city.
loop at all_customers.
  write: / all_customers-city,
           all_customers-name.
endloop.
```

Now, all data is available and ready for export to a file.

Opening a File

To open a file in the file system, use the open dataset statement followed by the name of the file:

```
parameters filename(128) default '/usr/tmp/testfile.dat'
                      lower case.
data msg_text(50).
open dataset filename for output in text mode
                   message msg_text.
if sy-subrc ne 0.
  write: 'File cannot be opened. Reason:', msg_text.
  exit.
endif.
```

Here, the end user can enter a file name on the selection screen in the parameter filename, which has the attribute lower case, since path and file name are case-sensitive for some operating systems. The open dataset command creates this file if it does not yet exist. Otherwise, the contents of the file will be overwritten by the new data.

If you wish to only append new data to an already existing file, use the `open dataset` command followed by the addition `for appending`. Then the new data will be appended to the existing data.

The addition `for output` at the `open dataset` command means that the file is opened for the ABAP/4 program to output data to it. In a similar way, you can open a file for input—i.e., ABAP/4 reads data from the file. The extension `in text mode` tells the program that data on the file will be lines of text. You can also use the addition `in binary mode`, which is also the default mode. The binary mode is applicable to raw data, which is not interpreted during the I/O operation. For example, executables of programs will be transferred in binary mode.

In general, the system shields you from all considerations concerning operating system dependencies. In this context, however, you have to pay attention to the operating system, since you are dealing directly with data in the file system. In particular, the file in the `open dataset` statement must be accessible by the system. Notice that we specified the file name with its full path. This path must exist in the underlying file system and follow the conventions of the operating system. When the call fails, the system return code `sy-subrc` is set to a non-zero value. The text of the error message is delivered in the field after the addition `message`. For instance, the path might not exist or you might not have the right to open the file since the system is not allowed to do this.

Transferring Data to a File

In a next step, data is sent to the file using the `transfer` statement.

```
loop at all_customers.
  transfer all_customers-name to filename.
endloop.
```

In this example, all customer names from the internal table all_customers are transferred to the file whose name is contained in the variable filename.

You can also transfer a complete record in a single step. The program reading the data then should provide the same structure. For example, consider the following source code of an export program:

```
loop at all_customers.
  transfer all_customers to filename.
endloop.
```

As a result, records with type customers are transferred to the file. Any program that reads data from this file should use records of the same type.

By default, data is transferred in the length of the respective field or structure. If you prefer to transfer a different number of bytes, add the parameter length to the transfer command followed by the actual length. Here is an example:

```
data len type i.
loop at all_customers.
  len = strlen( all_customers-name ).
  transfer all_customers-name to filename
                              length len.
endloop.
```

In this example, the actual length of each customer name is determined using the statement `len = strlen( all_customers-name )`. Then, the name is transferred in the appropriate length.

Closing a File

Although the system closes all open files at the end of a program run, it is good programming style to close the file explicitly. This is done with the `close` statement:

```
close dataset filename.
```

This statement closes the corresponding file. If you re-open it, every `transfer` or `read dataset` command starts at the very beginning of the file.

Reading Data from a File

Up to now you have seen how to write data to a file. The inverse operation—that is, reading the file contents—is executed with the `read dataset` statement. In our example, an importing program would look like this:

```
parameters filename(128) default '/usr/tmp/testfile.dat'
                         lower case.
data: msg_text(50),
      all_customer_names like customers-name occurs 100
                         with header line.
open dataset filename for input in text mode
             message msg_text.
if sy-subrc ne 0.
  write: 'File cannot be opened. Reason:', msg_text.
  exit.
endif.
```

```
do.
  read dataset filename into all_customer_names.
  if sy-subrc ne 0.
    exit.
  endif.
  append all_customer_names.
enddo.
loop at all_customer_names.
  write / all_customer_names.
endloop.
```

In this example, the file is opened for the read operation first. This is accomplished by the addition for input after the open dataset command. Then, the system return code sy-subrc has a non-zero value if the file cannot be opened. In the remaining part of the program, all customer names are read from the file using the read dataset command in a do loop. Since you usually do not know in advance how many entries exist in the file, you should query the system return code sy-subrc to avoid an infinite loop. At the end of the file, the return code has a non-zero value, and the program stops reading. Finally, the content of the internal table is displayed in a loop.

In the section "Transferring Data to a File" above, we've also discussed the technique of transferring complete records. In this case, the corresponding reading program will also work with records of the same type:

```
data all_customers like customers occurs 100
                with header line.
do.
  read dataset filename into all_customers.
  if sy-subrc ne 0.
    exit.
  endif.
  append all_customers.
enddo.
```

Here, all fields of the header line of the internal table all_customers are filled at each read dataset statement.

To ensure that the same data structures are used when writing to a file and reading from that file, refer to Dictionary structures or use common include files with data declarations for both programs.

Files in a Distributed R/3 System

When using the file interface, you need to take a look at the architecture of your R/3 System: in a small R/3 System, your PC or workstation is at the same time used as presentation server and as application server. In this case, you'll work with the file system of your PC or workstation when you use the transfer and read dataset commands explained in the sections above. In a large-scale system, however, the application server is often a different machine.

The R/3 System architecture is explained in Appendix A.

Since the ABAP/4 runtime system operates on the application server, a program using a transfer command writes data to the file system of the application server, and a read dataset statement reads data from there. In contrast, if you want to use the file system of your PC, which is where the presentation server runs, you should use functions of the ABAP/4 Development Workbench designed especially for this purpose:

- WS_DOWNLOAD: Save an internal table as a file on the presentation server

- WS_UPLOAD: Load a file from the presentation server to an internal table

Take a look at the following example programs that work with the local file system of your PC or workstation. First, here is a program writing data to a file on your PC:

```
parameters filename(128)
            default 'c:\users\default\testfile.dat'
                        lower case.
tables customers.
data all_customers like customers occurs 100
                 with header line.
select * from customers into table all_customers.
sort all_customers by city.
loop at all_customers.
  write: / all_customers-city,
           all_customers-name.
endloop.
call function 'WS_DOWNLOAD'
     exporting
          filename        = filename
     tables
          data_tab        = all_customers
     exceptions
          file_open_error = 1
          others          = 2.
case sy-subrc.
  when 1.
    write 'Error when file opened'.
    exit.
  when 2.
    write 'Error during data transfer'.
    exit.
endcase.
```

In this example, the file name can be entered by the end user on the selection screen. Reading the data from database table customers into the internal table all_customers is accomplished in the same way as in the preceding sections. Then the function WS_DOWN-LOAD is called with the file name as a parameter and with the internal table all_customers as source for the data to be transferred. The function has a set of exceptions, from which we explicitly used the exception file_open_error. The other possible error situations are handled via the generic exception others. Note that the service function WS_DOWNLOAD encapsulates all the administration for working with the file.

The inverse operation—reading from a file on your PC or workstation—is executed by the following sample program:

```
parameters filename(128) default 'c:\users\default\test-
file.dat'
                          lower case.
tables customers.
data all_customers like customers occurs 100
                with header line.
call function 'WS_UPLOAD'
    exporting
          filename      = filename
    tables
          data_tab      = all_customers
    exceptions
          file_open_error = 1
          others        = 2.
case sy-subrc.
  when 1.
    write 'Error when file opened'.
    exit.
  when 2.
    write 'Error during data transfer'.
    exit.
endcase.
loop at all_customers.
  write: / all_customers-name,
          all_customers-city.
endloop.
```

Here, data is read using the function WS_UPLOAD into the internal table all_customers, and this data is displayed in the final loop.

A Quick Review

Here is a review of some of the most important points in this chapter:

- The open dataset statement opens a file. The system return code indicates errors, and the message text from the operating system is available.

- Writing data is done using the transfer command.

- The close dataset statement finishes the file transfer.

- Data is read with the read dataset command. The end of the file is indicated by a non-zero value of the system return code.

- If presentation server and application server run on different machines, you can use specially-designed functions of the ABAP/4 Development Workbench for data transfer to files on your PC or workstation.

In the next chapter, you will see how to establish a direct program to program communication using the Remote Function Call.

CHAPTER

TWENTY-SEVEN

Remote Function Calls

- **An easy way to deal with communication protocols**

- **Calling a remote function**

- **Avoiding a waiting situation by using the asynchronous call**

This chapter goes into detail about the *Remote Function Call* (*RFC*), which offers an easy way to implement communication between application programs via ABAP/4 function calls. Using RFC, you need not worry about protocols or incompatibilities between different hardware or operating systems. RFC is similar to the Remote Procedure Call used in other programming environments.

The RFC can be very useful when you have a company with many subsidiaries that have their own systems. To provide the headquarters with up-to-date information, you can call remote functions that retrieve the desired data from its respective local databases. With the RFC, you can either wait for the answer—the *synchronous* call—or continue the processing of the calling program and receive the answer later—the *asynchronous* call.

Communication between Programs

In everyday life, people follow certain rules for communication. For example, if the telephone rings, you pick it up and say "Hello?" and wait for the caller to speak. In the same way, when you end the conversation, you say "Goodbye" to the other person and wait for that person to say "Goodbye" back to you. This is the part of the "protocol" for a telephone conversation in English. With file transfer, it is possible to implement simple communication between two programs. As a programmer, you have a similar set of rules to establish, namely which program begins to send the data to the common file, when the partner program is allowed to write its data to that file, and who closes the file. The rules that govern such a communication are called *protocol*. You can imagine that it is not very easy to invent such a protocol. You should be ready to react to various error situations. Different machines can, and in fact do, support incompatible internal representations of numbers. So the protocol has to take into account such peculiarities. Two machines might have different code pages—that is, printed characters are mapped differently on two machines. For example, one computer speaks English and the other German. In short, you may have a heterogeneous environment to take into account.

In the realm of computer networks, there are many such protocol conventions, the most famous perhaps being the TCP/IP protocol used over the Internet. These protocols organize the traffic of data between machines in the network. There are higher level protocols such as CPI-C, once introduced by IBM for communication between programs. The first way that two ABAP/4 programs communicated was based on this protocol, and you can still use it today as a basis for communication between programs. Although it might be quite appealing to invent communication protocol, it is rather tedious to do and maintain it over the life cycle of the program.

The Remote Function Call (RFC) of ABAP/4 is an easy method of communication between application programs through ABAP/4 function calls. The Remote Function Call relieves you from technical considerations about protocols.

Calling a Remote Function

The local call of a function (see Chapter 10) means that the function runs in the same system on the same machine as the calling program. With the remote call, the called function can run in a different system on a different machine in the network. From your perspective, nothing changes. The only difference is that the caller specifies an additional parameter in the function call: the *destination*.

A remote call, for example, can be useful, when your travel agency has grown big and there is one main office and lots of local offices that run their local programs. Every night, for instance, the main office starts the remote call to update the central database and do some reporting. So a remote function call might look like this:

```
parameters: date_1 type d,
            date_2 type d.
data:       l_agency(20),
            l_bookings like bookings occurs 50 with header
            line.
call function 'GET_LOCAL_BOOKINGS'
            destination 'FLORIDA'
            exporting
              from_date = date_1
              to_date   = date_2
            importing
              agency    = l_agency
            tables
              local_bookings = l_bookings.
```

By the specification of the destination parameter, the runtime system knows that the function call does not run locally, but rather runs on a system whose name is FLORIDA. The exporting parameters from_date and to_date specify the period that is to be considered. The function returns the name of the local travel agency through the importing parameter agency and the bookings of the chosen period in the internal table local_bookings.

Runtime Behavior of an RFC

What happens at runtime, when the remote call of the above example is carried out? At first, the system must find out what is meant by the destination FLORIDA. This target can be a different R/3 system, an R/2 system, a different application server within the same R/3 system, or an external application such as a C program. All destinations are contained in the database table rfcdes, where all the information that is necessary to identify the partner with logical name FLORIDA in the network is stored. You will see how to display and maintain the entries of the system table `rfcdes` in the "Maintaining Destinations" section, below.

When you execute the call, the runtime system converts data into a machine-independent representation and sends it over the communication lines to the partner. The system automatically takes care of the above-mentioned problems like different code pages or internal representation of data. On the partner side, the function GET_LOCAL_BOOKINGS is invoked, the work is done and data is sent back to the caller. In the partner system, the function GET_LOCAL_BOOKINGS should be declared as remotely callable in the interface description. This is necessary because then the ABAP/4 Development Workbench automatically generates a piece of code that serves as the entry routine (called a *stub*) for the incoming call. The stub receives the incoming data and routes it to the desired function. Then the function is carried out and results are sent back to the caller.

Since references cannot be held in a network, the parameters of a remotely called function can only be passed by value—that is, they are copied. To make a remote call faster, the runtime system copies the contents of a table over the network only in the first call. For all subsequent calls, only differences in the table contents are copied over the network.

Technically speaking, a new user session is created when a function in a system is remotely called. This session remains alive as long as the calling program lives. Therefore, if a function at the same target is called again, the runtime system can re-use the communication path between the systems and need not establish the communication again. In addition, if a function of the same function group is called at a later time, global variables of the function group still have the contents of the previous call. This behavior is very useful when the called functions retrieve a lot of re-usable data.

Advanced Features

In the simplest case, a remotely called function reads data from the database and returns this data to the caller. Using the techniques explained in Part VI (User Dialogs), the remote partner can also send screens. This is useful when you want to develop a dialog application distributed over the network.

> **NOTE** The functionality of sending screens from a remote system is supported from R/3 Release 3.0C on.

If a remotely called function requires additional information from the caller, which has not been provided by the interface parameters, you can use the fixed destination BACK. With this destination, the called function can call back any function in the caller's context without initiating a new communication line. In the travel agency example, the call back technique can be used when the remote agency has made bookings for local carriers. Then, the remotely called function could ask the caller whether information about a certain local carrier should be transmitted.

When developing a remotely callable function that will run in different production systems, you will often work in a single development system. In that case, it is helpful to test the function in the development system itself. For this reason, you can use the destination NONE, and the called function will be processed in the current system as if it was a remote system. In particular, the called function gets a new user session.

NOTE With the RFC technique, you can also call an external program written in the C language. Inversely, it is possible to call an ABAP/4 function from an external application.

Maintaining Destinations

To maintain a destination or add a new one, choose Utilities ➤ RFC Interface ➤ RFC Target Machine on the Function Administration screen. On the next screen, an overview of all RFC destinations appears as shown in Figure 27.1.

FIGURE 27.1:
An overview of the RFC destinations

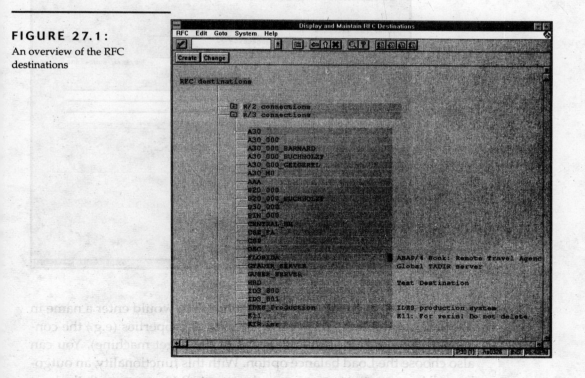

The RFC destinations are classified according to the *connection type*—for example, connections to an R/2 system, an R/3 system, or an external program.

If you want to create a new destination, click on the Create button. To maintain an existing destination, double-click on the destination's name. In both cases, a screen appears where you can create or change a destination as shown in Figure 27.2.

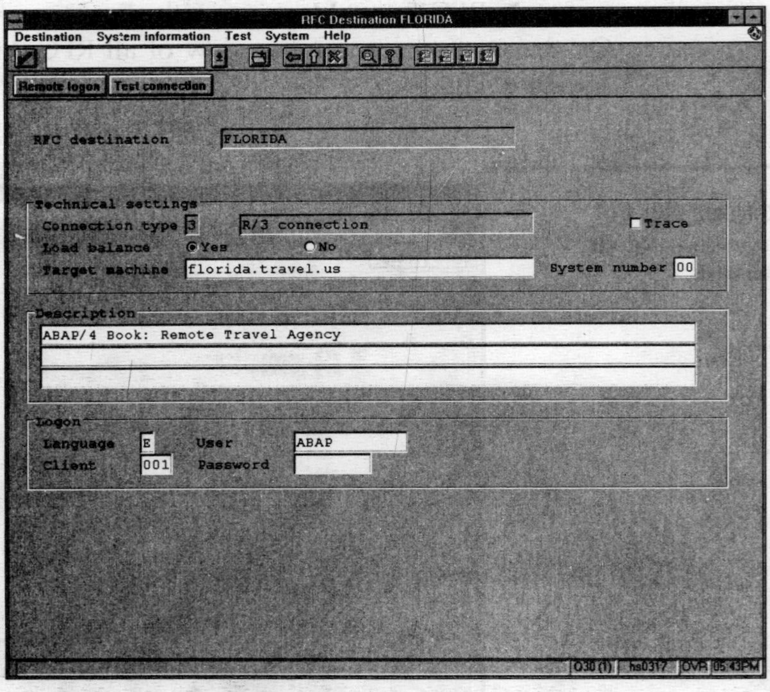

FIGURE 27.2:
The details of the FLORIDA destination

If you wanted to create a new destination, you would enter a name in the RFC destination text box and specify its properties (e.g., the connection type and the network name of the target machine). You can also choose the Load balance option. With this functionality, an outgoing call is connected to a server in the remote R/3 system with the least load. In other words, you will always log on to a machine with a maximum of free resources. In the middle portion of the RFC destination Maintenance screen, you would enter a short description. In the lower portion, enter the Logon data for the Remote Function Call. Finally, save the destination by clicking on the Save button.

You can test a connection through the Test connection button. If everything is OK, the remote system sends technical information about itself. Otherwise, you receive an error message. Since you specified the Logon data, you can directly logon to the remote system by clicking the Remote logon button. Then, the initial screen of the remote system appears, and you can start working there.

Dealing with Communication Errors

Of course there are a lot of possible errors that might occur. For instance, the caller must be notified when the target system is not available or the line breaks down. Similarly, runtime errors can happen during the execution of the remote call. To cover these situations, there are special system exceptions. The exception communication_failure tells the caller that something went wrong on the communication line during the execution of the call. You can add the optional parameter message followed by a field to get the detailed text of the error that occurred. A runtime error is given back via the exception system_failure. Here again, the caller can add the parameter message followed by a field to receive the associated error text. For example, if the remotely called function does not exist or is not declared as remotely callable, this situation is detected by the exception system_failure and the message text is available in the field after message. To meet all these possible situations, the above call should look like this:

```
parameters: date_1 type d,
            date_2 type d.
```

```
data:        l_agency(20),
             sys_msg(80),
             comm_msg like sys_msg,
             l_bookings like bookings occurs 50 with header
             line.
call function 'GET_LOCAL_BOOKINGS'
             destination 'FLORIDA'
             exporting
                from_date        = date_1
                to_date          = date_2
             importing
                agency           = l_agency
             tables
                local_bookings = l_bookings
             exceptions
                system_failure        = 1 message sys_msg
                communication_failure = 2 message comm_msg.
case sy-subrc.
   when 1.
      write: / 'system error', sys_msg.
      exit.
   when 2.
      write: / 'communication error', comm_msg.
      exit.
endcase.
```

The ABAP/4 Debugger also supports the debugging of such a remote call. This is very helpful when a runtime error occurs because the function module does not exist in the caller's system.

The Asynchronous Call

When calling a remote function as described above, the calling program cannot continue until the call returns. You can avoid this waiting situation by using the asynchronous call. Very often the calling program even does not need the result of the call to continue its work (for example, when a mail is sent). To make the call asynchronous, use the addition starting new task followed by a name for the task:

```
call function 'GET_LOCAL_BOOKINGS'
            destination 'FLORIDA'
            starting new task 'COLLECT_BOOKINGS'
            exporting
                from_date = date_1
                to_date   = date_2.
```

In this asynchronous call, the caller only passes from_date and to_date to the remote partner, but does not request a table with the bookings to be sent back immediately. So the calling program can continue its work without the need to wait for the call to come back. In the remote system the function GET_LOCAL_BOOKINGS runs in a separate user session with name COLLECT_BOOKINGS.

You can also use an asynchronous call when the caller needs data back at a later time. For example, there might be many local travel agencies in many different states, and you need their booking data only once a day. You can call all these agencies asynchronously, and the remote partners send their booking data to you when they retrieved this data from their database. This could be a fast solution for the problem of collecting distributed data. However, if the caller wants a direct feedback when the remote function has finished, you would need to poll the database periodically whether the data arrived or not. You can be notified automatically and receive the remote data when you use the addition performing on end of task, as shown below:

```
call function 'GET_LOCAL_BOOKINGS'
            destination 'FLORIDA'
            starting new task 'COLLECT_BOOKINGS'
            performing 'ANSWER' on end of task
            exporting
                from_date = date_1
                to_date   = date_2.
```

In this example, ANSWER is the name of a subroutine in the caller's system whose execution is triggered when the called function has finished its job in the remote system. If the addition performing on end of task is used, the communication line between both partners is held until the called function has finished and returns results to the AN-SWER form. You would declare such a form in the calling program as shown:

```
form answer using taskname.
  data:              l_agency(20),
                     sys_msg(80),
                     comm_msg like sys_msg,
                     l_bookings like bookings occurs 50 with header
                     line.
receive results from function 'GET_LOCAL_BOOKINGS'
            importing
              agency          = l_agency
            tables
              local_bookings = l_bookings
            exceptions
              system_failure = 1 message sys_msg
              communication_failure = 2 message comm_msg.
  case sy-subrc.
    when 0.
      update bookings from table l_bookings.
    when 1.
      write: / 'system error', sys_msg.
      exit.
    when 2.
      write: / 'communication error', comm_msg.
      exit.
    endcase.
endform.
```

As a result, when the remote function has finished its work and data must be sent back, the caller's runtime system receives a message from the remote partner and processes the form ANSWER. With the receive command, the form imports the data coming back and notifies the caller about errors. The command receive results from function is especially designed to represent the importing part of the asynchronous function call.

A Quick Review

Here are some of the more important points we covered in this chapter:

- The Remote Function Call establishes easy program-to-program communication between different remote R/3, R/2, or external systems.

- The synchronous RFC waits for data to come back.

- Using the asynchronous RFC the calling program need not wait and can continue its work. In this case, control is transferred to a special subroutine for receiving incoming data and error messages.

In the next chapter, you will see how to use OLE Automation from within ABAP/4 to invoke a desktop application.

CHAPTER

TWENTY-EIGHT

OLE Automation

- **Using OLE automation servers from within ABAP/4**

- **Creating an object and setting properties**

- **Invoking methods**

Object *Linking and Embedding* (OLE) is a technique introduced by Microsoft to incorporate objects of one application into another. The OLE Automation part of that technique can be considered as a call interface, by which it is possible to create references to objects of an application, call its methods, or set and get object properties.

Using OLE Automation Servers from ABAP/4

Through its Open Object Interface, the ABAP/4 language supports the OLE Automation technique. This enables you to integrate Desktop Applications into the R/3 system. Technically speaking, OLE Automation in ABAP/4 is based on the use of RFC. When called from an ABAP/4 program, the R/3 system acts as OLE client, and the external application as OLE server.

Because of its design, the Open Object Interface is not restricted to OLE Automation. It is an open interface to invoke objects of any technology like CORBA, which will be supported in future R/3 releases.

Creating an Object

Before using the objects of an OLE server, the server must be registered in the R/3 system. You can do this by choosing Development ➤ Programming Environment ➤ OLE2 ➤ OLE2 Setup on the ABAP/4 Development Workbench screen. On the next screen, you see the OLE server applications that are already registered in the system, and you can add a new application. Choose Development ➤ Programming Environment ➤ OLE2 ➤ OLE2 Typeinfo to load the type information for the OLE application into the R/3 system. This guarantees that the programs you develop for OLE automation are language-independent. Finally, to display a list of all available registered server applications and the descriptions of their objects, choose Development ➤ Programming Environment ➤ OLE2 ➤ OLE2 Object Browser. To work with such an object from within ABAP/4, first create it with the create statement:

```
include ole2incl.
data application type ole2_object.
create object application 'excel.application'.
if sy-subrc ne 0.
   write: / 'Error when opening excel.application', sy-msgli.
endif.
```

The create statement returns an object handle identified by a variable, here application. This variable must have the type ole2_object. The object's name follows the handle. In the example, we want to create an Excel application. The associated object's name is *excel.application*. If you prefer to work with object names in your native language, use the addition language followed by a field containing the desired language key. The default language is English. The system return code again notifies you about possible error situations. In case of an error, an error text can be found in the system field sy-msgli.

Object Properties

After the object has been successfully created, you will usually set some properties to be able to work with it. For example, to see the result of the create action, it is necessary to make the object visible on the screen. This means that the object's property of being visible must be set:

```
set property of application 'Visible' = 1.
If sy-subrc ne 0.
* Send an error message.
endif.
```

As a result of this `set property` command, the Excel application appears on the screen and you can work with it as usual. The addition `no flush` to the get command is useful to bundle subsequent calls and send them all at once. This improves the performance of OLE calls, since by default each call is transmitted individually to the OLE server.

You can also query properties of an object with the `get property` command:

```
data visible type i.
get property of application 'Visible' = visible.
```

The contents of the variable `visible` tells you whether the object is visible or not.

Calling Methods

The next step is to call methods of the object. Depending on the specific work you want the OLE Server to do, you need to call different methods. To proceed in this example, we will open an Excel spreadsheet and fill it with some of the flight data. In Excel, all the spreadsheets are contained in books, so first a new book must be opened. You do this by calling the following method:

```
data workbook type ole2_object.
call method of application 'Workbooks' = workbook.
call method of workbook     'Add'.
```

Here `application` is the object handle. The method returns the handle to another object in the variable `workbook`. The effect of calling these two methods is that a new document is created and added to your application. You can check for errors by querying the system return code and the message field. A method call can also pass parameters to the object with the addition `exporting`. Parameters are identified only by their position and must be enumerated in the call:

```
data sheet type ole2_object.
call method of application 'Worksheets' = sheet
               exporting #1 = 1.
call method of sheet 'Activate'.
```

Here the first worksheet is opened and made active. For the detailed description of a method's interface parameters, refer to the manual of your OLE server.

The complete example is listed below. Data from the `customers` table is transferred to the spreadsheet in the subroutine `fill_sheet`. The resulting spreadsheet is shown in Figure 28.1.

```
program excel.
include ole2incl.
tables: customers.
data: application type ole2_object,
      workbook    type ole2_object,
      sheet       type ole2_object,
      cells       type ole2_object.

create object application 'excel.application'.

set property of application 'visible' = 1.

call method of application 'Workbooks' = workbook.
perform errors.
call method of workbook 'Add'.
perform errors.
call method of application 'Worksheets' = sheet
               exporting #1 = 1.
perform errors.
call method of sheet 'Activate'.
perform errors.
perform fill_sheet.

form fill_sheet.
  data: row_max type i value 256,
        index   type i.
  field-symbols: <name>.
  select * from customers.
    index = row_max * ( sy-dbcnt - 1 ) + 1.
    do 4 times.
      assign component sy-index of structure customers to
<name>.
      call method of sheet 'Cells' = cells
```

```
                              exporting #1 = index.
              set property of cells 'Value' = <name>.
              add 1 to index.
         enddo.
       endselect.
    endform.


    form errors.
      if sy-subrc ne 0.
        write: / 'Error in OLE call', sy-msgli.
        exit.
      endif.
    endform.
```

FIGURE 28.1:

An Excel spreadsheet created from ABAP/4

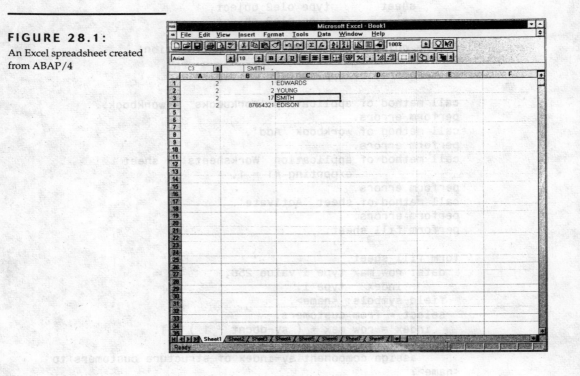

Deleting Object Links

Finally, when you want to leave the OLE application, first call the appropriate method to quit the application and then free the resources associated with the OLE object. This is done using the `free` command:

```
free object application.
```

From then on, there is no link to the created object and you cannot invoke methods.

A Quick Review

Here is a review of some of the points we covered in this chapter:

- You can invoke OLE objects from the ABAP/4 language.
- You create objects with the command `create object`.
- You can set properties by the `set property` command, and you can query them by `get property`.
- Call methods via `call method`.
- Release objects with the `free object` command.

In the appendices, we'll make a short tour through the architecture of the R/3 System, the ABAP/4 Query tool, and advanced features of the ABAP/4 Development Workbench. You'll also see how teamwork in a distributed environment is supported by the Workbench. Finally, a list of the most important system fields is included.

In the chapters of this book, we guided you from a brief sketch on basic principles into developing a full example application. We worked with the ABAP/4 Development Workbench and wrote small example programs in ABAP/4. We defined re-usable data objects in the Dictionary and also created various data objects in programs. We discussed in detail the two construction principles (records and internal tables) for building complex data objects. The Data Modeler, a graphical design tool using entity-relationship models, helped us in visualizing Dictionary tables and their mutual dependencies.

After covering elementary language constructs, we put special emphasis on the event-oriented character of the language. We demonstrated how to structure programs by using forms that are modularization units local to a single program and functions that are re-usable components that can be called from many different programs. One central area of interest in developing business applications is the interface to permanent data in a database. We introduced the methods of Open SQL for manipulating database tables from ABAP/4, and we described how to temporarily create snapshots of database tables in internal tables, the most powerful objects in the ABAP/4 language. In a later section, we worked with reports and re-usable Logical Databases for data retrieval.

User dialogs are essential as an interface to the end user. We created screens with menu bars, icons, and push buttons and sent messages to the end user in case of error situations. We presented the elaborated transaction concept of ABAP/4 to develop application programs with several screens guaranteeing consistency of the database data. Finally, we presented various open interfaces from within the ABAP/4 language to external components, starting from a simple file interface through the powerful Remote Function Call up to invoking applications following the standard for OLE Automation.

Throughout the whole text, you could follow all steps of writing an application program in a comprehensive application example. We hope that this book will be a valuable guideline whenever you work with ABAP/4 in SAP's R/3 system. Good luck!

APPENDICES

- Appendix A: Architecture of the R/3 System

- Appendix B: The ABAP/4 Query

- Appendix C: Advanced Features of the ABAP/4
  Development Workbench

- Appendix D: Teamwork in a Distributed
  Environment

- Appendix E: Important System Fields

APPENDIX

A

Architecture of the R/3 System

The R/3 system is a collection of standard business applications completely written in ABAP/4, and for this reason, it is platform independent. ABAP/4 is the central part of a middleware layer that eliminates dependencies from hardware, operating systems, or database management systems (see Figure A.1).

FIGURE A.1:

The layered structure of the R/3 system

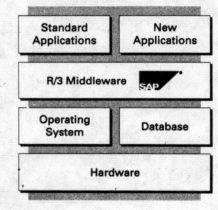

The R/3 middleware, also called R/3 Basis, is made up of the following components:

- GUI
- ABAP/4 runtime system
- Database interface
- Multi-user support
- ABAP/4 Development Workbench
- Workflow system
- Mail system

- Desktop integration
- Background processing
- Spool system
- System administration tools
- Communication interfaces to external systems

The R/3 system has been designed for distributed client/server computing based on a *three-tier architecture*. Logically, an R/3 system consists of three different layers:

- A database tier to store and retrieve business data
- An application tier for running the application logic
- A presentation tier for the GUI

Each of these services can be distributed across different hardware systems, as shown in Figure A.2.

FIGURE A.2:
The three-tier architecture of
the R/3 system

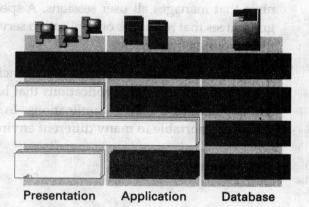

Presentation   Application   Database

If you do not need the highest possible degree of distribution, the R/3 architecture allows you to combine two or three levels on the same machine (see Figure A.3).

FIGURE A.3:

Scaling an R/3 system

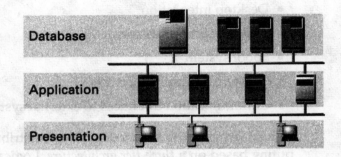

Using the different client/server distribution models, an R/3 system is scalable from a small size (one-tier system for a small number of users) up to a large scale environment (three-tier system for thousands of users). The services of an R/3 system can also be distributed in a heterogeneous environment with different operating systems and presentation software. The R/3 architecture minimizes network traffic using buffering and compression techniques for data exchange. This is very important for a client/server system, since it needs to rely on fast and stable communication. In addition, multi-user support is provided by the R/3 dispatching mechanism that manages all user sessions. A special load balancing method guarantees that resources of application servers are uniformly exploited, thus avoiding bottlenecks.

With the ABAP/4 Development Workbench as integral part of the R/3 Basis, you can develop applications that have the same properties as SAP's standard business applications. In particular, your own programs are portable to many different environments.

APPENDIX

B

The ABAP/4 Query

You can use the ABAP/4 Query tool to create simple database queries without the need to write a program. The ABAP/4 Query therefore targets users who want to define their own queries but who don't have either programming knowledge or much experience with the technical details of the R/3 system.

The ABAP/4 Query has all the features you are familiar with from other query products. In particular, you can retrieve information from any database table or from re-usable Logical Databases. Interactive features to drill-down into details or to condense information are supported as well. Tabular lists can be dynamically re-arranged and sorted by the end user. A distinctive feature is the ABAP/4 Query's support of different currencies. For example, when summing up currency-dependent values, the sum is automatically calculated for each individual currency.

It is also possible to dynamically calculate subtotals or to convert currencies. You can present a list or parts of a list with the R/3 graphics tool or transfer the data to an external spreadsheet.

The Role of Logical Databases in ABAP/4 Queries

Logical Databases are of central importance for creating reports since they provide different re-usable views on operative data in an R/3 system.

NOTE You find all you need about Logical Databases in Chapter 15.

Because of the importance of Logical Databases, ABAP/4 Query has been especially designed for use with them. Any Logical Database defined in the R/3 system can be the basis for a query. With ABAP/4 Query, the hierarchy of data as defined in the underlying Logical Database is made visible on the resulting list. So, you can not only create simply structured tabular lists, but also hierarchical lists where each line has a different structure. Using the ABAP/4 Query, you can also evaluate other data than those from a Logical Database. In this case, data must have a flat structure.

ABAP/4 Reports versus ABAP/4 Queries

As already explained in Chapters 15–17, an ABAP/4 report uses elements of the programming language to determine

- which data is to be retrieved,
- how data is interrelated,
- how it is sorted, and
- how it is arranged for output to the screen or printer.

The ABAP/4 Query supports a different approach. Here you do not code the way to get a result, but instead describe the desired list itself. The ABAP/4 Query tool then uses this description and automatically makes an ABAP/4 report that produces the desired list. This approach has the advantage that you can use the ABAP/4 Development Workbench for queries as well; for instance, you can use standard selection screens, work with variants, or run queries in the background.

> **NOTE** If you need a refresher on report variants or background processing, take a look at Chapter 18.

Data Access with the ABAP/4 Query

The ABAP/4 Query offers a user-specific environment that defines which data a user is allowed to analyze. In addition, the ABAP/4 Query uses views of Logical Databases called *Functional Areas*. This approach has three advantages: first, data can be protected against unauthorized access. Second, technical details like table and field names are hidden from the user. Third, it is possible to narrow or widen the range of information as provided by a Logical Database.

A Functional Area contains a subset of fields from the associated Logical Database, thus representing a view on the tables of the Logical Database. A Functional Area can also include information that is not contained in the Logical Database. In addition, you can create new information by combining existing data and putting it into fields of the Functional Area. In this sense, a Functional Area represents an extension of a Logical Database. For each Logical Database, you can create one or more Functional Areas. Each query is associated with one Functional Area. This association determines the range of query data that can be analyzed. Information provided by a Functional Area is not identified by technical field names, but rather by a declarative text. So, an ABAP/4 Query user need know neither the name of a table nor the name of a field containing a relevant piece of information.

Access rights in ABAP/4 Query are managed via *User Groups*. A User Group contains users with identical access authorization and a set of associated Functional Areas. Within a User Group, it is possible to access only that data that the associated Functional Areas provide. A user can be member of more than one group, and a Functional Area can be associated to more than one User Group. So, you have various possibilities for defining access rights for data analysis with the ABAP/4 Query, depending on your needs.

Elements of an ABAP/4 Query

Each query is based on a set of fields from the associated Functional Area. Data can be processed and presented on the screen in three different ways:

- as a basic list,
- as a statistic, or
- as a ranked list.

A *basic list* presents data in the order defined by the Functional Area. In a basic list, it is possible to sort the data depending on different criteria and to calculate sums and intermediate sums. A *statistic* shows statistical figures calculated from the basic data (for example, a sorted list of bookings). A *ranked list* is a specialization of a statistic—for example, the top ten customers of a travel agency.

A query can have a basic list, up to nine statistics, and up to nine ranked lists. Each of these partial lists is optional. The advantage of a query with several partial lists is that data is read only once and afterwards can be rearranged according to different aspects.

Creating a Query

The first step in the definition of a query is to choose a Functional Area. Depending on the User Group, you have the choice between different Functional Areas. The next step is the selection of fields from the Functional Area. A field should be selected if you need it on a list, as a sort criterion, or as a new selection criterion on the selection screen of the query. The selection screen always contains the criteria from the Functional Area.

In addition to the fields from the Functional Area, you can define local fields with a scope restricted to the query. Local fields typically are used to calculate figures derived from basic data. For the calculations, you can use standard formulas and elementary conditional expressions.

After the field selection for a query, you'll define its partial lists (basic list, statistics, and ranked lists). As mentioned above, any query list is defined by the layout description. For example, you can specify all of the following:

- which fields are displayed
- in which sequence the fields should appear
- which fields are sort criteria
- which fields will have sums and intermediate sums
- which special output options are needed (frames, colors, page breaks, new lines, fixed positions, output length, currencies, etc.)
- layout of page header and footer

At any time during the definition of a query, it is possible to run the query to see how the defined list looks so far.

Sample Queries

We'll illustrate the defining procedure in the example of a basic list where all lines have identical structure. The sample basic list will display an overview of all existing flight connections in a travel agency. Assume that there is a Functional Area based on a Logical Database. Having selected the desired fields like Carrier ID and Flight number (see Figure B.1), you can make additional specifications to define the basic list as shown in Figure B.2.

The resulting list is shown in Figure B.3.

FIGURE B.1:

Selecting fields from a
Functional Area

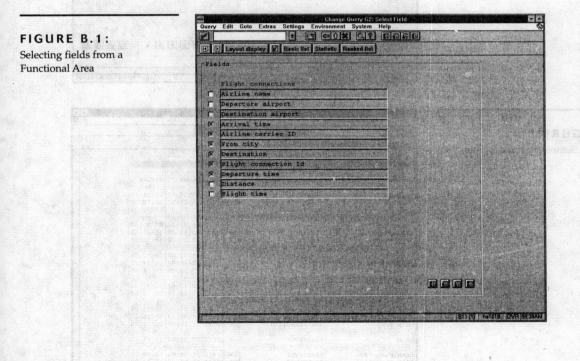

FIGURE B.2:

Definition of a basic list with a single line

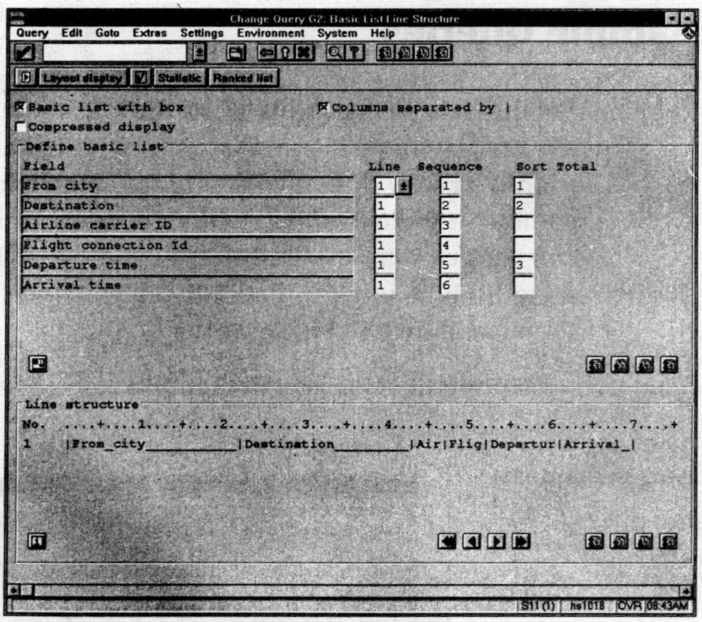

FIGURE B.3:

The sample basic list

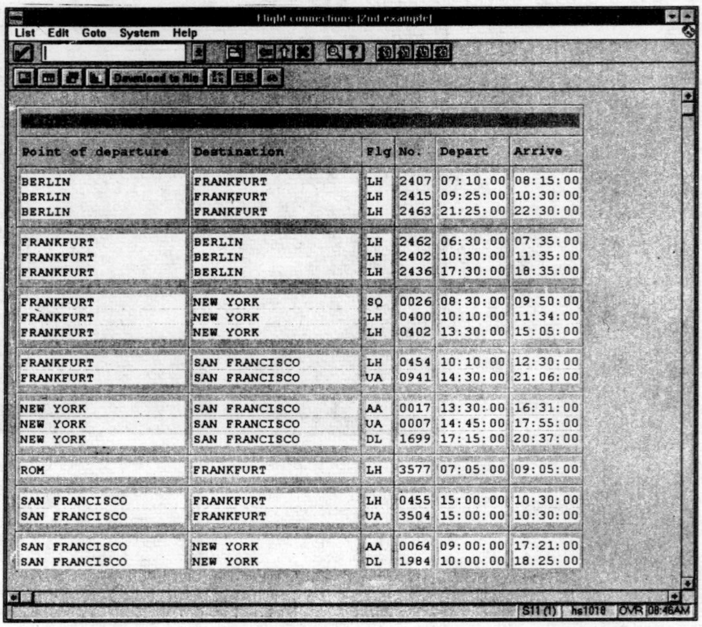

With ABAP/4 Query, you can evaluate and display hierarchical relationships of tables in a Logical Database. For example, to display the actual flights for each connection, you can define a basic list where details of a flight connection are displayed on one line and details of the actual flights on another (see Figure B.4).

FIGURE B.4:

Definition of a basic list with multiple lines

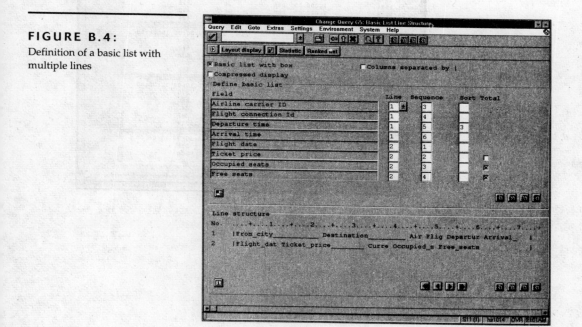

The resulting list itself is shown in Figure B.5.

Here, you can easily see the hierarchical relationship between the data: first details for a flight connection, then details for all flights of that connection.

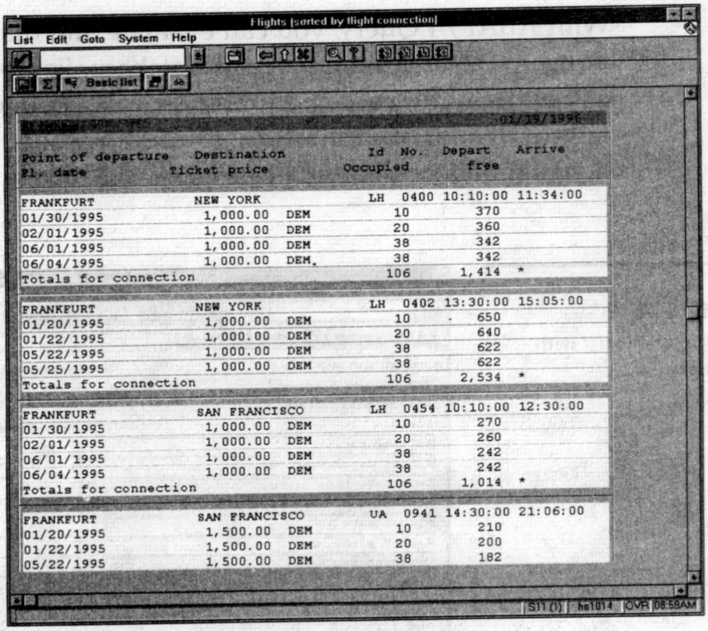

FIGURE B.5: The sample basic list with multiple lines

APPENDIX

C

Advanced Features of the ABAP/4 Development Workbench

In this appendix, we'll cover several advanced Workbench tools that can make your everyday life easier. For example, you'll learn how to insert complex statements into a program source and how to debug a program.

Elementary Workbench operations (for example, creating a program) are covered in Chapter 3.

Inserting Statements

Instead of keying in a complex statement (e.g., a select or call function statement), you can insert it in a program source by choosing the statement and potential additions or parameters (e.g., the where clause of a select statement) from one or more dialog boxes. To this end, select Edit ➤ Insert Statement on the ABAP/4 Editor screen. Then the system asks you to specify the type of the command, as shown in Figure C.1.

When you choose a select statement, you need only enter the name of a database table and then choose the fields of the table that are to be included in the where clause of the select statement. Finally, a template of a select statement is automatically put into the program source, as shown in Figure C.2.

In a similar way, you can insert call function commands, write statements for table structures from the Dictionary, and many more statements.

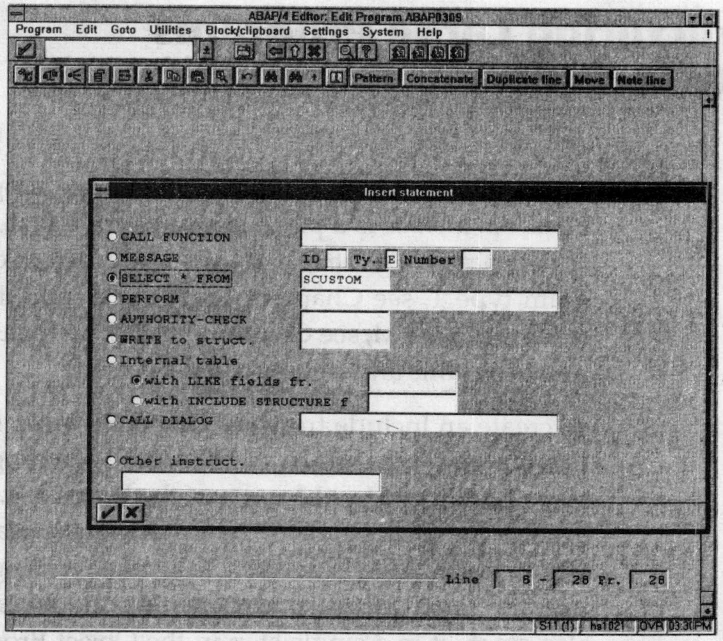

FIGURE C.1:

Inserting a complex statement template

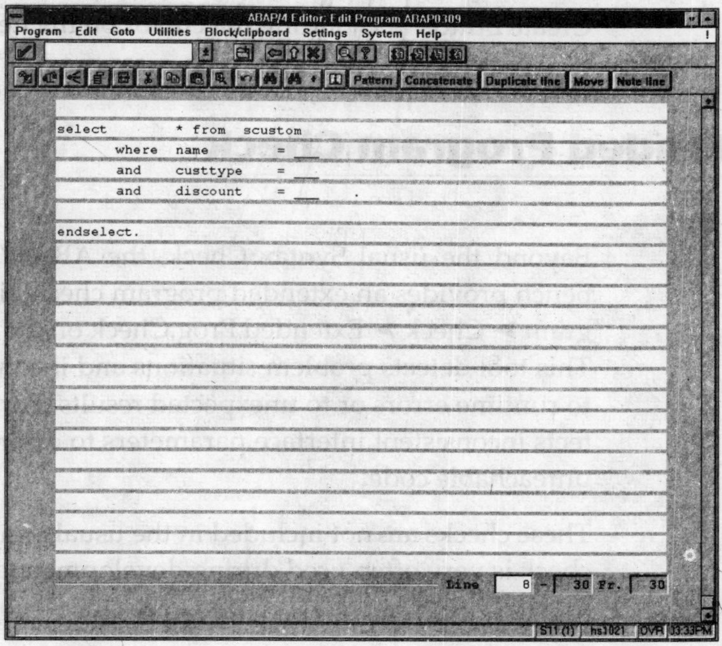

FIGURE C.2:

The source code with inserted select template

Structuring Large Programs with Includes

You can structure the source code of large programs by using Include Files. An *Include* is a piece of source code that is similar to a program: it has a name (e.g., abapincl) and attributes. In contrast to a report (program type 1, see Chapters 15–18) or a module pool of a transaction (program type M, see Chapters 19–22), an Include can only be inserted into programs and not executed by itself.

To create an Include from the Object Browser, set the program type to I on the attributes screen. In the source of a program, the include statement is followed by the name of the Include (e.g., abapincl) and incorporates the source code of the Include at the place in the main program where the Include is needed. Instead of writing the include statement into the main program and creating the Include separately, you can also create it in a single step in the Object Browser by clicking on the Create button and placing the cursor on the item Includes.

Extended Program Check

Beyond the usual Syntax Check, the ABAP/4 Development Workbench provides an extended program check via the menu choice Program ➤ Check ➤ Extended Prog.Check on the ABAP/4 Editor screen. This tool detects problem situations and inconsistencies that can lead to runtime errors or to unexpected results. For instance, the check detects inconsistent interface parameters to external functions and flags unreachable code.

These checks are not included in the usual Syntax Check, because this check is very often used during development and should therefore be very fast. In contrast, the extended program check has to investigate many objects of the system environment and is typically done at the end of the development process.

Debugging a Program

Runtime errors can occur during the development process, even if a program is syntactically correct and free of warnings from the extended program check. Even worse, a program may produce unexpected or unexplainable results. To investigate these kind of problems, ABAP/4 has a simple and efficient debugging facility with a lot of features supporting the search for an error. To find the faulty coding, you can do the following:

- stop the program anywhere during runtime,
- continue statement by statement,
- skip over subroutines, and
- check or change the contents of variables on the fly.

For instance, to stop a program at a given line of code, you can set a breakpoint in the source by positioning the cursor on the desired statement in the Editor screen and choosing Utilities ➤ Breakpoints ➤ Set from the menu bar. While running the program, the system stops at the marked statement, shows the surrounding piece of code, and enables you to continue in debugging mode (see Figure C.3).

In debugging mode, you can display the contents of fields in the lower part of the screen either by typing their names or by double-clicking on them in the displayed source code. Similarly, all lines of an internal table can be displayed by clicking on Table and entering the name of the table on the next screen. In addition, the call stack of events and active subroutines is accessible via Goto ➤ Active Call Stack.

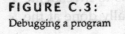

FIGURE C.3:

Debugging a program

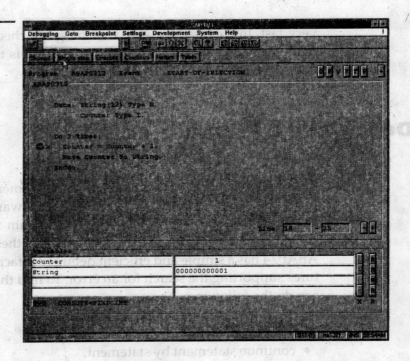

From the breakpoint, you can execute the debug program one statement at a time by clicking on the Single Step button. By clicking on the Execute button, you can execute a subroutine without stopping at each statement. Finally, when you choose Continue, you can process all statements up to the next breakpoint or to the end of the program (whichever comes first).

If you analyze a program in debugging mode, you can set further breakpoints at freely chosen events, subroutines, or statements. These dynamic breakpoints are specified on a special pop-up screen that appears when you choose the functions at Breakpoint ➤ Breakpoint At from the menu bar.

Using Double-Clicks to Create Objects and Display Their Definitions

When developing a program, you will often need new objects (for example, a variable). By double-clicking on an object name on the Editor screen, you can create this object or switch to the definition (e.g., to the defining data statement or to the definition of a subroutine). For example, if you are using a subroutine that has not yet been declared, double-clicking on the name of the subroutine brings up a dialog box asking you whether you want this subroutine to be created. When you confirm this action, you can choose the program or an Include into which to insert the definition of the subroutine. Short programs usually don't have Includes, and so you'll return to the main program in this case. Next, the definition of the subroutine (i.e., the form/endform statements) and some standard comment lines for a description of the subroutine are inserted in the program source.

The above approach of creating an object is very useful when you first design the usage of that object (e.g., the call of a subroutine) and plan to create the definition at a later time. This sequence of events happens often during the development process of an application program when you use the method of *Rapid Prototyping* (where the layout of the desired application program is implemented very early and its behavior is then discussed with end users and managers while demonstrating the first prototype). You can always create development objects (e.g., subroutines or Dictionary tables) using the Create button in the Object Browser of the ABAP/4 Development Workbench.

NOTE	You will see later in this Appendix how to get an overview of the different object types of a program, under the heading "Getting an Overview of All Parts of a Program."

Looking up the definition of an object is similar to creating an object. By double-clicking on the current object, you can switch to the definition; e.g., the defining data statement or the definition of a subroutine. Double-clicking a second time provides you with a Use List of this object (see the next section).

Working with Use Lists

For each object (e.g., a variable of a program or a Dictionary structure), you can get a Use List of this object by clicking on the Where-Used List button, which is available on nearly every screen of the ABAP/4 Development Workbench. For global objects like Dictionary structures, you will not only see all occurrences in the current program, but also in all other programs of the R/3 system. In contrast to simple textual search functions, the Use Lists also display the relevant context of each occurrence (e.g., the complete ABAP/4 command using a Dictionary table, which often extends to more than one line of code).

For example, the Use List of a database table named serptree lists all programs using this table. For each program, all occurrences can be displayed (see Figure C.4)

Double-clicking anywhere on a Use List brings up the corresponding program source, so you can directly navigate between all objects of a program and their definitions.

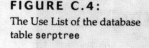

FIGURE C.4:

The Use List of the database table serptree

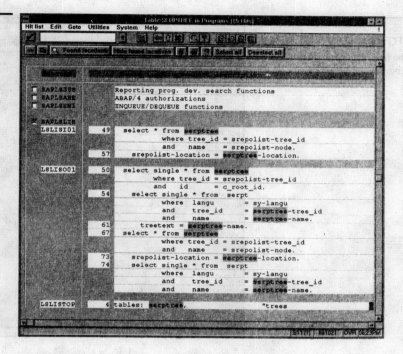

Getting an Overview of All Parts of a Program

The Object Browser displays a tree-like hierarchy of all the components (or subobjects) that make up a program. On the Object Browser screen, you can see a list of all the subobjects of a program, as shown in Figure C.5.

In short, these components are defined as follows:

- **Dictionary structures**: Tables and structures used in the current program (see Chapter 5).

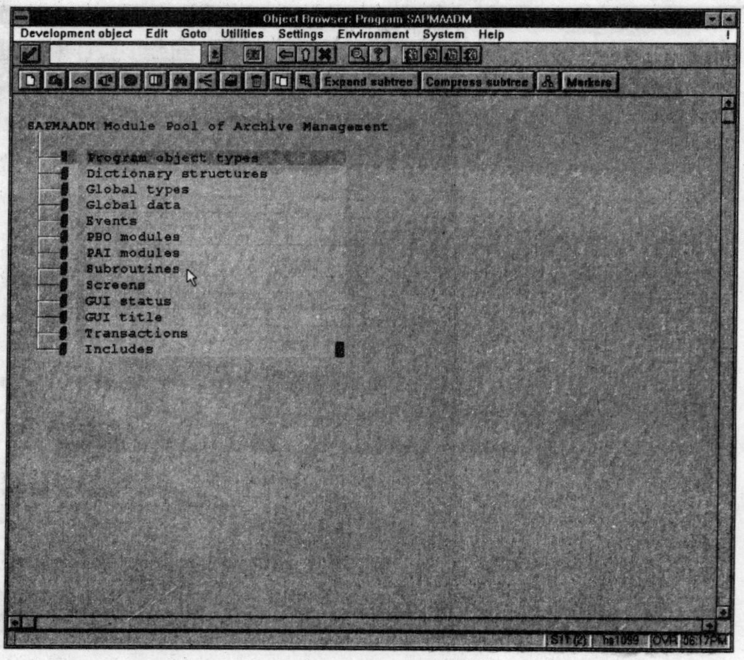

FIGURE C.5:

The tree of all components of a program

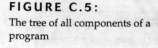

- **Global types and data**: Types and variables of the main program that are also available in all modularization units (e.g., subroutines or modules; see Chapter 4).

- **Events**: Event structure of a program according to the external flow of control (e.g., the action of the user; see Chapter 9).

- **PBO and PAI modules**: Modularization units associated with screens, which are called before or after the screen is displayed (see Chapter 19).

- **Subroutines**: Internal subroutines of the current program (see Chapter 10).

- **Screens**: Full screens or dialog boxes (see Chapters 19 and 22).

- **GUI statuses and titles**: Menu bars, buttons, and titles (see Chapter 19).

- **Transactions**: Programs performing database changes (see Chapter 21).

- **Includes**: Parts of program code that are textually inserted (see the section "Includes" in this appendix).

The precise meaning of the different types of program components is explained in the corresponding chapters.

By double-clicking on each component of the tree, you can expand or compress the corresponding subtree, displaying that element's components, as shown in Figure C.6.

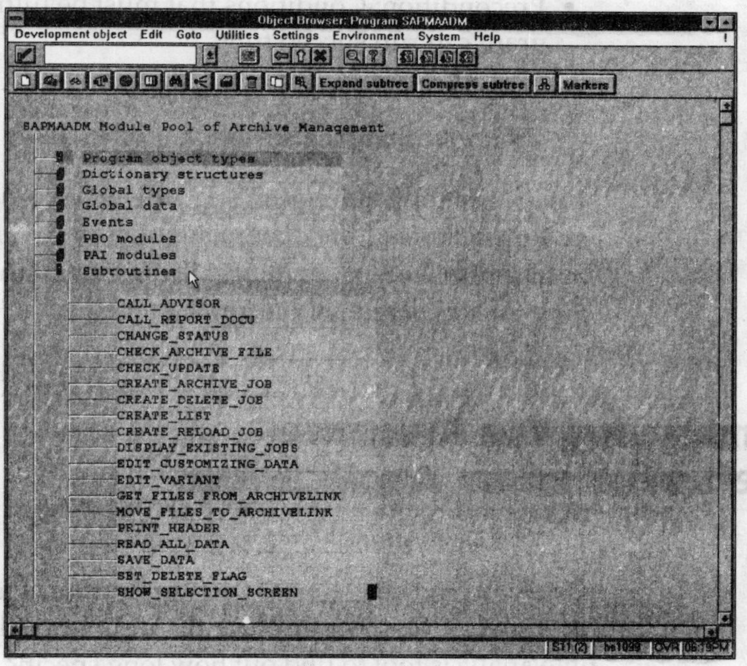

FIGURE C.6:

The object list of a program with an expanded subtree containing all subroutines

If you want to create a subobject of a type which does not yet occur in your program, double-click on the first entry Program Object Types (see Figure C.6) and select the object type (e.g., an Include) in the next dialog box.

Documenting a Program

You can edit documentation for each program by choosing Edit ➤ Documentation ➤ Display/Change from the menu bar of the Object Browser. The program documentation can be translated to different languages (like French or Spanish), and the documentation is structured by the following aspects:

- Description: General description of the program's purpose and functionality.
- Precondition: Conditions that must be fulfilled before the program can run successfully.
- Output: The result of the program.
- Example: Sample user input and results of a program run.

When executing a program (e.g., the module pool of a transaction), an end user can read the documentation of the currently active program in his or her Logon Language via the menu function Help ➤ Extended Help on any screen of the application.

Analyzing the Runtime Behavior of an Application

Once you have developed your application, it may not run fast enough or perhaps does not produce the desired result. You can use the runtime analysis tool to find out how long specific operations take during the run, and you can see a trace list of the subroutines that have been processed.

The runtime analysis is accessible by choosing Test ➤ Runtime Analysis from the menu bar of the ABAP/4 Development Workbench screen. First, specify the program you want to analyze, and then execute the program. The system creates a trace file that is evaluated in the next step. A statistical figure shows the time distribution among the various operations, the database, and the R/3 system. From there, you can switch to a hit list that displays the absolute time. Click on the button Absolute <-> % to switch to the display of the percentage of each operation with respect to the time for the whole run. You can also follow up the call hierarchy of subroutines or function calls, get statistical figures on how often a routine is called, or find out which program calls the routine.

By choosing Test ➤ SQL Trace from the Workbench screen, you can trace database calls to find out which tables are used by your applications and which database calls are issued during the run of a program. This is often useful since accessing a database table is more time consuming than accessing an internal table that is local to the program.

In addition to these analysis tools, further testing tools are available in the Test menu of the ABAP/4 Development Workbench.

The runtime analysis is accessible by choosing Test ➤ Runtime Analysis from the menu bar of the ABAP/4 Development Workbench screen. First, specify the program you want to analyze, and then execute the program. The system creates a trace file that is evaluated in the next step. A statistical figure shows the time distribution among the various operations, the database, and the R/3 system. From there, you can switch to a bit list that displays the absolute time. Click on the button Absolute <> % to switch to the display of the percentage of each operation with respect to the time for the whole run. You can also follow up the call hierarchy of subroutines or function calls, get statistical figures on how often a routine is called, or find out which program calls the routine.

By choosing Test ➤ SQL Trace from the Workbench screen, you can trace database calls to find out which tables are used by your applications and which database calls are issued during the run of a program. This is often useful since accessing a database table is more time consuming than accessing an internal table that is local to the program.

In addition to these analysis tools, further testing tools are available in the Test menu of the ABAP/4 Development Workbench.

APPENDIX

D

Teamwork in a Distributed Environment

The ABAP/4 Development Workbench can be used for small applications as well as for large-scale development projects where many people work together in a distributed system environment. Using the Workbench Organizer, you can establish a network of R/3 systems with well-defined transport paths from development or test systems into production systems. This guarantees you a high degree of security in developing and maintaining a production system, since errors in the test phase do not affect the target system.

If you want to create a test object—that is, an object that you are using just to practice a technique or try out a new idea (for example, a program or Dictionary structure)—you can declare it a *local object*, as we did with our sample program. Local objects cannot be transported to another system.

> **NOTE**
>
> A local development object (e.g., a Dictionary table) can immediately be used by every developer in the same system. In other words, a local object is not a private object of the person who created it.

However, if you create or change an object in a development system that will be used in production systems, you have to assign a development class to this object. We will discuss the use of development classes in more detail in the section below. A new or changed object is automatically included in a *Task*. A Task can be put together into a *Change Request*, which determines which objects are transported to the production system. For example, if you decided that you wanted your sample program to be implemented in the production system, you would have to assign it to a development class instead of designating it a local object. Suppose you create it in an R/3 system named *ABC*. Your sample program would then be included in a Task named *ABCK001234*, which could be combined with other Tasks to a Change Request, e.g., *ABCK001235* (the numbers of Correction and Change Requests are automatically determined by the Workbench). This Change Request would specify how and when your sample program would be transported from the development system into the actual production system, where it would be available to the end users.

Development Classes

Development classes support the distributed development of large applications. A set of development objects (for example, programs or Dictionary tables) make up a development class, and development classes are in turn components of the R/3 system. In practice, within a development class, objects for an application area are strongly related to each other, but those objects are only loosely connected to the rest of the system.

Objects within a development class can be displayed in the Object Browser. Simply type the name of the class on the Object Browser's first screen (our sample class has the name *SLDB*) and click on the Display button, as shown Figure D.1.

The objects of the specified class will appear in a screen, as shown in Figure D.2.

Each development class is under the administration of one developer. When creating a class (e.g., the sample class *ZTST*), you'll attach the class to an original R/3 system (also called its *integration system*) where the objects of the class are created and changed (e.g., the system *ABC*). At the same time, you'll assign a *consolidation system* to a development

FIGURE D.1:
Displaying the SLDB development class in the Object Browser

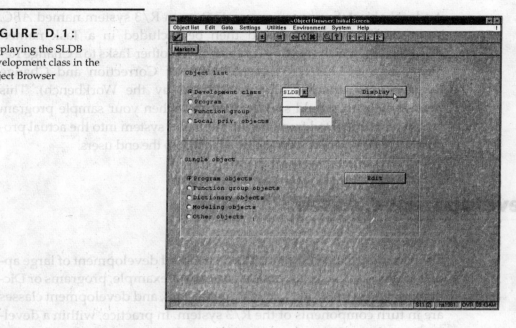

FIGURE D.2:
The list of objects that make up the SLDB development class

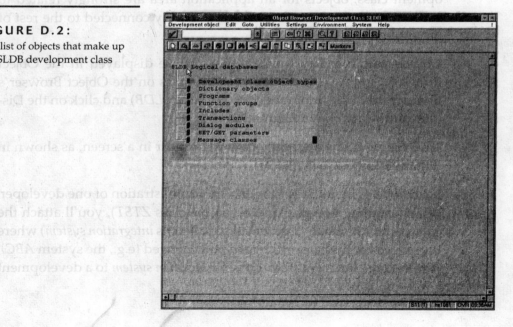

class. This system is the default target for transports of objects from your development class (e.g., the system *XYZ*).

You can find out the integration and consolidation systems for a class by double-clicking on the name of the development class in the Development Class screen you saw above in Figure D.2. You can see the information for the SLDB class displayed in Figure D.3.

FIGURE D.3:

Integration and consolidation system information for the SLDB development class

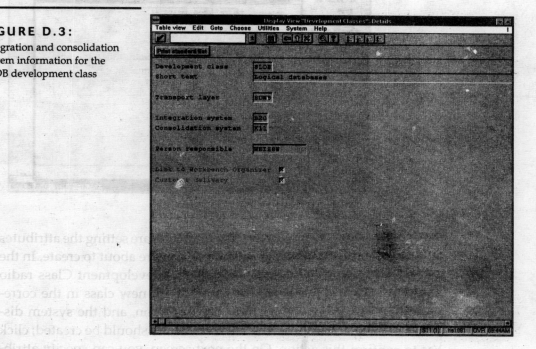

When you create a new object (for example, a program that will display a list of customer's first names) that is strongly connected to an existing object (for example, a program that will display a list of customer's last names), assign the same development class to the new object (see Figure D.4). If you begin a new object that really isn't related to any other existing objects, give the new object a new development class.

FIGURE D.4:

Assigning a development class
to a program

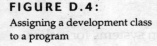

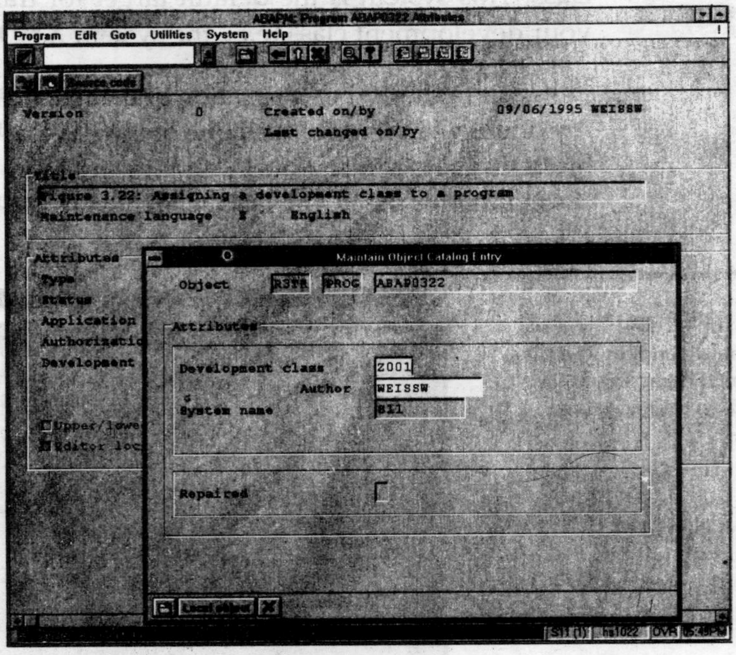

You create a new development class when you are setting the attributes in the Object Browser for the new object you are about to create. In the Object Browser's first screen, click on the Development Class radio button to select it and enter the name of the new class in the corresponding text box. Click on the Display button, and the system displays a dialog box asking whether a new class should be created; click Yes to confirm this action. On the next screen, you can specify attributes of the new class and save the new class by clicking on the Save button. SAP's customers can create their own classes in a name area reserved for customer development. According to SAP's general naming conventions, the names of all classes created by the developer of an SAP customer must begin with the letters *Y* or *Z*. This is because the R/3 system itself is written in ABAP/4 using the same development tools and naming conventions. Thus, there would be a conflict if a developer used a class name that began with something else—it might be the same name that an internal R/3 system class uses, so the new class would overwrite the internal one.

Creating Tasks and Change Requests

As we mentioned above, in addition to being assigned to a class, new or changed objects are assigned to Tasks. In turn, a group of Tasks makes up a Change Request. So, a Task can have one or more objects and a Change Request can consist of one or more Tasks. Each Task is owned by a single developer and contains the development objects (programs, Dictionary structures, etc.) assigned to that developer.

When you create or change an object, a Change Request and a Task are created by the system. The system then guides you through the different steps of filling in the information needed by the Request. For example, you must enter a short description to briefly sketch the reason why you created this Request, and you must provide documentation describing the reason in detail (for example, how does it affect the system's functionality).

Each time a new developer joins a project, you can add that person to the Change Request. The system automatically creates a Task for the new developer. You can change the owner of a Task, but until a Change Request is released, only the owner can change a Task's objects.

Releasing Tasks and Change Requests

The Workbench Organizer is used for managing Change Requests and transports. You can access the Organizer by selecting Environment ➤ Workbench Organizer in the Object Browser menu bar. When the Organizer's main screen appears (see Figure D.5), click on the Display button in the screen's left part to get a list of all Change Requests for a developer.

FIGURE D.5:
The Workbench Organizer's
Initial screen

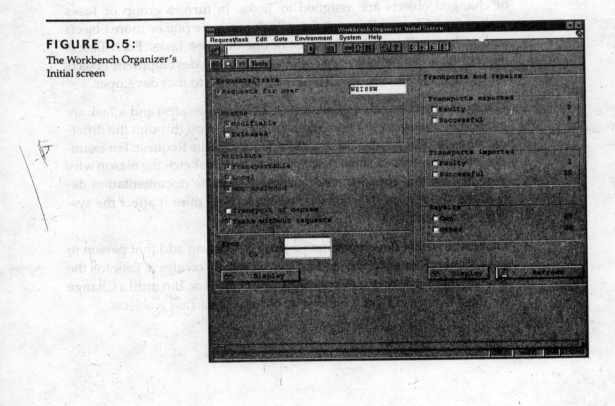

By default, you get your own Requests, since the system takes your logon name as the value in the Requests For User field on the screen in Figure D.5. The resulting list of Change Requests is shown in Figure D.6.

Releasing a Change Request automatically triggers the transport of that Request's objects from the development system to a target system. But before you can release a Change Request, you must release that Request's Tasks. In the Workbench Organizer Requests screen, select each Task and click on the Release button in the Application toolbar.

Once you have released the Tasks, the process of releasing a Change Request is very similar. Again, on the Workbench Organizer Requests screen, click on the Change Request to select it, and then click on the Release button in the Application toolbar. The objects are exported

FIGURE D.6:

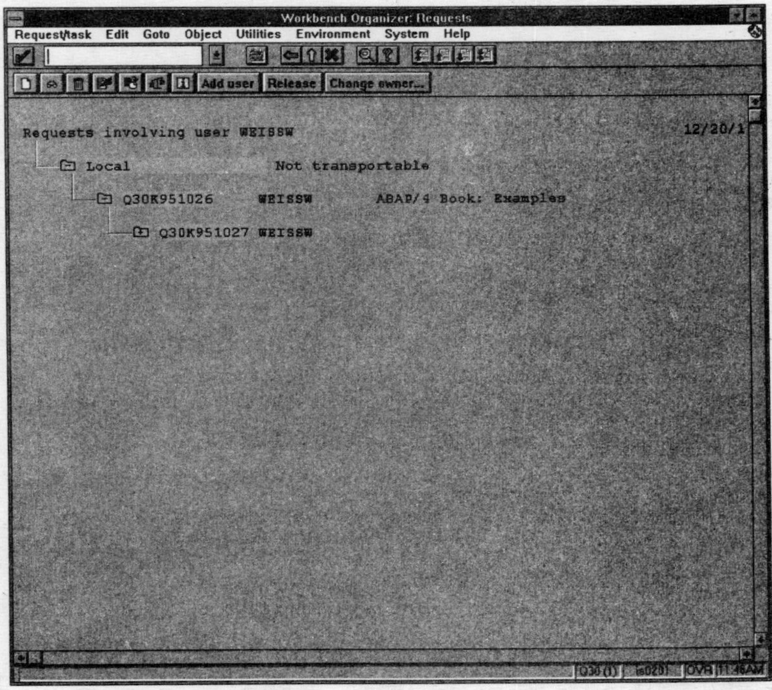

The Workbench Organizer's Requests screen, displaying Change Requests for a user

from the development system, and they will be imported into the destination system at a later time. The objects belonging to the released Tasks are locked—i.e., they aren't usable for a developer in a new Task until the corresponding Change Request is released and all objects have been exported.

No specific knowledge of the underlying R/3 operating system is required to execute these transports. The Workbench Organizer provides a tool for tracking released objects. To track an object, select Goto ➤ Logs ➤ Transport Log on the Workbench menu bar. The transport log will appear, and you can check it for possible import errors in the target system. So, you can implement a team-oriented development of applications, with the Workbench Organizer covering all organizational aspects.

APPENDIX

E

Important System Fields

The most important ABAP/4 system fields are listed below:

System field	Meaning
sy-datum	Date
sy-uzeit	Time
sy-tzone	Time zone difference to GMT
sy-dayst	Daylight Savings Time active
sy-mandt	Client number
sy-uname	User
sy-langu	SAP logon language key
sy-sysid	R/3 System ID
sy-saprl	R/3 Release
sy-dbsys	Database system
sy-opsys	Operating system
sy-tcode	Transaction code
sy-cprog	Main program
sy-repid	Report name
sy-subrc	Return value
sy-index	Loop index
sy-tabix	Table line
sy-fdpos	Location of string
sy-dbcnt	Number of elements with DB operations
sy-batch	Background processing active

System field	Meaning
sy-dynnr	Number of current screen
sy-dyngr	Screen group of current screen
sy-pfkey	Current GUI status
sy-msgid	Message ID
sy-msgty	Message type (E,I,W,…)
sy-msgno	Message number
sy-msgv1	Message variable
sy-msgv2	Message variable
sy-msgv3	Message variable
sy-msgv4	Message variable
sy-uline	Underline
sy-vline	Vertical bar
sy-pagno	Current page
sy-colno	Current column
sy-linno	Current line in list
sy-linct	Number of list lines
sy-cucol	Cursor position (column)
sy-curow	Cursor position (row)
sy-lsind	Number of stacked list
sy-winco	Cursor column in window
sy-winro	Cursor position in window
sy-tvar0	Text var. for text elements
sy-tvar1	Text var. for text elements
sy-tvar2	Text var. for text elements

System field	Meaning
sy-tvar3	Text var. for text elements
sy-tvar4	Text var. for text elements
sy-tvar5	Text var. for text elements
sy-tvar6	Text var. for text elements
sy-tvar7	Text var. for text elements
sy-tvar8	Text var. for text elements
sy-tvar9	Text var. for text elements

You can get an overview of all system fields by reading the ABAP/4 Help function for the structure sy in the Editor.

INDEX

Note to the Reader: Throughout this index **boldfaced** page numbers indicate primary discussions of a topic. *Italicized* page numbers indicate illustrations.

Symbols and Characters

A

C

D

E

F

G

M

T

u

y

x

z

ABAP/4—Developing SAP's R/3 Applications Companion CD-ROM

The ABAP/4 book's companion CD contains the source code of the example programs in the book, together with the documentation about the ABAP/4 commands. It also includes demonstrations of various parts of the R/3 System.

Installation Instructions

To run the navigation tool of the CD-ROM, follow the steps below:

1. Put the CD in your CD-ROM drive.
2. Open the File Manager.
3. Click on the CD-ROM drive icon.
4. Choose the file CDSETUP.EXE in the root directory of your CD and press ⏎.
5. Follow the instructions on the screen.

The CD-ROM contains a folder called ABAPBOOK with programming examples (folder PROGRAMS) and the ABAP/4 keyword documentation from the R/3 System (folder DOCU). For more information on how to use the programs and documentation, refer to the file README.TXT in the ABAPBOOK folder.

This DEMOR3 CD should be used for personal purposes only. Neither this CD nor any part of it may be copied, reproduced, or translated into another language, without the prior consent of Sybex and SAP AG. The information contained is subject to change without notice and does not represent a commitment on the part of SAP AG in the future. Unless otherwise noted, SAP AG is the source of all presentations and visuals.

NOTE   The code from this book can be found on the companion CD. In addition to the code, SAP and Sybex have provided a number of useful and informative documents from SAP's European marketing team. Many of these are in English and German, some are also in Spanish, French and Italian, and others are only in their original German form.